EASTERN EUROPEAN POETS SERIES #32

Know this: lofty or low, this science has been given to us on earth not for the earth.

A SCIENCE NOT FOR THE EARTH

SELECTED POEMS AND LETTERS

YEVGENY BARATYNSKY

Translated from the Russian by Rawley Grau

Edited by Rawley Grau and Ilya Bernstein

EASTERN EUROPEAN POETS SERIES
UGLY DUCKLING PRESSE
2015

A SCIENCE NOT FOR THE EARTH
Yevgeny Baratynsky

Translations, Introduction, and Notes © Rawley Grau, 2015

Eastern European Poets Series #32
Series Editor: Matvei Yankelevich
Guest Translations Editor: Ilya Bernstein

ISBN 978-1-937027-13-1
First Edition, First Printing, 2015

Ugly Duckling Presse
232 Third Street #E303
Brooklyn, NY 11215
www.uglyducklingpresse.org

Distributed in the USA by SPD/Small Press Distribution.
Distributed in Canada via Coach House Books by Raincoast Books.
Distributed in the UK by Inpress Books.

Cover design by Caitlin Keogh. Maps drawn by Pierie Korostoff.
Portrait of Baratynsky from an engraving by A. Münster, based on a
drawing by A. Lebedev (1820s).

Typeset by Emmalea Russo, Rebekah Smith, and Don't Look Now!,
with assistance from Bianca Andia, Siddhartha Lokanandi, and
Brenna Pladsen. The type is Minion and Univers.

Printed and bound by Thomson-Shore in Dexter, Michigan.
Covers printed by Prestige Printing in Brooklyn, New York.

The translation and layout were supported by the Federal Agency for
Press and Mass Communication under the federal target program,
Culture of Russia (2012–2018). The publisher would like to thank the
Russian Institute for Translation for this grant.

We would also like to acknowledge the support of the National
Endowment for the Arts and the New York State Council on the Arts.

NYSCA

State of the Arts

ART WORKS.

ИНСТИТУТ ПЕРЕВОДА

AD VERBUM

TABLE OF CONTENTS

DUSK

POEMS 1839–1844

LETTERS

NOTES

SCIENCE AND THE MYSTERIES OF SOULS

"HE IS ORIGINAL BECAUSE HE THINKS"

Born at the start of the nineteenth century, Yevgeny Abramovich Baratynsky achieved his first fame in his early twenties with a succession of well-crafted poems lamenting the pains of love and the torments of existence. For Russia's reading public, the sorrow in these elegies was augmented by the personal tragedy that defined the poet's image: he was a young man in disgrace, compelled to serve in the army as a sub-officer*—a humiliating rank for a nobleman—in a remote outpost on the Finnish coast.

The facts, to be sure, were somewhat different. At the age of sixteen, Baratynsky had participated in the theft of five hundred rubles and a gold-framed snuffbox from the father of a schoolmate. For this foolish act, something more than a schoolboy prank and wholly unbecoming a future army officer, he was expelled from the prestigious Corps des Pages military academy and forbidden by Emperor Alexander I from entering any service, civil or military, unless he chose to enlist as an ordinary sol- dier. This Baratynsky did, and after serving a year in the guards in St. Petersburg, where he began writing poetry in earnest, he was transferred to an infantry regiment in Finland—not as further punishment but at the request of his mother and uncles, who believed it would improve his chances for promotion (also, his new commanding officer was a relative). The poet's time in Finland, then, was hardly the "exile" he and his friends made it out to be; in fact, his regiment was often posted in St. Petersburg, less than two hundred miles away. Apart from boredom, the main hard- ship Baratynsky suffered was the uncertainty of his status: although he came from a highly distinguished family, his army rank deprived him of

---

* *Unter-ofitser*, a non-commissioned officer, roughly equivalent to a corporal or sergeant.

the basic rights of nobility and meant he could not choose his own path. Essentially, his future was on hold.

But what captivated Baratynsky's first readers was not just this romantic image, nor even his elegant poetic style with its carefully turned phrases. The most striking thing about his poems, what set them apart from the countless other elegies of the day, was their obvious intelligence: the emotions were observed in detail and analyzed to the nuance. The sorrow was heartfelt but dry-eyed, calibrated by reason and expressed with wry understanding. Such a dissection of the heart, not lessening the feeling but sharpening it, bringing it into focus, was something quite new in the genre. Aleksandr Pushkin, his great contemporary, described Baratynsky's achievement in no uncertain terms: "He is original in our country because he thinks. He would be original anywhere else, too, because he thinks in his own way, correctly and independently, while at the same time he feels strongly and deeply."*

By the mid-1820s, however, Russia's progressive critics were calling for a serious-minded, robust poetry, and the gentle genre of the elegy was denounced as trivial and self-absorbed. Agreeing with their overall assessment (which applied more to his many imitators than to his own work), Baratynsky turned to a verse in which the intellectual aspect became even more pronounced. The concerns of his earlier poems—the vicissitudes of emotion and the contradictions of existence—were now presented directly, without the frame of unhappy love or malicious fate, and the more or less conventional persona of the elegies—the disenchanted lover, the melancholy singer in the wilds of nature—gave way to that of the observant, endlessly questioning poet-thinker.

The years 1825 and 1826 were a time of dramatic change for both Baratynsky and Russia. In the space of a year and a half, he at last received his promotion, bid good riddance to Finland and the army, courted and soon married a smart, congenial young woman, and settled permanently in Moscow. Meanwhile, his nemesis, Alexander I, died unexpectedly

---

* Aleksandr Pushkin, "Baratynskiy" (1830), in *Polnoye sobraniye sochineniy v desyati tomakh*, 4th ed., vol. 7, *Kritika i publitsistika* (Leningrad: Nauka, 1978), 153. Here and throughout, all translations from the Russian are mine.

without obvious heir, and the revolutionary stirrings among the younger nobility, having fermented for a decade, rose to the surface in an attempted coup d'état against the new ruler, Nicholas I, in December 1825. The revolt was quickly suppressed, and Russia's intellectuals despaired of effecting any real political change in the country. The Enlightenment paradigms of rationalism and constitutionalism, which had inspired the Decembrists (as the rebels came to be called), were now discredited, and a new generation looked for answers in German idealism, in romanticism, and, increasingly, in the mystical traditions of the Russian Orthodox Church.

This was nowhere more true than in Moscow, where the youth were "besotted with transcendental philosophy," as Baratynsky wrote Pushkin in January 1826.* But despite this somewhat mocking remark, Baratynsky himself took an active role in the city's main literary-philosophical circle, a group of men a few years younger than himself who, before the Decembrist uprising put an end to such formal associations, had been the Lovers of Wisdom Society. He attended their salons, contributed to their journals, and helped with plans for new publications. By 1830, their intellectual leader, the brilliant critic and thinker Ivan Kireyevsky, was one of his closest friends. But while the group's idealistic philosophy, based largely on the thought of the German metaphysician Friedrich Schelling, left traces on his poetry, Baratynsky never fully embraced it. In the same 1826 letter to Pushkin, he described his attitude to the new "German aesthetics" as a mixture of attraction and skepticism: "What I like in it is its particular poetry, but it seems to me its principles can be refuted philosophically." A similar duality characterized his attitude to Kireyevsky's circle as a whole: however much he was drawn to their ideas, he never relinquished the rational doubt he had inherited from the French Enlightenment. If the lyric persona of Baratynsky's early elegies often found himself unable to love, despite desperately wanting to, then in the poems of the late 1820s and 1830s he struggles to believe—in the righteousness of God, in transcendent truth, and even in poetry itself—yet cannot dismiss the questions posed by reason: he is unable not to think.

---

* Letter 34, in the present book, p. 325.

By the late 1830s, Baratynsky had more or less broken off relations with Kireyevsky and his circle, both for personal reasons and because of widening philosophical differences: they were moving towards a more overt Slavophilism, rejecting the Western influences Baratynsky admired and professing a more fanatical devotion to Russian Orthodoxy. It was around this time that Baratynsky seems to have entered a period of depression, precipitated by his growing alienation from Moscow's intellectual life, his increasingly time-consuming responsibilities for his family's properties, and, undoubtedly, also Pushkin's untimely, senseless death in January 1837. Much of this dark mood is reflected in the poems of Baratynsky's last book, the exquisite *Dusk*, which appeared in 1842.

His spirits lightened considerably after a brief visit to St. Petersburg in 1840. Although his animus towards Moscow's literary circles remained strong, he found new purpose in practical activities, specifically, in the planning and construction of a sawmill on his Muranovo estate in the Moscow suburbs. The goal was to develop a timber business that would provide sufficient regular income for him to travel to Western Europe and, eventually, resettle in St. Petersburg. In September 1843, with the enterprise showing satisfactory results, Baratynsky and his wife, Nastasya, with three of their seven children, at last embarked on the long-anticipated trip. During a six-month stay in Paris, he attended the city's famous literary salons, met the luminaries of the day, and got to know the Russian émigré community. Although he found Parisian life fatiguing, it also seems to have been fulfilling: in a poem composed during the sea voyage from Marseilles to Naples in the spring of 1844, he writes euphorically of having resolved "many tumultuous questions" in France. Indeed, that particular poem, "The Pyroscaphe," expresses an exuberance so unlike his previous work that some see it as heralding a new period in his verse. Sadly, however, Baratynsky died in Naples three months later, leaving behind a poetic legacy that explores the basic questions of existence with unflinching honesty and incisive wit.

Most remarkably, his work examines the nature of poetry itself: What purpose does it serve? What knowledge can it offer the modern age? What does the poet have to say and to whom does he say it? And who pays any attention to him? Few poets have dared to question with such urgency the premises of their practice. If Baratynsky's answers seem tentative, partial, or contradictory, we should not be surprised. Unlike many philosophical poets, he did not begin with an established system of belief (Christianity, rationalism, Schellingianism) that he then tried to put into verse; his poetry does not so much profess a position as test the validity of various positions, and opposing ideas are given almost equal weight. When a definitive conclusion appears to be reached in one poem, we find it challenged in others. Still, there is a strong coherence throughout Baratynsky's lyric verse as he seeks salvation and truth in poetry even as he fears it might destroy him or, worse, turn out to be mere self-delusion.

THE POET'S SCIENCE

A few stanzas into the long meditative poem "Autumn" (completed in early 1837), Baratynsky paints a wonderfully detailed picture of a farmer harvesting and milling his grain—with creaking wagons, smoking kilns, ringing flails, and noisy millstones. When his labors are done and the grain is stored, he is ready for winter: "there is delightful warmth inside his cottage, / hospitality and foamy beer." But then, in a sudden introspective pivot, the poet addresses a different sort of laborer:

> But you, as you enter the autumn of your days,
> O plowman of the fields of life,
> . . . .
> are you rich, too, like the tiller of the soil?

At thirty-six and on the cusp of middle age, Baratynsky is clearly posing the question to himself. What does he have to show for all his work? In contrast to the farmer's productive fields, the poet surveys only barren thickets; instead of foamy beer, all he can offer his guests is food in which "the same taste is in every dish / and is, like the grave, terrifying."

The question of what his work can offer the world was especially pertinent for a Russian poet in the late 1830s. This was a time when there was a general feeling that the age of poetry had passed and what society needed was the kind of critical examination that only prose could provide. If poetry had any role left at all, it was to inspire the passions. As the critic Vissarion Belinsky asserted in a review of Baratynsky's 1835 collected works: "In our age, our cold, prosaic age, what we need in poetry is fire and more fire; otherwise, it is hard to get us burning."[*] But Baratynsky was not interested in firing people up: *that* sort of poet he derides in a later stanza in "Autumn," describing him as an insipid "proclaimer of the common wisdom" who easily inflames the crowd and wins its approval.

The poet who refuses to cater to the received ideas of the day cannot hope for such confirmation. If he wants to find meaning in his bitter-tasting work, he is offered only two options in "Autumn." The first, intellectual and cynical, is to subdue his plaintive heart in the "sardonic triumph" of the mind and accept the "soul-numbing chill" of experience. The second option is sentimental yet visionary: spurred by sorrow, he makes himself believe in a land of recompense where he falls prostrate with humility before the now-vindicated deity. But as comforting as it may be, visionary faith in a righteous God is no more or less valid than the cynical acceptance of dreary experience. And certainly, the mind's sardonic triumph has its own particular appeal.

Ultimately, it does not matter how such a poet consoles himself. Either way, he reaches an impasse when it comes to what he can offer the world:

> know this: what is within you, you can never
> translate to any earthly sound;
> the fickle children of life's vain endeavors
> cannot be taught what you have learned;
> know this: lofty or low, this science has
> been given to us on earth not for the earth.

This is the point where poetry fails: the impossibility of translating into words the poet's inner revelation—a science that is not for the earth.

---

[*] V. G. Belinsky, review of *The Poems of Yevgeny Baratynsky*, in *The Telescope* (1835), quoted in *Chronicle*, 330–331. (See pp. 476–480 for elaboration of the short titles used in the footnotes.)

Can we find a ray of hope in this surprising word *science*? In the first half of the nineteenth century, after all, the notion of science was closely linked to *enlightenment* and offered the reassurance of order, logic, and coherence—a system of rational knowledge. In this sense, it stands in sharp contrast to the turmoil, contradiction, and conflict of the world so often portrayed in Baratynsky's poems.

But what we find when we examine his work as a whole are two distinctly opposing attitudes towards science and rational knowledge. In three of his key poems, science plays a negative, even destructive role. In "The Last Death" (1827), a future of astounding scientific progress is envisioned—with artificial islands, flying machines, and controlled-climate agriculture (among other things we might recognize today). But in this future, the emphasis on the life of the mind eventually brings the human race to extinction, after which nature reclaims the earth and "deep silence" is "enthroned throughout the world." In "The Last Poet" (1835), set in modern Greece amid a resurgence of technology and commerce, a poet is born who warns of the emptiness of any science that does not submit to love and beauty. But he is silenced by the laughter of his audience, the followers of Urania, the muse of science, and throws himself into the sea. Science again leads to a deathly silence in "Signs" (written no later than 1839), where modern man's rational attitude to nature—conducting tests "with crucible, measure, and balance"—has made it impossible for him to understand her language of omens: "And Nature closed up her heart to mankind, / and on earth all prophecy vanished."

The idea that scientific progress and the privileging of rationality over intuitive feeling separate man from nature, and from himself, is fully consonant with the romanticism of the day. But what sets Baratynsky apart from other romantics is the insight that rational thought is an inevitable part of poetic practice and inseparable from language itself. By the very fact that its medium is language, poetry is, as it were, contaminated by the same analytic impulse that destroys our connections with nature, with our own feelings, and with life itself. This is the tragedy examined in the poem "Thought, always thought!" in which the "unfortunate word-artist" has no escape from consciousness. Unlike other artists, who deal with such sensate forms as sculpture, music, and painting, the poet is doomed to gaze into the "sharp ray" of thought, before which "earthly life turns pallid."

The desire for escape from consciousness—for sleep, for "oblivion"—runs through Baratynsky's work from his earliest poems to his last. But at the same time he embraces poetry as an intellectual medium that is obliged to investigate all facets of experience, from the sublime to the abject. In other words, if poetry cannot provide an escape from consciousness or access to transcendent truth, then it can at least be an instrument to uncover the truth of this present life. In the preface to his narrative poem *The Concubine* (1831), Baratynsky argued that rather than banning "immoral" literature,

> does it not make more sense to look at it from a different perspective: not to demand of it practical moral teachings, but to see in it a science like other sciences, to seek in it *knowledge*, and nothing else?*

When one of his critics expressed shock at the comparison—"Literature, a science *like other sciences*—this is quite strange! ... Art and science are completely different things!"†—and insisted that literature's highest morality lay in its sublime nature, Baratynsky responded:

> a creative work cannot be either sublime or moral in any way other than by faithfully reflecting reality, in any way other than by being true.‡

Baratynsky approaches Baudelaire's revolutionary understanding of poetry as a vehicle for exploring modern experience. In the poem "Blessed is the man who holy things discloses" (1839), Baratynsky declares: "Two

---

* Preface to *The Concubine*, published in Ye. A. Baratynsky, *Poems 1982*, 463 (italics in the original).

† Nikolay Nadezhdin, review of *The Concubine*, in *The Telescope* (1831), quoted in *Chronicle*, 263 (italics in the original).

‡ Ye. A. Baratynsky, "Antikritika" (1831), in *Razuma velikolepnyy pir: O literature i iskusstve*, ed. Ye. N. Lebedev (Moscow: Sovremennik, 1981), 124.

provinces, both radiance and shadow, / we take as equal objects of our study," and goes so far as to compare the insights of poetry with Isaac Newton's discovery of the law of gravity:

> The fruit falls from the apple tree, and heaven's
> law is apprehended by the mind of man!
> Thus sometimes nothing but the mere suggestion
> imparts to us the wild meaning of sin.

But if Newton belongs to the order of scientists condemned in "Signs" for subjecting nature to tests, Baratynsky shows us a different kind of research in "On the Death of Goethe" (1832), where the great German writer is eulogized as the consummate poet-investigator. More akin to the pre-scientific humans in "Signs" who read and respond to omens, he understands the language of nature intuitively:

> He breathed one life with the natural world:
>   he made sense of the brook's babbling waters,
> the speech of the tree leaves he understood,
>   and felt how the grass germinated,
> he knew how to read the book of the stars,
> and with him the waves of the ocean conversed.

Yet his knowledge is also expressed in distinctly scientific terms: "He studied, he probed the entirety of man!" In Goethe there is no divide between the rational mind and intuitive feeling. Indeed, he has experienced life on earth so completely that no afterlife, no "land of recompense," is needed—or if there is a heaven, then he can enter it as a completely pure soul. But Goethe is the exception, and Baratynsky writes of him almost with envy, as if aware that his own highly syllogistic verse is far different from the German's "science," which emanated from a heart still able to respond to nature with wholeness and empathy.

The fate of the modern poet, alienated from society and doomed to consciousness, is the main theme of Baratynsky's book *Dusk*, which today is recognized as the first Russian work in which a collection of poems was published as a coherent lyric entity (a practice that would become standard only some fifty years later).* The poems in *Dusk* echo each other: the poem "Thought, always thought!", for instance—where the poet is contrasted to non-verbal artists who can enjoy freedom from conscious- ness—is followed by "The Sculptor," where just such an artist, consumed with passion for his statue, merges with it in a "victory of bliss." While critics often describe the dominant theme in *Dusk* as the poet's prob- lematic relationship to society, a no less important concern is the poet's conflicted attitude to his own poetic gift. In "The Last Poet," the disheart- ened poet buries his "useless gift" in the primordial sea; in "Novinskoye," the poet's response to a woman's seduction is not the passion she expects but Apollonian inspiration; in "To a Wise Man," poetry is described as a source of necessary distress; in "Gusting winds and violent weather," the aging poet can no longer turn to song for relief from oppressive thoughts—and so on. The climax of this theme comes in "Autumn," where the poet is made to confront the utter futility of his life's work:

> But no response will be found for the word
> that has transcended the passions of earth.

The question of where such a response can be found is then taken up in the poem that concludes Baratynsky's book, "Rhyme." Here the word- artists of antiquity are contrasted to the modern poet. The Greek singer or Roman orator could count on an enthusiastic response from his audi- ence, and as a result:

> he knew just who his was; he could
> discern how mighty was the god
> who governed his majestic word.

---

* The lyric unity of *Dusk* was first examined in detail by I. L. Almi, "Sbornik Ye. A. Boratynskogo 'Sumerki' kak liricheskoye yedinstvo," *Voprosy literatury: Metod. Stil'. Poetika* 8 (Vladimir: Vladimirskiy gosudarstvennyy pedogogicheskiy institut im. P. I. Lebedeva-Polyanskogo, 1973), 23–81. The poet Aleksandr Kushner, mean- while, made the case for *Dusk* as the first Russian "book of verse" in "Kniga stikhov," *Voprosy literatury*, 1975, no. 3, 179. On the title page of *Dusk*, the book is described with the singular noun *sochineniye*—"a work."

The modern poet, however, has no such sympathetic audience; consequently, he is filled with doubt as to the validity of his poetic gift:

> The poet in our age knows not
> whether he truly sails the heights,
> how great is his creative notion.
> Yourself both judge and under judgment,
> explain your fevered restlessness:
> A gift sublime? An absurd disease?
> Resolve this unresolvable question.

Still, in "Rhyme," Baratynsky does find an answer for the poet—and it is thrillingly modern, with implications that were not fully explored until the experimental poetry of the twentieth century. If the poet has no audience to confirm his gift, if he cannot translate his "science" for the children of the earth, he must find the validating response elsewhere: in the fabric of poetry itself, in the play of language, and specifically, in rhyme:

> Amid the lifeless sleep that is
> the world, amid its tomb-like coldness,
> it's you alone, O Rhyme, who gladden
> the poet's heart with your caress.
> Like the dove of the ark, it's you alone
> who come back from his native shore
> bearing a living branch for him;
> it's you alone in your response
> who reconcile him to the surge
> divine, and recognize his dreams!

The turn to poetry for validation is not a new theme for Baratynsky. As a young man on the brink of despair in St. Petersburg in 1818, he found his calling in "the good Muses' family," as he reminds his friend in "To Delvig" (1822). More specifically, in "Finland" (1820), one of Baratynsky's first major works, the poet claims that he needs no audience: "I have sufficient compensation / for all my sounds in sounds, and for my dreams in dreams." And in "A child, I would the forest echo" (1831), he recounts how he was first drawn to poetry by the "golden play" of rhyme: "How sounds to sounds making reply / once coddled me in their embrace!" In "Rhyme," this embrace is raised to a higher level, as a reply made to the poet himself—a living branch from his native shore. Here we have a different "land of recompense" from the one in "Autumn"—not a transcendent heaven that proves the righteousness of God, but a harmony within language itself that makes the poet whole, reconciling him to his gift and confirming the truth of his inner revelation, his untranslatable science.

UNCOMMON CONNECTIONS

With "Rhyme," the otherwise somber *Dusk* ends on a joyful note: the discovery of the validating response in the very material of poetry. But even with this restorative confirmation, a profound gulf remains between the poet and the world, and his inner revelation remains untranslatable. This state of affairs can be seen, in fact, as an extension of the situation presented on a more personal level in Baratynsky's elegies of the 1820s. The critic Nikolay Melgunov noted the similarities between the two bodies of work as early as 1838:

> Baratynsky is primarily an elegiac poet, but in his second period he has raised *personal* sadness to a *general* philosophical significance; he has become the elegiac poet of contemporary humanity. "The Last Poet," "Autumn," and other poems are clear evidence of this.[*]

The modern-day critic Sergey Bocharov describes the "sadness" of the elegies as caused by failed connections: "This situation of non-coinciding, missed connection, the dissociating of emotions in time, is basic in Baratynsky's elegies."[†] Thus in "Complaint" (1820), a much-anticipated reunion comes too late, when the poet can no longer take joy in it; in

---

[*] N. A. Melgunov, letter to A. A. Krayevsky, April 14, 1838, quoted in *Chronicle*, 344 (italics in the original).

[†] S. G. Bocharov, "'Obrechyon bor'be verkhovnoy,'" in *O khudozhestvennykh mirakh* (Moscow: Sovetskaya Rossiya, 1985), 83.

"Disillusionment" (1821), the renewed affection of a former lover now brings only distress; and in "Confession" (1823), vows made in the first blaze of love do not survive love's passing. Timing, however, is only part of the problem. In "To..." ("The obvious infatuation...") (probably written in 1821), the disjuncture is more profound—between the poet's passionate words and the emptiness of his soul. He babbles "the nonsense of love" from mere habit, he says, comparing himself to a skeptic in a temple: "without belief he still burns incense / to gods now alien to his soul."

The image has fascinating implications: it is easy to see Baratynsky as a skeptic in the Temple of Poetry. And just as the sweet smell of incense cannot compensate for absent gods, so too the caress of rhyme and "the mysterious power of harmony" (as he puts it elsewhere) cannot bridge the gap between transcendent meaning and the experience of the world. Earthly life always pales before poetic thought, which like the vision in "Truth" (1823) ruins the sweetness of existence by revealing things for what they are. As Baratynsky laments in a late work, poetic inspiration is always the "herald of life's calamities."*

There is, however, a group of poems in which the poet envisions the possibility of a profound and gratifying connection to life. These are the works dedicated to his wife, Nastasya Baratynskaya. The theme of marital devotion is rare in nineteenth-century romanticism; the assumption was that the poet is inspired by falling in love or losing love, not by love's maturing. But Baratynsky's poems to his wife possess a particularly unusual timbre: their relationship is often portrayed in the context of his poetic calling, and she herself, far from being his inspiration, is seen as the antidote to the pains of both poetry and the world. In "Stanzas" (1827), where we find her first unmistakable appearance, she is identified in starkly mundane terms as "my young wife," and the poet prays to be allowed to "hide away" with her in the oblivion of the provinces. A few years later, in "Believe me, gentle one," she is presented explicitly as rival

---

* From "I love you, goddesses of song" (1842). It is hardly surprising, then, that Baratynsky so often wrote about abandoning verse—notably, in the poems "Epilogue" (1823), "A child, I would the forest echo" (1831), "A faithful record of impressions" (1834), and "[On the Planting of a Wood]" (1842).

to the muse: the poet tells her that inspiration "causes me such agitation / I can't breathe love in quietness" and begs her to "make the insurgent muse submit to your command." In one of his last poems, her validating role is very similar to that of rhyme: the poet recalls how her "miraculous love" transformed his hell into paradise and restored his faith in himself and in heaven ("When the poet, a child of doubt and passion").

By far the most remarkable work in this group is "Arbitrary was the pet name," in which Baratynsky describes a form of connection with his wife that transcends even mortality. At the same time, he suggests a solution to the key problem that plagues the poet in both "Autumn" and "Thought, nothing but thought!": the impossibility of expressing the fullness of one's inner being in a medium pervaded by consciousness. It is worth looking at the poem in its entirety.

It opens simply, even playfully:

> Arbitrary was the pet name
> I, adoring, gave my love—
> the unaccountable creation
> of my childish tenderness.

But we soon find ourselves quite explicitly in the realm of semiotics,[*] as the poet explains the peculiar power of the arbitrary name:

> Free of all apparent meaning,
> it's for me the symbol of
> feelings for which I could find no
> words in any human tongue.

As a sign that exists outside the bounds of conventional meaning, the pet name is able to express the untranslatable experience of love. And not only that: it is safe from corruption and exploitation by the world:

---

[*] A point underscored by Yury Lotman, who quotes these lines to illustrate how a word becomes "not just a conventional sign, but a symbol," in *Universe of the Mind: A Semiotic Theory of Culture*, trans. Ann Shukman (London and New York: I. B. Tauris and Co., 1990), 108.

Ablaze with love in all its fullness,
consecrated to love alone—
in this world of idle gossip
I don't want it to be known.
What's it to the world?

Like the poet's science in "Autumn," the arbitrary name is not for the earth. But unlike that science, its meaning can be communicated to another person—to the one the poet loves, or more specifically, to her "spirit," to *her* inner being:

But if
doubt should ever cause dismay
to her spirit—oh, this name
instantly will conquer it.

And because it is a word, a medium that is not dependent on physical senses, the arbitrary name can even transcend earthly life and be the means by which the couple's souls are joined in the afterlife:

And in the other world, beyond
the grave, where there are no faces,
where, sweet friend, for recognition
there are no earthly sensual signs—
with it I'll greet life undying,
into the depths I'll call it out,
and your soul will soon come flying
on its way to meet my soul.

The ability of the arbitrary name to ensure this otherworldly reunion recalls the way rhyme is able to bring the poet a living branch from his homeland. Rhyme too, we should note, is a largely arbitrary aspect of language, free of semantic logic (it is simply coincidence that, in English, *love* rhymes with *dove* and *above*, or *labor* with *neighbor* and *saber*; such facts are, literally, meaningless). But if rhyme can validate the truth of the poet's gift, here the pet name validates his soul's connection with another person, with another soul.

"Oh, the mysteries of souls!" the poet exclaims towards the end of "To My Tutor, the Italian," Baratynsky's last poem and a work unlike any other in his corpus. It begins as an affectionate, half-humorous reflection on the life of Giacinto Borghese, a man long dead, who fled to Russia from Italy during the Napoleonic Wars and became Baratynsky's childhood tutor. Family history merges into world history as the poet recalls his tutor's wartime stories and reflects on the deaths of their three protagonists: the Russian general Aleksandr Suvorov, Napoleon, and Giacinto himself. He then offers his own lyrical impressions of Naples, where he is writing the poem, and of the places he has visited, and this soon brings him to Virgil's tomb, Aeneas's descent into the Underworld, and the realm of the blessed dead—landing the poem squarely on a very familiar theme: the search for oblivion and freedom from life's anxieties. Who, Baratynsky asks, would not wish to die among the beauties of Naples?[*] And yet Giacinto died in Russia without regret. Then, after a pause, the poet interjects, "Oh, the mysteries of souls!" as he goes on to wonder at the English poet Byron being tormented by thought even in sunny Italy whereas Giacinto found peace in the snowy northern wilds.

The exclamation is a beautiful turn. The poem seems to stop for a moment in awe of the ineffable, untranslatable truth of each and every person's being. What can be said, after all, about Napoleon or Suvorov or Byron or Giacinto? What can be said about their torments, their strivings, their deaths, their souls?

Perhaps it is this awareness of the mysterious nature of souls that leads Baratynsky to reject one of the primary roles romanticism assigned the poet: that of the prophet who speaks to the souls of men. In the Russian canon, the central work expounding this doctrine is Pushkin's 1826 poem "The Prophet," in which the poet undergoes a painful transformation in the desert: a seraph opens his eyes and ears to the flight of angels and the movement of sea monsters; he tears out the poet's tongue and inserts the sting of a serpent; and cleaving his chest with a sword, he replaces the poet's heart with a burning coal. Then, almost dead, the poet hears

---

[*] A chilling question, as we know that just weeks after writing these lines he will himself die there.

the voice of God: "Arise, prophet, behold and hearken, / be filled with my will / and, traversing sea and land, / burn with my word the hearts of men." Although Baratynsky may well be recalling Pushkin's poem when he likens the poet to the prophet who "in the unspeaking desert / ... finds the light sublime," the comparison is made in verses that celebrate solitude and, indeed, solitary inebriation ("The Goblet" [1835]). In fact, whenever Baratynsky shows us poets who attempt to "burn the hearts of men," the results are disastrous—the prime example is "The Last Poet," but similar defeats are lamented in "Autumn" and, most personally, in "[On the Planting of a Wood]" (1842). In "What sounds are these?" (1841), Baratynsky goes so far as to command an aged singer to overturn his tripod—the three-legged stool that symbolizes prophetic authority—even as he assures him that he is "one of the chosen."

Baratynsky's muse does not burn hearts; she does not even dazzle, we are told in "My Muse" (1829). Her most notable feature is "the uncommon expression of her face"—which is in itself a striking characterization. It is even more so in Russian, where the adjective I have translated as "uncommon"—*neobshchiy*—is one of Baratynsky's typical negations, in which he appends the negative prefix *ne-* to a word to create a term with a very specific meaning (often, as here, a neologism). In this instance, the negated word, *obshchiy*, means "general, common to all, held in common." Hence, the muse's expression is not merely "unusual": it is "not general, not for general use." Her face, unlike the prophet's, is directed not towards the general society (*obshchestvo*), but towards a select few.

If in "Autumn" Baratynsky brings us to the limits of poetry—the impossibility of translating the poet's revelation into words—he has always underscored the limits of his own poetry, his own prophetic incapacity. Long before "My Muse," he describes himself in "Finland" as strumming "unresounding strings" (another Baratynskian negation), without the hope or need for an audience. But his most famous poem along these lines, written around 1828, begins with an explicit acknowledgment of his limited reach:

My gift is meager and my voice not loud ...

There is a "but," of course, and it is a rather surprising one—almost a non sequitur:

> but I'm alive, and my existence is
> beloved to somebody on the earth:

In other words, it does not really matter that his gift is insignificant because he lives and is loved in the present life. What compensates for his poetic deficiency is nothing other than his wife's love! (Although the indefinite pronoun "somebody" is deliberate—the fact of the love is what's important, not who the lover is—Nastasya is the obvious candidate here.) Baratynsky goes on to make another astonishing assertion:

> my descendant will find it years from now
> in my poems.

Mysteriously, by being loved on earth, the poet's existence (the Russian word *bytiyo* connotes his very being, the essence of his life) becomes substantial enough to be conveyed in poetry across time. This opens up an almost miraculous possibility:

> Who knows? His soul and mine
> may prove to be in intimate relation,
> and as I found a friend in my generation,
> a reader in posterity I'll find.

Love between souls in the present life (the Russian word *drug* expresses a depth of attachment often diluted in the English word *friend*) becomes the warranty of a possible intimacy between the souls of the poet and his reader in the future. The parallels with "Arbitrary was the pet name" are noteworthy: in both poems, love transforms the verbal creation into something that can carry the poet's soul across the depths of eternity, or the depths of time, to connect it with the soul of another.* In

---

* Interestingly, in describing his reaction to "My gift is meager," Osip Mandelstam uses an image closely related to "Arbitrary was the pet name"—that of hearing one's name being called: "I would like to know if there is anyone who encounters these lines

"My gift is meager," however, there is the added element of uncertainty: "Who knows?" Not everyone who reads Baratynsky's poems will become *his* reader, one to whom his muse reveals her "ungeneral" expression. The intimate bond of souls is essential; otherwise, the response to his work will be at best only careless praise.

In the poem "In days of limitless distractions," Baratynsky describes how as a young man immersed in the "discordant raptures" of the passions, he nevertheless carried in his soul "the ideal of sublime proportionalities," which allowed him to produce works of elegance. As he was writing these works, he tells us,

> ... I discerned the vast design
> of the world of poetry,
> and wanted to bestow on life,
> O lyre, this your harmony.

But as we have seen, throughout his lyrics Baratynsky records the impossibility of such a bestowal: poetry is unable to transform society, the poet is scorned and derided, and prophecy has vanished from the world. Again and again, poetry falls short and the discords of life cannot be made to rhyme. It is this tragic realization, perhaps more than anything else, that makes Baratynsky a modern poet. But if poetry cannot lend its harmony to life, we are offered another possibility, one that also feels very modern: that life, in the mysterious and intimate connection of souls, can lend its substance to poetry.

---

by Baratynsky who does not tremble with the kind of joyful, terrible shudder you feel when someone unexpectedly calls out your name" ("O sobesednike" [1913], in *Proza* [Ann Arbor, Mich.: Ardis, 1983], 17; for the whole passage from Mandelstam's essay, see the note to "My gift is meager and my voice not loud").

A POET NOT OF HIS TIME

If much of Baratynsky's poetry examines the problems of failed communication, missed connections, and non-coinciding responses (to recall Bocharov), we can say that the poet himself "coincided" with his own time for only a few years—from 1819 to about 1825—when his elegies and philosophical meditations met with an enthusiastic response from readers, who ranked him alongside Pushkin. For the remainder of his life, however, he was as a poet out of sync with his age.

When the same poems appeared in his first collection of verse in 1827, the critic Stepan Shevyryov, writing in the most progressive literary journal of the day, castigated the poet for "thinking in his poetry more than feeling" and lamented "the conspicuous influence of the French school" (that is, French neoclassicism).* His 1835 collection received an even harsher review from Vissarion Belinsky, who (like Shevyryov, his ideological opponent) found that the poems' "basic and primary element is the mind, occasionally reasoning thoughtfully on lofty human subjects, almost always skimming across them, but most often dissipating into wordplay or sparkling with witticisms." I have mentioned that Belinsky saw Baratynsky as lacking the "fire" required by "our prosaic age," but he also deplored his lack of "contemporaneity." "The true poet," Belinsky wrote, "must be a son of his time." Baratynsky's work, however, belonged to a previous age: "Is this poetry? Is this what we are being forced to read, we who know Pushkin's verses by heart? And some people say the eighteenth century is over!"†

Belinsky's review of *Dusk* in 1842 was no kinder. He saw the book as essentially irrelevant to the present day:

> Was it so long ago that every new poem by Mr. Baratynsky …
> excited the attention of the public and provoked interpretations

---

* S. P. Shevyryov, "Obozrenie russkoy slovesnosti 1827 god," in *The Moscow Messenger* (1828), quoted in *Chronicle*, 201.

† Belinsky, review of *The Poems of Yevgeny Baratynsky*, quoted in *Chronicle*, 330–331.

and debates among reviewers? But now, quietly, modestly, a book has appeared with the recent poems of this same poet—and it is no longer talked about and debated.

He blamed the failure on the poet's "unsustained struggle with thought," which "has done great harm to Mr. Baratynsky's talent."[*] A quarter-century later the much more sympathetic critic Mikhail Longinov compared the impression made by Baratynsky's book to that of "a specter appearing in the midst of surprised and baffled faces unable to make sense of what sort of ghost this was and what it wanted from its descendents."[†]

Baratynsky's contemporaries relegated him to the previous century, the age of Voltaire, with its witticisms and worldly skepticism. But what the nineteenth century wanted was transcendence and faith—in God, in human progress, in a self-assured, and reassuring, universal system (be it Schelling's or Hegel's philosophy or Russian Orthodox Christianity)— while Baratynsky offered only dichotomies and doubt, questioning even the power of poetry itself. Joseph Brodsky stated the problem succinctly: "Within a cultural tradition whose main tenor is consolation, Baratynsky is an oddity."[‡]

But if Baratynsky's work confounded his contemporaries, it resonated with a later age. He was rediscovered at the turn of the twentieth century by the Russian symbolist poets (Zinaida Gippius, Valery Bryusov, and Andrey Bely, among others), who perceived a Nietzschean pessimism in his later work. His influence can be felt in the next generation too, in the work of such major poets as Osip Mandelstam, Nikolay Zabolotsky, Anna Akhmatova, and Vladislav Khodasevich, while in the late twentieth century Brodsky, Aleksandr Kushner, and Viktor Krivulin, among others,

---

[*] V. G. Belinsky, review of *Dusk*, in *Notes of the Fatherland* (1842), quoted in *Chronicle*, 392. For a longer excerpt from Belinsky's review, see the notes to the poem "When death, O Poet, stops your voice."

[†] Mikhail Longinov, "Baratynskiy i yego sochineniya," *Russkiy arkhiv* 5, no. 2 (1867), col. 262.

[‡] Joseph Brodsky, biographical note in *An Age Ago: A Selection of Nineteenth-Century Russian Poetry*, selected and translated by Alan Myers (New York: Farrar Strauss Giroux, 1988), 158–159.

explored Baratynsky's significance for their own understanding of poetry in both prose and verse.[*]

This unusual history of reception (or non-reception) was lucidly explained for the English reader by the critic D. S. Mirsky in his *History of Russian Literature*:

> [Baratynsky's] poetry is, as it were, a short cut from the wit of the eighteenth-century poets to the metaphysical ambitions of the twentieth (in terms of English poetry, from Pope to T. S. Eliot). As in his earlier work he excelled in the lighter forms of (serious) wit, his later work is saturated with wit in the higher sense, which in his case would not be exactly the sense given to the word either by Donne or by Pope, but would be necessarily included in any definition of poetic wit broad enough to include both Pope and Donne.[†]

Although twentieth-century Russian poets embraced Baratynsky as one of their own, Soviet literary scholarship was more hesitant. For one thing, critics had to grapple with the damning assessment the poet had received from Vissarion Belinsky, whose authority was virtually unquestioned in official Soviet thought. For another, the exalted status of Pushkin in Russian culture took its toll: if Baratynsky was not portrayed as a kind of "envious Salieri" to Pushkin's "divine Mozart," his best hope was to be ranked as a distant second among Pushkin's contemporaries (the "Pushkin Pleiad"). Things began to change in the 1960s and 1970s with thoughtful studies of the poet by Lidiya Ginzburg, Irina Semenko, Inna Almi, Yury Mann, and later, Sergey Bocharov. But it was, tellingly, a Norwegian scholar, Geir Kjetsaa, who wrote the first serious critical biography of Baratynsky, in 1973, and it is only in the last twenty years, thanks largely to the work of Aleksey Peskov, that the poet's life has been thoroughly documented.[‡]

---

[*] A thorough discussion of Baratynsky's influence on twentieth-century Russian writers is found in Mariya Gelfond, *"Chitatelya naydu v potomstve ya…": Boratynskiy i poety XX veka* (Moscow: Biosfera, 2012).

[†] D. S. Mirsky, *A History of Russian Literature from Its Beginnings to 1900*, ed. Francis J. Whitfield (1958; repr. Evanston, IL.: Northwestern Univ. Press, 1999), 106.

[‡] On the importance of Kjetsaa's biography and Peskov's research, see "A Few

There is, indeed, a long tradition of Baratynsky being overlooked, undervalued, or simply denied "greatness." The reasons are themselves interesting. Belinsky called it a lack of "fire and more fire." Mirsky, in the inevitable comparison to Pushkin, noted that Baratynsky

> had not that divine, Mozartian lightness which produces the (false) impression that Pushkin's work cost him no labor—Baratynsky's obvious labor gives his verse a certain air of brittleness which is at poles' ends from Pushkin's elasticity.*

Vladimir Nabokov assessed the poet's status with all the exactitude of a lepidopterist:

> If in the taxonomy of talent there exists a cline between minor and major poetry, [Baratynsky] presents such an intermediate unit of classification. His elegies are keyed to the precise point where the languor of the heart and the pang of thought meet in a would-be burst of music; but a remote door seems to shut quietly, the poem ceases to vibrate (although its words may still linger) at the very instant that we are about to surrender to it. He had deep and difficult things to say, but never quite said them.†

Although Nabokov might cringe at being included in the same paragraph with Belinsky and Mirsky, his regret over the poet's "would-be burst of music" is not so different from the call for "fire and more fire" or the description of Baratynsky's "obvious labor."

But as I have tried to show, the lack of fire, the muffled music, and the unconcealed struggle we find in Baratynsky's lyric work are not failings: they are intrinsic to his understanding of poetry as a search for truth— a science—in an age when prophecy is no longer possible. They reflect his awareness that consciousness—thought—is inherent to language and

---

Preliminaries" (in the Letters section) and the "Introduction to the Notes."

   * Mirsky, *History of Russian Literature*, 106.

   † Vladimir Nabokov, commentary to his translation of Aleksandr Pushkin's *Eugene Onegin*, rev. ed. (Princeton, NJ: Princeton University Press, 1975), 2: 380.

cannot be easily dismissed, his frank admission that when you try to say something deep and difficult, it can never quite be said. Perhaps this is what makes him all the more able to communicate with our own unsentimental age, which has learned to be suspicious of claims to wholeness and to trust dissonance more than melody.

ABOUT THE TRANSLATIONS

The present volume collects eighty-seven poems by Baratynsky—nearly two-fifths of his entire lyric corpus. All of his most important lyric works are here, from the early elegies to his very last poems, including the entire contents of *Dusk*, presented as a separate section with the poems in their original order.* The other works are presented in approximate chronological order, based on the presumed date they were written or the date of their first publication. The book also includes 166 letters by Baratynsky—well over half of those that have survived. The overall goal is to introduce the English reader as fully as possible to the work, life, and thought of this extraordinary but long-neglected poet. The main omissions are Baratynsky's "descriptive poem" *Feasts*; the verse fairy tale *The Transmigration of Souls*; the long narrative poems *Eda*, *The Ball*, and *The Gypsy* (originally titled *The Concubine*); and the prose tale "The Ring." Their inclusion would have doubled the volume's size and considerably delayed its publication. And while the narrative poems have their own great beauty and originality, it is his lyric work for which Baratynsky is most prized.

Although I have been discussing the "untranslatability" of the poet's revelation as central to Baratynsky's understanding of poetry, I in no way wish to imply that his poetry is itself untranslatable. It is no more so than any body of verse.

Like most Russian poets of his day, Baratynsky wrote in regular metrical verse and, with the exception of a few poems in classical meters (the so-called elegiac couplet), his lines are rhymed and the rhymes are almost always exact. In my translations, I have tried to follow his metrical patterns as closely as possible. Although his early work is written in the conventional meters of the day, with the "standard" iambic tetrameter dominating, his later poems, especially in *Dusk*, display a fair degree of metrical experimentation (the very different alternating stanza forms of "The Last Poet" are particularly notable). I gave myself a much wider berth, however, when it came to rhyme: I wanted at the very least to

---

* Here we also place the epigram "To a Coterie," likely intended for *Dusk*.

"suggest" the rhyme schemes of the poems, but I did not worry too much about achieving exact or even close rhymes. I had in mind the Anglo-American tradition—which even in the nineteenth century was much "looser" than Russian prosody—and felt free to avail myself of its opportunities. Sight rhymes (e.g. *prove/love, come/home*) and near rhymes (*grace/praise, learn/born*) have long been accepted as legitimate, and over the past century, especially in British verse, partial rhymes, off-rhymes, and assonances have often stood in for true rhymes. I sometimes went further, pairing words with even fainter echoes, and when nothing close presented itself, I simply did without a rhyme. Given the remarkable precision with which Baratynsky expresses his ideas, my principal concern was to convey his meaning as faithfully as I could, without subtraction or addition. At the same time, I did not want to turn his harmonies into prose—in this regard, the decision to approximate his metrical forms proved essential. To a large degree, the poem itself defined the balance between semantic and prosodic elements. The effect of an epigram, for example, often depends on finding a witty and surprising rhyme.

Any translator of nineteenth- or even twentieth-century Russian poetry must address such questions of rhyme and meter. Baratynsky, however, presents a few particular challenges as well. I mentioned earlier his characteristic negated adjectives, which are often striking neologisms. In "My Muse," I chose to render the unusual adjective *neobshchiy* with the standard word "uncommon" because alternatives such as "ungeneral" or "ungeneric," although in some ways closer to the "feel" of the Russian, can be misconstrued or are completely off-key. In other instances, I may have more successfully approximated the neologistic effect: "termless spring" ("Left to Ruin"), "unalien life" ("Signs"), "unhypocritical requiem" ("When death, O Poet, stops your voice"), to cite a few.

As Belinsky and other contemporary reviewers noted, Baratynsky is also very fond of wordplay; he particularly likes juxtaposing words with related etymological roots, a rhetorical device known as polyptoton. He often does this in ways that are impossible to replicate in English. In the elegy "Disillusionment," for example, the speaker makes the dramatic pronouncement:

No more do I trust assurances,
no more do I believe in love …

which in Russian is expressed not only with anaphora, but also as a play on words with the root -ver-, relating to the idea of faith or belief: *veryu* ("[I] believe, trust"), *uveren'ya* ("assurances"), and *veruyu* ("[I] believe [as a creed]"):

Uzh ya ne veryu uveren'yam,
Uzh ya ne veruyu v lyubov'…

Given the important, if subtle, difference between the verbs *veryu* and *veruyu*—mistrust of the ex-lover's promises turns into renunciation of the creed of love—I chose to render these as two etymologically distinct words: *trust* and *believe*. In the last four lines, the Russian presents an even more intricate polyptotic matrix:

Ya splyu, mne sladko usyplen'ye;
Zabud' byvalyye mechty:
V dushe moyey odno volnen'ye,
A ne lyubov' probudish' ty.

I sleep—and I find slumber pleasant;
forget the dreams that are no more,
for in my soul you will awaken
mere agitation, but not love.

The quatrain opens with a play on the verb "to sleep" (with two variant roots, -sp- and -syp-)—*splyu* ("[I] sleep") and *usyplen'ye* ("falling asleep, being lulled to sleep")—which I render in my translation with two alliterative words related in meaning but etymologically distant: "sleep" and "slumber." In the lines that follow, the polyptoton is more subtle, almost subliminal. The word for "forget" (*zabud'*) and the adjective I translate as "that are no more" (*byvalyye*: "former") are both etymologically related to the verb "to be" with its variant roots -bud- and -by-, while in the last line the root -bud'-, in the Russian word for "awaken" (*probudish'*), sounds very much like the "to be" root -bud- but is etymologically unconnected (we could call this relation "pseudopolyptoton"). A clever translator might imitate the effect with something like: "forget the dreams that are foregone, / for in my soul you will beget ..."—but that introduces a stylistic aberration (the poetically marked "foregone," in the sense of "former," clashes with the otherwise conversational tone) and abandons the poem's important sleep imagery. Conversely, I sometimes produce Baratynsky-like polyptoton when it is not actually present in the Russian. For example, I translate the concluding lines of the poem "Death" as: "and you [are] the *solution* to all riddles, / the *dissolution* of all chains," where the original simply repeats the word *razreshen'ye*, which can express both ideas.

Another notable feature of Baratynsky's style is the occasional use of unusual archaic words and inflections. While adding an exalted dignity to the tone, they sometimes make it harder for readers to grasp the meaning. Similarly, although his syntax is often intricate, he occasionally makes it even more complex with strange inversions of normal word order. In both cases, the difficulties appear to be deliberately introduced, as obstacles that require the reader to stop and work out what the poet is saying.[*] This is all part of what Mirsky called Baratynsky's "obvious labor," in which the reader "assists all the time at the hardly won, but always complete, victory of the master over the resistant material."[†] Although I have not hesitated to use older words and elevated diction in my translation, I have avoided baffling archaisms as well as quaint antique words and inflections ("'twas," "doth," "ere," "alack," etc.), which tend to signal a clichéd notion of sentimental nineteenth-century verse. Similarly, I have resisted imitating the most extreme difficulties of Baratynsky's syntax: word order in English is much less flexible than in Russian, and awkward syntactical inversions generally suggest a lazy attempt to appease meter and rhyme, rather than the artist's struggle to express difficult ideas precisely. This

---

[*] An indication that the unusual archaisms and syntactical complexities are an intentional part of his poetics is the fact that they appear only in Baratynsky's later lyrics and in later revisions to earlier poems—verses written before 1830 are models of a smooth, elegant style—nor do we find such difficulties in his letters or prose.

[†] Mirsky, *History of Russian Literature*, 106.

does not mean I simplified Baratynsky's complex sentence structures. On the contrary, I tried as much as possible to reflect his subordinate clauses, parenthetical asides, and sometimes snaking syntax; I merely untangled the occasional knot.

I had no desire to turn Baratynsky into a modern American poet, but neither did I wish to embalm him in a pseudo-nineteenth-century style. I sought to produce something that offers present-day readers unhindered access to the poet's thought without disguising his roots in early-nineteenth-century poetry. My hope is that these translations are much more than "cribs" to the Russian, but also that they are not merely impressionistic "imitations" or the kind of museum pieces that one admires but does not cherish. If I have succeeded, they are living poems that, to some degree at least, can convey the poet's loved existence and find him readers not only in posterity but in a new language.

~ ~ ~

Translation is by its very nature a collaboration—first of all with the author himself, even if he has long passed from the earth. Many times I felt Yevgeny Abramovich looking over my shoulder as I tried to find the best words to carry his thoughts, emotions, and harmonies.

The second important collaborator is the reader. The translator himself is always his own first reader, but others are crucial. Over the past four years, I have been incredibly fortunate to have as my first "other reader" Ilya Bernstein, a man whose ear is well tuned to the nuances and cadences of both Russian and English poetry, who is himself a fine poet and translator, and who has been exceptionally generous in sharing with me his insights, reactions, and advice. His help was essential in elucidating numerous difficult passages in the Russian, and he kept me from making several embarrassing mistakes. Our discussions impelled me to delve deeper into the meaning of the poems and clarify my own thinking. It is no exaggeration to say that his mark is on nearly every one of the translated poems. He also read my translations of the letters, comparing them with the original Russian and French, and made many helpful comments. He has my heartfelt gratitude.

My first translations of Baratynsky's poems were made some thirty years ago when I was a graduate student at the University of Toronto. Professor R. D. B. Thomson played a crucial role in sharpening my understanding of Russian verse, and for this I offer him long-overdue thanks. I am also very grateful to the late Professor Gleb Žekulin, whose openhearted wisdom, kindness, and support are etched in my memory.

I am glad of this opportunity to express my thanks to the International Research and Exchanges Board (IREX), which made possible a nine-month research trip to the Soviet Union in 1984–1985. There I was able to discuss Baratynsky with a number of Russia's finest literary scholars: Lidiya Ginzburg, Irina Semenko, Sergey Bocharov, Yury Mann, and especially Inna Almi, with whom I spent an unforgettable winter's day in Suzdal and Vladimir. I am grateful to them all for the insights they shared in our conversations and for their excellent writings on the poet, which have profoundly shaped my own thinking. I am also deeply grateful for the friendship, hospitality, and inspiration I received from Viktor Krivulin and Natalya Kovalyova, and from my extraordinary, dear friend Sofya Lvovna Chernyavskaya. Professors Ginzburg and Semenko, Vitya and Sofya Lvovna are no longer with us, but I treasure their memory.

It was in Toronto that my work found its first "other" readers in Margaret Burgess and Serafima Roll—their love and support have remained a necessary part of my life even over great distances—and in Felix and Lenna Raskolnikov, whose good will and encouragement were essential to my well-being. To all these friends I am forever grateful (sadly, Felix too has left this world).

I would also like to thank my good friends Joy Connelly and Bill Kamberger, the first of my readers who had no Russian and so could give me a much-appreciated response to the translations as English poems. I am grateful as well to another friend, Jane Costlow, herself a close reader, translator, and scholar of Russian literature, who inspired me to seek a wider audience for my translations.

My very special thanks go to the late Tomaž Šalamun, without whom this publication would not have happened: he generously passed on an early version of my work to Matvei Yankelevich at Ugly Duckling Presse. I am also very grateful to Matvei for taking a chance on me, for connecting me with Ilya, and for being patient over many delays.

I also want to give special thanks to my friends Erica Johnson Debeljak, a skilled writer and astute reader who very kindly read through my translations of the letters and offered thoughtful comments and corrections, and Tony Čater, who has been an invaluable sounding board for me through the entire process.

While I have received much beneficial advice from several quarters, in the end I alone am responsible for whatever mistakes and misreadings are found in the translations and accompanying commentaries.

Finally, there is one other person I would like to thank. Throughout the past decade, my sanity, my rootedness in life, has been ensured by my partner, the friend of my soul, Saško Radomin, and I am grateful to him every day for his patience, support, and love.

Rawley Grau
January 2015
Ljubljana

1800	Yevgeny Abramovich Baratynsky is born February 19* to retired Lieutenant General Abram Andreyevich Baratynsky and his wife Aleksandra Fyodorovna, a former lady-in-waiting to the empress, on the Vyazhlya estate, near the town of Kirsanov in Tambov Province.
1804	Abram Baratynsky moves his family to the part of Vyazhlya known as Mara.
1809	The family moves to Moscow; Abram falls ill in November.
1810	Abram Baratynsky dies in Moscow on March 24.
1811	Aleksandra Baratynskaya returns to Mara with her seven children in the spring.
1812	In May, Yevgeny enters a boarding school in St. Petersburg to prepare for his examinations at the Corps des Pages. He is accepted into the military academy on October 9.
1815	Yevgeny and other classmates form a "society of avengers" to play practical jokes on their teachers.
1816	On February 19 (his sixteenth birthday), Yevgeny and a classmate steal 500 rubles in banknotes and a gold-framed tortoise-shell snuffbox from the father of a fellow "avenger." The incident is reported to Emperor Alexander I, who orders the boys expelled from the school. They are forbidden from entering any civil or military service unless they choose to enlist in the army as ordinary soldiers. Baratynsky goes to live with his uncle in Podvoyskoye-Goloshchapovo, in Smolensk Province. With the exception of six months in 1817, which he spends with his mother and siblings in Kirsanov and Mara, he remains in Podvoyskoye until September 1818.
1818	The family decides that Yevgeny's best option is to enter the guards as a rank-and-file soldier. Baratynsky arrives in St. Petersburg in October. He soon becomes friends with Anton Delvig, Wilhelm Küchelbecker, and Aleksandr Pushkin.

---

* Unless indicated otherwise, dates refer to the Julian calendar ("Old Style"). According to the Gregorian calendar ("New Style"), Baratynsky was born on March 2, 1800.

1819	On February 8, Baratynsky enlists in the Jaeger Life-Guard Regiment. Around the same time, without his knowledge, Delvig submits a few of Baratynsky's poems to *The Well-Intentioned*. His poems begin appearing regularly in St. Petersburg journals. Later in the year, Delvig and Baratynsky begin sharing an apartment.
1820	In January, Baratynsky is promoted to sub-officer and transferred to the Neyshlotsky Infantry Regiment, based in Fredrikshamn, Finland. His poems, along with those of his friends in the so-called "alliance of poets" are attacked for their celebration of carousing, sex, and liberal ideas. He writes "Finland" and the long poem *Feasts*.
1821	In February, he meets Sofya Ponomaryova in St. Petersburg and develops an infatuation for her that lasts to the following spring. During this time, he writes "Disillusionment," "The Kiss," and other elegies inspired by Ponomaryova. Critics begin mentioning him as one of Russia's finest poets. His regiment is posted in St. Petersburg for over a year, from May 1821 to August 1822, when they return to Rochensalm, Finland.
1823	In Rochensalm, Baratynsky begins work on the long narrative poem *Eda* and prepares his collected lyrics for publication. In December, he sends Vasily Zhukovsky his "confession" about the Corps des Pages incident and asks for his intercession with the tsar.
1824	Alexander I continues to refuse Baratynsky's promotion to the officer's rank of ensign. In the summer, again posted in St. Petersburg, Baratynsky becomes infatuated with Aleksandra Voyeykova. From mid-October to late January 1825, he lives with Nikolay Putyata in Helsingfors, where he gets to know Agrafena Zakrevskaya, the wife of the governor-general.
1825	In Fort Kyumen, soon after leaving Helsingfors, he begins writing the narrative poem *The Ball*, based on Zakrevskaya. On April 21, the emperor finally agrees to Baratynsky's promotion, restoring to him the rights of nobility. In the summer, when the regiment is again posted in St. Petersburg, Baratynsky becomes more intensely involved with Zakrevskaya. In the fall, after a short visit to Helsingfors, he goes to Moscow on leave to take care of his mother.
	Alexander I dies in November. An unsuccessful mutiny against the new emperor, Nicholas I, takes place in St. Petersburg on December 14—the "Decembrist Uprising." In the aftermath, many are arrested and sentenced to imprisonment or exile; among Baratynsky's friends, Küchelbecker and Aleksandr Bestuzhev are imprisoned, and Kondraty Ryleyev is executed as one of the leaders of the revolt.

1826	In late January, Baratynsky is permitted to retire from the army. His first book, *Eda and Feasts*, is published in February. He meets the Engelhardt family in February or March and marries Nastasya Engelhardt on June 9. He settles permanently in Moscow.
1827	During this time his closest friendships in Moscow are with Pushkin, Pyotr Vyazemsky, and Sergey Sobolevsky; he attends Zinaida Volkonskaya's literary salon and becomes involved with the group around *The Moscow Messenger*. He spends the summer and fall in Mara, where he completes the visionary poem "The Last Death." Baratynsky's first collection of lyrics, *Poems*, is published in late October.
1828	*The Ball* is published in December with Pushkin's *Count Nulin* as *Two Tales in Verse*.
1829	Baratynsky becomes friends with Ivan Kireyevsky and his mother, Avdotya Yelagina. In October, the Baratynskys go to Mara. He begins writing *The Concubine*.
1830	The Baratynskys return to Moscow in the spring. They spend the summer on the Engelhardts' suburban Muranovo estate, but are in Moscow throughout the cholera epidemic, which reaches the city in September.
1831	Delvig dies of a sudden illness in St. Petersburg on January 14. *The Concubine* is published in April. Fearing a return of cholera, the Baratynskys go to Kazan and Kaymary. Baratynsky works on materials for Kireyevsky's new journal, *The European*.
1832	In February, after publishing only two issues, *The European* is banned by Nicholas I on the grounds of promoting revolution. The Baratynskys return to Moscow in the early summer, and Baratynsky begins planning a new edition of his collected works. He is active in the literary salons hosted by Yelagina and Dmitry and Yekaterina Sverbeyev.
1833	In June, Baratynsky and his family leave for an extended stay in Mara, where he deals with estate business and revises his poems. During this period he writes "Left to Ruin." The family returns to Moscow in the spring of 1834.
1835	Baratynsky buys a house in Moscow. He is involved in the founding of *The Moscow Observer*, edited by Mikhail Pogodin and Stepan Shevyryov. His poem "The Last Poet" appears in the journal's first issue; "The Stillborn" appears in its second issue. After much delay, the two-volume *Poems of Yevgeny Baratynsky* is published in April.

1836	Around this time Baratynsky ends his close involvement with Kireyevsky and his circle. His father-in-law, Lev Engelhardt, dies in November, and Baratynsky assumes responsibility for all the Engelhardt properties.
1837	Pushkin dies on January 29 from wounds suffered in a duel. Baratynsky completes the long meditative elegy "Autumn," which appears in the issue of *The Contemporary* dedicated to Pushkin's memory.
1838	He makes plans to travel to Germany and Italy in the fall but cancels them, possibly because of the death of his four-year-old daughter.
1839	He makes plans to travel with his family to Odessa and the Crimea for the winter. In November he writes to Pyotr Pletnyov about his unhappiness in Moscow, saying he is "weary" and has "succumbed to gloom." He again cancels his travel plans for unknown reasons.
1840	He spends two weeks in St. Petersburg in February. He and Nastasya initially plan a trip to Paris, but then decide to move to St. Petersburg in the fall. Financial difficulties force them to cancel their plans.
1841	Baratynsky begins building a sawmill and brick factory in Muranovo, as well as completely reconstructing the manor house. The family moves to a rented house in nearby Artyomovo while construction is under way.
1842	Baratynsky's timber business begins operations. In May, his third collection of poems, *Dusk*, is published. In the fall, the family moves back to Muranovo. Baratynsky again contemplates a move to St. Petersburg. He writes "[On the Planting of a Wood]."
1843	In October, Baratynsky, Nastasya, and three of their seven children travel to Paris, where they stay until March. Baratynsky meets the writers Lamartine, Vigny, Sainte-Beuve, and Nodier, among others, as well as Russian émigrés.
1844	In April, the family travels by ship to Naples. Baratynsky writes "The Pyroscaphe" and "To My Tutor, the Italian." In the early morning of July 11 (NS) / June 29 (OS), he dies unexpectedly, after complaining of a violent headache during the night. His body is temporarily interred at the British Cemetery in Naples.
1845	Baratynsky is buried at the Alexander Nevsky Monastery in St. Petersburg on September 12 (NS) / August 31 (OS).

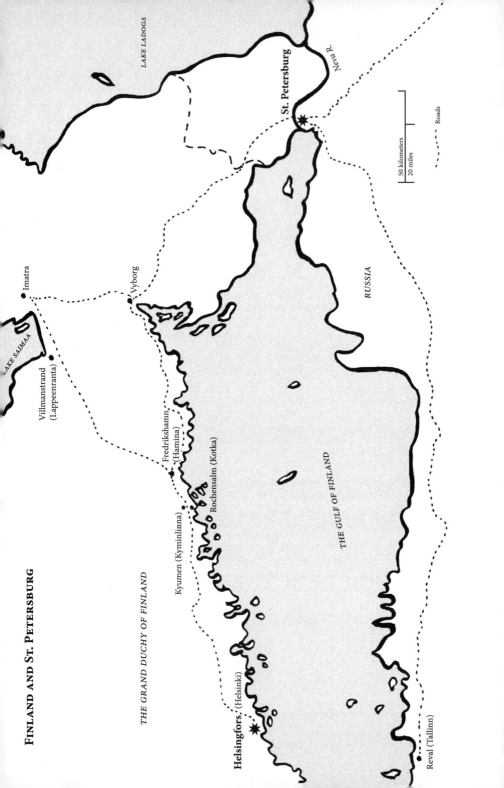

FINLAND AND ST. PETERSBURG

LAKE LADOGA

St. Petersburg

Neva R.

RUSSIA

50 kilometers
20 miles

- - - Roads

Imatra

Vyborg

LAKE SAIMAA

Villmanstrand
(Lappeenranta)

Fredrikshamn
(Hamina)

THE GRAND DUCHY OF FINLAND

Rochensalm (Kotka)

Kyumen (Kyminlinna)

THE GULF OF FINLAND

Helsingfors (Helsinki)

Reval (Tallinn)

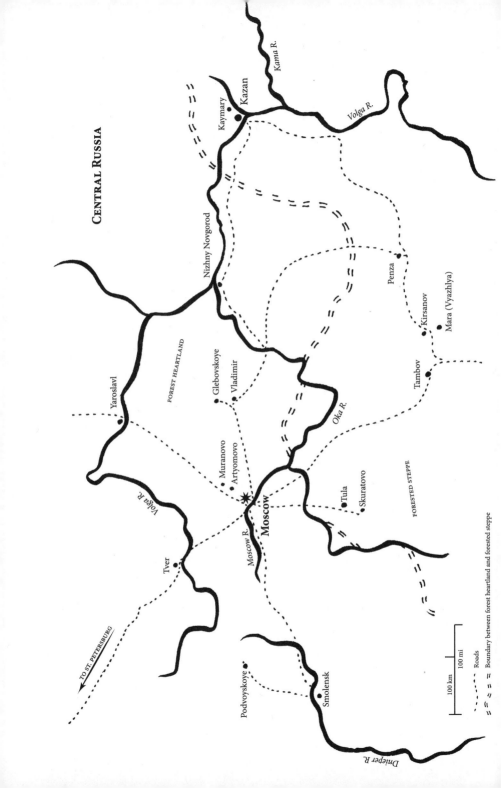

CENTRAL RUSSIA

Kama R.

Volga R.

Kazan

Kaymary

Nizhny Novgorod

Penza

Kirsanov

Mara (Vyazhlya)

FOREST HEARTLAND

Yaroslavl

Glebovskoye

Vladimir

Tambov

Muranovo

Artyomovo

Oka R.

FORESTED STEPPE

Tula

Skuratovo

Moscow

Volga R.

Moscow R.

Tver

TO ST. PETERSBURG

Podvoyskoye

Smolensk

Dnieper R.

100 mi

100 km

Boundary between forest heartland and forested steppe

Roads

POEMS 1820–1834

РОПОТ

Он близок, близок день свиданья,
Тебя, мой друг, увижу я!
Скажи: восторгом ожиданья
Что ж не трепещет грудь моя?
Не мне роптать, но дни печали,
Быть может, поздно миновали:
С тоской на радость я гляжу,
Не для меня ее сиянье,
И я напрасно упованье
В больной душе моей бужу.
Судьбы ласкающей улыбкой
Я наслаждаюсь не вполне:
Все мнится, счастлив я ошибкой,
И не к лицу веселье мне.

COMPLAINT

The day comes soon! We'll be together—
again, my friend, your face I'll see!
So tell my why my heart's not trembling
with the thrill of expectancy.
I've no right to complain, and yet
my sad days may have passed too late:
wistfully now I look on joy;
its radiance cannot be mine
and though I try, I try in vain
to waken hope in my sick soul.
And though fate smiles, I cannot take
full pleasure in its offering:
my happiness seems some mistake
and gaiety not right for me.

<1820>, <1827>

РАЗЛУКА

Расстались мы; на миг очарованьем,
На краткий миг была мне жизнь моя,
Словам любви внимать не буду я,
Не буду я дышать любви дыханьем!
Я все имел, лишился вдруг всего;
Лишь начал сон… исчезло сновиденье!
Одно теперь унылое смущенье
Осталось мне от счастья моего.

SEPARATION

We said farewell; for a moment my life had seemed—
for a brief moment—under an enchantment;
the words of love I now will hear no longer,
no longer will the breath of love I breathe.
I had the world, and suddenly it was lost;
sleep had but fallen... and the dream was gone!
Now only a forlorn embarrassment
remains to me from all my happiness.

<1820>, <1827>

ПОСЛАНИЕ К Б. ДЕЛЬВИГУ

Где ты, беспечный друг? где ты, о Дельвиг мой,
    Товарищ радостей минувших,
Товарищ ясных дней, недавно надо мной
    Мечтой веселою мелькнувших?

Ужель душе твоей так скоро чуждым стал
    Друг отлученный, друг далекой,
На финских берегах между пустынных скал
    Бродящий с грустью одинокой?

Где ты, о Дельвиг мой! ужель минувших дней
    Лишь мне чувствительна утрата,
Ужель не ищешь ты в кругу своих друзей
    Судьбой отторженного брата?

Ты помнишь ли те дни, когда рука с рукой,
    Пылая жаждой сладострастья,
Мы жизни вверились и общею тропой
    Помчались за мечтою счастья?

"Что в славе? что в молве? на время жизнь дана!" —
    За полной чашей мы твердили
И весело в струях блестящего вина
    Забвенье сладостное пили.

И вот сгустилась ночь, и все в глубоком сне —
    Лишь дышит влажная прохлада;
На стогнах тишина! сияют при луне
    Дворцы и башни Петрограда.

EPISTLE TO BARON DELVIG

Where are you, carefree friend? O Delvig, where are you,
    my comrade of delights now vanished,
my comrade of clear skies, which not so long ago
    shone like a happy dream above me?

Has he so soon become a stranger to your soul—
    your friend now gone, your friend now distant,
who with a lonely sadness amid the desolate rocks
    is wandering the shores of Finland?

Where are you, O my Delvig! Am I the only one
    who feels the loss of days now over?
Do you not search among the circle of your friends
    for me, your fate-uprooted brother?

Do you recall those days when we walked side by side,
    burning with thirst for passion's pleasure,
entrusted ourselves to life, and on a common road
    happiness' dream pursued together?

"What's fame to us? What's gossip? Our life is a brief span!"
    Thus we proclaimed with cups overflowing,
and merrily in streams of effervescent wine
    we drank the sweetness of forgetting.

And now the night grows thick, and all is deep in sleep—
    but the moist air is fresh with coolness.
In the marketplaces, silence! The towers and palaces
    of Peter's city gleam in moonlight.

К знакомцу доброму стучится Купидон,—
  Пусть дремлет труженик усталый!
"Проснися, юноша, отвергни,— шепчет он,—
  Покой бесчувственный и вялый.

Взгляни! ты видишь ли: покинув ложе сна,
  Перед окном, полуодета,
Томленья страстного в душе своей полна,
  Счастливца ждет моя Лилета?"

Толпа безумная! напрасно ропщешь ты!
  Блажен, кто легкою рукою
Весной умел срывать весенние цветы
  И в мире жил с самим собою;

Кто без уныния глубоко жизнь постиг
  И, равнодушием богатый,
За царство не отдаст покоя сладкий миг
  И наслажденья миг крылатый!

Давно румяный Феб прогнал ночную тень,
  Давно проснулися заботы,
А баловня забав еще покоит лень
  На ложе неги и дремоты.

И Лила спит еще; любовию горят
  Младые снежные ланиты,
И, мнится, поцелуй сквозь тонкий сон манят
  Ее уста полуоткрыты.

И где ж брега Невы? где чаш веселый стук?
  Забыт друзьями друг заочной,
Исчезли радости, как в вихре слабый звук,
  Как блеск зарницы полуночной!

And here is Cupid knocking at the door of his good friend—
    do not disturb the weary toiler!
"Wake up, my boy!" he whispers. "And cast aside the bonds
    of your insensible, dull slumber.

"Look! Do you see her? She has left her bed of rest
    and stands half-naked at the window;
passionate languor fills her soul—my fair Lilette
    is waiting for some lucky fellow!"

Mad crowd of murmurers, you criticize in vain!
    Blessed is he who in the springtime
with nimble hand knows how to pluck the flowers of spring,
    and with himself lives in contentment;

who undespairing sees this life in all its depth
    and with indifference abundant
will not, for all the world, yield one sweet moment of rest
    or pleasure's all too fleeting moment!

Night's shadow ruddy Phoebus has long ago expelled,
    the day's cares long ago have risen,
but laziness still keeps amusement's spoiled child
    safe in the bed of bliss and dozing.

Lilette, too, still is sleeping; her young and snowy cheeks
    are blazing with the warmth of love,
and her half-parted lips, it seems, through gauzy sleep
    are beckoning someone for a kiss.

And where are Neva's banks? The merry clink of cups?
    Their absent friend friends have forgotten;
delights have disappeared, like in a storm faint sounds,
    or like the flash of midnight lightning!

И я, певец утех, пою утрату их,
И вкруг меня скалы суровы,
И воды чуждые шумят у ног моих,
И на ногах моих оковы.

And I, singer of mirth, now sing the loss of it,
    and cheerless cliffs are all around me,
and alien waters now are thundering at my feet,
    and on my feet the shackles bind me.

1820

ФИНЛЯНДИЯ

В свои расселины вы приняли певца,
Граниты финские, граниты вековые,
    Земли ледяного венца
    Богатыри сторожевые.
Он с лирой между вас. Поклон его, поклон
    Громадам, миру современным;
    Подобно им, да будет он
    Во все годины неизменным!

Как все вокруг меня пленяет чудно взор!
    Там необъятными водами
    Слилося море с небесами;
Тут с каменной горы к нему дремучий бор
    Сошел тяжелыми стопами,
Сошел — и смотрится в зерцале гладких вод!
Уж поздно, день погас; но ясен неба свод,
На скалы финские без мрака ночь нисходит,
    И только что себе в убор
    Алмазных звезд ненужный хор
    На небосклон она выводит!
Так вот отечество Одиновых детей,
    Грозы народов отдаленных!
Так это колыбель их беспокойных дней,
    Разбоям громким посвященных!

Умолк призывный щит, не слышен скальда глас,
    Воспламененный дуб угас,
Развеял буйный ветр торжественные клики;
Сыны не ведают о подвигах отцов,
    И в дольном прахе их богов
    Лежат низверженные лики!

FINLAND

Within your crevices you have received the singer,
O granite rocks of Finland, granite rocks eternal,
    you stalwart heroes keeping watch
    over the icy crown of earth.
He has his lyre with him. He bows to you, he bows
    to these great bulks old as creation—
    may he, like them, also remain
    unchanged throughout the ages!

How wondrously does all around me capture my gaze!
    There, the sea in its boundless waters
    joins with the heavens undivided;
Here, from the stony mountain the drowsy pinewood has
    come down to it with plodding footsteps—
come down and is reflected in the smooth waters' glass!
It's late, the day is done; but the dome of the sky still glows,
upon the Finnish cliffs the night falls without darkness,
    and as if putting on her jewels
    brings out on the horizon's edge
    the diamond stars in a needless chorus.
So this is the homeland of Odin's sons, who once
    struck fear in the hearts of distant peoples!
So this is the cradle of their tumultuous days
    devoted to the din of pillage!

Soundless now is the shield of summons, the skaldic voice
    unheard, the blazing oak tree cold,
the raging winds have carried off the solemn cries—
the sons know nothing of the fathers' valiant deeds,
    and the countenances of their gods
    lie overthrown in the dust of the earth.

И все вокруг меня в глубокой тишине!
О вы, носившие от брега к брегу бои,
Куда вы скрылися, полночные герои?
      Ваш след исчез в родной стране.
Вы ль, на скалы ее вперив скорбящи очи,
Плывете в облаках туманною толпой?
Вы ль? дайте мне ответ, услышьте голос мой,
      Зовущий к вам среди молчанья ночи.
Сыны могучие сих грозных, вечных скал!
Как отделились вы от каменной отчизны?
Зачем печальны вы? зачем я прочитал
На лицах сумрачных улыбку укоризны?
И вы сокрылися в обители теней!
И ваши имена не пощадило время!
Что ж наши подвиги, что слава наших дней,
      Что наше ветреное племя?
О, все своей чредой исчезнет в бездне лет!
Для всех один закон, закон уничтоженья,
Во всем мне слышится таинственный привет
      Обетованного забвенья!

Но я, в безвестности, для жизни жизнь любя,
      Я, беззаботливый душою,
      Вострепещу ль перед судьбою?
Не вечный для времен, я вечен для себя:
      Не одному ль воображенью
      Гроза их что-то говорит?
      Мгновенье мне принадлежит,
      Как я принадлежу мгновенью!
Что нужды до былых иль будущих племен?
Я не для них бренчу незвонкими струнами;
Я, не внимаемый, довольно награжден
За звуки звуками, а за мечты мечтами.

And all that surrounds me is suspended in deep silence.
O you who carried war from one shore to another,
O heroes of the midnight realm, where have you gone?
    Your country holds no trace of you.
Is that you gazing at her cliffs with eyes of sorrow,
a nebulous multitude hovering in the clouds?
Is that you? Give me an answer, hear my voice calling
    amid the soundlessness of night!
You mighty sons of these terrible, timeless cliffs!
How were you separated from your stony homeland?
What are you grieving for? Why is it that I read
a smile of reproach upon your melancholy faces?
You too have disappeared into the world of shades!
    Time has not spared even your names!
What, then, are our great deeds, or the glory of our days?
    What, then, is our inconstant race?
Oh, all in turn will vanish in the abyss of years!
For everyone, one law: the law of annihilation.
In everything I hear a cryptic salutation:
    the promise of oblivion.

But I, in obscurity, loving life for the sake of life,
    who in my soul am free, untroubled,
    in the face of fate should I now tremble?
Not eternal for time, I am eternal for myself:
    Is it not the imagination only
    that hears some message in its storm?
    The moment—it belongs to me,
    just as I belong to the moment!
What need is there for past or future generations?
It's not for them I strum these unresounding strings:
although unheard, I have sufficient compensation
for all my sounds in sounds, and for my dreams in dreams.

1820, <1827>

ВОДОПАД

Шуми, шуми с крутой вершины,
Не умолкай, поток седой!
Соединяй протяжный вой
С протяжным отзывом долины.

Я слышу: свищет аквилон,
Качает елию скрыпучей,
И с непогодою ревучей
Твой рев мятежный соглашен.

Зачем с безумным ожиданьем
К тебе прислушиваюсь я?
Зачем трепещет грудь моя
Каким-то вещим трепетаньем?

Как очарованный, стою
Над дымной бездною твоею
И, мнится, сердцем разумею
Речь безглагольную твою.

Шуми, шуми с крутой вершины,
Не умолкай, поток седой!
Соединяй протяжный вой
С протяжным отзывом долины.

THE WATERFALL

Roar out, roar out from the steep summit!
Do not let up, O hoary stream!
Unite your voice's wailing scream
with the wailing answer of the valley.

I hear the whistling aquilon—
it rocks the spruce tree till it's groaning;
and with the tempest, wild and roaring,
your riotous roar is set in tune.

Why this insane anticipation
with which I listen to your voice?
Why am I trembling in my breast
with a kind of vatic trepidation?

I stand above your misty depths
as if transfixed by an enchantment,
and in my heart, it seems, I'm able
to comprehend your wordless speech.

Roar out, roar out from the steep summit!
Do not let up, O hoary stream!
Unite your voice's wailing scream
with the wailing answer of the valley.

1820

В АЛЬБОМ

Вы слишком многими любимы,
Чтобы возможно было вам
Знать, помнить всех по именам;
Сии листки необходимы;
Они не нужны были встарь:
Тогда не знали дружбы модной,
Тогда, бог весть! иной дикарь
Сердечый адрес-коледарь
Почел бы выдумкой негодной.
Что толковать о старине!
Стихи готовы. Может статься,
Они для справки обо мне
Вам очень скоро пригодятся.

IN AN ALBUM

You are adored by far too many
for you to possibly recall
their names or recognize them all:
these pages, therefore, are essential.
They were not needed in olden days—
back then none knew of modish friendship;
back then, God knows, those savages
would think such heart-directories
a most impractical invention.
But why talk now of ancient times?
The poem is ready. Very likely,
as a register of who I am
you'll soon find it will come in handy.

1821

РАЗУВЕРЕНИЕ

Не искушай меня без нужды
Возвратом нежности твоей:
Разочарованному чужды
Все обольщенья прежних дней!
Уж я не верю увереньям,
Уж я не верую в любовь
И не могу предаться вновь
Раз изменившим сновиденьям!
Слепой тоски моей не множь,
Не заводи о прежнем слова
И, друг заботливый, больного
В его дремоте не тревожь!
Я сплю, мне сладко усыпленье;
Забудь бывалые мечты:
В душе моей одно волненье,
А не любовь пробудишь ты.

DISILLUSIONMENT

Don't try to tempt me by restoring
your tenderness—there is no point:
all the enticements of the past are
strange to the disenchanted man.
No more do I trust assurances,
no more do I believe in love,
nor am I able to succumb
to dreams that once were traitorous.
My pain is blind—do not augment it,
say not a word about the past,
and, solicitous friend, do not
disturb the sick man when he's dozing.
I sleep—and I find slumber pleasant;
forget the dreams that are no more,
for in my soul you will awaken
mere agitation, but not love.

<1821>

ПОЦЕЛУЙ

Сей поцелуй, дарованный тобой,
Преследует мое воображенье:
И в шуме дня, и в тишине ночной
Я чувствую его напечатленье!
Сойдет ли сон и взор сомкнет ли мой,
Мне снишься ты, мне снится наслажденье;
Обман исчез, нет счастья! и со мной
Одна любовь, одно изнеможенье.

THE KISS

This kiss, which you presented as a gift,
continues to pursue my imagination:
in the noise of day, in the quiet of night
upon my lips I still feel its impression.
Should sleep descend on me and shut my eyes,
of you I dream, I dream of sweet sensation;
the illusion's gone—no happiness!—and I
have only love, have only enervation.

<1822>, <1827>

ДЕЛЬВИГУ

Дай руку мне, товарищ добрый мой,
Путем одним пойдем до двери гроба,
И тщетно нам за грозною бедой
Беду грозней пошлет судьбины злоба.
Ты помнишь ли, в какой печальный срок
Впервые ты узнал мой уголок?
Ты помнишь ли, с какой судьбой суровой
Боролся я, почти лишенных сил?
Я погибал: ты дух мой оживил
Надеждою возвышенной и новой.
Ты ввел меня в семейство добрых Муз;
Деля досуг меж ими и тобою,
Я ль чувствовал ее свинцовый груз
И перед ней унизился душою?
Ты сам порой глубокую печаль
В душе носил, но что? не мне ли вверить
Спешил ее? И дружба не всегда ль
Хоть несколько могла ее умерить?
Забытые фортуною слепой,
Мы ей назло друг в друге все имели
И, дружества твердя обет святой,
Бестрепетно в глаза судьбе глядели.

О! верь мне в том: чем жребий ни грозит,
Упорствуя в старинной неприязни,
Душа моя не ведает боязни,
Души моей ничто не изменит!
Так, милый друг! позволят ли мне боги
Ярмо забот сложить когда-нибудь
И весело на светлый мир взглянуть,
По-прежнему ль ко мне пребудут строги,

TO DELVIG

Give me your hand, my friend, and let us go
along the same road till we reach the grave,
and spiteful fate will send us blow on blow,
each one more terrible, but all in vain.
Do you recall that time, in all its gloom,
when first you visited my little room?
Do you recall the fate with which I struggled
almost to my last strength—how cruel its force?
I was perishing: my spirit you restored,
instilling in me hope, new and exalted.
You brought me to the good Muses' family—
dividing between you and them my time,
did I then feel my leaden destiny,
or in my soul bow down to it in shame?
You too sometimes would carry a deep sorrow
within your soul—what then? Did you not run
to open your heart to me? And did not always
friendship, if but a little, ease the pain?
Blind fortune had forgotten us, but we,
to spite her, had everything in each other,
and so, pronouncing friendship's sacred vow,
we looked fate in the eye and did not tremble.

You may be sure of this: no matter what
chance may threaten, stubborn in its old hatred,
my soul will not succumb to trepidation;
my soul is firm—nothing will alter it!
That's true, dear friend! Whether the gods allow me
one day to cast this yoke of care aside
and gaze with gladness on the shining world,
or do not change and stay unfriendly to me,

Всегда я твой. Судьей души моей
Ты должен быть и в вёдро и в ненастье,
Удвоишь ты моих счастливых дней
Неполное без разделенья счастье;
В дни бедствия я знаю, где найти
Участие в судьбе своей тяжелой:
Чего ж робеть на жизненном пути?
Иду вперед с надеждою веселой.
Еще позволь желание одно
Мне произнесть: молюся я судьбине,
Чтоб для тебя я стал хотя отныне,
Чем для меня ты стал уже давно.

I am forever yours. And you must be
the judge of my soul in fair or bitter weather;
my happy days you double—incomplete
is happiness if it is not divided.
In times of anguish I know where to find
a heart that feels the heavy fate I suffer:
so what have I to fear upon life's road?
Filled with a joyful hope I will march onward.
Allow me to express just one thing more,
just one more wish: I pray to destiny
that, from now on at least, for you I be
what you became for me so long ago.

<1822>, <1827>

ЭПИЛОГ

Чувствительны мне дружеские пени,
Но искренне забыл я Геликон
И признаюсь: неприхотливой лени
Мне нравится приманчивый закон;
Охота петь уж не владеет мною:
Она прошла, погасла, как любовь.
Опять любить, играть струнами вновь
Желал бы я, но утомлен душою.
Иль жить нельзя отрадою иною?
С бездействием любезен мне союз;
Лелеемый счастливым усыпленьем
Я не хочу притворным исступленьем
Обманывать ни юных дев, ни муз.

EPILOGUE

I'm not insensitive to friends' objections,
but truly, Helicon is now my past,
and I admit it: I like the seductive
regime of undemanding laziness.
The appetite for song no longer rules me:
it's gone away, died out, the same as love.
To love again? To play my strings once more?—
I'd like to, but my soul is much too weary.
Is living by some other joy forbidden?
This pact with idleness is what I choose;
I'm basking in a happy, drowsy slumber
and do not want, with feigned displays of fervor,
to trick either young maidens or the muse.

<1823>

ПРИЗНАНИЕ

Притворной нежности не требуй от меня:
Я сердца моего не скрою хлад печальной.
Ты пра́ва, в нем уж нет прекрасного огня
    Моей любви первоначальной.
Напрасно я себе на память приводил
И милый образ твой, и прежние мечтанья:
    Безжизненны мои воспоминанья,
    Я клятвы дал, но дал их выше сил.

    Я не пленен красавицей другою,
Мечты ревнивые от сердца удали;
Но годы долгие в разлуке протекли,
Но в бурях жизненных развлекся я душою.
Уж ты жила неверной тенью в ней;
Уже к тебе взывал я редко, принужденно,
    И пламень мой, слабея постепенно,
    Собою сам погас в душе моей.
Верь, жалок я один. Душа любви желает,
    Но я любить не буду вновь;
Вновь не забудусь я: вполне упоевает
    Нас только первая любовь.

Грущу я; но и грусть минует, знаменуя
Судьбины полную победу надо мной.
Кто знает? мнением сольюся я с толпой;
Подругу, без любви — кто знает? — изберу я.
На брак обдуманный я руку ей подам
    И в храме стану рядом с нею,
Невинной, преданной, быть может, лучшим снам,
    И назову ее моею;

CONFESSION

Do not demand of me pretended tenderness:
the mournful coldness of my heart I won't conceal.
You're right—it burns no longer with the beautiful
    blaze of my initial love.
In vain I've tried to summon into memory
your darling image and the things we once imagined—
    but lifeless now are all my recollections;
      I did make vows, but made them past my strength.

    I'm not in thrall to any other beauty—
jealous imaginings put far away from your heart—
but long years have passed with the two of us apart,
and in the storms of life my soul became distracted.
You lived there still, but as a wavering shadow,
and rarely, awkwardly, would I invoke your name,
    and, dwindling over time, the flame
    in my soul flickered out on its own.
Believe me, I'm the wretched one. My soul is craving
    love, but I will not love again—
I won't lose myself again: total intoxication
    belongs to our first love alone.

I'm sad. But sadness too will pass—and so betoken
    fate's total triumph over me.
Who knows? I'll come to think the way most people think
and without love may even—who knows?—choose a companion.
I'll offer her my hand in a marriage carefully pondered,
    stand at the altar by her side—
she innocent and, perhaps, to the finest dreams devoted—
    and I will call her mine.

И весть к тебе придет, но не завидуй нам:
Обмена тайных дум не будет между нами,
Душевным прихотям мы воли не дадим,
    Мы не сердца под брачными венцами,
    Мы жребии свои соединим.

Прощай! Мы долго шли дорогою одною;
Путь новый я избрал, путь новый избери;
Печаль бесплодную рассудком усмири
И не вступай, молю, в напрасный суд со мною.
    Невластны мы в самих себе
    И, в молодые наши леты,
    Даем поспешные обеты,
Смешные, может быть, всевидящей судьбе.

And you will hear the news, but do not envy us:
no exchange of secret thoughts will ever be between us;
we'll give no liberty to our innermost caprices,
    for what we join beneath the bridal crowns
    won't be our hearts—only our destinies.

Farewell! Long did we travel the same road together.
A new path I have chosen; a new path you should choose.
    Your fruitless sorrow let your reason soothe,
And, please, don't enter into pointless judgment with me.
    We have no power in ourselves,
    and in our youthful years we utter
    promises that are ill-considered
and maybe, to all-seeing fate, ridiculous.

<1823>, <1833>

БЕЗНАДЕЖНОСТЬ

Желанье счастия в меня вдохнули боги:
Я требовал его от неба и земли
И вслед за призраком, манящим издали,
    Жизнь перешел до полдороги;
Но прихотям судьбы я боле не служу:
Счастливый отдыхом, на счастие похожим,
Отныне с рубежа на поприще гляжу
    И скромно кланяюсь прохожим.

HOPELESSNESS

Desire for happiness the gods enkindled in me:
I claimed it as my right from heaven and from earth,
and so, chasing a specter that beckoned from afar,
    I reached the midpoint of life's journey.
But I no longer serve the vagaries of fate:
now happy in a rest that happiness resembles,
I stand henceforth and watch the arena from the side
    and bow to all who pass, most humbly.

<1823>, <1827>

ИСТИНА

О счастии с младенчества тоскуя,
    Все счастьем беден я,
Или вовек его не обрету я
    В пустыне бытия?

Младые сны от сердца отлетели,
    Не узнаю я свет;
Надежд своих лишен я прежней цели,
    А новой цели нет.

Безумен ты и все твои желанья —
    Мне тайный голос рек;
И лучшие мечты моей созданья
    Отвергнул я навек.

Но для чего души разуверенье
    Свершилось не вполне?
Зачем же в ней слепое сожаленье
    Живет о старине?

Так некогда обдумывал с роптаньем
    Я тяжкий жребий свой,
Вдруг Истину (то не было мечтаньем)
    Узрел перед собой.

"Светильник мой укажет путь ко счастью! —
    Вещала.— Захочу
И, страстного, отрадному бесстрастью
    Тебя я научу.

TRUTH

Happiness I have hungered for since childhood,
    and happiness still lack,
or could it be that I will never find it
    in the wilderness of life?

The dreams of youth have flown off from my heart,
    and I don't know the world;
I've lost the former goal of all my hopes,
    and there is no new goal.

You are insane, you and all your desires,
    an inner voice proclaimed,
and so my fantasy's finest creations
    I banished for all time.

But what's the point of the soul's disillusion
    if it is not complete?
Why in my soul does blind regret still linger
    for a time that is long past?

Once I was thus pondering and grumbling
    over my heavy fate,
when suddenly I saw (it was no daydream)
    the Truth before my eyes.

"My lamp shall light the way to happiness!"
    she prophesied. "Should I wish,
O man of passions, I could teach you all
    the joys of passionlessness.

Пускай со мной ты сердца жар погубишь,
    Пускай, узнав людей,
Ты, может быть, испуганный, разлюбишь
    И ближних и друзей.

Я бытия все прелести разрушу,
    Но ум наставлю твой;
Я оболью суровым хладом душу,
    Но дам душе покой."

Я трепетал, словам ее внимая,
    И горестно в ответ
Промолвил ей: "О гостья неземная!
    Печален твой привет.

Светильник твой — светильник погребальный
    Последних благ моих!
Твой мир, увы! могилы мир печальный,
    И страшен для живых.

Нет, я не твой! в твоей науке строгой
    Я счастья не найду;
Покинь меня: кой-как моей дорогой
    Один я побреду.

Прости! иль нет: когда мое светило
    Во звездной вышине
Начнет бледнеть, и все, что сердцу мило,
    Забыть придется мне,

Явись тогда! раскрой тогда мне очи,
    Мой разум просвети,
Чтоб, жизнь презрев, я мог в обитель ночи
    Безропотно сойти."

"With me you shall extinguish the heart's fever,
    shall learn what people are,
and then, perhaps alarmed, you shall stop loving
    your family and friends.

"I will ruin all the sweetness of existence,
    but I will instruct your mind.
Your soul I will immerse in bitter coldness,
    but I will bring her peace."

I trembled as I listened to her words and,
    in sorrowful reply,
I said to her: "O visitor unearthly!
    Your greeting is woe to me.

"This lamp of yours—it is a funeral lantern
    for the last good things I have.
Your peace—alas!—the sad peace of the coffin,
    dreaded by all who live.

"No, I am not yours! In your strict instruction
    I won't find happiness.
So leave me! Somehow I will go on stumbling
    along my road, alone.

"Farewell!—Or no! When in the starry heights
    my star begins to fade
and everything that's precious to my heart
    I will have to forget,

"visit me then! And then my eyes uncover,
    my reason fill with light,
that, hating life, I go down without murmur
    into the realm of night."

<1823>

39

К...

Мне с упоением заметным
Глаза поднять на вас беда:
Вы их встречаете всегда
С лицом сердитым, неприветным.
Я полон страстною тоской,
Но нет! рассудка не забуду
И на нескромный пламень мой
Ответа требовать не буду.
Не терпит Бог младых проказ
Ланит увядших, впалых глаз.
Надежды были бы напрасны,
И к вам не ими я влеком.
Любуюсь вами, как цветком,
И счастлив тем, что вы прекрасны.
Когда я в очи вам гляжу,
Предавшись нежному томленью,
Слегка о прошлом я тужу,
Но рад, что сердце нахожу
Еще способным к упоенью.
Меж мудрецами был чудак:
"Я мыслю,— пишет он,— итак,
Я несомненно существую".
Нет! любишь ты, и потому
Ты существуешь,— я пойму
Скорее истину такую.
Огнем, похищенным с небес,
Япетов сын, гласит преданье,
Одушевил свое созданье,
И наказал его Зевес
Неумолимый, Прометея
К скалам Кавказа приковал,

TO...

The obvious infatuation
in my eyes when I look up at you
dooms me, for in return you show
a face of frosty indignation.
The ache of passion fills my soul,
but no! I won't abandon reason,
and no response will I compel
to this my ardor so unseemly.
God suffers not the youthful tricks
of sunken eyes and pallid cheeks.
To hope would be a vain endeavor,
and hope's not why I'm drawn to you.
I admire you as I would a flower,
am happy because you're beautiful.
And when I look into your eyes,
surrendering to a tender languor,
I grieve a little for the past,
but I am glad to find my heart
still able to feel infatuation.
There once was a philosopher,
a peculiar man, who wrote the words:
"I think and therefore, without question,
I am." But no! You love and that
is why you are—this is a truth
that sooner wins my recognition.
With fire he'd stolen from the skies,
Iapetus' son (so says tradition)
engendered life in his creation,
and Zeus, who would not be appeased,
punished Prometheus: he left him
shackled on the Caucasian rocks,

41

И сердце вран ему клевал;
Но, дерзость жертвы разумея,
Кто приговор не осуждал?
В огне волшебных ваших взоров
Я занял сердца бытие:
Ваш гнев достойнее укоров,
Чем преступление мое;
Но не сержусь я, шутка водит
Моим догадливым пером.
Я захожу в ваш милый дом,
Как вольнодумец в храм заходит.
Душою праздный с давних пор,
Еще твержу любовный вздор,
Еще беру прельщенья меры,
Как по привычке прежних дней
Он ароматы жжет без веры
Богам, чужим душе своей.

a raven pecking at his heart.
Who, understanding well the victim's
boldness, has not condemned the verdict?
In the fire of your magic eyes
I seized upon my heart's true being:
the wrath you show is more deserving
of blame than any crime of mine.
But I'm not angry; my shrewd pen is
guided by nothing more than jest.
I walk into your lovely house
like a skeptic entering a temple.
My soul empty a long, long time,
the nonsense of love I still declaim,
still ply the tactics of enticement,
just as, following a habit of old,
without belief he still burns incense
to gods now alien to his soul.

<1824>, <1827>

А. А. В—ОЙ

Очарованье красоты
   В тебе не страшно нам:
Не будишь нас, как солнце, ты
   К мятежным суетам;
От дольней жизни, как луна,
   Манишь за край земной,
И при тебе душа полна
   Священной тишиной.

TO A. A. V.

Beauty's enchanting power, in you,
      is nothing that we fear:
you do not rouse us, like the sun,
      to stormy activity.
From mortal life you, like the moon,
      call us beyond earth's realm,
and in your presence the soul is filled
      with holy quietness.

1824?, <1826>

ОНА

Есть что-то в ней, что красоты прекрасней,
Что говорит не с чувствами — с душой;
Есть что-то в ней над сердцем самовластней
Земной любви и прелести земной.

Как сладкое душе воспоминанье,
Как милый свет родной звезды твоей,
Какое-то влечет очарованье
К ее ногам и под защиту к ней.

Когда ты с ней, мечты твоей неясной
Неясною владычицей она:
Не мыслишь ты — и только лишь прекрасной
Присутствием душа твоя полна.

Бредешь ли ты дорогою возвратной,
С ней разлучась, в пустынный угол твой —
Ты полон весь мечтою необъятной,
Ты полон весь таинственной тоской.

SHE

There's something in her more sublime than beauty,
which speaks not to the emotions, but the soul,
something that rules your heart more absolutely
than any earthly love or earthly charm.

Like a memory in which the soul takes pleasure,
like your natal star, which shines with gentle light,
a kind of magic power draws you to her,
to her protection, prostrate at her feet.

When you are next to her, she is obscurely
the reigning sovereign of your dream obscure.
You do not think—and nothing but the presence
of the sublime one permeates your soul.

And when you leave her, as you make the journey
along the road back to your lonely room,
you are filled with a dream beyond all measure,
you are filled with a longing you can't explain.

1824?, <1827>

ОПРАВДАНИЕ

Решительно печальных строк моих
Не хочешь ты ответом удостоить;
Не тронулась ты нежным чувством их
И презрела мне сердце успокоить!
Не оживу я в памяти твоей,
Не вымолю прощенья у жестокой!
Виновен я: я был неверен ей;
Нет жалости к тоске моей глубокой!
Виновен я: я славил жен других…
Так! но когда их слух предубежденный
Я обольщал игрою струн моих,
К тебе летел я думой умиленной,
Тебя я пел под именами их.
Виновен я: на балах городских,
Среди толпы, весельем оживленной,
При гуле струн, в безумном вальсе мча
То Делию, то Дафну, то Лилету
И всем троим готовый сгоряча
Произнести по страстному обету;
Касаяся душистых их кудрей
Лицом моим; объемля жадной дланью
Их стройный стан; — так! в памяти моей
Уж не было подруги прежних дней,
И предан был я новому мечтанью!
Но к ним ли я любовию пылал?
Нет, милая! когда в уединенье
Себя потом я тихо проверял,
Их находя в моем воображенье,
Тебя одну я в сердце обретал!
Приветливых, послушных без ужимок,
Улыбчивых для шалости младой,

JUSTIFICATION

You are determined, then: you will not deign
to respond to the tearful lines I wrote you.
Unmoved by their deep feeling, you disdain
to give my heart a single word of comfort.
I shall not be revived among your thoughts;
you, so unkind, will offer no forgiveness.
I am guilty: I did betray your trust,
but you will have no pity on my anguish.
I am guilty: I sang the praise of others—
that's true enough. But even as I flattered
their vain attention with my lyre's play,
I was with you in the sweet subject matter:
you were my song, I only used their names.
I am guilty: among the gleeful throng
at the balls in the city, to the sound
of violins, in the mad waltz I whirled
first Delia, then Daphne, then Liletta,
and to all three I was prepared to utter
a vow of passion, caught up in the thrill
of the moment, feeling their perfumed curls
against my cheek, my ardent hand embracing
their slender waists—all that is true! The girl
I once had cherished now escaped me
and I surrendered to new reveries.
But did I ever burn with love for them?
No, dearest! Later, when I quietly
in solitude examined what I felt,
I may have found them in my fantasy,
but you alone I found within my heart.
Welcoming, willing girls, who make no faces
but always have a smile for youthful fun—

Из-за угла пафосских пилигримок
Я сторожил вечернею порой;
На миг один их своевольный пленник,
Я только был шалун, а не изменник.
Нет! более надменна, чем нежна,
Ты все еще обид своих полна…
Прости ж навек! но знай, что двух виновных,
Не одного, найдутся имена
В стихах моих, в преданиях любовных.

I would await these Paphian pilgrimesses
around the corner when the day was done.
For a moment I made myself their captive,
but this was not betrayal, only mischief.
No use! You are more arrogant than tender,
and cling to all the ways you've been offended…
Goodbye forever, then! But know this well:
two guilty names, not one, will be remembered
in my verse, and in the tales of love we tell.

<1824>, <1827>

ЧЕРЕП

Усопший брат! кто сон твой возмутил?
Кто пренебрег святынею могильной?
В разрытый дом к тебе я нисходил,
Я в руки брал твой череп желтый, пыльной!

Еще носил волос остатки он;
Я зрел на нем ход постепенный тленья.
Ужасный вид! как сильно поражен
Им мыслящий наследник разрушенья!

Со мной толпа безумцев молодых
Над ямою безумно хохотала;
Когда б тогда, когда б в руках моих
Глава твоя внезапно провещала!

Когда б она цветущим, пылким нам
И каждый час грозимым смертным часом
Все истины, известные гробам,
Произнесла своим бесстрастным гласом!

Что говорю? Стократно благ закон,
Молчаньем ей уста запечатлевший;
Обычай прав, усопших важный сон
Нам почитать издревле повелевший.

Живи живой, спокойно тлей мертвец!
Всесильного ничтожное созданье,
О человек! уверься наконец,
Не для тебя ни мудрость, ни всезнанье!

THE SKULL

Departed brother! Who has disturbed your rest?
Who has defiled the sanctity of the tomb?
I went down to you, into your ransacked house;
I took in my hands your yellowed, dusty skull.

It still bore bits of hair; I could detect
on it the slow advance of decomposition.
A horrid sight! How powerful its effect
upon the thinking heir of such destruction!

Above the pit, the gang of mad young men
I'd come here with were laughing their heads off madly.
If only there in my hands, if only then,
your head had suddenly started prophesying!

If only it had spoken then to us—
flourishing, ardent, and every moment threatened
by death—pronouncing in a passionless voice
all verities with which tombs are acquainted.

But what am I saying? Blest be a hundred times
that law which seals the mouths of skulls with silence.
Custom is right in its age-old command
that we respect the departed's solemn slumber.

Let the living live; the corpse, decay in peace!
O paltry creation of the Almighty—
O man! now be assured at last of this:
you are not made for wisdom or all-knowing.

Нам надобны и страсти и мечты,
В них бытия условие и пища:
Не подчинишь одним законам ты
И света шум и тишину кладбища!

Природных чувств мудрец не заглушит
И от гробов ответа не получит:
Пусть радости живущим жизнь дарит,
А смерть сама их умереть научит.

We need our passions and our dreams; they are
the condition and the food of our existence:
never will you subject to the same law
the noise of the world and the graveyard's silence.

The wise man will not stifle innate feeling;
no answer from the tomb will ever reach him.
Let life bestow its joys upon the living,
and as for dying, death itself will teach them.

<1824>, <1826>

БУРЯ

Завыла буря; хлябь морская
Клокочет и ревет, и черные валы
Идут, до неба восставая,
Бьют, гневно пеняся, в прибрежные скалы.

Чья неприязненная сила,
Чья своевольная рука
Сгустила в тучи облака
И на краю небес ненастье зародила?
Кто, возмутив природы чин,
Горами влажными на землю гонит море?
Не тот ли злобный дух, геены властелин,
Что по вселенной розлил горе,
Что человека подчинил
Желаньям, немощи, страстям и разрушенью
И на творенье ополчил
Все силы, данные творенью?
Земля трепещет перед ним:
Он небо заслонил огромными крылами
И двигает ревущими водами,
Бунтующим могуществом своим.

Когда придет желанное мгновенье,
Когда волнам твоим я вверюсь, океан?
Но знай: красой далеких стран
Не очаровано мое воображенье.
Под небом лучшим обрести
Я лучшей доли не сумею;
Вновь не смогу душой моею
В краю цветущим расцвести.
Меж тем от прихоти судьбины,

THE STORM

The storm begins to howl; the heaving
depths of the sea are thrashing, roaring, and black waves,
 advancing, rising to the heavens,
crash, foaming angrily, against the coastal cliffs.

 Whose adversarial force is this?
 Whose willful and capricious hand
 amassed the clouds into storm clouds and
on the brink of the heavens spawned the gusting winds?
 Who is disrupting nature's pattern,
in watery mountains driving the sea onto the land?
Is it not that spiteful spirit, the ruler of Gehenna,
 who flooded the universe with pain,
 who subjugated humankind
to lusts and frailty, to passions and destruction,
 and who marshaled against creation
 every force creation owned?
 The earth now trembles at his sight:
with his enormous wings he has blotted out the heavens
 and moves the waters, roaring and seething,
 by the power of his mutinous might.

 When will the moment come, so eagerly awaited?
When will I entrust myself, Ocean, to your billows?
 But know that it is not the beauty
of distant climes that captures my imagination.
 Beneath a better sky to find
 a better lot is past my knowledge,
 and even in a land of blossoms,
 my soul will never blossom again.
 Whether it come by the whim of fate,

Меж тем от медленной отравы бытия,
В покое раболепнем я
Ждать не хочу своей кончины;
На яростных волнах, в борьбе со гневом их,
Она отраднее гордыне человека!
Как жаждал радостей младых
Я на заре младого века,
Так ныне, океан! я жажду бурь твоих!

Волнуйся, восставай на каменные грани;
Он веселит меня, твой грозный, дикий рев,
Как зов к давно желанной брани,
Как мощного врага мне чем-то лестный гнев.

or whether by the sluggish poison of existence,
    I do not wish, meantime, to wait
    in servile peace for my extinction.
To die on raging billows, wrestling with their wrath,
is far more gratifying to the pride of man!
    As I hungered for the thrills of youth
    when my own youth was in its dawn,
I now am hungering, O Ocean, for your storms!

So toss and churn, rise up against your stony borders:
your wild and terrible roar fills me with joy,
    like the summons to a long-desired battle,
like the anger, somehow flattering, of a mighty foe.

1824

***

Отчизны враг, слуга царя,
        К бичу народов — самовластью
Какой-то адскою любовию горя,
        Он незнаком с другою страстью.
Скрываясь от очей, злодействует впотьмах,
        Чтобы злодействовать свободней.
Не нужно имени: у всех оно в устах,
Как имя страшное владыки преисподней.

* * *

The fatherland's foe, the tsar's valet—
　　he burns with a kind of love infernal
for the scourge of the nations, for autocracy;
　　with no other passion is he familiar.
Hiding from sight, he does his evil in the shadows,
　　that evil may be more freely done.
No need for a name: it's on the lips of everybody,
like the dread name of the prince of the nether realm.

Late 1824–early 1825

***

Как много ты в немного дней
Прожить, прочувствовать успела!
В мятежном пламени страстей
Как страшно ты перегорела!
Раба томительной мечты!
В тоске душевной пустоты,
Чего еще душою хочешь?
Как Магдалина плачешь ты,
И как русалка ты хохочешь!

* * *

How much you have in so few days
managed to live, managed to feel!
And in your passions' violent flames
how terribly you have burned out!
Slave to exhausting fantasies!
In the ache of your soul's emptiness,
what now might be your soul's desire?
You're weeping like the Magdalene
and wildly laughing like a siren!

Late 1824—early 1825

НАДПИСЬ

Взгляни на лик холодный сей,
    Взгляни: в нем жизни нет;
Но как на нем былых страстей
    Еще заметен след!
Так ярый ток, оледенев,
    Над бездною висит,
Утратив прежний грозный рев,
    Храня движенья вид.

INSCRIPTION

Look, if you will, at this cold face;
    observe: no life is there.
And yet how evident the trace
    of passions that once were.
Thus raging torrents turn to ice,
    suspended above the deep,
and sound no more their awesome voice,
    yet motion's semblance keep.

<1825>

СТАНСЫ

В глуши лесов счастлив один,
Другой страдает на престоле;
На высоте земных судьбин
И в незаметной, низкой доле
Всех благ возможных тот достиг,
Кто дух судьбы своей постиг.

Мы все блаженствуем равно,
Но все блаженствуем различно;
Уделом нашим решено,
Как наслаждаться им прилично,
И кто нам лучший дал совет,
Иль Эпикур, иль Эпиктет?

Меня тягчил печалей груз;
Но не упал я перед роком,
Нашел отраду в песнях муз
И в равнодушии высоком,
И светом презренный удел
Облагородить я умел.

Хвала вам, боги! предо мной
Вы оправдалися отныне!
Готов я с бодрою душой
На все угодное судьбине,
И никогда сей лиры глас
Не оскорбит роптаньем вас!

STANZAS

Happy is one in the forest wilds,
another sits on a throne in torment:
at the height of earthly destinies,
or in a lowly lot unnoticed,
all possible good has he attained
who knows the spirit of his fate.

We all are equal in our bliss,
but in our bliss we all are different;
our lot determines just what is
the right way to take pleasure in it,
and who's the better one to teach us:
Epicurus or Epictetus?

A weight of sorrows held me down,
but I was not crushed by destiny;
I found joy in the Muse's song,
and in lofty equanimity,
and knew how to ennoble a fate
for which the world had but contempt.

Praise be to you, O gods! Henceforth
before me you are justified!
With buoyant soul I am prepared
for all fate pleases to decide,
and never will my lyre's strains
again offend you with complaints.

<1825>

СТАНСЫ

Судьбой наложенные цепи
Упали с рук моих, и вновь
Я вижу вас, родные степи,
Моя начальная любовь.

Степного неба свод желанный,
Степного воздуха струи,
На вас я в неге бездыханной
Остановил глаза мои.

Но мне увидеть было слаще
Лес на покате двух холмов
И скромный дом в садовой чаще —
Приют младенческих годов.

Промчалось ты, златое время!
С тех пор по свету я бродил
И наблюдал людское племя
И, наблюдая, восскорбил.

Ко благу пылкое стремленье
От неба было мне дано;
Но обрело ли разделенье,
Но принесло ли плод оно?..

Я братьев знал; но сны младые
Соединили нас на миг:
Далече бедствуют иные,
И в мире нет уже других.

STANZAS

The chains that fate had laid upon me
fell from my hands and once again
I'm seeing you, my native steppeland,
the first love that I ever had.

The vaulted steppeland sky I longed for,
the currents in the steppeland air—
I let my eyes linger upon you
in breathless sensual delight.

But sweeter it was when I caught sight of
the woods that climb the slope of two hills
and the modest house within the fruit grove,
the haven of my childhood years.

You passed so quickly, golden days!
And ever since, I've roamed the world
and contemplated the human race,
and contemplating it, I mourned.

Heaven endowed me with an ardent
determination for the good.
But did it meet with understanding?
But did it bring forth any fruit?

I did know brothers—for but an instant
we were united by youthful dreams:
some far away in misery languish;
others are in this world no more.

Я твой, родимая дуброва!
Но от насильственных судьбин
Молить хранительного крова
К тебе пришел я не один.

Привел под сень твою святую
Я соучастницу в мольбах:
Мою супругу молодую
С младенцем тихим на руках.

Пускай, пускай в глуши смиренной,
С ней, милой, быт мой утая,
Других урочищей вселенной
Не буду помнить бытия.

Пускай, о свете не тоскуя,
Предав забвению людей,
Кумиры сердца сберегу я
Одни, одни в любви моей.

I belong to you, beloved woods!
To beg for shelter I have come,
for refuge from the violent fates—
but I have not come here alone.

I bring beneath your sacred bower
a co-participant in these prayers:
she is my young wife, and she carries
a quiet infant in her arms.

O let me, let me, hiding away here
in the humble wilds with my love, with her,
forget the existence of any other
topography in the universe.

Let me, with no regret for the world,
surrendered to oblivion,
preserve as idols of my heart
only, only the ones I love.

1827

ПОСЛЕДНЯЯ СМЕРТЬ

Есть бытие; но именем каким
Его назвать? Ни сон оно, ни бденье;
Меж них оно, и в человеке им
С безумием граничит разуменье.
Он в полноте понятья своего,
А между тем, как волны, на него
Одни других мятежней, своенравней,
Видения бегут со всех сторон:
Как будто бы своей отчизны давней
Стихийному смятенью отдан он;
Но иногда, мечтой воспламененный,
Он видит свет, другим не откровенный.

Созданье ли болезненной мечты
Иль дерзкого ума соображенье,
Во глубине полночной темноты
Представшее очам моим виденье?
Не ведаю; но предо мной тогда
Раскрылися грядущие года;
События вставали, развивались,
Волнуяся, подобно облакам,
И полными эпохами являлись
От времени до времени очам,
И наконец я видел без покрова
Последнюю судьбу всего живого.

Сначала мир явил мне дивный сад;
Везде искусств, обилия приметы;
Близ веси весь и подле града град,
Везде дворцы, театры, водометы,
Везде народ, и хитрый свой закон

THE LAST DEATH

There is a state of being—but what name
to give it? It is neither sleep nor waking.
It lies between the two, and in a man
it is the place where madness borders reason.
He's still in full possession of his mind,
but all the while, like waves, each one more wild,
each one more unpredictable than the other,
visions come rushing at him from every side—
it is as if he had been handed over
to his primal homeland's elemental strife.
But sometimes, blazing with imagination,
he sees a light that is from others hidden.

What was the vision that appeared to me,
emerging from the depths of midnight darkness—
the invention of disordered fantasy,
or the conception of a mind audacious?
I do not know, but it was then I saw
the years that are to come reveal themselves.
Events arose, unfolded, undulated
like billows of cloud, and from time to time
they coalesced into entire epochs,
before my eyes assuming visible form,
until, without a veil, at last I witnessed
the final destiny of all things living.

A wondrous garden I thought the world at first:
everywhere signs of art, signs of abundance;
cities and villages, one after the next;
everywhere palaces, theaters, fountains;
everywhere man—and all of nature's force

Стихии все признать заставил он.
Уж он морей мятежные пучины
На островах искусственных селил,
Уж рассекал небесные равнины
По прихоти им вымышленных крил;
Все на земле движением дышало,
Все на земле как будто ликовало.

Исчезнули бесплодные года,
Оратаи по воле призывали
Ветра, дожди, жары и холода,
И верною сторицей воздавали
Посевы им, и хищный зверь исчез
Во тьме лесов, и в высоте небес,
И в бездне вод, сраженный человеком,
И царствовал повсюду светлый мир.
Вот, мыслил я, прельщенный дивным веком,
Вот разума великолепный пир!
Врагам его и в стыд и в поученье,
Вот до чего достигло просвещенье!

Прошли века. Яснеть очам моим
Видение другое начинало:
Что человек? что вновь открыто им?
Я гордо мнил, и что же мне предстало?
Наставшую эпоху я с трудом
Постигнуть мог смутившимся умом.
Глаза мои людей не узнавали;
Привыкшие к обилью дольных благ,
На все они спокойные взирали,
Что суеты рождало в их отцах,
Что мысли их, что страсти их, бывало,
Влечением всесильным увлекало.

he had subdued to his ingenious laws.
Already he was, on artificial islands,
making a home of the rebellious seas;
already he was dividing up the heavens
at the whim of the wings he had conceived.
And everything on earth was breathing motion,
and everything on earth seemed jubilation.

The years of barren fields had disappeared;
the plowmen at their will called forth the weather,
the winds and the rains, the heat and the cold,
and everything they sowed repaid their labor
with faithful bounty; gone was the beast of prey
from the dark forest, from the heights of the sky,
from the watery abyss, for man had slain it,
and everywhere there reigned a luminous peace.
Now this—I thought, by the wondrous age enchanted—
now this is Reason's magnificent feast!
To its enemies' chagrin and their instruction,
this is what enlightenment has accomplished!

Centuries passed by. And before my eyes
another vision slowly started forming.
What is man now? What new discoveries
are his?—I proudly wondered. And what was shown me?
The age that now had taken shape I could
but barely grasp with my bewildered mind.
My eyes no longer recognized these people.
Accustomed to a wealth of earthly goods,
they contemplated everything serenely
that in their fathers had caused great unrest,
that once had held their fathers' thoughts and passions
in the grip of an all-powerful attraction.

Желания земные позабыв,
Чуждаяся их грубого влеченья,
Душевных снов, высоких снов призыв
Им заменил другие побужденья,
И в полное владение свое
Фантазия взяла их бытие,
И умственной природе уступила
Телесная природа между них:
Их в эмпирей и в хаос уносила
Живая мысль на крылиях своих;
Но по земле с трудом они ступали,
И браки их бесплодны пребывали.

Прошли века, и тут моим очам
Открылася ужасная картина:
Ходила смерть по суше, по водам,
Свершалася живущего судьбина.
Где люди? где? скрывалися в гробах!
Как древние столпы на рубежах,
Последние семейства истлевали;
В развалинах стояли города,
По пажитям заглохнувшим блуждали
Без пастырей безумные стада;
С людьми для них исчезло пропитанье;
Мне слышалось их гладное блеянье.

И тишина глубокая вослед
Торжественно повсюду воцарилась,
И в дикую порфиру древних лет
Державная природа облачилась.
Величествен и грустен был позор
Пустынных вод, лесов, долин и гор.
По-прежнему животворя природу,

Earthly desires forgotten, they eschewed
such primitive attractions, and the summons
of spiritual dreams, of lofty dreams, instead
supplanted in them every other purpose;
and their entire being was subject to
the absolute control of Fantasy,
and in their world the nature of the body
gave way before the nature of the mind:
on wings of living thought they were transported
to the Empyrean or to Chaos' realm;
but on the earth they moved with heavy footsteps,
and many of their marriages were childless.

Centuries passed again, and before my eyes,
a horrifying spectacle now opened:
Death walked abroad, on land, across the seas—
the fate of the living world I saw unfolding.
Where were the people? Where? In sepulchers!
Like ancient pillars marking the frontiers,
the last of the families were dying embers.
Abandoned and in ruins the cities stood,
and in the fields, now overgrown with brambles,
the herds wandered—without a shepherd, mad.
With people gone, so was the food they needed;
I heard the echo of their famished bleating.

And afterwards, deep silence was enthroned
throughout the world, majestical and solemn;
and regal Nature once again put on
the wild purple of an era long forgotten.
Grand and melancholy was the scene
of empty valleys, mountains, woods, and streams.
And as before, bestowing life on Nature,

На небосклон светило дня взошло,
Но на земле ничто его восходу
Произнести привета не могло.
Один туман над ней, синея, вился
И жертвою чистительной дымился.

on the horizon the light of the day appeared,
but now upon the earth nothing was able
to utter any greeting at its ascent.
There was only the mist, dark blue and twisting,
like cleansing smoke from a sacrificial victim.

<1827>

УВЕРЕНИЕ

Нет, обманула вас молва,
По-прежнему дышу я вами,
И надо мной свои права
Вы не утратили с годами.
Другим курил я фимиам,
Но вас носил в святыне сердца;
Молился новым образам,
Но с беспокойством староверца.

ASSURANCE

No, you have been deceived by talk;
I breathe you as I did before,
and you have not lost any rights
over me with the passing years.
Incense I burned to others, but you
I held in my heart's sanctuary;
to new icons I prayed—that's true,
but with an Old Believer's worry.

1828?

ФЕЯ

Порою ласковую фею
Я вижу в обаянье сна,
И всей наукою своею
Служить готова мне она.
Душой обманутой ликуя,
Мои мечты ей лепечу я;
Но что же? странно и во сне
Непокупное счастье мне:
Всегда дарам своим предложит
Условье некое она,
Которым, злобно смышлена,
Их отравит иль уничтожит.
Знать, самым духом мы рабы
Земной насмешливой судьбы;
Знать, миру явному дотоле
Наш бедный ум порабощен,
Что переносит поневоле
И в мир мечты его закон!

THE FAIRY

From time to time a smiling fairy
I see within the spell of dream,
and she is ready to serve me gladly
with all the science she commands.
My heart believes her and rejoices;
I babble out my dearest wishes—
But then what? Even in dream's caress
strange is unbartered happiness:
for with the gifts the fairy brings
invariably there's some condition
by which with spiteful intuition
she makes them vile or worthless things.
Our very spirit, then, must serve
a fate that mocks us here on earth:
the waking world, it seems, has so
enfettered our unfortunate brain
we helplessly apply its law
even in reverie's domain.

1828?

***

Мой дар убог, и голос мой не громок,
Но я живу, и на земли мое
Кому-нибудь любезно бытие:
Его найдет далекий мой потомок
В моих стихах; как знать? душа моя
Окажется с душой его в сношенье,
И как нашел я друга в поколенье,
Читателя найду в потомстве я.

* * *

My gift is meager and my voice not loud,
but I'm alive, and my existence is
beloved to somebody on the earth:
my descendant will find it years from now
in my poems. Who knows? His soul and mine
may prove to be in intimate relation,
and as I found a friend in my generation,
a reader in posterity I'll find.

<1828>

БЕСЕНОК

Слыхал я, добрые друзья,
Что наши прадеды в печали,
Бывало, беса призывали;
Им подражаю в этом я.
Но не пугайтесь: подружился
Я не с проклятым сатаной,
Кому душою поклонился
За деньги старый Громобой;
Узнайте: ласковый бесенок
Меня младенцем навещал
И колыбель мою качал
Под шепот легких побасенок.
С тех пор я вышел из пеленок,
Между мужами возмужал,
Но для него еще ребенок.
Случится ль горе иль беда,
Иль безотчетно иногда
Сгрустнется мне в моей конурке —
Махну рукой: по старине
На сером волке, сивке-бурке
Он мигом явится ко мне.
Больному духу здравьем свистнет,
Бобами думу разведет,
Живой водой веселье вспрыснет,
А горе мертвою зальет.
Когда в задумчивом совете
С самим собой, из-за угла
Гляжу на свет и, видя в свете
Свободу глупости и зла,
Добра и разума прижимку,
Насильем сверженный закон,

THE LITTLE DEMON

I've heard it said, good friends, that when
our forefathers were feeling down,
they'd ask a demon to come round;
in this I like to copy them.
Don't be alarmed: I've not befriended
accursed Satan, to whom that fool
old Thunderclap once made a present—
for ready money—of his soul.
Listen and learn: when I was a baby
a little demon visited me;
he'd rock my cradle lovingly
to the whisper of some silly fable.
I gave up diapers long ago,
with men became a man, but I'll be
always a child for him, I know.
Should sorrow occur, or some disaster,
or sometimes, for no reason at all,
I just feel sad in my little chamber,
I wave my arm and as of old,
on Gray Wolf's back, or Sivka-Burka's,
he's there before me in a second.
My ailing spirit he whistles to health,
with magic beans dispels my thoughts,
sprinkles the water of life on mirth,
on sorrow pours the water of death.
And when, in pensive council with
myself, I look from behind a corner
out at the world, and there I see
folly and evil at liberty,
goodness and reason always hampered,
law overthrown by violence,

Я слабым сердцем возмущен;
Проворно шапку-невидимку
На шар земной набросит он;
Или, в мгновение зеницы,
Чудесный коврик-самолет
Он подо мною развернет,
И коврик тот в сады жар-птицы,
В чертоги дивной царь-девицы
Меня по воздуху несет.
Прощай, владенье грустной были,
Меня смущавшее досель:
Я от твоей бездушной пыли
Уже за тридевять земель.

enraged, my feeble heart protests—
nimbly he tosses over the earth
the cap of invisibility,
or, in the twinkling of an eye,
a flying carpet he unfurls
beneath my feet and wondrously
it bears me swiftly through the air
to the gardens of the Firebird,
the palace of the Maiden Tsar.
Farewell to you, sad truth's dominion,
so far you've caused me only pain:
I've left your heartless dust behind me
and now am thrice-nine lands away.

1828

СМЕРТЬ

Смерть дщерью тьмы не назову я
И, раболепною мечтой
Гробовый остов ей даруя,
Не ополчу ее косой.

О дочь верховного Эфира!
О светозарная краса!
В руке твоей олива мира,
А не губящая коса.

Когда возникнул мир цветущий
Из равновесья диких сил,
В твое храненье Всемогущий
Его устройство поручил.

И ты летаешь над твореньем,
Согласье прям его лия,
И в нем прохладным дуновеньем
Смиряя буйство бытия.

Ты укрощаешь восстающий
В безумной силе ураган,
Ты, на брега свои бегущий,
Вспять повращаешь Океан.

Даешь пределы ты растенью,
Чтоб не покрыл гигантский лес
Земли губительною тенью,
Злак не восстал бы до небес.

DEATH

Death I call not Daughter of Darkness,
nor in some slavish fantasy
do I endow her with a ghastly
skeleton and arm her with a scythe.

O daughter of the highest Aether!
O beauty radiant with light!
It is the olive branch of peace you
hold in your hand, not a deadly scythe.

When from the balance of wild forces
the bright and blossoming world appeared,
its orderly configuration
the Almighty gave into your care.

And so above creation flying,
you pour out concord on its strife;
you are a cool breeze, pacifying
the raucous tumult of this life.

You tame the hurricane uprising
in all the madness of its force,
and you turn back the ocean racing
again and again onto its shores.

On plant life you place limitations,
lest a gigantic forest cast
over the earth its mortal shadow
and grass climb up into the skies.

А человек! святая дева!
Перед тобой с его ланит
Мгновенно сходят пятна гнева,
Жар любострастия бежит.

Дружится праведной тобою
Людей недружная судьба:
Ласкаешь тою же рукою
Ты властелина и раба.

Недоуменье, принужденье,
Условье смутных наших дней;
Ты всех загадок разрешенье,
Ты разрешенье всех цепей.

And what of man? O holy maid!
At your appearance, from his cheek
at once the flush of anger fades,
the fever of lustful passion flees.

In you, who are most just, converge
the divergent fates of humankind:
the lord who rules, the slave who serves
you caress with the selfsame hand.

Bewilderment, coercion—such is
the order of our troubled days,
and you the solution to all riddles,
the dissolution of all chains.

<1828>, <1833>

ОТРЫВОК
(СЦЕНА ИЗ ПОЭМЫ "ВЕРА И НЕВЕРИЕ")

Он
Под этой липою густою
Со мною сядь, мой милый друг;
Смотри, как живо все вокруг!
Какой зеленой пеленою
К реке нисходит этот луг!
Какая свежая дуброва
Глядится с берега другого
В ее веселое стекло!
Как небо чисто и светло!
Все в тишине; едва смущает
Живую сень и чуткий ток
Благуханный ветерок:
Он сердцу счастье навевает!
Молчишь ты?

Она
                О любезный мой!
Всегда я счастлива с тобой
И каждый миг равно ласкаю.

Он
Я с умиленною душой
Красу творенья созерцаю.
От этих вод, лесов и гор
Я на эфирную обитель,
На небеса подъемлю взор
И думаю: велик Зиждитель,
Прекрасен мир! Когда же я
Воспомню тою же порою,

FRAGMENT
(A SCENE FROM THE POEM *BELIEF AND UNBELIEF*)

He:
Beneath this leafy linden tree
come, my dear friend, sit down with me.
Look! Everything's so bright and vivid!
How green the carpet of this meadow,
sloping away down to the river!
How fresh that grove of trees appears
reflected from the opposite shore
in the water's genial mirror.
How luminous the sky, how clear!
And all is still—the lively leaves,
the sensitive current barely are
disturbed by the sweet-smelling breeze,
which fills my heart with happiness!
But you're so quiet.

She:
                    Oh, my dearest!
I'm always happy when I'm with you
and every moment equally cherish.

He:
When I behold creation's glory,
my soul is filled with tender bliss.
From these waters and hills and forests,
I lift my eyes up to the skies,
to the aethereal dwelling place,
and think: how great the Architect,
how beautiful the world! And when
at the same moment I remember

Что в этом мире ты со мною,
Подруга милая моя...
Нет сладким чувствам выраженья,
И не могу в избытке их
Невольных слез благодаренья
Остановить в глазах моих.

Она
Воздай тебе Создатель вечный!
О чем еще его молить!
Ах! об одном: не пережить
Тебя, друг милый, друг сердечный.

Он
Ты грустной мыслию меня
Смутила. Так! сегодня зренье
Пленяет свет веселый дня,
Пленяет Божие творенье;
Теперь в руке моей твою
Я с чувством пламенным сжимаю,
Твой нежный взор я понимаю,
Твой сладкий голос узнаю...
А завтра... завтра... как ужасно!
Мертвец незрящий и глухой,
Мертвец холодный!.. Луч дневной
В глаза ударит мне напрасно!
Вотще к устам моим прильнешь
Ты воспаленными устами,
Ко мне с обильными слезами,
С рыданьем громким воззовешь:
Я не проснусь! И что мы знаем?
Не только завтра, сей же час
Меня не будет! Кто из нас

that you are with me in this world,
my darling friend, there are no words
to capture all the sweet emotions!
They overwhelm me: I can't stop
the tears of gratitude welling up
in my eyes uncontrollably.

She:
May our eternal God reward you!
What else is there to ask of him!
Oh! Only this: not to outlive
you, my dear friend, my heart's companion.

He:
With this sad thought of yours, you have
upset me. It's true! Today my gaze is
enthralled by the day's cheerful light,
enthralled by all of God's creation;
today I press within my hand
your hand with such a fervent feeling;
your tender eyes I understand,
your sweet-toned voice I can distinguish…
Tomorrow, though—tomorrow—horror!
A corpse unseeing and unhearing,
a cold, dead corpse! The light of day
will strike my eyes to no avail!
And uselessly your burning lips
you'll press against my lips, and with
copious tears and violent sobbing
you will call out to me—and I
shall not wake up! And who can say?
Not just tomorrow, this very moment
I might be gone! Tell me, who wouldn't

В земном блаженстве не смущаем
Такою думой?

Она
                    Что с тобой?
Зачем твое воображенье
Предупреждает Провиденье?
Бог милосерд, друг милый мой!
Здоровы, молоды мы оба,
Еще далеко нам до гроба.

Он
Но все ж умрем мы наконец,
Все ляжем в землю.

Она
                    Что же, милый?
Есть бытие и за могилой,
Нам обещал его Творец.
Спокойны будем: нет сомненья,
Мы в жизнь другую перейдем,
Где нам не будет разлученья,
Где все земные опасенья
С земною пылью отряхнем.
Ах! как любить без этой веры!

Он
Так, Всемогущий без нее
Нас искушал бы выше меры;
Так, есть другое бытие!
Ужели некогда погубит
Во мне он то, что мыслит, любит,
Чем он созданье довершил,

amid such earthly bliss be upset
by such a thought?

She:
                        What's wrong? Why let
your imagination get ahead
of what belongs to Providence?
God is all-merciful, dear friend!
We both are young and full of health—
the grave's still very far from us.

He:
But even so, we die in the end,
we all lie in the ground.

She:
                        What of it?
There is a life beyond the grave:
for this we have our Maker's promise.
So let's be calm; there is no doubt:
we'll pass from this life to another,
where we will always be together,
where, when we shed our earthly dust,
we shed all earthly trepidation.
Without this faith, how could we love?

He:
Yes, otherwise the Almighty One
would be testing us beyond all measure!
Yes, there must be a life to come!
For is it possible he could ever
destroy in me what thinks and loves,
the pinnacle of his creation,

В чем, с горделивым наслажденьем,
Мир повторил он отраженьем
И сам себя изобразил?
Ужели Творческая сила
Лукавым светом бытия
Мне ужас гроба озарила,
И только?.. Нет, не верю я.
Что свет являет? Пир нестройный!
Презренный властвует; достойный
Поник гонимою главой;
Несчастлив добрый, счастлив злой.
Как! не терпящая смешенья
В слепых стихиях вещества,
На хаос нравственный воззренья
Не бросит мудрость Божества?
Как! между братьями своими
Мы видим правых и благих,
И превзойден детьми людскими,
Не прав, не благ Создатель их?..
Нет! мы в юдоли испытанья,
И есть обитель воздаянья;
Там, за могильным рубежом,
Сияет день незаходимый,
И оправдается Незримый
Пред нашим сердцем и умом.

Она
Зачем в такие размышленья
Ты погружаешься душой?
Ужели нужны, милый мой,
Для убежденных убежденья?
Премудрость вышнего Творца
Не нам исследовать и мерить;

in which, with proud delight, he has
doubled the world as a reflection
and made an image of himself?
For is it possible the Creator's
power illumines, in the deceitful
light of this life, only the horror
of the grave? No, I don't believe it.
What do we see? A feast disordered!
The contemptible reign, and the worthy
must bow their persecuted heads;
the wicked are happy, unhappy the good.
How can this be? If no confusion
in matter's blind affairs it brooks,
will not then the Deity's wisdom
direct its gaze on moral chaos?
How can this be? Among our brothers
we see men who are good and just—
so is their Maker not good, not just?
Is he outdone by his human children?
No! We are in a vale of trials
and there is a land of recompense;
and there, beyond the grave's confine,
a day is shining, never-waning,
and the Unseen One is vindicated
before our heart, before our mind.

She:
My dear, why is your soul so laden
with ruminations such as these?
Do the persuaded really need
such explanations to persuade them?
The sublime wisdom of our Maker
is not for us to measure and probe,

В смиреньи сердца надо верить
И терпеливо ждать конца.
Пойдем: грустна я в самом деле,
И от мятежных слов твоих,
Я признаюсь, во мне доселе
Сердечный трепет не затих.

with humble hearts we must believe
and wait the end with quiet patience.
Let's go. I really do feel sad,
and even now—I won't dissemble—
inside my heart I still am trembling
from the disturbing things you said.

<1829>

МУЗА

Не ослеплен я музою моею:
Красавицей ее не назовут,
И юноши, узрев ее, за нею
Влюбленною толпой не побегут.
Приманивать изысканным убором,
Игрою глаз, блестящим разговором
Ни склонности у ней, ни дара нет;
Но поражен бывает мельком свет
Ее лица необщим выраженьем,
Ее речей спокойной простотой;
И он, скорей чем едким осужденьем,
Ее почтит небрежной похвалой.

MY MUSE

I am not dazzled by my muse—nobody
would ever say that she is beautiful,
and young men, catching sight of her, would hardly
dash off, a lovesick legion, in pursuit.
She has neither the gift nor the desire
to captivate with elegant attire,
sparkling conversation, the play of eyes;
but sometimes the world is struck, for just a moment,
by the uncommon expression of her face,
the peaceful simplicity of her words—
and rather than pronounce its caustic judgment,
will honor her instead with careless praise.

<1829>

ПОДРАЖАТЕЛЯМ

Когда печалью вдохновенный
Певец печаль свою поет,
Скажите: отзыв умиленный
В каком он сердце не найдет?
Кто, вековых проклятий жаден
Дерзнет осмеивать ее?
Но для притворства всякий хладен,
Плач подражательный досаден,
Смешно жеманное вытье!
Не напряженного мечтанья
Огнем услужливым согрет,
Постигнул таинства страданья
Душемутительный поэт.
В борьбе с тяжелою судьбою
Познал он меру высших сил,
Сердечных судорог ценою
Он выраженье их купил.
И вот нетленными лучами
Лик песнопевца окружен,
И чтим земными племенами,
Подобно мученику, он.
А ваша муза площадная,
Тоской заемною мечтая
Родить участие в сердцах,
Подобна нищей развращенной
Молящей лепты незаконной
С чужим ребенком на руках.

TO IMITATORS

When the singer, by sorrow inspired,
sings of a sorrow that is his own,
tell me, whose heart would then deny him
a warm, emotional response?
Who, eager for eternal curses,
would dare mock his unhappiness?
But pretense has no power to sway us;
the parroted lament annoys us;
affected moans are ludicrous.
Warmed by the ever-obliging fire
of his unlabored reverie,
the soul-disturbing poet fathoms
the mysteries of suffering.
In battle with an onerous fate
he's learned the strength of higher forces:
the expression of his pain was bought
at the price of his heart's convulsions.
And now the image of the singer
is wreathed in incorruptible rays;
he is revered by all the nations,
and, like a holy martyr, praised.
But your vulgar muse, who with her borrowed
anguish believes she will inspire
true sympathy in people's hearts,
is like some depraved beggarwoman
beseeching illicit alms while holding
another's baby in her arms.

<1829>

***

Чудный град порой сольется
Из летучих облаков;
Но лишь ветр его коснется,
Он исчезнет без следов.
Так мгновенные созданья
Поэтической мечты
Исчезают от дыханья
Посторонней суеты.

* * *

Now and then a wondrous city
from floating clouds will coalesce,
but the wind need only touch it,
and it's gone without a trace.
Thus the momentary inventions
of poetic fantasy
vanish at the merest breath of
meaningless activity.

<1829>

***

Где сладкий шепот
Моих лесов?
Потоков ропот,
Цветы лугов?
Деревья голы;
Ковер зимы
Покрыл холмы
Луга и долы.
Под ледяной
Своей корой
Ручей немеет;
Все цепенеет,
Лишь ветер злой,
Бушуя, воет
И небо кроет
Седою мглой.

Зачем, тоскуя,
В окно слежу я
Метели лёт?
Любимцу счастья
Кров от ненастья
Оно дает.
Огонь трескучий
В моей печи;
Его лучи
И пыл летучий
Мне веселят
Беспечный взгляд.
В тиши мечтаю
Перед живой

* * *

Where's the sweet whisper
of my green forests?
The murmur of streams,
the meadow flowers?
The trees are naked,
and winter's blanket
covers the hills,
the meadows and dales.
The brook beneath
its icy crust
has lost its voice.
And all is numb.
But the angry wind
rampages and wails,
draping gray fog
across the skies.

Why through the window
do I watch, rueful,
the flight of the wind?
The window gives shelter
from the foul weather
to fortune's friend.
My stove is warm
with a crackling blaze;
its glowing rays
and flying sparks
are able to cheer
my happy eyes.
I dream in silence
before the lively

Его игрой,
И забываю
Я бури вой.

О Провиденье,
Благодаренье!
Забуду я
И дуновенье
Бурь бытия.
Скорбя душою
В тоске моей,
Склонюсь главою
На сердце к ней,
И под мятежной
Метелью бед,
Любовью нежной
Ее согрет,
Забуду вскоре
Крутое горе,
Как в этот миг
Забыл природы
Гробовый лик
И непогоды
Мятежный крик.

play of its flame,
and have forgotten
the wail of the storm.

O Providence,
to you be thanks!
The gusting winds
of this life's storms
I'll also forget.
When my soul mourns,
lost in regret,
I'll lay my head
against her heart.
Beneath the furious
blizzard of sorrows,
safe in the warmth
of her tender love,
I'll soon forget
the bitterest woes—
just as, this moment,
I forgot nature's
sepulchral face,
and the foul weather's
violent cries.

1831?

МОЙ ЭЛИЗИЙ

Не славь, обманутый Орфей,
Мне Элизийские селенья:
Элизий в памяти моей
И не кропим водой забвенья.
В нем мир цветущий старины
Умерших тени населяют,
Привычки жизни сохраняют
И чувств ее не лишены.
Там жив ты, Дельвиг! там за чашей
Еще со мною шутишь ты,
Поешь веселье дружбы нашей
И сердца юные мечты.

MY ELYSIUM

Deluded Orpheus, do not sing
to me of the Elysian mansions:
Elysium's in my memory,
unsprinkled by oblivion's water.
There in the flowering world of the past
the shadows of the dead reside;
they keep to the routines of life
and its emotions still possess.
You are alive there, Delvig, jesting
with me still over a cup of wine;
you sing the gladness of our friendship
and the heart's ever-youthful dreams.

1831

***

Бывало, отрок, звонким кликом
Лесное эхо я будил,
И верный отклик в лесе диком
Меня смятенно веселил.
Пора другая наступила,
И рифма юношу пленила,
Лесное эхо заменя.
Игра стихов, игра златая!
Как звуки, звукам отвечая,
Бывало, нежили меня!
Но все проходит. Остываю
Я и к гармонии стихов —
И как дубров не окликаю,
Так не ищу созвучных слов.

* * *

A child, I would the forest echo
awaken with a ringing cry,
and the faithful answer in the wildwood
flooded me with confused delight.
Then came a different season and
rhyme captivated the young man,
taking the forest echo's place.
The play of verse, what golden play!
How sounds to sounds making reply
once coddled me in their embrace!
But everything passes. I grow colder
even to the harmony of verse—
and just as I call to the woods no longer,
I no longer seek concordant words.

1831

***

В дни безграничных увлечений,
В дни необузданных страстей
Со мною жил превратный гений,
Наперсник юности моей.
Он жар восторгов несогласных
Во мне питал и раздувал;
Но соразмерностей прекрасных
В душе носил я идеал:
Когда лишь праздников смятенья
Алкал безумец молодой,
Поэта мерные творенья
Блистали стройной красотой.

Страстей порывы утихают,
Страстей мятежные мечты
Передо мной не затмевают
Законов вечной красоты;
И поэтического мира
Огромный очерк я узрел,
И жизни даровать, о лира!
Твое согласье захотел.

* * *

In days of limitless distractions,
in days of passions unrestrained,
a twisted genius lived beside me;
he was my youth's own bosom friend.
The fever of discordant raptures
he nurtured and inflamed in me,
but in my soul the ideal I carried
of sublime proportionalities:
whenever the young madman thirsted
for holidays of turbulence,
the measured creations of the poet
shone with beauty and elegance.

The passions' vehemence subsides,
the passions' reveries unruly
do not obscure before my eyes
the laws of everlasting beauty—
and I discerned the vast design
of the world of poetry,
and wanted to bestow on life,
O lyre, this your harmony.

1831

* * *

Мой неискусный карандаш
Набросил вид суровый ваш,
Скалы Финляндии печальной;
Средь них, средь этих голых скал,
Я, дни весны моей опальной
Влача, душой изнемогал.
В отчизне я. Перед собою
Я самовольною мечтою
Скалы изгнанья оживил
И, их рассеянно рисуя,
Теперь с улыбкою шепчу я:
Вот где унылый я бродил,
Где, на судьбину негодуя,
Я веру в счастье отложил.

* * *

My artless pencil has set down
a quick sketch of your austere form,
O cliffs of melancholy Finland.
Among these naked cliffs I spent
the days of my disfavored spring,
my spirit faltering within me.
I am at home now. Here, before me,
submitting to a willful fancy,
I've brought my exile's cliffs to life.
And as I draw them absently,
now with a smile I softly say:
This is where, hopeless, I wandered once,
where railing at fate I laid aside
what belief I had in happiness.

1831?

НА СМЕРТЬ ГЕТЕ

Предстала, и старец великий смежил
    Орлиные очи в покое;
Почил безмятежно, зане совершил
    В пределе земном все земное!
Над дивной могилой не плачь, не жалей,
Что гения череп — наследье червей.

Погас! но ничто не оставлено им
    Под солнцем живых без привета;
На все отозвался он сердцем своим,
    Что просит у сердца ответа;
Крылатою мыслью он мир облетел,
В одном беспредельном нашел ей предел.

Все дух в нем питало: труды мудрецов,
    Искусств вдохновенных созданья,
Преданья, заветы минувших веков,
    Цветущих времен упованья.
Мечтою по воле проникнуть он мог
И в нищую хату, и в царский чертог.

С природой одною он жизнью дышал:
    Ручья разумел лепетанье,
И говор древесных листов понимал,
    И чувствовал трав прозябанье;
Была ему звездная книга ясна,
И с ним говорила морская волна.

Изведан, испытан им весь человек!
    И ежели жизнью земною
Творец ограничил летучий наш век,

ON THE DEATH OF GOETHE

She appeared—and in peace the great old man
    shut his eyes, the eyes of an eagle;
unprotesting he slept, for in earth's domain
    he'd accomplished all that is earthly.
Weep not over this wondrous grave, do not mourn
that the genius's skull is bequeathed to the worm.

He is gone! But beneath the living sun
    he left nothing without his greeting:
with his heart he responded to everything
    that petitions the heart for an answer.
The wide world he traveled on winged thought,
whose bound he found in the boundless alone.

All nourished his spirit: the works of the wise
    and artists' inspired creations,
the tales and testaments of olden times,
    the hopes of flowering ages.
Through fantasy he could enter at will
both the poor man's hut and the palace of kings.

He breathed one life with the natural world:
    he made sense of the brook's babbling waters,
the speech of the tree leaves he understood,
    and felt how the grass germinated,
he knew how to read the book of the stars,
and with him the waves of the ocean conversed.

He studied, he probed the entirety of man!
    And if the Creator restricted
to this earthly life our life's brief span,

И нас за могильной доскою,
За миром явлений, не ждет ничего:
Творца оправдает могила его.

И если загробная жизнь нам дана,
    Он, здешней вполне отдышавший
И в звучных, глубоких отзывах сполна
    Все дольное долу отдавший,
К Предвечному легкой душой возлетит,
И в небе земное его не смутит.

and nothing beyond the tombstone,
beyond the world of appearances, waits,
the Creator is justified now by his grave.

And if we are granted a life past the tomb,
    then he, who has breathed this life fully
and in resonant, deep responses returned
    in full to the world all that's worldly—
he will rise, light in soul, to the One Before Time,
and the earthly will not trouble him in the skies.

1832

***

К чему невольнику мечтания свободы?
Взгляни: безропотно текут речные воды
В указанных брегах, по склону их русла;
Ель величавая стоит, где возросла,
Невластная сойти. Небесные светила
Назначенным путем неведомая сила
Влечет. Бродячий ветр не волен, и закон
Его летучему дыханью положен.
Уделу своему и мы покорны будем,
Мятежные мечты смирим иль позабудем;
Рабы разумные, послушно согласим
Свои желания со жребием своим —
И будет счастлива, спокойна наша доля.
Безумец! не она ль, не вышняя ли воля
Дарует страсти нам? и не ее ли глас
В их гласе слышим мы? О, тягостна для нас
Жизнь, в сердце бьющая могучею волною
И в грани узкие втесненная судьбою.

* * *

What good are fantasies of freedom to the prisoner?
Just look: without complaint the waters of the river
flow in appointed banks along the channel's incline;
the spruce, in majesty, stands right where it has grown,
powerless to step away. The lights that shine in the heavens
are drawn by a force unknown along a designated
path. The roving wind blows not at will: there is
a law set down that governs its every fickle breeze.
So we too will submit to what we've been allotted,
will calm rebellious dreams or let them be forgotten;
rational slaves, we will, in all docility,
refashion our desires to fit our destiny—
and thus our lot will be a happy, peaceful one.
Madman! Is it not that—is it not a higher will
that gives our passions to us? And is not the voice
we hear in them its voice? Oh, how it weighs on us,
this life, beating inside our hearts a mighty billow,
and yet constrained by fate to flow in straits so narrow.

<1833>

***

Когда исчезнет омраченье
Души болезненной моей?
Когда увижу разрешенье
Меня опутавших сетей?
Когда сей демон, наводящий
На ум мой сон, его мертвящий,
Отыдет, чадный, от меня,
И я увижу луч блестящий
Всеозаряющего дня?
Освобожусь воображеньем,
И крылья духа подыму,
И пробужденным вдохновеньем
Природу снова обниму?

Вотще ль мольбы? напрасны ль пени?
Увижу ль снова ваши сени,
Сады поэзии святой?
Увижу ль вас, ее светила?
Вотще! я чувствую: могила
Меня живого приняла,
И, легкий дар мой удушая,
На грудь мне дума роковая
Гробовой насыпью легла.

* * *

When will the darkness disappear
from my debilitated soul?
When will I see the nets untied
that have me tangled in their cords?
When will this demon who encumbers
my mind with a deadening slumber
depart, infernal one, from me,
and I will see a ray of splendor
from all-illuminating day?
Will be in my imagination
set free, will lift my spirit's wings,
and with awakened inspiration
embrace nature once again?

Are prayers in vain? Have complaints no power?
Will I ever again see your bowers,
O gardens of holy Poetry?
Will I see you, her shining beacons?
In vain! I feel it: the tomb has taken
me alive, and upon my breast,
suffocating my delicate gift,
implacable thought has laid itself
like an earthen mound upon a grave.

<1833>

***

Болящий дух врачует песнопенье.
Гармонии таинственная власть
Тяжелое искупит заблужденье
И укротит бунтующую страсть.
Душа певца, согласно излитая,
Разрешена от всех своих скорбей;
И чистоту поэзия святая
И мир отдаст причастнице своей.

* * *

Canticles heal the spirit in affliction.
The mysterious power of harmony
is able to redeem the heavy error
and pacify the passions' mutiny.
The singer's soul, poured out in full concordance,
from all her tribulations is released,
and holy poetry imparts her pureness
to her communicant and gives her peace.

<1833>

О мысль! тебе удел цветка:
Он свежий манит мотылька,
Прельщает пчелку золотую,
К нему с любовью мошка льнет,
И стрекоза его поет;
Утратил прелесть молодую
И чередой своей поблек —
Где пчелка, мошка, мотылек?
Забыт он роем их летучим,
И никому в нем нужды нет;
А тут зерном своим падучим
Он зарождает новый цвет.

* * *

O thought, the flower's fate is yours!
When fresh, the butterfly it lures,
the golden bee it fascinates;
to it with love the midge will cling,
of it the dragonfly will sing—
but when its youthful charm abates
and all its brightness fades away,
where then are bee, midge, butterfly?
Forgotten by their winged troops,
it's of no use to anyone.
But just now, in the seed it drops,
a brand new flower is being born.

<1833>

***

О, верь: ты, нежная, дороже славы мне.
Скажу ль? Мне иногда докучно вдохновенье:
    Мешает мне его волненье
    Дышать любовью в тишине!
Я сердце предаю сердечному союзу:
    Приди, мечты мои рассей!
Ласкай, ласкай меня, о друг души моей!
И покори себе бунтующую музу.

* * *

Believe me, gentle one: you're dearer than glory to me.
Shall I say it? I sometimes tire of inspiration:
    it causes me such agitation
    I can't breathe love in quietness.
My heart I here surrender to the alliance of hearts:
    Come and dispel my reveries!
Caress me, oh, caress me, friend of my soul,
and make the insurgent muse submit to your command.

<1833>

***

Есть милая страна, есть угол на земле,
Куда, где б ни были: средь буйственного стана,
В садах Армидиных, на быстром корабле,
Браздящем весело равнины океана,
Всегда уносимся мы думою своей,
    Где, чужды низменных страстей,
Житейским подвигам предел мы назначаем,
Где мир надеемся забыть когда-нибудь
    И вежды старые сомкнуть
    Последним, вечым сном желаем.

. . . .
. . . .
. . . .
. . . .
. . . .
. . . .
. . . .
. . . .

    Я помню ясный, чистый пруд;
    Под сению берез ветвистых,
Средь мирных вод его три острова цветут;
Светлея нивами меж рощ своих волнистых,
За ним встает гора, пред ним в кустах шумит
И брызжет мельница. Деревня, луг широкой,
А там счастливый дом… туда душа летит,
Там не хладел бы я и в старости глубокой!
Там сердце томное, больное обрело
    Ответ на все, что в нем горело,
И снова для любви, для дружбы расцвело
    И счастье вновь уразумело.
Зачем же томный вздох и слезы на глазах?

* * *

There is a lovely country, a corner on the earth,
to where, wherever we are—amid the camp's commotion,
or in Armida's gardens, or on a speeding ship
as merrily it furrows the vast plains of the ocean—
to where we're always carried by the musings of our mind;
        where, to the baser passions strange,
we demarcate the compass of this life's endeavors,
and where we hope someday to leave the world behind,
        and long to shut our aged eyes
        in our last, our eternal slumber.

. . . .
. . . .
. . . .
. . . .
. . . .
. . . .
. . . .
. . . .

        I remember a pond, clear and clean:
        beneath a canopy of birches,
amid its peaceful waters, three islands are in bloom;
beyond it, bright with fields between the rippling orchards,
rises a hill; in front, among the thickets, a mill
rumbles and splashes. A village; then a great wide meadow;
and then, the happy house... There flies my soul—
there I would never grow cold, not even in my dotage!
There did my heart, infirm and languishing, obtain
        an answer to all that burned within it,
and there, for love, for friendship, it blossomed once again,
        and happiness again it comprehended.
So why this languid sigh, and in my eyes these tears?

Она, с болезненным румянцем на щеках,
Она, которой нет, мелькнула предо мною.
Почий, почий легко под дерном гробовым:
        Воспоминанием живым
        Не разлучимся мы с тобою!
Мы плачем… но прости! Печаль любви сладка,
        Отрадны слезы сожаленья!
Не то холодная, суровая тоска,
        Сухая скорбь разуверенья.

She, with a sickly flush upon her cheek, appeared—
she, who does not exist, appeared in a glimmer before me.
Rest, gently rest beneath the hillock of your grave:
    our memories are still alive,
    and in them we will not be parted.
We weep… Forgive us! The sorrow of love is sweet,
    and tears of pity have their pleasure.
So different is this from heartache, cold and grim,
    the arid grief of disillusion.

<1833>

* * *

Весна, весна! как воздух чист!
   Как ясен небосклон!
Своей лазурию живой
   Слепит мне очи он.

Весна, весна! как высоко
   На крыльях ветерка,
Ласкаясь к солнечным лучам,
   Летают облака!

Шумят ручьи! блестят ручьи!
   Взревев, река несет
На торжествующем хребте
   Поднятый ею лед!

Еще древа обнажены,
   Но в роще ветхий лист,
Как прежде, под моей ногой
   И шумен и душист.

Под солнце самое взвился
   И в яркой вышине
Незримый жавронок поет
   Заздравный гимн весне.

Что с нею, что с моей душой?
   С ручьем она ручей
И с птичкой птичка! с ним журчит,
   Летает в небе с ней!

* * *

It's spring! It's spring! How clean the air!
    How luminous the sky!
So vibrant is its azure that
    it robs me of my eyes.

It's spring! It's spring! How high the clouds
    are sailing overhead,
upon the wings of a gentle breeze,
    caressing the sun's rays.

The noisy brooks! The shining brooks!
    The river, with a roar,
on its triumphant back bears off
    the ice it's broken through.

Still naked stand the trees, but in
    the grove the withered leaf
is as before—both loud and fragrant
    underneath my feet.

Invisible, a lark has flown
    to just below the sun,
and sings, up in the dazzling heights,
    a hymn to hail the spring.

What's going on? What's with my soul?
    With the brook she is a brook,
with the bird a bird—with the one she purls,
    with the other soars aloft!

Зачем так радует ее
    И солнце и весна!
Ликует ли, как дочь стихий,
    На пире их она?

Что нужды! счастлив, кто на нем
    Забвенье мысли пьет,
Кого далеко от нее
    Он, дивный, унесет!

Why is she so delighted by
        the sunshine and the spring?
Is she, child of the elements,
        rejoicing at their feast?

Why ask! Happy the man who drinks
        the oblivion of thought,
who's carried far away from it
        by this miraculous feast!

<1833>

***

Своенравное прозванье
Дал я милой в ласку ей:
Безотчетное созданье
Детской нежности моей;
Чуждо явного значенья,
Для меня оно символ
Чувств, которых выраженья
В языках я не нашел.
Вспыхнув полное любовью
И любви посвящено,
Не хочу, чтоб суесловью
Было ведомо оно.
Что в нем свету? Но сомненье
Если дух ей возмутит,
О, его в одно мгновенье
Это имя победит;
Но в том мире, за могилой,
Где нет образов, где нет
Для узнанья, друг мой милой,
Здешних чувственных примет,
Им бессмертье я привечу,
К безднам им воскликну я,
Да душе моей навстречу
Полетит душа твоя.

* * *

Arbitrary was the pet name
I, adoring, gave my love—
the unaccountable creation
of my childish tenderness.
Free of all apparent meaning,
it's for me the symbol of
feelings for which I could find no
words in any human tongue.
Ablaze with love in all its fullness,
consecrated to love alone—
in this world of idle gossip
I don't want it to be known.
What's it to the world? But if
doubt should ever cause dismay
to her spirit—oh, this name
instantly will conquer it.
And in the other world, beyond
the grave, where there are no faces,
where, sweet friend, for recognition
there are no earthly sensual signs—
with it I'll greet life undying,
into the depths I'll call it out,
and your soul will soon come flying
on its way to meet my soul.

<1833>

ЗАПУСТЕНИЕ

Я посетил тебя, пленительная сень,
Не в дни веселые живительного мая,
Когда зелеными ветвями помавая,
Манишь ты путника в свою густую тень,
    Когда ты веешь ароматом
Тобою бережно взлелеянных цветов,—
    Под очарованный твой кров
    Замедлил я моим возвратом.
В осенней наготе стояли дерева
    И неприветливо чернели;
Хрустела под ногой замерзлая трава,
И листья мертвые, волнуяся, шумели;
    С прохладой резкою дышал
    В лицо мне запах увяданья;
Но не весеннего убранства я искал,
    А прошлых лет воспоминанья.
Душой задумчивый, медлительно я шел
С годов младенческих знакомыми тропами;
Художник опытный их некогда провел.
Увы! рука его изглажена годами!
Стези заглохшие, мечтаешь, пешеход
Случайно протоптал. Сошел я в дол заветный,
Дол, первых дум моих лелеятель приветный!
Пруда знакомого искал красивых вод,
Искал прыгучих вод мне памятной каскады;
    Там, думал я, к душе моей
Толпою полетят виденья прежних дней…
Вотще! лишенные хранительной преграды,
    Далече воды утекли,
    Их ложе поросло травою,
Приют хозяйственный в нем улья обрели

I paid my visit to you, captivating bower,
not in the joyful days of life-restoring Maytide,
when, beckoning with verdant branches,
you lure the wanderer into your leafy shade,
     when you exude the sweet aroma
of blossoms you have nurtured with a fond concern—
     I had been slow in my return
     underneath your enchanted cover.
The trees were standing in autumnal nakedness,
     their aspect dark and uninviting;
under my foot I heard the crunch of frozen grass
and the noise of the dead leaves rustling;
     with a stinging chill, my nostrils were
     filled with the odor of decay—
yet springtime garb was not what I was seeking here,
     but memories from a time gone by.
My soul absorbed in thought, lingeringly I walked
along footpaths I had known from my earliest childhood;
     a skillful artist laid them out—
alas, his hand has been erased by the passing decades!
One might believe some rambler trampled, as if by chance,
these overgrown trails. I went down to a dell I treasured—
that dell, the friendly nurturer of my first reflections!
I looked for the pretty waters of a familiar pond,
looked for the splashing waters of a cascade remembered;
     There, I thought, my soul would be
engulfed in swarming visions of a former day...
Vain hope! Bereft of any barrier to detain them,
     the waters had drained far away
     and grass had overrun the pond bed,
beehives had turned it into a haven for industry,

И легкая тропа исчезла предо мною.
Ни в чем знакомого мой взор не обретал!
Но вот по-прежнему, лесистым косогором,
Дорожка смелая ведет меня… обвал
      Вдруг поглотил ее… Я стал
И глубь нежданную измерил грустным взором,
С недоумением искал другой тропы.
      Иду я: где беседка тлеет
И в прахе перед ней лежат ее столпы,
      Где остов мостика дряхлеет.
      И ты, величественный грот,
Тяжело-каменный, постигнут разрушеньем,
      И угрожает уж паденьем,
Бывало, в летний зной, прохлады полный свод!
Что ж? пусть минувшее минуло сном летучим!
Еще прекрасен ты, заглохший Элизей,
      И обаянием могучим
      Исполнен для души моей.
Тот не был мыслию, тот не был сердцем хладен,
      Кто, безымянной неги жаден,
Их своенравный бег тропам сим указал,
Кто, преклоняя слух к таинственному шуму
Сих кленов, сих дубов, в душе своей питал
      Ему сочувственную думу.
Давно кругом меня о нем умолкнул слух,
Прияла прах его далекая могила,
Мне память образа его не сохранила,
Но здесь еще живет его доступный дух;
      Здесь, друг мечтанья и природы,
      Я познаю его вполне:
Он вдохновением волнуется во мне,
Он славить мне велит леса, долины, воды;
Он убедительно пророчит мне страну,

and in front of me the tenuous footpath vanished.
In nothing could my eyes find anything they knew!
But now, just as before, a little lane was boldly
          leading me through the wooded slope—
and suddenly was swallowed in fallen rocks... I stopped
and with a sad gaze measured the unexpected hollow,
looking in confusion for another path to follow.
          I go on—to where the summerhouse
is rotting, its columns lying before it in the dust;
to where the little bridge's skeleton is crumbling.
And you, magnificent grotto with your heavy stones,
          you too have not escaped destruction;
          your vaulted chamber, which was once
so cool in summer's heat, now threatens to collapse.
What of it? Let the past pass like a fleeting dream!
Beautiful are you still, my overgrown Elysium,
          and permeated with a charm
          that wields a power over my being.
Not in his thought, not in his heart was he unfeeling
          who, eager for a nameless pleasure,
marked out the whimsical direction of these trails;
who, inclining his ear to the mysterious murmur
of these oak trees, these maples, nourished in his soul
          a correspondent contemplation.
Long has it been since I heard any mention of him,
          a distant grave has taken his dust,
my memory has not preserved for me his face,
but his accessible spirit here is living still;
          here, a friend of reverie and nature,
          I recognize him utterly:
as inspiration he is stirring inside of me,
he commands me to praise the woods and dells and waters;
he prophesies for me, convincingly, a land

Где я наследую несрочную весну,
Где разрушения следов я не примечу,
Где в сладостной тени невянущих дубров,
     У нескудеющих ручьев,
     Я тень священную мне встречу.

where I will inherit a termless spring,
where I will see no traces of deterioration,
where, in the sweet shade of groves that never decay,
by streams that never run dry,
I'll meet the shade I hold as sacred.

1833–1834

***

Вот верный список впечатлений
И легкий и глубокий след
Страстей, порывов юных лет,
Жизнь родила его — не гений.
Подобен он скрыжали той,
Где пишет ангел неподкупный
Прекрасный подвиг и преступный —
Все, что творим мы под луной.
Я много строк моих, о Лета!
В тебе желал бы окунуть
И утаить их как-нибудь
И от себя и ото света…
Но уж свое они рекли,
А что прошло, то непреложно,
Года волненья протекли,
И мне перо оставить можно.
Теперь я знаю бытие.
Одно желание мое —
Покой, домашние отрады.
И, погружен в самом себе,
Смеюсь я людям и судьбе,
Уж не от них я жду награды.
Но что? с бессонною душой,
С душою чуткою поэта
Ужели вовсе чужд я света?
Проснуться может пламень мой,
Еще, быть может, я возвышу
Мой голос, родина моя!
Ни бед твоих я не услышу,
Ни славы, струны утая.

* * *

A faithful record of impressions
is here before you, both deep and light
the mark of passions, of youthful flights:
life has given birth to it—not genius.
It's like that tablet upon which
fine deeds and crimes are both inscribed
by an angel who cannot be bribed—
all that we do beneath the moon.
So many of my lines I've wished
to drown, O Lethe, in your waters,
and in some way to keep them hidden
both from myself and from the world…
But they said what they had to say,
and what is past is past transforming.
The years of turbulence are over,
and I can put my pen away.
I know now what existence is.
My sole desire now is peace,
the joys of family and home.
And so, immersed within myself,
I laugh at people and at fate.
No more I seek reward from them.
But what then? With this sleepless soul,
a poet's sensitive soul, can I be
wholly detached from the world around me?
The flame in me may waken still;
one day, perhaps, I'll lift again
my voice, O my beloved land!
Neither your sorrows will I hear,
nor glory, while I hide my strings.

1834

DUSK

КНЯЗЮ ПЕТРУ АНДРЕЕВИЧУ ВЯЗЕМСКОМУ

Как жизни общие призывы,
Как увлеченья суеты,
Понятны вам страстей порывы
И обаяния мечты;
Понятны вам все дуновенья,
Которым в море бытия
Послушна наша ладия.
Вам приношу я песнопенья,
Где отразилась жизнь моя:
Исполнена тоски глубокой,
Противоречий, слепоты,
И между тем любви высокой,
Любви добра и красоты.

Счастливый сын уединенья,
Где сердца ветреные сны
И мысли праздные стремленья
Разумно мной усыплены;
Где, другу мира и свободы,
Ни до фортуны, ни до моды,
Ни до молвы мне нужды нет;
Где я простил безумству, злобе
И позабыл, как бы во гробе,
Но добровольно, шумный свет,—
Еще порою покидаю
Я Лету созданную мной,
И степи мира облетаю
С тоскою жаркой и живой.
Ищу я вас, гляжу: что с вами?
Куда вы брошены судьбами,
Вы, озарявшие меня

TO PRINCE PYOTR ANDREYEVICH VYAZEMSKY

No less than the common demands of life,
no less than meaningless diversions,
you understand the passions' surges
and the enchantments of reverie;
you understand all of the winds
to which our ship is obedient
sailing the ocean of existence.
To you I bring these canticles,
in which you see my life reflected,
one that is filled with a deep sorrow,
with blindness and with contradiction,
but also with an exalted love,
a love for goodness and beauty.

The happy child of a seclusion
where the heart's ever-changing dreams
and the mind's futile aspirations
I sensibly have lulled to sleep;
where, a friend of peace and freedom,
neither for fortune nor for fashion
nor for opinion have I need;
where I've forgiven spite and madness,
and forgotten, as if dead and buried,
but willingly, the noisy world—
even now from time to time I leave
this Lethe of my own creation
and fly across the world's vast steppe
with a sorrow ardent and alive.
I search for you, I look to see
how you are, where the fates have cast you,
you who have illumined my life

И дружбы кроткими лучами,
И светом высшего огня?
Что вам дарует провиденье?
Чем истытует небо вас?
И возношу молящий глас:
Да длится ваше упоенье,
Да скоро минет скорбный час!

Звезда разрозненной Плеяды!
Так из глуши моей стремлю
Я к вам заботливые взгляды,
Вам высшей благости молю,
От вас отвлечь судьбы суровой
Удары грозные хочу,
Хотя вам прозою почтовой
Лениво дань мою плачу.

with the soft radiance of friendship
and with a loftier fire's light.
What gift does providence now send you?
What trial must you endure from heaven?
And I lift up an imploring voice:
May your happiness long continue!
May the hour of anguish quickly pass!

Star from a Pleiad now dispersed!
Thus from my wilderness I turn
my eyes towards you, full of concern,
and plead for you the highest grace.
Unfeeling fate's terrible blows
I want but to deflect from you,
though in epistolary prose
I'm lax in rendering my due.

1834

ПОСЛЕДНИЙ ПОЭТ

Век шествует путем своим железным;
В сердцах корысть, и общая мечта
Час от часу насущным и полезным
Отчетливей, бесстыдней занята.
Исчезнули при свете просвещенья
Поэзии ребяческие сны,
И не о ней хлопочут поколенья,
Промышленным заботам преданы.

Для ликующей свободы
Вновь Эллада ожила,
Собрала свои народы
И столицы подняла:
В ней опять цветут науки,
Носит понт торговли груз,
И не слышны лиры звуки
В первобытным рае муз!

Блестит зима дряхлеющего мира,
Блестит! Суров и бледен человек;
Но зелены в отечестве Омира
Холмы, леса, брега лазурных рек.
Цвстст Парнас! Пред ним, как в оны годы,
Кастальский ключ живой струею бьет;
Нежданный сын последних сил природы,
Возник Поэт: идет он и поет.

Воспевает, простодушной,
Он любовь и красоту,
И науки, им ослушной,
Пустоту и суету:

The age proceeds along its iron path:
hearts swell with greed; the general fantasy
grows hourly more blatant and more brash
as it pursues mundane utility.
Beneath enlightenment's illumination
poetry's childish dreams have disappeared,
and people worry over other matters,
surrendered to industrial concerns.

For a liberty triumphant,
Hellas has returned to life;
she has gathered up her peoples
and her capitals rebuilt.
Science flourishes once more,
Pontus bears commercial cargo,
but the lyre cannot be heard
in the Muses' ancient garden.

The winter of the crumbling world is gleaming,
and how it gleams! Yet man is grim and pallid.
But green are the hills in the land of Homer,
the forests and the banks of azure rivers.
Parnassus blooms! There, as in olden years,
a living stream beats from Castalia's spring;
the unsought child of nature's waning powers,
the Poet appears. He goes forth and sings.

With a simple heart he praises
love and beauty in his song,
telling of how vain and empty
science is that heeds them not.

Мимолетные страданья
Легкомыслием целя,
Лучше, смертный, в дни незнанья
Радость чувствует земля.

Поклонникам Урании холодной
Поет, увы! он благодать страстей;
Как пажити Эол бурнопогодной,
Плодотворят они сердца людей;
Живительным дыханием развита,
Фантазия подъемлется от них,
Как некогда возникла Афродита
Из пенистой пучины вод морских.

И зачем не предадимся
Снам улыбчивым своим?
Бодрым сердцем покоримся
Думам робким, а не им!
Верьте сладким убежденьям
Вас ласкающих очес
И отрадным откровеньям
Сострадательных небес!

Суровый смех ему ответом; персты
Он на струнах своих остановил,
Сомкнул уста вещать полуотверсты,
Но гордыя главы не преклонил:
Стопы свои он в мыслях направляет
В немую глушь, в безлюдный край; но свет
Уж праздного вертепа не являет,
И на земле уединенья нет!

Momentary sufferings
curing with light-mindedness.
Mortal, in days of ignorance
better does the earth feel bliss.

He sings to cold Urania's acolytes
(alas!) of passions and the grace they bring:
Like stormy Aeolus, who sows the fields,
so do the passions seed the hearts of men;
grown ripe beneath their vitalizing breath,
from them the imagination rises up,
as the goddess Aphrodite once appeared
from out the foamy tumult of the deep.

Why, then, do we not surrender
to the smiling dreams we dream?
But instead we meekly bend our
eager hearts to timid schemes.
Do not doubt the sweet persuasions
that you see in loving eyes,
nor the joyous revelations
from the sympathetic skies.

Grim laughter the response he gets. He stops
his fingers as they fall upon the strings;
his lips, half-parted, ready to speak out,
he shuts, but still he holds his proud head high:
in his mind's eye he turns his footsteps toward
the voiceless wilds, a land unvisited,
but there is no empty cave left in the world,
and on the earth there is no solitude.

Человеку непокорно
Море синее одно:
И свободно, и просторно,
И приветливо оно;
И лица не изменило
С дня, в который Аполлон
Поднял вечное светило
В первый раз на небосклон.

Оно шумит перед скалой Левкада.
На ней певец, мятежной думы полн,
Стоит… в очах блеснула вдруг отрада:
Сия скала… тень Сафо!.. песни волн…
Где погребла любовница Фаона
Отверженной любви несчастный жар,
Там погребет питомец Аполлона
Свои мечты, свой бесполезный дар!

И по-прежнему блистает
Хладной роскошию свет:
Серебрит и позлащает
Свой безжизненный скелет;
Но в смущение приводит
Человека вал морской,
И от шумных вод отходит
Он с тоскующей душой!

Man has all the world subdued,
all except the dark blue sea:
it is free and it is wide,
it is ever welcoming;
and its face it has not altered
from the time Apollo first
lifted over the horizon
the eternal light of day.

It roars beneath the cliffs of Leucas. There,
filled with tempestuous thoughts, the singer stands...
and suddenly joy flashes in his eyes:
This cliff... the shade of Sappho... and the song
of the waves... Where Phaon's lover had once buried
the hapless fire of her rejected love,
in this same spot now he, Apollo's pupil,
would bury his dreams, bury his useless gift.

And the world, just as before,
gleams in its cold opulence,
silvering and gilding the bones
of its lifeless skeleton.
But the billows of the sea
fill man with embarrassment,
and from the booming waters he
walks away with an aching heart.

<1835>, <1842>

165

***

Предрассудок! он обломок
Давней правды. Храм упал;
А руин его потомок
Языка не разгадал.

Гонит в нем наш век надменный,
Не узнав его лица,
Нашей правды современной
Дряхлолетнего отца.

Воздержи младую силу!
Дней его не возмущай;
Но пристойную могилу,
Как уснет он, предку дай.

* * *

Superstition—it's a fragment
of bygone truth. The temple's fallen,
and today's descendant cannot
guess the language of its ruins.

Arrogant, our age condemns it,
but we fail to recognize
the wizened face of the father
of our modern verities.

Temper, then, your youthful strength
and do not disturb his days,
but when your ancestor sleeps,
make for him a decent grave.

<1841>

НОВИНСКОЕ

А. С. Пушкину

Она улыбкою своей
Поэта в жертвы пригласила,
Но не любовь ответом ей,
Взор ясный думой осенила.
Нет, это был сей легкий сон,
Сей тонкий сон воображенья,
Что посылает Аполлон
Не для любви — для вдохновенья.

NOVINSKOYE

to A. S. Pushkin

She smiled at him and with her smile
invited the poet to be her victim,
but it wasn't love that in reply
clouded his clear eyes with reflection.
No, it was that gossamer dream,
that subtle dream of imagination,
the dream none but Apollo sends,
meant not for love, but inspiration.

1827?, <1842>

ПРИМЕТЫ

Пока человек естества не пытал
　　Горнилом, весами и мерой,
Но детски вещаньям природы внимал,
　　Ловил ее знаменья с верой;

Покуда природу любил он, она
　　Любовью ему отвечала:
О нем дружелюбной заботы полна,
　　Язык для него обретала.

Почуя беду над его головой,
　　Вран каркал ему в опасенье,
И замысла, в пору смирясь пред судьбой,
　　Воздерживал он дерзновенье.

На путь ему выбежав из лесу волк,
　　Крутясь и подъемля щетину,
Победу пророчил, и смело свой полк
　　Бросал он на вражью дружину.

Чета голубиная, вея над ним,
　　Блаженство любви прорицала.
В пустыне безлюдной он не был одним:
　　Нечуждая жизнь в ней дышала.

Но, чувство презрев, он доверил уму;
　　Вдался в суету изысканий…
И сердце природы закрылось ему,
　　И нет на земле прорицаний.

SIGNS

Before man subjected nature to tests
    with crucible, measure, and balance;
as long as he, childlike, heeded her voice
    and trustingly sought out her omens;

as long as he loved her, Nature bestowed
    her love on him in return,
devising a language for him, like a friend
    overflowing with friendly concern.

Perceiving calamity over his head
    a raven would cry out a caution,
and man would humble himself before fate
    and curb his too-daring intention.

Or a wolf from the woods, running onto his path
    and circling and bristling its fur,
would prophesy victory, and so his host
    he then fearlessly led into war.

Or a pair of turtledoves gliding aloft
    foretold of the rapture of love.
In the unpeopled wasteland he wasn't alone—
    it breathed with unalien life.

But disdaining his feelings he trusted his mind
    and delved into vain explorations,
and Nature closed up her heart to mankind,
    and on earth all prophecy vanished.

<1839>

171

***

Всегда и в пурпуре и в злате,
В красе негаснущих страстей,
Ты не вздыхаешь об утрате
Какой-то младости твоей.
И юных граций ты прелестней!
И твой закат пышней, чем день!
Ты сладострастней, ты телесней
Живых, блистательная тень!

* * *

Always arrayed in gold and crimson,
in the beauty of passions that never fade,
you are not one to mourn the passing
of a sort of youth you once enjoyed.
You are lovelier than our young graces,
your setting sun outshines the day!
More sensuous are you, more fleshly
than are the living, resplendent shade!

1840

***

Увы! Творец непервых сил!
На двух статейках утомил
Ты кой-какое дарованье!
Лишенный творческой мечты,
Уже, в жару нездравом, ты
Коверкать стал правописанье!

Неаполь возмутил рыбарь,
И, власть прияв, как мудрый царь,
Двенадцать дней он градом правил;
Но что же? — непривычный ум,
Устав от венценосных дум,
Его в тринадцатый оставил.

* * *

An author past his prime! Too bad
you spent what little gift you had
on a pair of measly articles.
Bereft of all creative thought,
in fevered madness now you start
tampering with the spelling rules!

Naples was once turned upside down
by a fisherman who seized the crown
and twelve days governed with great wisdom.
But then what? His beleaguered mind,
unused to thoughts of royal kind,
on Day Thirteen just up and quit him.

<1842>

НЕДОНОСОК

Я из племени духо́в,
Но не житель Эмпирея,
И, едва до облаков
Возлетев, паду, слабея.
Как мне быть? Я мал и плох;
Знаю: рай за их волнами,
И ношусь, крылатый вздох,
Меж землей и небесами.

Блещет солнце — радость мне!
С животворными лучами
Я играю в вышине
И веселыми крылами
Ластюсь к ним, как облачко;
Пью счастливо воздух тонкой,
Мне свободно, мне легко,
И пою я птицей звонкой.

Но ненастье заревет
И до облак, свод небесный
Омрачившись, вознесет
Прах земной и лист древесный:
Бедный дух! Ничтожный дух!
Дуновенье роковое
Вьет, крутит меня, как пух,
Мчит под небо громовое.

Бури грохот, бури свист!
Вихорь хладный! Вихорь жгучий!
Бьет меня древесный лист,
Удушает прах летучий!

THE STILLBORN

I am of the spirit tribe
but dwell not in the Empyrean;
flying up, I barely touch
the clouds, then lose strength and plummet.
What to do? I'm small and frail;
paradise lies past their billows—
this I know, and so I flail,
a winged sigh, between earth and heaven.

Should the sun shine, what delight!
The life-giving rays become
playmates to me in the heights;
in gay wings I cuddle them,
clasp them like a little cloud.
Happily the thin air drinking,
I'm so free, I feel so light,
I sing out just like a songbird.

But should stormy winds begin
howling, blackening the vault of
heaven, lifting to the clouds
the dust of the earth, the tree leaf—
O poor spirit! paltry spirit!—
merciless, the fateful blast
whirls me like a feather, spins me,
hurls me to the thundering skies.

How the tempest whistles, crashes!
How the whirlwind chills and scorches!
Now the tree leaf bruises, bashes!
Flying dust now suffocates me!

Обращусь ли к небесам,
Оглянуся ли на землю —
Грозно, черно тут и там;
Вопль уныло я подъемлю.

Смутно слышу я порой
Клик враждующих народов,
Поселян беспечных вой
Под грозой их переходов,
Гром войны и крик страстей,
Плач недужного младенца…
Слезы льются из очей:
Жаль земного поселенца!

Изнывающий тоской,
Я мечусь в полях небесных,
Надо мной и подо мной
Беспредельных — скорби тесных!
В тучу прячусь я, и в ней
Мчуся, чужд земного края,
Страшный глас людских скорбей
Гласом бури заглушая.

Мир я вижу как во мгле;
Арф небесных отголосок
Слабо слышу… На земле
Оживил я недоносок.
Отбыл он без бытия:
Роковая скоротечность!
В тягость роскошь мне твоя,
О бессмысленная вечность!

Whether I look up to heaven
or to earth cast down my gaze,
all is black and full of terror—
desolate the cry I raise.

Dimly, now and then, I hear
shouts rise up from hostile nations,
screams of carefree villagers
fleeing from the storming armies,
war's thunder, the passions' cry,
the wailing of a child with fever…
Tears are streaming from my eyes—
I am grieving for earth's people.

Moaning in anguish, to and fro
I'm tossed across the fields of heaven,
over me and under me
boundless, yet for grief too narrow.
In a stormcloud I hide, I fly,
to the realm of earth a stranger,
the dread voice of human woe
muffling in the voice of tempest.

The world I see as in a fog;
faintly I make out the echo
of celestial harps… On earth,
life I've given to a stillborn.
Without being, it was gone—
terrible such evanescence!
How your bounty weighs me down,
O eternity so senseless!

<1835>

179

АЛКИВИАД

Облокотясь перед медью, образ его отражавшей,
    Дланью слегка приподняв кудри златые чела,
Юный красавец сидел, горделиво-задумчив, и, смехом
    Горьким смеясь, на него мужи казали перстом;

Девы, тайно любуясь челом благородно-открытым,
    Нехотя взор отводя, хмурили брови свои.
Он же глух был и слеп; он, не в меди глядясь, а в грядущем,
    Думал: к лицу ли ему будет лавровый венок?

ALCIBIADES

Resting his cheek on one hand before the bronze-mirrored image,
   with the other he lifts golden curls off his brow:
Thus did the beautiful youth sit, haughtily pensive, while men were
   laughing their bitter laughs, pointing their fingers at him.

Girls, covertly admiring his forehead so noble and open,
   loath to avert their eyes, wrinkled their faces to frowns.
Deaf, though, was he and blind, surveying not bronze but the future,
   asking himself: Will not laurels look fine on his brow?

<1835>

РОПОТ

Красного лета отрава, муха досадная, что ты
     Вьешься, терзая меня, льнешь то к лицу, то к перстам?
Кто одарил тебя жалом, властным прервать самовольно
     Мощно-крылатую мысль, жаркой любви поцелуй?
Ты из мечтателя мирного, нег европейских питомца,
     Дикого скифа творишь, жадного смерти врага.

COMPLAINT

Poison of glorious summer, maddening insect, why do you
    buzz around tormenting me, now at my face, now my hand?
Who was it gave you that stinger, able to willfully shatter
    thought in its strong-winged flight, love in its ardent embrace?
You turn the placid dreamer, the pupil of Europe's enticements,
    into a Scythian brute wild for the death of his foe.

<1841>

МУДРЕЦУ

Тщетно меж бурною жизнью и хладною смертью, философ,
    Хочешь ты пристань найти, имя даешь ей: покой.
Нам, из ничтожества вызванным творчества словом тревожным,
    Жизнь для волненья дана: жизнь и волненье — одно.

Тот, кого миновали общие смуты, заботу
    Сам вымышляет себе: лиру, палитру, резец;
Мира невежда, младенец, как будто закон его чуя,
    Первым стенаньем качать нудит свою колыбель!

TO THE WISE MAN

Vainly, philosopher, do you, between stormy life and death's coldness,
    hope to discover a harbor—you have a name for it: *Peace.*
Called out of nothingness by the unsettling word of creation,
    we're given life for disquiet: life and disquiet are one.

He who is left untouched by the common misfortunes some other
    worry invents for himself: chisel, or palette, or lyre.
Ignorant still of the world but seemingly sensing its order,
    with his first whimper the babe forces his crib to be rocked.

<1840>

***

Филида с каждою зимою,
Зимою новою своей,
Пугает большей наготою
Своих старушечьих плечей.
И, Афродита гробовая,
Подходит, словно к ложу сна,
За ризой ризу опуская,
К одру последнему она.

* * *

Sweet Phyllis with each winter's season,
in a new winter all her own,
sends chills through us as she exposes
more of her cronish collarbone.
Thus our sepulchral Aphrodite
proceeds as if to sweet repose,
dropping one garment, then another,
as to her final rest she goes.

<1841>

БОКАЛ

Полный влагой искрометной,
Зашипел ты, мой бокал!
И покрыл туман приветный
Твой озябнувший кристалл…
Ты не встречен братьей шумной,
Буйных оргий властелин,—
Сластолюбец вольнодумной,
Я сегодня пью один.

Чем душа моя богата,
Всё твое, о друг Аи!
Ныне мысль моя не сжата
И свободны сны мои;
За струею вдохновенной
Не рассеян данник твой
Бестолково оживленной
Разногласною толпой.

Мой восторг неосторожный
Не обидит никого,
Не откроет дружбе ложной
Таин счастья моего;
Не смутит глупцов ревнивых
И торжественных невежд
Излияньем горделивых
Иль святых моих надежд!

Вот теперь со мной беседуй,
Своенравная струя!
Упоенья проповедуй
Иль отравы бытия;

THE GOBLET

Filled with effervescent liquid,
ah, my goblet, how you hiss!
Your chilled crystal is enveloped
in a most inviting mist…
Now no boisterous brotherhood
hails you, orgiastic lord—
a freethinking sybarite,
today I will drink alone.

All the riches of my soul
belong to you, my friend Aÿ!
Now my thought is unconstrained,
and the dreams I dream are free.
Your vassal cannot be distracted
once across the inspired stream
by the senselessly excited
crowd and its cacophony.

My incautious jubilation
will not cause the least offense,
nor divulge to seeming friendship
secrets of my happiness,
nor dismay the envious cretin
and the solemn simpleton
by revealing my ambitions,
whether prideful or divine.

So, then, talk a while with me,
willful, unpredictable liquid!
Preach to me of ecstasy,
or the poisons of existence;

Сердцу милые преданья
Благодатно оживи
Или прошлые страданья
Мне на память призови!

О бокал уединенья!
Не усилены тобой
Пошлой жизни впечатленья,
Словно чашей круговой;
Плодородней, благородней,
Дивной силой будишь ты
Откровенья преисподней
Иль небесные мечты.

И один я пью отныне!
Не в людском шуму пророк —
В немотствующей пустыне
Обретает свет высок!
Не в бесплодном развлеченье
Общежительных страстей —
В одиноком упоенье
Мгла падет с его очей!

graciously revive the stories
that are dearest to my heart,
or bring to my recollection
sufferings I once endured.

O my goblet of seclusion!
you, unlike the loving cup,
do not sharpen the sensation
of the pettiness of life;
more prolific and more noble,
with marvelous ability
you waken chthonic revelations,
or celestial reveries.

So henceforth I drink alone!
Not among the din of man,
but in the unspeaking desert
the prophet finds the light sublime!
Not in the futile diversion
of communal manias,
but in lonely exultation
will the fog fall from his eyes.

<1835>

***

Были бури, непогоды,
Да младые были годы!

В день ненастный, час гнетучий
Грудь подымет вздох могучий;

Вольной песнью разольется,
Скорбь-невзгода распоется!

А как век-то, век-то старой
Обручится с лютой карой,

Груз двойной с груди усталой
Уж не сбросит вздох удалой:

Не положишь ты на голос
С черной мыслью белый волос!

* * *

Gusting winds and violent weather—
youthful years could want no better!

In dark days, in times distressing,
a mighty sigh will lift the breast and

spill out in a song of freedom,
sing away all care-misfortune!

But when age, that elder season,
weds itself to cruel chastisement,

the bold sigh relieves no longer
the weary breast its double burden:

there can be no harmonizing
whitened hair with black surmisings.

<1839>

***

На что вы, дни! Юдольный мир явленья
    Свои не изменит!
Все ведомы, и только повторенья
    Грядущее сулит.

Недаром ты металась и кипела,
    Развитием спеша,
Свой подвиг ты свершила прежде тела,
    Безумная душа!

И, тесный круг подлунных впечатлений
    Сомкнувшая давно,
Под веяньем возвратных сновидений
    Ты дремлешь; а оно

Бессмысленно глядит, как утро встанет,
    Без нужды ночь сменя,
Как в мрак ночной бесплодный вечер канет,
    Венец пустого дня!

* * *

What use are you, days? This earthly existence
    will never change its forms.
They all are known, and only repetitions
    the future promises.

You dashed about and churned—and not for nothing—
    in your hurry to unfold,
and while the body lingered you accomplished
    your task, O reckless soul!

The tight compass of sublunary impressions
    is long ago complete
for you, who slumber now beneath recurring
    dream-images, but it

senselessly watches as the morning rises,
    replacing night in vain,
as barren evening sinks into night's darkness,
    crowning the empty day!

<1840>

КОТТЕРИИ

Братайтеся, к взаимной обороне
Ничтожностей своих вы рождены;
Но дар прямой не брат у вас в притоне,
Бездарные писцы-хлопотуны!
Наоборот союзным на благое
Реченного достойные друзья,
"Аминь, аминь,— вещал он вам,— где трое
Вы будете — не буду с вами я".

TO A COTERIE

So have your brotherhood! For you were born to
defend each other's insignificance.
But true Talent is no brother to your warren,
you talentless pack of busy scriveners!
Friends worthy not of that which once was uttered
to those allied for good—but the inverse:
"Amen, amen, where three of you are gathered,"
he tells you, "I will not be in your midst."

<1842>

АХИЛЛ

Влага Стикса закалила
Дикой силы полноту
И кипящего Ахилла
Бою древнему явила
Уязвимым лишь в пяту.

Обречен борьбе верховной,
Ты ли долею своей
Равен с ним, боец духовный,
Сын купели новых дней?

Омовен ее водою,
Знай, страданью над собою
Волю полную ты дал,
И одной пятой своею
Невредим ты, если ею
На живую веру стал.

ACHILLES

Styx's icy waters tempered
the fullness of his wild strength
and to the ancient battle rendered
fiery Achilles vulnerable
nowhere except in his heel.

Doomed to the most exalted struggle,
how do you compare to him,
you who are the spirit's warrior,
child of a latter-day baptism?

Washed in its waters, know this:
you have given suffering
full rein over you, and only
in your heel are you kept safe
from harm—if it is but firmly
placed upon a living faith.

<1841>

***

Сначала мысль, воплощена
В поэму сжатую поэта,
Как дева юная, темна
Для невнимательного света;
Потом, осмелившись, она
Уже увертлива, речиста,
Со всех сторон своих видна,
Как искушенная жена
В свободной прозе романиста;
Болтунья старая, затем
Она, подъемля крик нахальной,
Плодит в полемике журнальной
Давно уж ведомое всем.

* * *

At first the thought, when it's made flesh
in the concise poem of the poet,
is like a young girl, still obscure
to the eyes of a heedless world.
Then it grows bolder and becomes
more artful and more smooth of tongue,
displaying itself on every side,
like a woman of experience
in the free prose of the novelist.
Finally, an old chatterbox,
it instigates a shameless clamor
and brings forth in opinion columns
what everyone knew long ago.

<1838>

***

Еще как Патриарх не древен я; моей
Главы не умастил таинственный елей:
Непосвященных рук бездарно возложенье!
И я даю тебе мое благословенье
Во знаменьи ином, о дева красоты!
Под этой розою главой склонись, о ты,
Подобие цветов царицы ароматной,
В залог румяных дней и доли благодатной.

* * *

I am not yet ancient as a Patriarch; my head
was never anointed with the oil of sacrament:
giftless the laying on of hands unconsecrated.
And the benediction I bestow on you, O maiden
of beauty, under a different sign is given here.
Beneath this rose incline your head, you who are
the very likeness of the flowers' fragrant empress,
in pledge of rosy days and a portion full of blessing.

1839

***

Толпе тревожный день приветен, но страшна
Ей ночь безмолвная. Боится в ней она
Раскованной мечты видений своевольных.
Не легкокрылых грез, детей волшебной тьмы,
　　Видений дня боимся мы,
　　Людских сует, забот юдольных.

　　Ощупай возмущенный мрак:
　　Исчезнет, с пустотой сольется
　　Тебя пугающий призрак,
И заблужденью чувств твой ужас улыбнется.

О сын Фантазии! ты благодатных Фей
Счастливый баловень, и там, в заочном мире,
Веселый семьянин, привычный гость на пире
　　Неосязаемых властей!
　　Мужайся, не слабей душою
　　Перед заботою земною:
Ей исполинский вид дает твоя мечта;
Коснися облака нетрепетной рукою —
Исчезнет; а за ним опять перед тобою
Обители духов откроются врата.

* * *

Clamorous day is welcome to the crowd, but night,
soundless, fills it with dread. It fears in it
capricious visions of unchained imagination.
Not light-winged chimeras, spawn of the enchanted dark—
    we fear the visions of the day,
      the cares of earth, human commotion.

    Place your hand upon the troubled gloom:
    it disappears—the phantom that
    alarmed you fades to emptiness
and your horror smiles at how your senses were deceived.

O child of Fantasy! You are the fortunate
pet of the gracious Fairies, and there, in the world unseen,
a cheerful family man, a regular at the feast
    of powers incorporeal.
    Have courage, then; do not despair
    when you are faced with earthly care:
it's your imagination that makes it seem colossal.
Just touch the cloud with untrembling hand—
it disappears: behind it once again the portal
will open up for you into the spirits' land.

<1839>

205

***

Здравствуй, отрок сладкогласный!
Твой рассвет зарей прекрасной
Озаряет Аполлон!
Честь возникшему Пииту!
Малолетную Хариту
Ранней лирой тронул он.

С утра дней счастлив и славен,
Кто тебе, мой мальчик, равен?
Только жавронок живой,
Чуткой грудию своею,
С первым солнцем, полный всею
Наступающей весной!

* * *

Hail to you, my sweet-voiced child!
On your dawn Apollo shines
his beautiful radiance!
All honor to the newborn Poet!
He has touched with his precocious
lyre the heart of a young Grace.

Glad and glorious in your morning,
who, my boy, can be your rival?
Only the lark, who brightly sings,
his breast so alive with feeling,
as he greets the sun's arrival
full of all the coming spring.

<1841>

***

Что за звуки? Мимоходом
Ты поешь перед народом,
Старец нищий и слепой!
И, как псов враждебных стая,
Чернь тебя обстала злая,
Издеваясь над тобой.

А с тобой издавна тесен
Был союз камены песен,
И беседовал ты с ней,
Безымянной, роковою,
С дня, как в первый раз тобою
Был услышан соловей.

Бедный старец! слышу чувство
В сильной песне… Но искусство…
Старцев старее оно:
Эти радости, печали —
Музыкальные скрыжали
Выражают их давно!

Опрокинь же свой треножник!
Ты избранник, не художник!
Попеченья гений твой
Да отложит в здешнем мире:
Там, быть может, в горном клире,
Звучен будет голос твой!

* * *

What sounds are these? On your travels,
you perform before the people,
aged father, poor and blind!
And the evil rabble presses
round you like a pack of vicious
dogs and taunts you without end.

But the bond has long been strong
between you and the muse of song:
with her—fateful and unnamed—
you have happily conversed
ever since the day you first
heard the song of the nightingale.

Poor old man! I hear the heart
in your powerful song, but art—
it is older than old men.
These same joys and tribulations—
music tablets have expressed them
since time immemorial.

Overturn your tripod, father!
You're one of the chosen—no mere artist!
Let your genius put aside
in this world below all worries:
there, perhaps, in heaven's chorus
will your voice at last resound.

<1841>

***

Всё мысль да мысль! Художник бедный слова!
О жрец ее! тебе забвенье нет;
Всё тут, да тут и человек, и свет,
И смерть, и жизнь, и правда без покрова.
Резец, орган, кисть! счастлив, кто влеком
К ним чувственным, за грань их не ступая!
Есть хмель ему на празднике мирском!
Но пред тобой, как пред нагим мечом,
Мысль, острый луч! бледнеет жизнь земная!

* * *

Thought, always thought! Unfortunate word-artist!
Thought's priest! For you there's no oblivion.
Again and again, always the world and man
and death and life and truth without a cover.
Brush, organ, chisel—happy the man inclined
to these sensate things, who stays within their border!
Drunkenness awaits him at the world's feast!
But before you, as before a sword unsheathed—
O thought, sharp ray!—this earthly life turns pallid.

<1840>

СКУЛЬПТОР

Глубокий взор вперив на камень,
Художник Нимфу в нем прозрел,
И пробежал по жилам пламень,
И к ней он сердцем полетел.

Но, бесконечно вожделенный,
Уже он властвует собой:
Неторопливый, постепенный
Резец с богини сокровенной
Кору снимает за корой.

В заботе сладостно-туманной
Не час, не день, не год уйдет,
А с предугаданной, с желанной
Покров последний не падет,

Покуда, страсть уразумея
Под лаской вкрадчивой резца,
Ответным взором Галатея
Не увлечет, желаньем рдея,
К победе неги мудреца.

THE SCULPTOR

His deep gaze fixed upon the stone,
the artist saw the Nymph inside,
and fire raced through every vein
and in his heart he flew to her.

But soon, consumed with endless yearning,
he's master of himself again:
the gradual chisel without hurry
removes one layer and then another
from the goddess concealed within.

In a sweet fog of concentration
an hour, a day, a year goes by,
but the final veil falls not away from
the one foreguessed, the one desired,

until, the passion recognizing
beneath the chisel's sly caress,
Galatea answers with her eyes and
flushed with desire draws the wise man
on to the victory of bliss.

<1841>

ОСЕНЬ

1

И вот сентябрь! замедля свой восход,
    Сияньем хладным солнце блещет,
И луч его в зерцале зыбком вод
    Неверным золотом трепещет.
Седая мгла виется вкруг холмов;
    Росой затоплены равнины;
Желтеет сень кудрявая дубов,
    И красен круглый лист осины;
Умолкли птиц живые голоса,
Безмолвен лес, беззвучны небеса!

2

И вот сентябрь! и вечер года к нам
    Подходит. На поля и горы
Уже мороз бросает по утрам
    Свои сребристые узоры.
Пробудится ненастливый Эол;
    Пред ним помчится прах летучий,
Качаяся, завоет роща, дол
    Покроет лист ее падучий,
И набегут на небо облака,
И потемнев, запенится река.

3

Прощай, прощай, сияние небес!
    Прощай, прощай, краса природы!
Волшебного шептанья полный лес,

AUTUMN

1

And now it's September! Rising with delay,
        the sun shines with colder radiance,
and in the water's wavering glass its ray
        shimmers with an uncertain gold.
The hilltops are swaddled in a gray mist,
        the lowlands are sodden with dew;
yellow now is the oak tree's curly crown;
        the round leaf of the aspen is red;
the birds' bright chatter is no more to be heard,
hushed is the woodland, soundless are the skies.

2

And now it's September! The evening of the year
        approaches. Already each morning
the hoarfrost scatters its silvery designs
        across the fields and on the mountains.
Inclement Aeolus will soon awake,
        and whirling dust will flee before him;
the grove, swaying, will start to howl, its leaves
        will fall and cover up the ground,
and a great mass of cloud will fill the sky,
and the river, darkening, begin to foam.

3

Farewell, farewell to the radiance of the skies!
        Farewell, farewell to nature's charms!
To woods alive with magic whisperings

Златочешуйчатые воды!
Веселый сон минутных летных нег!
    Вот эхо в рощах обнаженных
Секирою тревожит дровосек,
    И скоро, снегом убеленных,
Своих дубров и холмов зимний вид
Застылый ток туманно отразит.

4

А между тем досужий селянин
    Плод годовых трудов сбирает:
Сметав в стога скошенный злак долин,
    С серпом он в поле поспешает.
Гуляет серп. На сжатых бороздах
    Снопы стоят в копнах блестящих
Иль тянутся вдоль жнивы, на возах,
    Под тяжкой ношею скрыпящих,
И хлебных скирд золотоверхий град
Подъемлется кругом крестянских хат.

5

Дни сельского, святого торжества!
    Овины весело дымятся,
И цеп стучит, и с шумом жернова
    Ожившей мельницы крутятся.
Иди, зима! На строги дни себе
    Припас оратай много блага:
Отрадное тепло в его избе,
    Хлеб-соль и пенистая брага;
С семьей своей вкусит он без забот
Своих трудов благословенный плод!

and waters plated with golden scales!
To happy dreams of fleeting summer pleasures!
    And now the woodsman with his ax
disturbs an echo in the naked forest,
    and, before long, the frozen stream
will hazily reflect the wintry view
of oak groves and hillsides whitened with snow.

4

Meanwhile, the able rustic gathers in
    the fruits of his toil over the year;
he's raked the valleys' new-mown grain in ricks
    and hurries with his sickle to the field.
To and fro it swings. Along the fresh-reaped furrows,
    sheaves stand resplendent in haycocks
or are pulled across the harvested field in wagons
    that creak under their heavy load,
and soon a golden-topped city of grain
rises in stacks around the peasant huts.

5

Glad days of sacred rural ceremony!
    Smoke rises gaily from the kilns,
the flail rings out, and noisily the millstones
    revolve in the awakened mill.
So come, winter! Against harsh days the plowman
    has set aside an ample store:
there is delightful warmth inside his cottage,
    hospitality and foamy beer.
Surrounded by his family, he will taste,
free of all care, his labor's blessed fruits.

6

А ты, когда вступаешь в осень дней,
　　　Оратай жизненного поля,
И пред тобой во благостыне всей
　　　Является земная доля;
Когда тебе житейские бразды,
　　　Труд бытия вознаграждая,
Готовятся подать свои плоды,
　　　И спеет жатва дорогая,
И в зернах дум ее сбираешь ты,
Судеб людских достигнув полноты,—

7

Ты так же ли, как земледел, богат?
　　　И ты, как он, с надеждой сеял;
И ты, как он, о дальнем дне наград
　　　Сны позлащенные лелеял...
Любуйся же, гордись восставшим им!
　　　Считай свои приобретенья!..
Увы! к мечтам, страстям, трудам мирским
　　　Тобой скопленные презренья,
Язвительный, неотразимый стыд
Души твоей обманов и обид!

8

Твой день взошел, и для тебя ясна
　　　Вся дерзость юных легковерий;
Испытана тобою глубина
　　　Людских безумств и лицемерий.
Ты, некогда всех увлечений друг,
　　　Сочувствий пламенный искатель,

6

But you, as you enter the autumn of your days,
　　O plowman of the fields of life,
and your earthly lot appears before your eyes
　　in all its generosity,
and as the furrows of this life get ready
　　to offer up their bounty to you
and so reward the labor of existence,
　　and as the precious harvest ripens,
and you, in grains of thought, gather it in,
now at the prime of human destiny—

7

are you rich, too, like the tiller of the soil?
　　Like him, with hope you sowed your seed;
like him, you too have nurtured gilded dreams
　　of a distant day of recompense—
Well, now it's here! Admire it, be proud,
　　and add up all you have obtained!...
Alas! For dreams and passions and worldly toil
　　you now have nothing but disdain,
and the stinging, indeflectible shame
of your soul's delusions and indignities.

8

Your day has come, and now you clearly see
　　how brazen were youthful certainties;
you have experienced in all their depth
　　man's follies and hypocrisies.
You, once a friend to every lunacy,
　　an ardent seeker of fellow feeling,

Блистательных туманов царь — и вдруг
　　Бесплодных дебрей созерцатель,
Один с тоской, которой смертный стон
Едва твоей гордыней задушен.

9

Но если бы негодованья крик,
　　Но если б вопль тоски великой
Из глубины сердечныя возник,
　　Вполне торжественный и дикой,—
Костями бы среди своих забав
　　Содроглась ветреная младость,
Играющий младенец, зарыдав,
　　Игрушку б выронил, и радость
Покинула б чело его навек,
И заживо б в нем умер человек!

10

Зови ж теперь на праздник честный мир!
　　Спеши, хозяин тароватый!
Проси, сажай гостей своих за пир
　　Затейливый, замысловатый!
Что лакомству пророчит он утех!
　　Каким разнообразьем брашен
Блистает он!.. Но вкус один во всех
　　И, как могила, людям страшен:
Садись один и тризну соверши
По радостям земным своей души!

the tsar of brilliant mists—now suddenly
    you're contemplating barren thickets,
alone with an anguish whose mortal groan
is barely stifled by your arrogance.

9

But if such a cry of indignant rage,
    if such a wail of mighty anguish,
were to rise up from the depths of your heart,
    fully majestic, fully savage—
the frivolous youth would shudder in his bones
    in the middle of his amusements;
the child at his play would burst into tears
    and let go of his toy, and gladness
would quit his forehead never to return,
and the man in him would die a living death.

10

So now invite the honest world to a feast!
    Unstinting host, do not delay!
And seat your guests around a table laid
    with ingenuity and wit.
What savory delights it promises!
    With what variety of viands
it shines!… But the same taste is in every dish
    and is, like the grave, terrifying.
Sit down, then, all alone and hold a wake
for all the joys your soul once knew on earth.

11

Какое же потом в груди твоей
     Ни водворится озаренье,
Чем дум и чувств ни разрешится в ней
     Последнее вихревращенье:
Пусть в торжестве насмешливом своем
     Ум бесполезный сердца трепет
Угомонит и тщетных жалоб в нем
     Удушит запоздалый лепет,
И примешь ты, как лучший жизни клад,
Дар опыта, мертвящий душу хлад.

12

Иль, отряхнув видения земли
     Порывом скорби животворной,
Ее предел завидя невдали,
     Цветущий брег за мглою черной,
Возмездий край, благовестящим снам
     Доверясь чувством обновленным,
И бытия мятежным голосам,
     В великом гимне примиренным,
Внимающий, как арфам, коих строй
Превыспренный не понят был тобой,—

13

Пред Промыслом оправданным ты ниц
     Падешь с признательным смиреньем,
С надеждою, не видящей границ,
     И утоленным разуменьем:
Знай, внутренней своей вовеки ты
     Не передашь земному звуку

11

Whatever shining revelation might
        then make a home within your breast,
however this final whirlwind of thoughts
        and feelings might be there resolved—
let your mind in sardonic triumph allay
        the futile tremble of your heart
and stifle within it the now-too-late
        babble of unavailing laments,
and as life's finest treasure you will accept
experience's gift, a soul-numbing chill.

12

Or, shaking off the visions of the earth
        in a surge of life-giving sorrow;
discerning its boundary not far away,
        a flowering shore beyond the blackness,
a land of recompense; with feeling revived,
        trusting in dreams of joyous tidings;
and hearkening to the riotous voices of life
        now reconciled in a great anthem,
as if to harps whose harmonies had been
too exalted for you to comprehend—

13

before justified Providence you fall
        prostrate with grateful humility,
filled with a hope that knows no bounds, with all
        your understanding now appeased—
know this: what is within you, you can never
        translate to any earthly sound;

И легких чад житейской суеты
  Не посвятишь в свою науку;
Знай, горняя иль дольная, она
Нам на земле не для земли дана.

14

Вот буйственно несется ураган,
  И лес подъемлет говор шумный,
И пенится, и ходит океан,
  И в берег бьет волной безумной:
Так иногда толпы ленивый ум
  из усыпления выводит
Глас, пошлый глас, вещатель общих дум,
  И звучный отзыв в ней находит,
Но не найдет отзыва тот глагол,
Что страстное земное перешел.

15

Пускай, приняв неправильный полет
  И вспять стези не обретая,
Звезда небес в бездонность утечет;
  Пусть заменит ее другая:
Не явствует земле ущерб одной,
  Не поражает ухо мира
Падения ее далекий вой,
  Равно как в высотах эфира
Ее сестры новорожденный свет
И небесам восторженный привет!

the fickle children of life's vain endeavors
    cannot be taught what you have learned;
know this: lofty or low, this science has
been given to us on earth not for the earth.

14

Now comes the hurricane in violent rage,
    the forest raises a noisy clamor,
the ocean churns, advancing, and its wave
    crashes madly against the shoreline.
Thus sometimes a voice, an insipid voice,
    proclaimer of the common wisdom,
rouses the crowd's lethargic mind from its doze
    and resonant response finds in it.
But no response will be found for the word
that has transcended the passions of earth.

15

Should a star in the heavens lose her way
    and not regain her proper bearing
but veer instead into the great abyss,
    and should a second star replace her,
the earth will not notice the loss of the first—
    the distant wail of her descent
will never strike the ear of the world;
    nor will it mark the newborn light
of her sister in the aethereal heights
or her elated greeting to the heavens.

16

Зима идет, и тощая земля
В широких лысинах бессилья,
И радостно блиставшие поля
Златыми класами обилья,
Со смертью жизнь, богатство с нищетой —
Все образы годины бывшей
Сравняются под снежной пеленой,
Однообразно их покрывшей:
Перед тобой таков отныне свет,
Но в нем тебе грядущей жатвы нет!

16

Winter is coming. And the scraggly land
    in vast bald tracts of impotence
and fields that once had jubilantly gleamed
    with the bounty of golden grain,
both death and life, riches and poverty—
    all of the forms of the year now over—
will be made equal beneath a shroud of snow,
    covering all of them uniformly...
Such is the world before you from now on,
but in it, for you, there is no harvest to come.

Late 1836 – early 1837, <1841>

***

Благословен святое возвестивший!
Но в глубине разврата не погиб
Какой-нибудь неправедный изгиб
Сердец людских пред нами обнаживший.
Две области: сияния и тьмы
Исследовать равно стремимся мы.
Плод яблони со древа упадает:
Закон небес постигнул человек!
Так в дикий смысл порока посвящает
Нас иногда один его намек.

* * *

Blessed the man who holy things discloses!
But he is not lost in the abyss of vice
who before our eyes some iniquitous
perversion in the human heart exposes.
Two provinces, both radiance and shadow,
we take as equal objects of our study.
The fruit falls from the apple tree, and heaven's
law is apprehended by the mind of man!
Thus sometimes nothing but the mere suggestion
imparts to us the wild meaning of sin.

1839

РИФМА

Когда на играх Олимпийских,
На стогнах греческих недавних городов,
Он пел, питомец Муз, он пел среди валов
Народа, жадного восторгов мусикийских,—
В нем вера полная в сочувствие жила:
     Свободным и широким метром,
     Как жатва, зыблемая ветром,
     Его гармония текла.
Толпа вниманием окована была,
     Пока, могучим сотрясеньем
Вдруг побежденная, плескала без конца
     И струны звучные певца
     Дарила новым вдохновеньем.
     Когда на греческий амвон,
     Когда на римскую трибуну
Оратор восходил, и славословил он
     Или оплакивал народную Фортуну,
И устремлялися все взоры на него,
     И силой слова своего
Вития властвовал народным произволом, —
     Он знал, кто он; он ведать мог,
     Какой могучий правит бог
     Его торжественным глаголом.
     Но нашей мысли торжищ нет,
     Но нашей мысли нет форума!..
     Меж нас не ведает поэт,
     Высок полет его иль нет,
     Велика ль творческая дума.
     Сам судия и подсудимый,
     Скажи: твой беспокойный жар —
     Смешной недуг иль высший дар?

RHYME

When at the Olympian competitions
or in the public squares of the young Greek city-states
he sang, the Muses' ward—sang in the midst of waves
of people hungering for musical elation—
there lived within him then full faith in sympathy:
    with meter broad and unconstrained,
    like grain swaying beneath the wind,
    unhindered flowed his harmony.
The multitudes stood riveted in their attention
    till all at once a great convulsion
swept over them and they applauded without end
    and on the singer's sounding strings
    bestowed again new inspiration.
    When the orator mounted the podium
    in Ancient Greece, when he ascended
the tribunal in Ancient Rome, and would extol
    the nation's fortune or lament it,
and the eyes of every person there were turned his way,
    and the rhetorician had full sway
through the power of his speech over the people's will—
    he knew just who he was; he could
    discern how mighty was the god
    who governed his majestic word.
    But no agora for our thought
    is there, and for our thought no forum!...
    The poet in our age knows not
    whether he truly sails the heights,
    how great is his creative notion.
    Yourself both judge and under judgment,
    explain your fevered restlessness:
    A gift sublime? An absurd disease?

Реши вопрос неразрешимый!
Среди безжизненного сна,
Средь гробового хлада света,
Своею ласкою поэта
Ты, Рифма! радуешь одна.
Подобно голубю ковчега,
Одна ему, с родного брега,
Живую ветвь приносишь ты;
Одна с божественным порывом
Миришь его твоим отзывом
И признаешь его мечты!

Resolve this unresolvable question.
Amid the lifeless sleep that is
the world, amid its tomb-like coldness,
it's you alone, O Rhyme, who gladden
the poet's heart with your caress.
Like the dove of the ark, it's you alone
who come back from his native shore
bearing a living branch for him;
it's you alone in your response
who reconcile him to the surge
divine, and recognize his dreams!

<1840>, 1843?

POEMS 1839–1844

***

Мою звезду я знаю, знаю,
    И мой бокал
Я наливаю, наливаю,
    Как наливал.
Гоненьям рока, злобе света
    Смеюся я:
Живет не здесь — в звездах Моэта
    Душа моя!
Когда ж коснутся уст прелестных
    Уста мои,
Не нужно мне ни звезд небесных,
    Ни звезд Аи!

* * *

My star I know, I know my star,
　　and this my glass
I fill, I fill my glass just as
　　I have before.
Fate's wrath, the malice of the world—
　　I laugh at these:
not here—my soul lives in the stars,
　　in Moët's stars.
But when her lovely lips are pressed
　　against my lips,
I need no stars—not those above,
　　nor yours, Aÿ!

<1839>

***

На все свой ход, на все свои законы.
Меж люлькою и гробом спит Москва;
Но и до ней, глухой, дошла молва,
Что скучен вист и веселей салоны
Отборные, где есть уму простор,
Где властвует не вист, а разговор.
И погналась за модой новосветской,
Но погналась старуха непутем:
Салоны есть,— но этот смотрит детской,
А тот, увы! глядит гошпиталем.

* * *

Everything has its pace, has its own laws.
From the cradle to the grave, Moscow is snoozing,
but even she, though deaf, had heard the news:
card games are boring, salons are more amusing
(with the right people)—there the mind has space,
and conversation rules the day, not whist.
So off she ran, chasing the latest fashion,
but in her haste the old dame got it wrong:
there are salons—but this one's a kindergarten
and that one, alas, looks like a veterans' home.

1840–1843?

С КНИГОЮ "СУМЕРКИ"

С. Н. К.

Сближеньем с вами на мгновенье
Я очутился в той стране,
Где *в оны дни* воображенье
Так сладко, складно лгало мне.
На ум, на сердце мне излили
Вы благодатные струи
И чудотворно превратили
В день ясный *сумерки* мои.

WITH THE BOOK *DUSK*

to S. N. K.

We became friends, and for a moment
I found myself back in that land
where "in the old days" the imagination
told me such lovely, lilting lies.
You poured out on my heart, my mind,
the streams of your benevolent grace
and with miraculous power turned
my *dusk* into the clearest day.

1842

[НА ПОСЕВ ЛЕСА]

Опять весна; опять смеется луг,
И весел лес своей младой одеждой,
И поселян неутомимый плуг
Браздит поля с покорством и надеждой.

Но нет уже весны в душе моей,
Но нет уже в душе моей надежды,
Уж дольный мир уходит от очей,
Пред вечным днем я опускаю вежды.

Уж та зима главу мою сребрит,
Что греет сев для будущего мира,
Но праг земли не перешел пиит,—
К ее сынам еще взывает лира.

Велик Господь! Он милосерд, но прав:
Нет на земле ничтожного мгновенья;
Прощает он безумию забав,
Но никогда пирам злоумышленья.

Кого измял души моей порыв,
Тот вызвать мог меня на бой кровавый;
Но подо мной, сокрытый ров изрыв,
Свои рога венчал он злобной славой!

Летел душой я к новым племенам,
Любил, ласкал их пустоцветный колос,
Я дни извел, стучась к людским сердцам,
Всех чувств благих я подавал им голос.

[ON THE PLANTING OF A WOOD]

Again it's spring; again the meadow laughs,
the woods delight to wear their youthful clothing,
and never wearying, the rustic's plow
furrows the fields, obedient and hoping.

But there is no more springtime in my soul;
but in my soul there is no hope remaining;
already this world is fading from my sight;
my eyelids droop before the day eternal.

Already that winter is silvering my head
which warms the plantings for the world to come;
but the poet has not crossed the earth's threshold—
his lyre still is summoning her sons.

Great is the Lord! He is merciful but just:
not a moment on the earth is without meaning;
he may forgive the lunacy of mirth,
but never feasts of evil-minded scheming.

The one whom my soul's vehemence had crushed
might well have challenged me to bloody battle,
but when he dug beneath me a hidden pit,
he crowned his horns with a malicious glory.

The younger generations my soul embraced:
their barren-flowered grain I loved, I nurtured;
I knocked at people's hearts day after day,
offering a voice for every fine emotion.

Ответа нет! Отвергнул струны я,
Да кряж другой мне будет плодоносен!
И вот ему несет рука моя
Зародыши елей, дубов и сосен.

И пусть, простяся с лирою моей,
Я верую: ее заменят эти,
Поэзии таинственных скорбей,
Могучие и сумрачные дети.

No answer! I have cast my strings aside:
may new, unbroken soil be fertile for me!
And so my hand is bringing to this ground
the embryos of spruces, pines, and oak trees.

And let me, as I bid my lyre farewell,
believe that one day these will supersede it:
born of a poetry of mysterious woe,
these towering and dusk-enshrouded children.

1842

***

Когда твой голос, о Поэт,
Смерть в высших звуках остановит,
Когда тебя во цвете лет
Нетерпеливый рок уловит,—

Кого закат могучих дней
Во глубине сердечной тронет?
Кто в отзыв гибели твоей
Стесненной грудию восстонет,

И тихий гроб твой посетит,
И над умолкшей Аонидой,
Рыдая, пепел твой почтит
Нелицемерной панихидой?

Никто!— но сложится певцу
Канон намеднишним Зоилом,
Уже кадящим мертвецу,
Чтобы живых задеть кадилом.

* * *

When death, O Poet, stops your voice
amid its most exalted music;
when in the flower of your years
fate cannot wait and intercepts you—

who will be moved deep in his heart
at the setting of your mighty days?
Whose chest will tighten? Who will start
to moan on hearing of your death?

Who will shed tears at your quiet grave
for the now-silent Aonian?
And who will honor your ashes with
an unhypocritical requiem?

Nobody!—But the singer will get
a canon composed by Zoilus-come-lately,
who, burning incense for the dead,
swings the censer to strike the living.

<1843>

***

Люблю я вас, богини пенья,
Но ваш чарующий наход,
Сей сладкий трепет вдохновенья, —
Предтечей жизненных невзгод.

Любовь Камен с враждой Фортуны —
Одно. Молчу! Боюся я,
Чтоб персты, падшие на струны,
Не пробудили вновь перуны,
В которых спит судьба моя.

И отрываюсь, полный муки,
От Музы, ласковой ко мне.
И говорю: до завтра, звуки!
Пусть день угаснет в тишине!

* * *

I love you, goddesses of song,
but when you arrive, enchanting me,
that sweet tremor of inspiration
is herald of life's calamities.

The Muses' love and Fortune's malice
are one. I keep quiet. I am fearful
lest fingers falling on the strings
awake the lightning bolts again
in whose midst my fate lies sleeping.

And so I draw back, full of torment,
from the Muse and her caress,
and say to sounds: Until tomorrow!
But let the day in silence end.

<1843>

МОЛИТВА

Царь небес! Успокой
Дух болезненный мой!
Заблуждений земли
Мне забвенье пошли!
И на строгий Твой рай
Силу серцу подай!

PRAYER

King of Heaven, grant rest
to my spirit distressed!
Of the earth's erring ways
let no memory remain!
And give my heart strength
for Thy paradise stern!

1842–1843

***

Когда, дитя и страсти и сомненья,
Поэт взглянул глубоко на тебя,
Решилась ты делить его волненья,
В нем таинство печали полюбя.

Ты, смелая и кроткая, со мною
В мой дикий ад сошла рука с рукою;
Рай зрела в нем чудесная любовь.

О, сколько раз к тебе, святой и нежной,
Я приникал главой моей мятежной,
С тобой себе и небу веря вновь.

* * *

When the poet, a child of doubt and passion,
looked at you with a gaze that pierced the marrow,
you decided then to share his agitation,
loving in him the mystery of sorrow.

Courageous and meek, you went with me down
into my wild hell, your hand holding mine;
miraculous love saw paradise there.

Oh, how many times have I pressed my rebellious
head against you, who are holy and gentle,
trusting, with you, in myself and heaven once more.

1843–1844

ПИРОСКАФ

Дикою, грозною ласкою полны,
Бьют в наш корабль средиземные волны.
Вот над кормою стал капитан.
Визгнул свисток его. Братствуя с паром,
Ветру наш парус раздался недаром:
Пенясь, глубоко вздохнул океан!

Мчимся. Колеса могучей машины
Роют волнистое лоно пучины.
Парус надулся. Берег исчез.
Наедине мы с морскими волнами;
Только что чайка вьется за нами
Белая, рея меж вод и небес.

Только вдали, океана жилица,
Чайке подобна, вод его птица,
Парус развив, как большое крыло,
С бурной стихией в томительном споре,
Лодка рыбачья качается в море:
С брегом набрежное скрылось, ушло!

Много земель я оставил за мною;
Вынес я много смятенной душою
Радостей ложных, истинных зол;
Много мятежных решил я вопросов,
Прежде чем руки марсельских матросов
Подняли якорь, надежды символ!

С детства влекла меня сердца тревога
В область свободную влажного бога;
Жадные длани я к ней простирал.

THE PYROSCAPHE

Tender with terrible, wild caresses,
Mediterranean waves strike our vessel.
There stands the captain, above the ship's bow.
His whistle rings out. With the steam joining forces,
our sail opens up to the wind with a purpose:
foaming, the sea lets forth a deep sigh.

Full speed ahead. The wheels of the mighty
engine dig into the billowing waters.
Taut is the sail. The shore's vanished from sight.
We are alone, face to face, with the sea wave;
only a gull, just behind us, is weaving,
effortless, white, between water and sky.

Only a fisherman's boat, the sea's tenant,
just like the seagull a bird of these waters,
its sail unfurled like an oversized wing,
in weary dispute with the blustery weather
rocks back and forth on the waves in the distance—
shoreline and shore life have faded, have gone!

Many the lands I have left far behind me;
many false joys and genuine evils
I have withstood in my turbulent soul;
many tumultuous questions I settled
before the hands of the Marseillais sailors
lifted the anchor—a symbol of hope!

Ever since childhood, my heart's trepidation
has drawn me towards the sea-god's free kingdom;
to it I hungrily stretched out my palms.

Темную страсть мою днесь награждая,
Кротко щадит меня немочь морская,
Пеною здравия брызжет мне вал!

Нужды нет, близко ль, далеко ль до брега!
В сердце к нему приготовлена нега.
Вижу Фетиду: мне жребий благой
Емлет она из лазоревой урны:
Завтра увижу я башни Ливурны,
Завтра увижу Элизий земной!

Now my dark passion is being rewarded:
maritime sickness obligingly spares me;
the sea wave will spray me with health-giving foam!

Whether the shore's near or far is no matter:
my heart will greet it with ready affection.
Thetis I see—from her azure urn
she chooses for me a benevolent fortune:
tomorrow I'll see the towers of Leghorn,
tomorrow I'll see Elysium on earth!

1844

ДЯДЬКЕ-ИТАЛЬЯНЦУ

Беглец Италии, Жьячинто, дядька мой,
Янтарный виноград, лимон ее златой
Тревожно бросивший, корыстью уязвленный,
И в край, суровый край, снегами покровенный,
Приставший с выбором загадочных картин,
Где что-то различал и видел ты один!
Прости наш здравый смысл, прости, мы та из наций,
Где брату твоему всех меньше спекуляций.
Никто их не купил. Вздохнув, оставил ты
В глушь севера тебя привлекшие мечты;
Зато воскрес в тебе сей ум, на всё пригодный,
Твой итальянский ум, и с нашим очень сходный!
Ты счастлив был, когда тебе кое-что дал
Почтенный, для тебя богатый генерал,
Чтоб, в силу строгого с тобою договора,
Имел я благодать нерусского надзора.
Благодаря богов, с тобой за этим вслед
Друг другу не были мы чужды двадцать лет.

Москва нас приняла, расставшихся с деревней.
Ты был вожатый мой в столице нашей древней.
Всех макаронщиков тогда узнал я в ней,
Ментóра моего полуденных друзей.
Увы! оставив там могилу дорогую,
Опять увидели мы вотчину степную,
Где волею небес узнал я бытие,
О сын Авзонии, для бурь, как ты свое,
Но где, хотя вдали твоей отчизны знойной,
Ты мирный кров обрел, а позже гроб спокойной.

TO MY TUTOR, THE ITALIAN

Italy's refugee, Giacinto, my old tutor,
you left her amber grape, her golden lemon behind you
in great anxiety, and stung with lust for gain,
arrived in an austere land, a snow-enveloped land,
with an array of paintings that were so enigmatic
no one but you could say, could see, what they depicted!
Forgive our common sense! Forgive us—we are a nation
that offers such as you least chance for speculation.
Nobody bought your pictures. You sighed and said farewell
to the dreams that had enticed you to our northern wilds.
But then that mind of yours, eternally resourceful,
your Italian mind revived, which is so like a Russian's!
You had a bit of luck when a general most worthy—
wealthy he seemed to you—gave you a little something
so that, by the strict terms of his, and your, decision,
I might enjoy the grace of non-Russian supervision.
From then on, you and I (for this I thank the gods)
in the twenty years that followed never were at odds.

Moscow received us when we quit the countryside;
in the ancient capital you were my loyal guide.
The whole macaroni tribe who lived there I met then—
all of my good mentor's meridional friends.
And leaving there, alas, a precious grave behind us,
we once again beheld our steppeland patrimony,
where, by the will of heaven, the life I came to know
was one of storms—like yours, son of Ausonia!—
but where you found, though far from your own sultry home,
a safe and quiet shelter and, later, a peaceful tomb.

Ты полюбил тебя призревшую семью
И, с жизнию ее сливая жизнь свою,
Ее событьями в глуши чужого края
Былого своего преданья заглушая,
Безропотно сносил морозы наших зим;
В наш краткий летний жар тобою был любим
Овраг под сению дубов прохладовейных.
Участник наших слез и праздников семейных,
В дни траура главой седой ты поникал;
Но ускорял шаги и членами дрожал,
Как в утро зимнее, порой, с пределов света,
Питомца твоего, недавнего корнета,
К коленам матери кибитка принесет
И скорбный взор ее минутно оживет.

Но что! радушному пределу благодарной,
Нет! ты не забывал отчизны лучезарной!
Везувий, Колизей, грот Капри, храм Петра
Имел ты на устах от утра до утра,
Именовал ты нам и принцов и прелатов
Земли, где зрел, дивясь, суворовских солдатов,
Входящих вопреки тех пламенных часов,
Что, по твоим словам, со стогнов гонят псов,
В густой пыли побед, в грозе небритых бо́род,
Рядами стройными в классический твой город;
Земли, где год спустя тебе предстал и он,
Тогда Буонапарт, потом Наполеон,
Минутный царь царей, но дивный кондотьери,
Уж зиждущий свои гигантские потери.

Скрывая власти глад, тогда морочил вас
Он звонкой пустотой революцьонных фраз.
Народ ему зажег приветственные плошки;

The family that took you in you grew to love,
and blending your own life into the life they led,
muffling in their events, in the wilds of a foreign country,
the legends and traditions from your past existence,
you bore without complaint the Russian winter's frost;
in our brief summer's heat, the place you loved the most
was that ravine beneath the oak wood's cooling branches.
Partaking in our tears and family celebrations,
in days of mourning you would hang your hoary head,
but then you quickened your step, trembling in every limb,
when on a winter's morn, at times, from the great world,
a covered sleigh arrived, delivering your ward,
the newly made cornet, back to his mother's arms,
and for a minute life returned to her worried eyes.

But still! Though grateful to our country for its welcome,
you never did forget the radiant land you hailed from!
The Colosseum, Capri, St. Peter's, Vesuvius
from one day to the next were ever on your lips;
you rattled off for us the names of princes, prelates,
from that land where, amazed, you watched Suvorov's soldiers
come marching into town despite the blazing hours
(which, in your words, could drive the dogs out of the squares),
in a storm of beards unshaven, caked in their victories' dust,
into your classical city, marching in ordered rows;
that land, where, one year later, you also would see him—
then still *Buonaparte*, soon *Napoléon*—
a fleeting king of kings but wondrous *condottiere*,
already laying the ground for losses beyond comparing.

Hiding his thirst for power, back then he dazzled you all
with the ringing, empty phrases of revolution's call.
To welcome him the people lit their earthen lamps,

Но ты, ты не забыл серебряные ложки,
Которые, среди блестящих общих грез,
Ты контрибуции назначенной принес;
Едва ты узнику печальному британца
Простил военную систему корсиканца.

Что на твоем веку, то ль благо, то ли зло,
Возникло, при тебе — в преданье перешло:
В Альпийских молниях, приемлемый опалой,
Свой ратоборный дух, на битвы не усталой,
В картечи эпиграмм Суворов испустил.
Злодей твой на скале пустынной опочил;
Ты сам глаза сомкнул, когда мирские сети
Уж поняли тобой взлелеянные дети;
Когда, свидетели превратностей земли,
Они глубокий взор уставить уж могли,
Забвенья чуждые за жизненною чашей,
На итальянский гроб в ограде церкви нашей.

А я, я с памятью живых твоих речей,
Увидел роскоши Италии твоей!
Во славе солнечной Неаполь твой нагорной,
В парах пурпуровых и в зелени узорной,
Неувядаемой,— амфитеатр дворцов
Над яркой пеленой лазоревых валов;
И Цицеронов дом, и злачную пещеру,
Священную поднесь Камены суеверу,
Где спит великий прах властителя стихов,
Того, кто в сей земле волканов и цветов
И ужасов и нег взлелеял эпопею,
Где в мраки Тенара открыл он путь Энею,
Явил его очам чудесный сад утех,
Обитель сладкую теней блаженных тех,

but you, you never forgot, amid the shining dreams
cherished by one and all, those silver spoons—your share
of the designated tribute to the conqueror.
Hardly could you forgive the Briton's mournful captive
the military system the Corsican established.

Whatever in your lifetime, whether good or ill,
had happened, it became a tale for you to tell:
from Alpine lightning blasts returning to disfavor,
yet not too weary to fight another battle, Suvorov
released his warrior spirit in a volley of epigrams.
Upon a desolate rock, your enemy breathed his last.
And you, too, shut your eyes, when the children you had raised
already understood this world's entangled nets;
already witnesses to earthly permutations,
drinking the cup of life yet alien to forgetting,
they now could let their gazes linger pensively
on the Italian tombstone in our churchyard wall.

And I, I with your words alive in memory,
have seen the opulence of your fair Italy!
Your clifftop Naples in the glory of the sun,
in purple mists, and in its patterned foliage, green
and never withering—a palaced amphitheater
rising above a bright carpet of azure billows;
and the house of Cicero, and that verdurous cave—
for the Muse's true believer still hallowed to this day—
where sleeps the mighty dust of poetry's own sovereign,
of him who in this land of blossoms and volcanoes,
of horrors and delights, nurtured the epic work
in which he led Aeneas into Taenarum's murk
and to his eyes revealed a wondrous garden of pleasures,
the lovely dwelling place of the shadows of the blessèd,

Что, крепки в опытах земного треволненья,
Сподобились вкусить эфирных струй забвенья.

Неаполь! До него среди садов твоих
Сердца мятежные отыскивали их.
Сквозь занавес веков еще здесь помнят виллы
Приюты отдыхов и Мария и Силлы.
И кто, бесчувственный, среди твоих красот
Не жаждал в их раю обресть навес иль грот,
Где б скрылся, не на час, как эти полубоги,
Здесь Лету пившие, чтоб крепнуть для тревоги,
Но чтоб незримо слить в безмыслии златом
Сон неги сладостной с последним, вечным сном.

И в сей Италии, где все — каскады, розы,
Мелезы, тополи и даже эти лозы,
Чей безымянный лист так преданно обник
Давно из божества разжалованный лик,
Потом с чела его повиснул полусонно,—
Все беззаботному блаженству благосклонно,
Ужиться ты не мог и, помня сладкий юг,
Дух предал строгому дыханью наших вьюг,
Не сетуя о том, что за пределы мира
Он улететь бы мог на крылиях зефира!

О тайны душ! меж тем как сумрачный поэт,
Дитя Британии, влачивший столько лет
По знойным берегам груди своей отравы,
У миртов, у олив, у моря и у лавы,
Молил рассеянья от думы роковой,
Владеющей его измученной душой,
Напрасно! (уст его, как древле уст Тантала,
Струя желанная насмешливо бежала!)—

who, tempered in the tests of earth's tumult, were found
worthy to taste the ethereal streams of oblivion.

Naples! Within your gardens, even before his time,
unquiet hearts had hoped to find oblivion's stream.
Here villas still recall, through a veil of centuries,
havens where Marius and Sulla took their ease.
And who, amid your beauties, could be so aloof
as not to long for, here, in their paradise, a roof,
a grotto in which to hide, not for an hour like them,
demigods drinking of Lethe for strength to meet alarms,
but in golden mindlessness to merge, unseen, the sweet
sleep of delicious pleasure with the last, eternal sleep?

And in this Italy, where everything—cascades,
roses and lemon balm, poplars, even those vines
whose nameless leaves had once enwreathed with such devotion
a face now long ago from deity demoted,
and later, drowsily, had drooped down off its brow—
where everything inclines to blissful, carefree joy,
you could not find your place, and so, remembering
the gentle south, gave up your spirit to the winds
of our ferocious blizzards, all without regretting
that it might else have flown this world upon a zephyr!

Oh, the mysteries of souls! That melancholy bard,
the child of Britain, dragging from shore to sultry shore
the poisons in his breast over so many years,
from myrtles and olive trees, from lava, from the sea
begged for distraction from the fateful rumination
to which his tortured soul was held in subjugation—
and all in vain! (the stream, long sought, escaped his lips
tauntingly, as it once had those of Tantalus)—

Мир сердцу твоему дал пасмурный навес
Метелью полгода скрываемых небес,
Отчизна тощих мхов, степей и древ иглистых!
О, спи! безгрезно спи в пределах наших льдистых!
Лелей по-своему твой подземельный сон,
Наш бурнодышащий, полночный аквилон,
Не хуже веющий забвеньем и покоем,
Чем вздохи южные с душистым их упоем!

while your heart found its peace under the cloudy roof
of skies six months a year hidden by whirling snows,
in the land of conifers and steppes and scraggly mosses!
O, sleep! Sleep dreamlessly within our icy borders!
And may your subterranean slumber be caressed
by our storm-breathing aquilon, wind of the north,
which blows no worse the balm of rest and all-forgetting
than southern sighs with their perfumed intoxication.

1844

LETTERS

Just over three hundred letters by Baratynsky have survived, in some cases only as copies or sporadic publications in nineteenth- or early-twentieth-century journals. And it was not until the end of the twentieth century—more than 150 years after the poet's death—that all his surviving letters were collected in a single volume, as part of the remarkable *Letopis' zhizni i tvorchestva Ye. A. Boratynskogo* [*A Chronicle of the Life and Work of Ye. A. Boratynsky*] (Moscow, 1998), compiled by the late Aleksey M. Peskov (1953–2009). Peskov's edition of the letters, and especially his meticulous efforts to establish as nearly as possible when each one was written (Baratynsky only rarely dated his letters), has greatly facilitated my own work here.

Three hundred letters is not a large number for a lifetime of correspondence (even given the poet's professed laxness in "epistolary prose"), and we can assume that many have been lost. We know, for example, that within hours after Baron Delvig died, in January 1831, his friends burned whatever they could find of his private papers; they were afraid the police would seize them and find things in his correspondence that might incriminate the letter-writers. Consequently, we have today only one letter from Baratynsky to a man who was probably his closest friend. We are also told that a collection of some three hundred letters, compiled by Modest Gofman before the First World War and intended for a third, never-published, volume of his edition of Baratynsky's complete works (1914–1915), "disappeared in the revolutionary turmoil" that followed the war. While this group may have included letters we know from existing versions, there may well have been many that had never been published.

What we have, then, is a record with gaps and imbalances. For example, the more than fifty surviving letters to Ivan Kireyevsky give us a very clear picture of this friendship, if only from one side of it (Kireyevsky's letters to Baratynsky have not reached us), at least for the period 1829 to 1834. On the other hand, only three letters to Aleksandr Pushkin have survived and, as mentioned, only one to Delvig—two other crucial relationships in the poet's life. There are many letters to his good friend Nikolay Putyata, but after 1837, when Putyata became Baratynsky's brother-in-law, these mostly concern the management of their wives' properties. The poet's youth in St. Petersburg and Finland and his efforts to regain his social status can be followed in his letters with relative ease, but the emotional struggles of the second half of the 1830s, when Baratynsky felt increasingly ostracized from the literary world, are much less well documented.

Of the 307 letters published by Peskov, many of which are little more than brief notes, I have translated 166, somewhat more than half. In making my selection, I wanted as much as possible to follow the major trajectories in Baratynsky's life: his expulsion from the Corps des Pages and attempt to regain his honor, his career as a poet, his most significant personal relationships, and his efforts to gain financial security for his family. But of course, these letters are much more than a record of his life: they also reveal the poet's moral and intellectual character and show patterns of thought that shape his poetry. My primary concern in making this selection was, indeed, to provide a background to the poems. To a large extent, of course, this background is biographical—we find here a somewhat different perspective on Finland than the one expressed in the poems; we learn more about Baratynsky's relationships with the women who inspired a number of his works (notably, Agrafena Zakrevskaya and Nastasya Baratynskaya); and we see how the conflict between poetic inspiration and the demands of mundane reality—a major theme in his work—is related to his increasing immersion in the "material worries" of supporting a growing family. But the letters also provide us with a psychological background, reflecting the poet's deep-rooted tension between a desire for excitement and a desire for tranquility, his skepticism about popular ideas and commitment to finding an authentic view, his yearning for mutual understanding and his fear of being misunderstood, among other currents.

The translated letters are often equipped with brief headnotes, while other biographical commentary—filling in the gaps, as it were—seeks to provide enough context for a more or less coherent narrative. The notes at the end of the book offer further clarification for the more obscure names and events mentioned in the letters.

For the sake of simplicity, dates are given in the Julian calendar, which was used in Russia until 1918. As Baratynsky writes in a letter from Paris (Letter 160), Russia was "twelve days younger than other nations," so January 1, 1844, in St. Petersburg was January 13, 1844, in Paris. For important historical and biographical dates, and for letters written from abroad, both Gregorian ("New Style") and Julian ("Old Style") dates are provided, as follows: "July 11 (NS) / June 29 (OS), 1844" (the date of the poet's death).

The presumed dates for the letters (given in square brackets) are all based on Peskov's *Chronicle*. The vast majority are necessarily approximate. A postmark, for instance, can tell us only when a letter was sent (or received); in such cases, the estimated date may be expressed as "January, before the 19th, 1826." Often, however, all that can be established is that a letter was written in a certain month or season.

As was standard practice for a Russian nobleman in the early nineteenth century, Baratynsky generally used Russian in letters to other men but French when writing to women. There are interesting exceptions: as a boy, he writes his mother in Russian when he feels particularly contrite about something; his use of Russian in a letter to the philosophically inclined Avdotya Yelagina is perhaps a sign of respect; he writes to his sister-in-law in Russian when dealing with a business matter; and his later letters to his wife are mostly in Russian. Still, of the letters presented here, thirty-seven were written in French and have been translated directly from that language. While the Russian letters have all been translated from Peskov's *Chronicle*, the sources for the French letters come from various publications (indicated on p. 478).

The reader will undoubtedly notice the different forms of the poet's surname that appear in the letters and commentary. During Baratynsky's lifetime two spellings of his family name were in currency: Баратынскій (Baratynsky) and Боратынскій (Boratynsky). In most official documents, such as school and military records, the former was used. The *Bar-* spelling was also used for all but one of his published works, and it is the spelling we consistently find in his friends' letters and in the contemporary press. It was also used in the edition of his works published in 1869 by his son Lev (who noted, however, that the *Bor-* spelling was "more correct"). Indeed, with a few notable exceptions, this spelling has been used in the great bulk of literary scholarship until very recently (the trend appears to be shifting). I have followed that practice here: it was under the *Bar-* spelling that Baratynsky became a poet. In his private correspondence, however, and generally within the family, the name was spelled *Boratynsky*, which, indeed, more closely reflects its etymological derivation from the Boratyn Castle (today in Ukraine) inherited by the poet's Polish ancestors in the fourteenth century. The situation is somewhat further complicated by the fact that Baratynsky signed the letters he wrote in French with what was then the usual transliteration of the name—*Boratinsky*. Rather than standardizing the spelling one way or another, I have decided to let all these apparent inconsistencies stand.

Similarly, I have preserved Baratynsky's use of French names in the letters he wrote in French. Thus, he signs himself "Eugène" or simply "E.", not "Yevgeny" or "Ye."; he refers to his sisters as "Sophie" and "Natalie," not "Sofya" and "Natalya," etc.—all standard practice. Occasionally, however, he inserts a Russian name in Cyrillic (usually in its affectionate form): he might call his wife "Настинька" ("Nastinka") instead of "Nastasie" or his sister-in-law "Соничка" ("Sonichka") instead of "Sophie." In such cases, I have simply transliterated the Russian.

Speaking of names, the reader should remember that Russian has separate feminine forms for Slavic surnames ending in *-ov, -ev, -in, -yn*, and *-y* (or *-oy*): namely, *-ova, -eva, -ina, -yna*, and *-aya*, respectively. Thus, Baratynsky's mother was Aleksandra *Baratynskaya*, Nikolay Karamzin's daughter was Sofya *Karamzina*, etc. Other names are not affected (e.g. Sofya Lvovna *Engelhardt*).

As a general rule, I have preserved as much as possible the conventions and courtesies of nineteenth-century Russian epistolary practice. The use of a person's first name and patronymic was (more or less as today) a sign of politeness, respect, or deference (e.g. Baratynsky always refers to his uncle as "Pyotr Andreyevich"). A man of Baratynsky's generation and class normally addressed close male friends by their full first names (Delvig addresses Baratynsky as "Yevgeny" in his letters), surnames ("dear Kireyevsky," "my dear Pletnyov"), or titles ("dear prince"). Diminutives (e.g. "Mitya" for "Dmitry") were not used between men nearly as often as they are today in Russia.

I have also preserved the nineteenth-century Russian units of measurement in my translation. Their approximate equivalents are as follows:

> 1 arshin = 28 inches
> 1 verst = 0.66 miles
> 1 pood = 36 pounds
> 1 quarter (*chetvert*) = 287 pounds
> 1 arpent = 0.84 acres
> 1 desyatina = 2.7 acres

Then, as now, the currency used in Russia was the ruble (1 ruble = 100 kopeks). Rubles existed in two forms, paper (banknotes, or "assignation rubles") and silver (the silver ruble was about three and a half times the value of the banknote). Money, it should be noted, is an underlying theme of these letters, from the 500 rubles (in banknotes) that Baratynsky and his schoolmate stole from a friend's father, to the amounts for which he sells the publication rights to his poems (Pushkin helped him get the price up to 7,000 rubles—Letter 101), to his expectations for the sale of his timber—5,000 rubles per *desyatina* (about 1,850 rubles per acre—Letter 138), to the 32,000 rubles he borrowed from a moneylender that would require a whole year's revenue (and then some) to pay back (Letter 166). To these numbers, add the price of the rye he needs to feed his peasants during a famine (40,000 rubles for 2,000 quarters, or 574 tons—Letter 104), the 300-ruble annual salary of Baratynsky's estate manager (Letter 115), and the cost of an overpriced dinner at a St. Petersburg restaurant (65 rubles—Letter 126), and you will have some idea of monetary values in the 1830s and 1840s (and the vast differences in living standards between the gentry and the peasants).

Finally, a word about my handling of verse quotations in these letters. In general, unless the verses appear in the first section of this book, I do not attempt a metrical or rhymed translation but provide only a close translation (in prose, as it were), with slashes indicating approximate line breaks. When the quotation is in French, the original is supplied in the body of the text with the translation in a footnote; the same method is used for other French phrases (Letter 132 is an exception). When Baratynsky's letters include entire poems that appear in the first section of the book, a footnote directs the reader to the appropriate page.

All the translations from Russian and French, both in the letters and the notes, are mine.

— R. G.

273

I.
THE CORPS DES PAGES
(1812–1816)

Yevgeny Baratynsky was born into a noble family of high-rank-
ing military officers. His father, Abram Andreyevich Baratynsky
(1767–1810), had served directly under Emperor Paul I and at-
tained the rank of major general. Three of Abram's brothers also
had very distinguished careers: Ilya Andreyevich was a rear admi-
ral, Bogdan Andreyevich, a vice admiral, while Pyotr Andreyevich
eventually became (under Emperor Alexander I) a lieutenant
general and a senator. The Baratynsky brothers owed their suc-
cess largely to the patronage of their relative Yekaterina Ivanovna
Nelidova, a lady-in-waiting to the Empress Maria Fyodorovna
and an intimate (though probably platonic) friend and influential
adviser to Paul. When Nelidova fell out of favor with the tsar in
1798, Abram Baratynsky was forced into retirement. He and his
wife, Aleksandra Fyodorovna Baratynskaya, née Cherepanova
(1777–1853)—like Nelidova, a graduate of the Smolny Convent's
Institute for Noble Maidens and a former lady-in-waiting to the
empress—settled in Tambov Province on the Vyazhlya estate, a
gift from Paul to Abram and Bogdan. It was here Yevgeny was born
on March 2 (NS) / February 19 (OS), 1800.

Abram could have returned to service, and St. Petersburg, after
Paul's assassination in a palace coup in 1801 and Alexander's as-
cension to the throne, but he chose instead to remain in retirement.
A few years later, after quarreling with his brothers, he moved his
young family to a new house on a separate part of the estate, called
Mara. In 1809, the family moved to Moscow (the reasons are un-
clear), and after just a few months Abram became seriously ill. He
died March 24, 1810, leaving Aleksandra to look after seven chil-
dren: Yevgeny (the eldest), Sofya (born 1801), Irakly (1802), Lev
(1806), Sergey (1807), Natalya (1809), and Varvara, born in 1810,
three months after Abram's death. Later that same year, Yevgeny
and Irakly were "enrolled" in the prestigious Corps des Pages mili-
tary academy in St. Petersburg—which meant only that they were
ensured a place at the academy when they reached the appropri-
ate age, provided they passed the entrance exams. In the spring of
1811, Aleksandra Baratynskaya moved the family back to Mara.

So it was that in early May, 1812, the twelve-year-old Yevgeny,
escorted by an aunt, arrived in St. Petersburg with hopes of con-

tinuing the family's military tradition. He spent the summer at a boarding school preparing for the Corps des Pages exams. His chance, it seems, came sooner than expected. Napoleon's forces invaded Russia in June, and the calamitous Battle of Borodino was fought outside Moscow on September 7 (NS) / August 26 (OS). New officers were needed to replace the fallen, and the next day thirty-eight "pages" (as the students were known) were quickly graduated, made officers, and sent into active service. Vacancies opened, and Yevgeny was admitted to the Corps des Pages on October 9.

1. TO HIS MOTHER, ALEKSANDRA FYODOROVNA BARATYNSKAYA, IN MARA.

This is, apparently, the first letter Baratynsky wrote to his mother from the Corps des Pages, and it is one of the very few times he wrote her in Russian. We do not know what the boy had done to upset her; perhaps it was simply that he had not written to her before now.

[December (?), 1812, Saint Petersburg]

Dear Maminka,

I was very sad to hear that I had the misfortune of upsetting you, but I will be better from now on. I have been at the Corps des Pages two months now. I took an examination and was placed in the 4th class [*the youngest class*], in Mr. Vasily Osipovich Kristafovich's section. Oh, Maminka, what a good officer he is, and he knows my uncle, too. As soon as I was accepted, he invited me to his quarters and told me everything concerning the Corps, even about which pages I should be friends with. I go to see him every evening with the other pages who visit him. He only invites the ones who are well behaved. I am very surprised that you did not receive the news from me about Uncle Pyotr Andreyevich's departure to Sveaborg, for I wrote you about it twice. I have started geography again, and I am translating from French into Russian and from Russian into French and from German into Russian. I am also studying Russian history now and have already gone through three periods and am learning about the 4th one, the reign of Grand Duke Yury II Vsevolodovich; I have also started geometry. We get up at 5 o'clock, at ½ past 5 have prayers until 6, then go to tea until ½ past 6, and then to classes from 7 to eleven, have dinner at 12, and then classes from 2 to 4, and at 7 o'clock and 8 o'clock we go to bed. I am sending you a list of expenses upon my entering the Corps. Farewell, dear Maminka, stay well. I kiss my little brothers and sisters. I remain your loving son

Yevgeny Boratynsky

2. TO HIS MOTHER, IN MARA (IN FRENCH).

During the school holidays, Yevgeny remained in St. Petersburg with his uncle Pyotr Andreyevich Baratynsky. At the time of this letter, however, Pyotr Andreyevich was in Mara to fetch Yevgeny's brother Irakly, who, like Yevgeny, was going to attend a boarding school in St. Petersburg and then enter the Corps. Another uncle, Ilya Andreyevich, had recently gone to his country estate.

[August (?), 1814, St. Petersburg]

My very dear Maman,

My uncle has just left for the countryside. I will stay here alone. I wait impatiently for the arrival of Pyotr Andreyevich and my brother. What pleasure it will be for me to have him tell of everything you have been doing in my absence; he will speak to me endlessly of you, of my brothers, my sisters, of everyone I hold most dear in the world.

The venerable Nikolay Antonovich is letting my brother stay with him and I will have the pleasure of seeing him always near me. Of all the gifts the supreme being has bestowed on us, nothing inspires such gratitude in me as imagination and hope. Through the first we are sustained in unhappiness, in absence; the hope of seeing again the object of our desires sweetens the time we are apart. Imagination transports me into your arms, dear Maman; it seems just as if I am talking to you. I would like some good Magician to put a spell on me, in such a way that it would always seem I was with you. This work would earn him all my gratitude. You wish to send me the little émigrés, my dear Maman, but there is no need, since I have already read the book three or four times. Farewell, my dear, my tender Maman; stay as well as I desire you to be. May God grant me the grace of seeing you again one day. I kiss my uncles' hands and those of my aunt; I embrace my brothers and my sisters. Be so good as to give my compliments to Monsieur Bories. I have the honor of being your very humble and very obedient servant and son

Eugène Boratinsky

3. TO HIS MOTHER, IN MARA (IN FRENCH).

[September or early October, 1814, Saint Petersburg]

My dearest Maman,

I am rushing so I can use Apollon Nikolayevich's departure to write you. Our examination is over. I remain in the same class. I am quite upset at not being able to tell you that I won the award, as I did last year, but you know that this does not always happen. I hope, however, to win it next year. At present, in my moments of leisure, I occupy myself by translating or composing little stories, and to tell you the truth, there is nothing I love more than poetry. I would very much like to be an author. Next time I will send you a kind of little novel, which I have almost finished. I would very much like to know what you say about it. If you think I have some talent, I will strive to improve myself by learning the rules. But truly, Maman, I have seen a number of published Russian translations that were so badly translated I don't know how the author had the audacity to present such foolish things to public judgment—and to complete the effrontery, he put his name to them. I assure you, without vanity, that I could have made much better translations. To give you some idea, I will tell you that he translated the French expression, *"Il jetait feu et flamme"** as: *"Ognyom i plamenem rykal."†* What is very good in French is very bad in Russian, and this is the most beastly expression [*l'expression la plus animal*] I have ever seen. Please forgive me if I speak ill of this poor devil, but I would like him to hear everything people say about him so he will lose the appetite for torturing our ears with the truly barbaric expressions he employs. But here I am, like a true French journalist, writing you a satire on bad

---

* He spewed fire and flame.

† With fire and flame he roared.

authors. Forgive me, my dear Maman, I know well that it does not become me to set myself up as a judge in an art where I am such a novice, but I have always felt it is no indiscretion to tell your mother what you think. Farewell, my dear Maman. I am well. I embrace my sisters and brothers.

Eugène Boratinsky

P.S. Please let me know if you received this letter sealed or unsealed.

4. TO HIS MOTHER, IN MARA (IN FRENCH).

The "faults" Baratynsky mentions here are probably the bad grades he received on his exams (most likely in German, algebra, and geometry), which meant he had to repeat a year.

[November (?), 1814, St. Petersburg]

My dear Maman,

I just received your letter and do not know how to tell you all the pleasure I felt seeing that you love me as ever and forgive my faults. I truly needed this consolation. It has put me at peace with myself, and I clearly see how preferable it is to all the pleasures of dissipation. I spend every holiday at my uncle's [Pyotr Baratynsky's], who has kindly hired a mathematics teacher for me, and I have already made some progress. Do I dare repeat my request concerning the navy? I beg you, my dear Maman, please grant me this favor. My own interests, which you say are so dear to you, absolutely demand it. I know how much it must cost your heart to see me in such a dangerous service. But tell me, do you know of a place in the universe—apart from the realm of the Ocean—where a man's life would not be exposed to a thousand dangers, where death would not snatch a son from his mother, father, sister? Everywhere the smallest puff of air is capable of destroying that fragile impulse we call our existence. Whatever you might say, dear Maman, there are things that are dependent on us, but there are other things whose behavior is entrusted to Providence. Our actions, our thoughts depend on us, but I cannot believe that our death depends on whether we choose to serve on the land or on the sea. What, is it really possible that destiny, having marked the end of my road, should execute its sentence on the Caspian Sea yet not know how to reach me in

Petersburg? I beg you, my dear Maman, do not constrain my inclination. I cannot serve in the Guards; they are too much out of harm's way. When there is war, they do nothing but remain shamefully idle. And you call that living! No, unmixed tranquility is not a life. Believe me, my dear Maman, one can get used to anything except tranquility and boredom. I would rather be perfectly unhappy than perfectly tranquil; at least a lively and profound feeling would occupy my entire soul; at least the sense of my misfortunes would remind me that I was alive. And truly, I feel that I must always have something dangerous to interest me; without it, I am bored. Imagine, my dear Maman, a furious tempest and me on the top deck, as if commanding the enraged sea, a wooden plank between me and death, the sea monsters amazed by the marvelous instrument, the child of man's genius, commanding the elements. And then... I will write to you as often as possible about all the beautiful things I see. And consider, too, my dear Maman, if I enter the navy, we will see each other in two years, not five. In two years, my dear Maman, I will kiss you, I will see you, I will speak with you—my dear Maman, imagine my happiness! Will you be indifferent to it? I cannot believe this—and even if destiny condemns me to perish at sea in a few years, I will have seen you again, I will have tasted that happiness. Are not a few moments of joy preferable to a long succession of tedious years? And so, my dear Maman, I hope you will not refuse me this favor. You say you are quite happy about my attraction to the works of the mind, but you must admit there is nothing more ridiculous than a young man who plays the pedant, who believes himself an author simply because he has translated two or three pages of Florian's *Estelle*, with thirty orthographical mistakes and in a pompous style he believes ornate, who thinks he has the right to criticize everything, without being able himself to either distinguish or feel the beautiful works he admires; he praises them with enthusiasm because others find them admirable, though he has never read them himself. Indeed, my dear Maman, I have this shortcoming and am trying to rid myself of it. I have very often praised the *Iliad*, which I read while still in Moscow and at such a tender age that not only could I not feel its beauty, I could not understand its content. I hear it praised everywhere so I praise it like a monkey. I am acquainted with many people who do not take the trouble to think and who let their own opinion be determined by public opinion, and indeed, these people, not excepting myself, bear a great resemblance to those automatons that move by springs hidden in their bodies. But this is a very long letter and I do not wish to bore you too much.

Farewell, my dear Maman. God grant we see each other soon. I remain your very humble and very obedient servant, as fashion puts it, and your obedient, your tender and appreciative son, as my heart puts it.

— *Eugène de Boratinsky*

P.S. Please send me some towels. I only have two left.

Baratynsky turned sixteen on February 19, 1816. There were no classes that week because of the Shrovetide holidays, and the pages were allowed to visit their families. Baratynsky and his schoolmate Dmitry Khanykov did not go home, however. Instead they went to see Pavel Nikolayevich Priklonsky, the father of another schoolmate and a chamberlain at the imperial court. While Baratynsky distracted Priklonsky with small talk, Khanykov stole five hundred rubles in banknotes and a gold-framed tortoise-shell snuffbox from the chamberlain's study. Priklonsky notified the school of the theft, and, on February 22, the school director reported the incident to the emperor. On February 25, Alexander I ordered that Baratynsky and Khanykov be expelled from the Corps des Pages. In addition, they were forbidden to enter either the military or civil service, unless they joined the army as rank-and-file soldiers. Essentially, they lost all their privileges as nobility. By March 1, Baratynsky had returned to his Uncle Pyotr Andreyevich's house.

5. TO HIS MOTHER, IN MARA.

Aleksandra Baratynskaya was, presumably, notified of the expulsion soon after it happened and wrote to her son (the letter has not survived). He answered her in Russian.

[Mid- to late March, 1816, St. Petersburg]

My dear Maminka. I do not know how to express to you everything I am now feeling. Can I someday hope to receive forgiveness for the misdeeds I have done? I am not so much upset by the punishment I have received as by the thought that I have caused you so much anguish. Oh, be assured that your tears are very dear to me. How can I ever worthily repay you for all your kindness and love to me? Instead of somehow expressing my gratitude to you, I am so ungrateful as to fill your life with anguish over my bad behavior. Believe me, dear Maminka, your tears mean far more to me than any punishment. Now, thanks be to God, I am forgiven, but the mere thought that you are still sad and angry makes me grieve even more instead of rejoicing at this. I hope to rectify my guilt through my future behavior and again be worthy of your love. Forgive me, sweet Maminka, deliver me from the torment I endure when I think about your anguish.

I remain your all-obedient and penitent son,

Yevgeny Boratynsky

Over the summer of 1816, Baratynsky's mother and uncles considered various options for Yevgeny, who, they were sure, would soon be pardoned. On June 29, his mother wrote from Mara to her brother-in-law Bogdan Andreyevich Baratynsky: "The Kamenskaya sisters [influential friends of his mother's] have written to me and, in the name of Katerina I. [Nelidova, who still had influence at court through her friendship with the Dowager Empress], have advised me to bring him home to our village [Mara], promising that after a year he will be forgiven—but how until then can I protect him from the many things that are inevitable at his age!" Eventually, they decided it would be best if Yevgeny was under a man's supervision, and so in July or August, he was sent to live with Bogdan Andreyevich on the Baratynskys' ancestral country estate Podvoyskoye-Goloshchapovo, in Smolensk Province.

[Between August and October, 1816,
Podvoyskoye-Goloshchapovo]

My dear Maman,

We pass the time here quite agreeably, dancing, singing, laughing; everything seems to breathe happiness and joy. There is but one idea which tarnishes in my eyes all these trappings of pleasure: that is the lack of permanence that attaches to them and the fact that I will soon see myself torn away from all these delights. I feel I have a nasty character, and what somehow causes my unhappiness is that I see too far in advance all the disagreeable things that can happen to me. There was a time when I did not think of such things! But this time has flown like a dream, or at least it was as short as the moments of happiness accorded the human life. My dear Maman, there has been much debate about happiness—does this not seem like beggars arguing over the philosopher's stone?

Such a man, in the midst of everything that seems to make him happy, carries a hidden poison that eats at him and renders him incapable of any feeling of pleasure. A sorrowful spirit, a well of boredom and sadness— that is what he carries in the tumult of joy, and I know this man well.

Might not happiness, by chance, be a certain combination of ideas that render us incapable of thinking of anything but that which fills our heart, which is filled in a way that does not allow us to reflect on what it feels?

Might not insouciance be an even greater happiness?

Might it not be the task of the being of beings, of the Eternal One… to make the soul susceptible to this feeling when it wishes to reward some of these little atoms that snatch a few blades of grass from the mud, our common mother?

O atoms for a day! O my companions in infinite smallness! Have you ever perceived this invisible hand that directs us on this anthill of the human race? Which of us has been able to anatomize those moments so brief in human life?—As for me, it never occurred to me.

Il le faut avouer telle est la vie humaine:
Chacun a son lutin qui toujours le promène
  Des chagrins aux amusements.
Des cinq sens tout au plus, malgré moi, je dépens,
L'homme est fait, je le sens, d'une pâte divine,
Nous serons tous un jour des esprits glorieux,
Mais dans ce monde-ci l'âme est un peu machine.
  La nature change à nos yeux,
  Et le plus triste Héraclite,
  Quand ses affaires vont mieux,
  Redevient un Démocrite.[*]

These verses are by a certain heretic who some people think is always wrong but whose verses are often filled with truth and power; I speak of Voltaire. I think this is one of the best things ever written about this mystical controversy. But I see that I will soon bore you with my philosophy. The passion for argument is not one of my lesser faults, and I do not intend to rid myself of it.

To conclude all this jumble, I will tell you that I was in a very bad mood when I started my letter, right up to the end of the second page, where I interrupted myself to have coffee with my aunts, and now I am not at all in the mood to talk about physical ills or moral ones.

I spent two days at my aunt Marfa Aleksandrovna's, who was indeed as affectionate towards me as if I were her own son. We paid a visit to our ancestors, the brave Slavic knights who undoubtedly died in the wars against Lithuania in defense of hearth and home. I wonder if perhaps you are unfamiliar with the country. So let me tell you that, after a little village named Kaprespino, on the shore where the Obsha River, rolling its silver waters, washes the green hills of the little canton of Bely on the road to Petersburg, 5 versts from Podvoyskoye, whose very name seems

---

* One must confess that such is human life: / Everyone has his imp, who always leads him / from sorrows to amusements. / In spite of myself, I depend, at the very most, on the five senses; / man is made, I feel it, of a divine dough; / we will all be glorious spirits one day, / but in this world, the soul is a bit of a machine. / Nature changes before our eyes, / and the saddest Heraclitus, / when his affairs are going better, / becomes a Democritus.

to proclaim battles, one sees... But now my uncle is coming to interrupt me in the middle of my peroration to hurry me to finish my letter—that is really too bad. Farewell, my dear Maman. And now here is my aunt Katerina Andreyevna, who wants to write a few words to you.

My aunt would like to write to you but she does not have time now. She tells me to send you her regards. Kiss my sisters and brothers for me.

E. Boratinsky

II.
ST. PETERSBURG AND FINLAND
(FALL 1818–SUMMER 1825)

Apart from six months spent with his mother in Tambov Province, Baratynsky lived for nearly two years on his uncle's estate in Podvoyskoye. During this period his family made several unsuccessful attempts to gain a pardon for him and have his status as a nobleman confirmed. In September 1818, his uncles Ilya and Bogdan took him to Moscow, where they were joined by his mother, in yet another effort to plead his case to people with influence at court. In the end, however, it was decided that he would have better chances of a pardon if he joined the army. And so in the fall of 1818, Baratynsky returned to St. Petersburg to enlist as a rank-and-file soldier.

7. TO HIS MOTHER, IN MOSCOW OR MARA (IN FRENCH).

[Between November and December (?), 1818, St. Petersburg]

I did not send you my address because I myself did not yet know where I would be living. I have taken an apartment with Monsieur Schlechtinsky—we have three nice rooms which must still be furnished, but furniture is cheap here. Address your letters: *In the Semyonovsky Regiment, in the house of the coffeehouse keeper Yezhevsky.* This is a fine old fellow, who knew my father in Gatchina. He tells me all sorts of little things, all sorts of anecdotes, which I listen to with great pleasure. He has a wife and a rather well-brought-up daughter, who speaks bad French and provincial Russian, plays the piano like our goddesses from Orzhevka, has read a few of Madame Radcliffe's novels, and complains that nothing in nature corresponds to the sublime affections of her heart. This whole little world is rather amusing. In my last letter I told you of a certain Madame Ein-Gross, whose acquaintance I made—well, this is a woman of gold. She is extremely well educated—that is to say, she knows more than I do. She plays the harp divinely, reads a great deal, loves painting, poetry, literature, and she is even capable of having her own feelings about all the arts. She and I discuss everything—friendship, love, infatuations, Epicureanism, stoicism—all such things are laid on the table. I am going to visit her every afternoon until I get bored with it; I should confess, however, that while waiting for something better, this is a divine woman, and I might even be inclined to fall in love with her, but have no fear on my account: I am too foolish for any serious folly.

Farewell, my good Maman. Do you not find all this a bit cavalier? Think what you will of me, but also remember that I love you with all my heart. Yesterday evening Madame E.-G. reminded me very vividly of Sophie; she was playing "La Tyrolienne" on the harp. Do you know she even resembles her a little in her person?

On February 8, 1819, Baratynsky was enlisted as a regular soldier in the Jaeger Life-Guard Regiment, based in St. Petersburg. It was around this time, or a little earlier, that he became friends with Aleksandr Pushkin, Anton Delvig, Wilhelm Küchelbecker, and other poets in St. Petersburg's progressive literary scene. Baratynsky had written a few occasional poems on his uncle's estate, and Delvig now encouraged him to devote himself more seriously to poetry. He even had a few of Baratynsky's poems published in a literary journal without his knowledge. The two became close friends and in August, when Baratynsky's roommate Andrey Shlyakhtinsky left the city, Delvig took his place.

On January 3, 1820—realizing that Yevgeny would have a better chance of success in the regular army, as opposed to the Guards—his uncles succeeded in having him transferred to the Neyshlotsky Infantry Regiment, under the command of Colonel Yegor Alekseyevich Lutkovsky, a distant relative of the family. The Neyshlotsky Regiment was headquartered in the Grand Duchy of Finland (which had become part of the Russian Empire some ten years earlier), in the town of Fredrikshamn (present-day Hamina). There Baratynsky met the aspiring poet Nikolay Konshin, who arranged for him to join the company he commanded in the regiment's 1st Battalion.

Baratynsky spent most of 1820 in Finland. It was during this period that he established himself as one of Russia's finest poets, with such works as the elegy "Separation," "Epistle to Baron Delvig," and, especially, the elegy "Finland," which he read at a meeting of the Free Society of Lovers of Russian Literature on a short trip to St. Petersburg in April.

In December he was given a three-month leave, most of which he spent in Mara with brief stops in St. Petersburg at either end. Meanwhile, Lutkovsky recommended Baratynsky for promotion to the officer's rank of ensign (which would have restored his rights as a nobleman), but Alexander refused.

Baratynsky returned to Finland in March 1821. His family continued their efforts on his behalf.

8. TO SERGEY UVAROV, IN ST. PETERSBURG.

Anna Nikolayevna Bantysh-Kamenskaya, a friend of Baratynsky's mother from the Smolny Institute, had asked Uvarov (then president of the Imperial Academy of Sciences) for his help with Baratynsky's promotion, and Uvarov in turn had requested that the young man provide him with a written account of his situation.

March 12, 1821, Fredrikshamn

Your Excellency,
Gracious Sir,
Sergey Semyonovich,

You have commanded me to present You with an account of sub-officer Boratynsky—I gratefully fulfill your command.

After his expulsion from the Corps des Pages, Boratynsky enlisted as a soldier in the Guards regiment; a year later, he was promoted to sub-officer and transferred to the Neyshlotsky Infantry Regiment. He is now being put forward by his commander for the rank of ensign, but his promotion is dependent on a higher commander.

Here you have everything that relates to him—now comes what relates also to Your Excellency: to return to a man his name and freedom, to return him to society and his family; to give him that selfhood without which his soul's activity will perish; in a word: to resurrect the dead.

All this you will do and all this is possible for you to do. I would not be so bold to speak in such a way if Anna Nikolayevna had not compelled me almost to have faith in Your Excellency.

To the number of those who are obliged to you, add one more grateful man.

With the most profound respect,
I have the honor, gracious Sir, to be
Your Excellency's most obedient servant,

Yevgeny Boratynsky

> From May 1, 1821 to August 1, 1822, the Neyshlotsky Regiment was posted in St. Petersburg. During these fifteen months Baratynsky immersed himself in the capital's social and literary life; at the same time he engaged in a serious flirtation with the salon hostess Sofya Dmitriyevna Ponomaryova, to whom he wrote the poems "In an Album" ("You are adored by far too many"), "The Kiss," and "Disillusionment," among others.

9. TO HIS MOTHER, IN MARA (IN FRENCH).

> In May 1822, his twenty-year-old sister Sofya (Sophie) arrived on her first visit to the city. She stayed until August.

> *[July 21 or 22, 1822, St. Petersburg]*

I gave Sophie the title of angel not because such was my pleasure but because she deserved it. If she continues to conduct herself as well as she does today, I will not hesitate to promote her to the Seraphim. She has a music teacher; she wears new dresses, which she has made for her; she accompanies us to the theater with pleasure and asks nothing better than to trot around the city—is this not all perfectly angelic? We have just celebrated Ilya Andreyevich's nameday at the home of my uncle here—the dinner was extremely merry and my angel extremely amiable. My angel is coming into her own in Petersburg, and this gives me great pleasure. As for me, well, carefree and indifferent as usual in everything that concerns myself, I am enjoying without distraction the happiness of having my Sophie: I love the feeling that she is near me; I watch her just *being*, and that is enough for me. At the same time, I would wish—for who does not desire something?—I would wish to never leave her, to follow her everywhere she goes—and since she is my angel, I hope, indeed, that she will one day bring me back to you. My affairs are in the same state as ever. There is a promise to intercede for me with the emperor when our regiments move out, which will be towards the end of August; it is possible that the emperor, in keeping with his custom, will refuse. If that happens, I have decided to ask for my retirement, if you do not object. I am not ambitious for distinctions, and as splendid as the rank of *praporshchik*[*] may be, it holds little temptation for my disillusioned soul. But you need to know that, for my plan to be realized, my philosophy is not enough. My uncle must take the matter into hand; if you would write him a word about this, my dear Maman, only to make him see that my project does not frighten you and that your son, renouncing all ranks in the world, can, by striving to please you, obtain a rank of distinction by your side. Forgive the brevity of my letters; I can in no way compete with Sophie. She is an angel, so with all my heart I consent to your loving her more than me. Farewell, my dear Maman; a thousand respects to my dear aunts.

E. B.

10. TO HIS MOTHER, IN MARA (IN FRENCH).

> Throughout most of 1823, Baratynsky was with his regiment in Rochensalm (in present-day Kotka), on the Finnish coast.

> *[April, before the 22nd, 1823, Rochensalm]*

You were no doubt astonished to receive the invisible bonnet sealed as a letter.

I had prepared a better envelope for it, but heavy parcels are not accepted here.

Our post office is only for letters and it was under the title of letter that my sister's talisman was accepted. I was about to make my devotions as devotedly as I could, and now Easter is on the way. I wish you a Happy Easter with all my heart.

---

[*] Ensign (the lowest officer rank).

The holidays will be magnificent where you are; springtime is already well advanced and I can imagine the beautiful sky and beautiful sunshine you must be having. We are not as well favored; the beautiful days have not yet come to us and the winds that blow from the sea make the air cold and damp. This depresses me, because I love the spring and cannot wait for its arrival. I pass the time rather monotonously, but I am far from being bored. I am following your advice: I do a lot of walking. I amuse myself by climbing our rocks, which are starting to become as beautiful as they are able to be—the green moss that covers them creates a very beautiful effect when the sun shines from above.

Forgive me if I write to you only about the weather, but I assure you that this is what occupies me the most here. Being almost alone with nature, she has become my true companion and I speak to you of her in Rochensalm as I might speak to you of Delvig in Petersburg. I continue to read German. God knows if I am making any progress; at least I am boring all the officers who possess this language with my questions and my enthusiasm for speaking it. These gentlemen are a very funny sort of people; as German as they are, they only know how to speak their language but do not have the ability to read it, and I am forced to skip over places I haven't been able to understand with a dictionary—rarely are they able to help me. Thus the days go by, and what gives me pleasure is that the more they go by the closer I am to my goal, to the day when I will be able to add to the pleasure of having seen Finland the pleasure of leaving it for a long time.

Farewell, my dear Maman, I expect you are very busy right now with your trees and your vegetable garden, and I imagine this with satisfaction, as it is a joy for you. Warm regards to my sisters.

My respects and felicitations to my dear aunt.

11. TO KONDRATY RYLEYEV AND ALEKSANDR BESTUZHEV, IN ST. PETERSBURG.

> In August or September of 1823, Baratynsky sold the rights to publish his collected poems to the poets Ryleyev and Bestuzhev, who edited the literary almanac *The Pole Star*. Baratynsky had also agreed to participate in a joint translation (with Ryleyev, Delvig, Pyotr Pletnyov, and others) of the play *Les Machabées* (1822) by the French writer Alexandre Guiraud.

[Between October and December (?), 1823, Rochensalm]

Dear brothers Bestuzhev and Ryleyev! Excuse me for not writing to you when I sent you the parcel with the rest of my drivel, as an honest man would have done. I am sure you have as much good-heartedness as there is laziness and muddledness in me. Let me get down to business. Please take it upon yourselves, dear brothers, to classify my poems. In my first notebook they have been copied without any order at all; the second book of elegies in particular needs to be rechecked; I would like my poems to present a certain mutual connection in their arrangement; they are to some degree capable of this. A second thing: please find out exactly which verses the honest censor will not allow; I might be able to rewrite them. Third: Delvig writes me that I will receive *The Maccabees* from you, dear Ryleyev; please send it as soon as possible: I'll do what I can about the translation. But in fact, I would be sincerely glad if they could manage without me. Fourth: O friends and brothers! Please do your best to present my children to the world in a nice clean dress! Books, like people, are often judged by their clothes.

Farewell, my dears. I wish you everything I myself do not have: pleasure, relaxation, happiness—rich dinners, good wine, affectionate lovers. I remain, in all the boredom of my Finnish existence, your deeply devoted

Boratynsky

12. TO VASILY ZHUKOVSKY, IN ST. PETERSBURG.

> Zhukovsky, perhaps Russia's most revered living poet, had close ties to the imperial family: he had taught Russian to the German princesses who married the tsar's brothers Nicholas and Michael and was a favorite of the Dowager Empress. He agreed to do what

he could for Baratynsky, but first he asked him for a detailed account of what had happened at the Corps des Pages.

[December, before the 25th, 1823, Rochensalm]

You impose a strange obligation on me, worthy Vasily Andreyevich; I would say *difficult*, if I didn't know you so well. When you require me to tell you the story of my wayward life, I am sure you are ready to listen to it with that generous kindness to which my readiness to make a confession rather unfavorable to myself perhaps gives me the right.

There has always been something particularly unlucky about my fate, and this serves as my main and overall justification: everything has contributed to the destruction of my good qualities and the development of my nefarious ones. The chain of events and impressions that turned me from, truly, a very good boy into an almost total scoundrel is a curious one.

At the age of 12, I entered the Corps des Pages, vividly remembering my mother's last tears and last instructions and firmly determined to fulfill them devoutly and, as people say in a school for children, to serve as an example of diligence and good behavior.

The head of my section at the time was a certain Kr—vich [Kristafovich] (he is now deceased, which, unfortunately for me, he was not yet so at the time)—a man limited in every way except in his passion for fault-finding. He disliked me from the first glance, and from my first day at the Corps treated me as if I were an inveterate mischief-maker. Affectionate with the other children, he was particularly rough towards me. His unfairness embittered me: children are no less proud than adults; offended pride demands revenge, and I resolved to avenge myself against him. In big calligraphic letters (we had a decent teacher for penmanship) I wrote the word *drunkard* on a slip of paper and pasted it to the broad back of my enemy. Unfortunately, some of my schoolmates saw my prank and, as we say, informed on me. I sat under arrest for three days, angry at myself and cursing Kr—vich.

My first prank did not make me an actual mischief-maker, but I was already a scoundrel in the opinion of my masters. I was the recipient of their constant and often unjust insults. Instead of giving me every possible chance to regain their favor, they in their inexorable severity took from me the hope and desire of ever winning their mercy.

Meanwhile, my heart drew me towards several schoolmates who were not on the best terms with the school administration, but it drew me to them not because they were mischief-makers but because I could feel (here I cannot say *observed*) better inner qualities in them than in my other schoolmates. You know that high-spirited boys fight among themselves and tease their teachers and tutors not because they want to go without dinner but because they possess greater vitality in their character, greater restlessness in their imagination, and in general, greater fervor in their feelings than other children do. So I was not yet a brute when I became friends with those children of my own age with similar qualities to me, but my masters saw things differently. I had not yet done any particular mischief, but a year after I entered the Corps they already considered me a monster.

What can I tell you? Even now I vividly remember the moment when, walking back and forth in our recreation hall, I told myself: well, then, I'll be a mischief-maker in actual fact! The thought of having no regard for anything, of throwing off every constraint, exhilarated me; a joyful feeling of freedom stirred my soul; it seemed to me I had found a new existence.

I will skip over the second year of my life at the Corps—it contains nothing remarkable—but I have to tell you about the third year, which includes the outcome you know about. We had the custom each year after the final examination of not doing anything for a few weeks—a right we obtained by I don't know what means. During this period those of us who had money on hand would buy books to read from Stupin's filthy shop, located right next to the Corps. And what books they were! *Glorioso, Rinaldo Rinaldi*, robbers in all possible forests and underground hideouts! And I, unfortunately, was one of the most ardent readers! Oh, if only Don Quixote's nurse, may she rest in peace, had been mine! With what determination she would have tossed in the oven all this robber nonsense, worth about as much as the medieval knight nonsense that caused her unfortunate master to lose interest in the world. The books I have been talking about, and in particular, Schiller's *Karl Moor*, inflamed my imagination; the robber's life seemed to me the most enviable in the world, and being restless and enterprising by nature, I came up with the idea of forming a society of avengers, which would have the goal of tormenting our masters as much as possible.

A description of our society would, perhaps, be entertaining and interesting in its main idea, taken from Schiller, and in the rest of its entirely juvenile details. There were five of us. We would gather in the attic every evening after supper. By general agreement we ate nothing at the common table but instead took away as much food from there as we could carry in our pockets and then feasted freely on this in our hideout. Here it was we lamented our fate together; here we thought up all kinds of practical jokes, which we later carried out in earnest. Sometimes our teachers would find their hats nailed to the window sills where they had put them; sometimes our officers would arrive home with the ends of their scarves cut off. Once we sprinkled ground-up Spanish fly in our inspector's snuffbox, which made his nose swell up. Recounting everything would be impossible. Whenever we thought up a prank, we drew lots to choose the perpetrator; he alone would have to answer if caught. But the most daring pranks I usually took upon myself as leader.

Sometime later (to my unhappiness) we accepted one more comrade into our society—this, indeed, was the son of that chamberlain who, I believe, is known to you because of my misfortune and also his. We had long noticed that he had a little too much money on him; we found it incredible that his parents would give a 14-year-old boy 100 to 200 rubles a week. He took us into his confidence and we learned that he had pilfered the key to his father's bureau, where there were large piles of banknotes, and that he was taking a few bills from there every week.

Once we possessed his secret, it goes without saying that we started using his money too. Our attic suppers became much tastier than before: we ate sweets by the pound. But this blessed life did not last long. Our comrade's mother, who at the time lived in Moscow, became dangerously ill and wished to see her son. He was granted leave to go and, as a sign of his devotion, left the unfortunate key with me and a boy named Kh—ov [Khanykov], who was his relative: "Take it! It will come in handy," he told us with the most touching emotion, and indeed, it came in much too handy for us!

Our comrade's departure sent us into a great depression. Farewell, pies and pastries—we were forced to give up everything. But this was too hard for us—we had accustomed ourselves to luxury. We needed some ideas; we thought and thought and finally came up with something!

I should tell you that a year before this time I had been introduced to the chamberlain in question by chance, and this chance occurrence belongs to those chance occurrences in my life on which I could base a system of predestination. I had been in the sick ward at the same time as his son and, in the boredom of a long convalescence, had constructed a small puppet theater. Once after visiting my comrade, he greatly praised my toy and added that he had long ago promised just such a thing to his little daughter but had not yet been able to find one that was well made. I offered him mine with a good heart; he accepted the gift, paid me many compliments, and asked me to visit him sometime with his son, but I never took advantage of the invitation.

Kh—ov, meanwhile, as a relative, had often been in his house. It occurred to us that what one scoundrel could do, another could as well. But Kh—ov told us that, because of various earlier pranks, he was already under suspicion in the house and would be carefully watched, so he absolutely needed a comrade who could at least occupy the servants and distract attention from him. I had not yet been, but had the right to be, in that unfortunate house. I decided to help Kh—ov. The Christmas holidays arrived, and we were released to our families. Deceiving the duty officers, each in his own way, all five of us left the Corps building and met up at Molinari's [sweet shop]. Kh—ov and I were supposed to pay our visit to the person in question, accomplish (if possible) our intended task, and return with an answer to our comrades, who were obliged to wait for us in the sweet shop.

We each had a shot of liquor for courage and set off on the most dishonorable road in the world.

Must I tell you the rest? We were too successful in accomplishing our intended task, but, in a chain of circumstances of which I myself can offer no clear account, our theft did not remain secret and we were both expelled from the Corps with the stipulation that we could not be accepted into any service, unless we wished to enter the military as privates.

I dare not try to justify myself, but a good-hearted and, of course, too compassionate person, wishing to lessen my misdeed in your eyes, would say: remember that at the time he was not yet 15 years old; remember that in military academies it is only called theft when something is stolen from one of your own and everything else is considered legitimate acquisition (*des bonnes prises**) and that among all his comrades he would have had trouble finding even one or two detractors if he had carried off his mischief successfully; remember how many different circumstances had over time introduced the idea to his imagination. Besides, isn't his action more an act of willfulness? If he had been truly wicked, and therefore already somewhat experienced and careful, he would have easily calculated that he was subjecting himself to great danger for the sake of fairly trivial gain; he would not have kept a kopek of the stolen money for himself but would have given it all to his comrades. What prompted him to such a dishonorable business? The youthful daring typical of the Corps and an imagination corrupted by bad books. The only thing we can deduce from this is that he was more susceptible than others to every sort of impression, and that with a different education, with different, more enlightened and attentive teachers, the very susceptibility that facilitated his ruin would have helped him surpass many of his schoolmates in everything useful and noble.

After my expulsion from the Corps, I moved around between different Petersburg boarding schools for about a year. Their proprietors, when they found out that I was the boy everyone was talking about at the time, refused to keep me. I was ready a hundred times to take my own life.

Finally, I went to the countryside, to my mother. I will never forget our first meeting! She had sent me off fresh and rosy-cheeked; I returned thin and pale, with sunken eyes, like the son in the Gospel returning to

---

* Fair game.

his father: *But when he was yet a great way off, his father saw him, and had compassion, and ran, and fell on his neck, and kissed him.* I expected reproaches but found only tears and bottomless affection, which moved me all the more because I was all the less worthy of it. In the course of four years, no one had spoken to my heart; it trembled powerfully at this living appeal to it; the light of this appeal dispelled the phantoms that had darkened my imagination; surrounded by the minutiae of the essential civic life, I came to know more intimately its conditions and was horrified both by my deed and by its consequences. My health did not sustain this emotional turmoil: I fell into a severe nervous fever and [my family] barely managed to summon me back to life.

At the age of 18, at my own wish, I entered the Jaeger Guards Regiment as a private; by chance I got to know some of our young poets and they shared their love of poetry with me. I do not know if my attempts have been successful for the world, but I know for certain that they have been the salvation of my soul. A year later, at the recommendation of the Grand Duke Nicholas Pavlovich, I was promoted to the rank of sub-officer and transferred to the Neyshlotsky Regiment, where I have now been for four years.

You know how unsuccessful all the recommendations made about me by my command have been. Year after year they have recommended me for promotion, and year after year the vain hope of imminent pardon has sustained me, but now, I confess to you, I am beginning to fall into despair. It is not my service, which I am used to, that is a burden to me; it is the contradictory nature of my position that weighs on me. I do not belong to any social estate, although I do possess a kind of title. I have no proper right to the hopes, the pleasures, of any of the estates. I must wait in idleness, at least in psychological idleness, for a change in my fate—must wait, perhaps, still more new years! I dare not offer my resignation, although, having entered service at my own free will, I should have the right to leave it when it seems reasonable to me; but such a resolve might be understood as willfulness. The only thing left for me to do is to repent that I voluntarily placed chains on myself that were too heavy. One must endure deserved misfortune patiently—I do not dispute this; but this is beyond my strength and I begin to feel that its long duration has not only killed my soul but even enfeebled my reason.

There, worthy Vasily Andreyevich, you have my story. I thank you for the interest you take in me; for me it is more than precious. Your good heart is my guarantee that my confessions will not weaken your regard towards one who by accident has done much that is dishonorable but who by inclination has always loved what is good.

With all my soul I remain your devoted

Boratynsky

13. TO VASILY ZHUKOVSKY, IN ST. PETERSBURG.

[March 5, 1824, Rochensalm]

Illness prevented me, worthy Vasily Andreyevich, from expressing my gratitude to you for the touching lines you sent me through Delvig. In them you thank me for my letter as if I had obliged you by taking the trouble to write it, while you forget that it is you alone who are doing me the good service; you remember only that I am unhappy and in need of consolation. Believe me, gratitude is no burden to me, especially gratitude towards you. I loved you, I wept over your verses, before I could ever have foreseen that the beautiful qualities of your heart might be beneficial to me.

Such good reports about my affair have reached me that, indeed, I am afraid to believe them. I entrust my fate to you, my Genius-Protector. You have begun, and you will finish. You will restore to me that common human existence of which I have been so long deprived that I have lost the habit of considering myself the same sort of human being as others; and then I will say, along with you: Praise be to poetry; poetry is virtue, poetry is strength—but in one poet alone, in you, are all its great qualities united.

May your days be as beautiful as your heart is, as beautiful as your poetry. A better wish cannot be imagined by one who is devoted to you to the depths of his soul,

Boratynsky

Efforts to win Baratynsky's promotion continued throughout 1824, and not only from Zhukovsky's side. In the spring of that year, Count Arseny Andreyevich Zakrevsky was appointed governor-general of Finland and the commander of the Russian army's Independent Finland Corps. Urged by his friend, the poet Denis Davydov, Zakrevsky took a personal interest in Baratynsky's case and petitioned the emperor on his behalf.

That summer, from June 10 to August 5, the Neyshlotsky Regiment was stationed in St. Petersburg. This was when Baratynsky became infatuated with the brilliant Aleksandra Andreyevna Voyeykova, Zhukovsky's goddaughter and the wife of the journalist Aleksandr Voyeykov. "To A. A. V." ("Beauty's enchanting power in you") and, probably, "She" are among the poems he wrote for her. Hailed as "our Peri" (a beautiful fairy in Persian mythology), Voyeykova had many admirers, including Aleksandr Turgenev and the poets Nikolay Yazykov and Ivan Kozlov.

14. TO HIS MOTHER, IN MARA (IN FRENCH).

[September, 1824, Rochensalm]

We are going to leave Rochensalm, my dear Maman. Zakrevsky, at my colonel's request, has permitted him to occupy a large and beautiful house in Kyumen, a house that belongs to the crown. It is merely seven versts from our former quarters. The colonel is taking me with him as a support. What is remarkable is that I will be living in the same two small rooms in this house that Suvorov once lived in when he was building the Kyumen fort. But we will not be there until the beginning of October. Letters can be addressed to Rochensalm, as before.

I lead a very calm, very tranquil, and very regular life. I work a little in the morning in my quarters; I dine at the colonel's and ordinarily spend the evening at his house playing boston with the ladies for a kopek a card: it's quite true I always lose, but at least I appear to be gallant and, besides, it's a distraction.

We are having a beautiful autumn; it seems to be compensating us for the bad summer we had. I love the autumn. Nature is very touching in the beauty of its farewell. It is a friend who is about to leave us and one delights in its presence with a melancholy love that fills the entire soul.

The colonel has received a letter from Rzhev which contains extraordinary news. A food shortage there has led to an actual insurrection. The peasants are abandoning their homes and leaving. More than three thousand people have left the district. All of the serfs. These moves are not happening without violence. They begin by grabbing whatever they can find in their masters' houses; they gather in bands and take vows to each another, some against their lords, others against the government, and others against Ar. [Arakcheyev]. This is a bad sort of fun. Have you had any news of it?

15. TO NIKOLAY KONSHIN.

Konshin, Baratynsky's company commander, had been the poet's closest friend in Finland. They exchanged a number of verse epistles and together wrote caustic epigrams on the local society. The epigrams created such ill will that Konshin was forced to retire; he left Finland in January 1824 and later joined the civil service in the town of Kostroma. In September, he wrote to Baratynsky, informing him of his recent marriage.

[2nd half of September–before Oct. 11, 1824, Rochensalm]

I received your letter, dear Konshin. It breathes with happiness and I am sincerely glad that at least one of our number has found the fulfillment of his heart's hopes. I share your opinion about your lovely life-companion; a certain feeling, a feeling that has never deceived either you or me, tells me, and told me before, that she will bring you all possible joy. God grant that the days to follow be like the first ones—and why not hope!

We had a dance recently for Nortman's silver anniversary; it was great fun. There were people there from Fr—hamn [Fredrikshamn], including your Amalia. Lutkovsky, a bit maliciously, was telling people in her presence about your marriage, your income being increased to 20 thousand, and your hopes of eventually getting 50 (you know what our Yegor is like). The poor girl didn't know where to look and was blanching and blushing in turn. Serves her right.

Almost everyone here, having heard that I had a letter from you and was about to answer, told me to send their regards—Natalya Nortman very warmly.

I live as I can, neither cheerful nor bored. From idleness I chase after Annette; I usually spend Sundays at Lutkovsky's. At home I write verse and convalesce from a wound inflicted by love: but this wound is not of the heart.

Stepanov has been promoted to general. We had a most excellent pie at his place. Our ladies complain about A. I.'s pride: she used to complain about theirs. Thus the wheel of fortune turns.

To visit you—this is one of those castles in the air which a person considers as such but nevertheless builds for his own pleasure. I would sincerely like to see how you live and admire your happiness, but I doubt it will happen. I am not free to do as I choose and God only knows if I ever will be in this life.

You speak to me of our accounts. If you can, send something: I cleaned myself out completely in Petersburg.

Klercker's living a happy life too. I was at his place and read in his eyes, which never lie, that he is satisfied with his fate. Düsterloh went to Livonia for the waters—I'm the only one remaining from our old brotherhood.

Farewell, I wish you a lastingly warm life in your family, simplicity in your feelings, and constant trust, the basis of matrimonial happiness. It seems to me that this happiness must always be kept somewhat "on a diet" and that any immoderation is disastrous for it. It's funny that I, a bachelor, am giving advice to you, a married man, but this is from a good heart and an old habit for philosophizing.

Boratynsky

My warmest regards to the gracious Madame Avdotya Yakovlevna.

16. TO NIKOLAY PUTYATA, IN HELSINGFORS (HELSINKI).

In May 1824, General Zakrevsky carried out an inspection of the 1st and 2nd battalions of the Neyshlotsky Regiment in the town of Villmanstrand, on Lake Saimaa in eastern Finland. Baratynsky made a strong impression on Zakrevsky's aide-de-camp, Nikolay Putyata, who later recalled: "He was thin, pale, and his features expressed a deep despondency. In the course of the inspection, I introduced myself to him and we talked about his friends in

Petersburg." In early October, Putyata wrote to Baratynsky, inviting him, at Zakrevsky's request, to spend some time at the Finland Corps headquarters in Helsingfors.

October 11, 1824 [Rochensalm]

I received your letter, my kind protector, and I do not know how to thank you for your generous proposal other than by accepting it with the liveliest gratitude. I would surely be frightened by your capital, if you had not given me the hope of finding in you both a guide and a protector. Indeed, regardless of what awaits me in Helsingfors, a chance that gives me the satisfaction of spending a few days with you and strengthening an acquaintance that is so flattering, so pleasing to me, I consider a very fortunate chance in my life.

Not knowing your name, I could not employ the usual form in the heading of my letter. Please excuse me for this and be assured that it in no way diminishes the genuine respect and complete devotion with which I remain, gracious sir, your most humble servant.

Ye. Boratynsky

17. TO ALEKSANDR TURGENEV, IN ST. PETERSBURG.

Aleksandr Turgenev had been the director of the Department of Religious Affairs at the Ministry of Public Education and Religious Affairs until the ministry was closed in the spring of 1824. Like his close friend Zhukovsky, he, too, had offered to do what he could for Baratynsky. In Helsingfors, however, the poet heard some troubling news about his case from Zakrevsky and so was now advising Turgenev not to press matters. The narrative poem Baratynsky mentions is *Eda*, about the love between a simple Finnish girl and a Russian soldier.

October 31 [1824], Helsingfors

Your Excellency,
  Gracious Sir,
    Aleksandr Ivanovich!

If I were not deeply touched by your magnanimous concern, I would have no heart. I will not say another word about my gratitude: you are like no one else; there is not a misanthrope alive who would not be reconciled to people if he met you among them. There is much I could add, but my business is not to assess but to feel.

Arseny Andreyevich [Zakrevsky] is right in wishing to wait a little with the recommendation for promotion; the true reason for this is decisive. On the last report about me, there was the following note written in the hand of our gracious monarch: "Make no further recommendation until commanded." This is also why I was not recommended for promotion in Petersburg. You understand that, after such a decision, Arseny Andreyevich cannot make any recommendation about me except verbally and that he would be subjecting himself to an almost certain refusal if he submitted a written recommendation. It is undoubtedly better to wait; two months will pass by unnoticed, and by now I am used to being patient.

Although Your Excellency finds it worthy to inquire about my poetic occupations, perhaps I am acting immodestly if I tell you that I have written a small narrative poem and if I request your permission to send you a copy of it. Verses are all I possess and this offering would be a widow's mite.

With true respect and complete devotion, I have the honor of being Your Excellency's obedient servant,

Ye. Boratynsky

18. TO IVAN KOZLOV, IN ST. PETERSBURG (IN FRENCH).

> Although some twenty years older than Baratynsky, Kozlov had only begun writing poetry in 1821, after losing his sight (the poor man was also paralyzed in the legs). If the following letter is authentic, Baratynsky must have received the manuscript for Kozlov's Byronesque narrative poem *The Monk* while he was in Helsingfors.

January 7 [1825, Helsingfors]

Here we are in a new year, my amiable Monsieur Kozlov; may it be a happy one for you and fertile in beautiful inspirations. I received your

Monk and read it with the most palpable pleasure; in several places it touched me deeply. You call it your cherished child, and you have every reason to cherish it: this is a very good work, in my opinion. The situations are strong, the style full of life and brilliant in colors; you have poured your soul into it. The places where you imitate Byron surpass him, as far as I can tell. The four verses from *The Giaour*:

> And my hungry arms trembled / and embraced only air; / deceived
> by the vision, they / pressed against my breast, alone.

are beautiful in Russian.

But where Byron himself might want to imitate you is the ending of your poem. It speaks remarkably to the imagination; its romanticism is remarkably national, and I believe you are the first to have captured this so well. Continue along this path, my dear poet, and you will do marvels. I will return your notebook to you next week; I have made a copy for my own use, for I don't want only to read you, I want to study you.

I blush to speak of *Eda* after *The Monk*, but for better or worse, I have finished my scribbling. I think a little too much vanity may have led me astray: I did not want to follow the beaten path, I did not want to imitate either Byron or Pushkin; that is why I threw myself into prosaic details, forcing myself to put them into verse, and so I made nothing but rhymed prose. Wanting to be original, I was only odd.

Tell our celestial Peri that I was as moved by her regards as is possible for an inhabitant of the earth, that I kiss the hem of her robe of a thousand colors, and that I appreciate her heart of a thousand virtues.

My affairs are going from bad to worse. You, who live in Petersburg, know that my current protector has asked to be allowed to resign. Now my promotion will be delayed for at least another year. All of this is making me more of a rhymer than ever, proving to me that my only place is in the world of poetry, as there is none for me in the real world.

We get almost all the journals here. In *Mnemosyne*, there is a polemical piece by Küchelbecker that I find to be very well thought out and very well written. Our Frérons have responded to it without intelligence and in bad faith. Our hacks are true literary monopolists: they have reinforced opinion, they have set themselves up as our judges through their usurious means, and there is almost no help for it! They are all of the same party and seem to have formed a front against what is beautiful and honest. One Grech, one Bulgarin, and one Kachenovsky form the triumvirate that rules Parnassus! You must agree: this is rather sad. We should support *Mnemosyne*, we should help Polevoy's journal succeed, because otherwise our works' reputation will depend on the degree of good will the above-named gentlemen have towards us. Talk about this with our friends; I am truly upset by this.

Farewell, my very dear friend. Please convey my respects to Madame Kozlova and wish her a happy new year from me.

Yours entirely,

E. Boratynsky

P.S. Things have changed: the general is staying, and I am reborn.

19. TO WILHELM KÜCHELBECKER, IN MOSCOW.

On January 24, 1825, General Zakrevsky left Helsingfors for St. Petersburg with his aide-de-camp Nikolay Putyata, who was traveling on to Moscow. Baratynsky asked Putyata to deliver this letter to his friend, the poet and critic Wilhelm Küchelbecker, along with some poems for *Mnemosyne*, the semi-annual almanac Küchelbecker co-published with Vladimir Odoyevsky. As it turned out, Putyata did not find Küchelbecker in Moscow and so left the poems with Odoyevsky.

[Around January 24, 1825, Helsingfors]

My dear Wilhelm, this letter will be delivered to you by Nikolay Vasilyevich Putyata, a man who respects your gifts, your character, and your heart, and therefore wishes to have a closer acquaintance with you. We have been sharing quarters in Helsingfors for more than two months; if there are any details about me that might be interesting to you, you can ask him whatever you wish; he will tell you everything that is impossible to put in a letter.

It has been a long time, much too long, since I wrote you, but you yourself are at fault for not sending me your address. When you sent me the first volume of *Mnemosyne*, you did not honor me with even two lines of your handwriting; in spite of this, I wished to thank you for a gift I found so pleasing, but I could not, for I did not know your place of residence. So I decided to wait to resume our correspondence when your journal had made you so famous that a person could address letters to you as people once did to the mathematician Euler: *To Monsieur Küchelbecker, in Europe.* Please don't be angry at this joke, old comrade, and accept my sincere greeting, which comes from a good heart.

It was with true pleasure that I read your conversation with Bulgarin in the 3rd volume of *Mnemosyne*. That is how comic articles should be written! Your article is filled with moderation, courtesy, and in many places true eloquence. Your opinions I find indisputably just. The responses you've received have been stupid and hypocritical.

Do not abandon your publication and continue to speak the truth. I am sure more and more people will buy it. But I would advise you to make it at least a monthly. You know that journals get all their interest from an interest in the day-to-day situations they deal with; time goes by, and the effect is lost.

I am sending you a few things for your journal; I'd send more if I had it, but you're welcome to whatever I have. Farewell, dear Wilhelm; do me a favor and answer me; write me how you live and what's going on with you. Our old acquaintance gives me the right to demand of you a certain trust. I am the same as ever in my heart, and I hope you haven't changed either. Your devoted

Boratynsky

20. TO ALEKSANDR IVANOVICH TURGENEV, IN ST. PETERSBURG.

January 25, 1825, Helsingfors

Your Excellency,
   Gracious Sir,
      Aleksandr Ivanovich!

Arseny Andreyevich [Zakrevsky] left for Petersburg on the 24th of this month, giving me every possible hope of his patronage; I know very well that I owe his good favor to your intercession alone. Now, when my fate so decisively hangs on his recommendation, please do not refuse to remind him of the concern with which you honor me and so encourage Arseny Andreyevich to carry out what he has promised.

With this letter I am also sending you the verse narrative I mentioned in one of my letters. If you appreciate, not the work itself, but the feeling with which I offer it to Your Excellency, you will be satisfied with me and graciously accept this insignificant monument of my lively gratitude.

With true respect and complete devotion I have the honor of being, gracious sir, Your Excellency's most obedient servant.

Ye. Boratynsky

This letter will be delivered to Your Excellency by Arseny Andreyevich's aide-de-camp, Mukhanov. If in your good favor to me you should desire to inquire in detail about my circumstances, he has first-hand knowledge of them and will be sufficiently able to answer all Your Excellency's questions.

21. TO HIS MOTHER, IN MARA (IN FRENCH).

> After Zakrevsky's departure, Baratynsky returned from Helsingfors to his regiment's base at Fort Kyumen (present-day Kymenlinna), near Rochensalm. He traveled as far as Rochensalm with Agrafena Fyodorovna Zakrevskaya (the general's wife) and an aide-de-camp, who continued on to St. Petersburg.

[February 10, 1825, Kyumen]

It is from Kyumen I write you, my good Maman, where my good Lutkovsky and his wife have received me with the same friendship as ever. I saw them again with palpable pleasure, and how could it have been otherwise? I have spent five years with them, filled always with their kindnesses, always received as one of their best friends. It is to them I owe every softening of my exile.

The general [Zakrevsky] bid me farewell in the most gracious manner and promised to do all that depended on him to win my promotion. I believe he will keep his word. But even if he does not succeed despite all his good will, I will preserve a lively gratitude towards him for all the charms of my stay in Helsingfors. The three months I spent there will always be an agreeable memory for me.

I left a day after him with Madame [Zakrevskaya]. Nothing could be merrier than the short journey we made together. We had with us that same Miss I have told you about and one of the aides-de-camp, a very intelligent young man. Our dinners and suppers could not have been more agreeable. We parted all three of us the best of friends, and this trip gave me, at least for a few moments, a very great taste for the life of adventurers. How is your health, my good Maman? I have not written to you in a long time, but traveling always causes interruptions in one's correspondence. It has also been a while since I have received any news from Mara.

Farewell, my dear Maman! May God grant you good health and soothe your soul: this is my daily wish and I repeat it in my letters as much from habit as from feeling.

22. TO NIKOLAY PUTYATA, IN MOSCOW.

The beautiful Agrafena Zakrevskaya—referred to here as "Alcina" (the name of a sorceress in Ariosto's *Orlando Furioso*) and "our Tsarina"—was notorious for her many love affairs. Baratynsky and Putyata both harbored a deep passion for her (as would Pushkin a few years later). She is the subject of a number of Baratynsky's poems, including "How much you have in so few days," "Inscription," "Assurance," and "The Fairy."

[Late February, 1825, Kyumen]

In noisy Moscow you did not forget this Finnish recluse—thank you: *that it may be well with thee and thou mayest live long on the earth.* I am sorry you were unable to see Küchelbecker; he is an interesting man in many respects and sooner or later he will be very prominent among our writers as a kind of Rousseau. He has great gifts, and in character he is very much like the Genevan eccentric: the same sensitivity and mistrustfulness, the same restless pride, which leads him to express immoderate opinions in order to distinguish himself by a particular manner of thought, and at times the same exultant love for truth, the good, the beautiful, for the sake of which he is ready to sacrifice everything. A man worthy of both respect and pity, born for the love of fame (and maybe even for fame) and for unhappiness. Thank you for taking my poetic children under your wing: you have made decent arrangements for all of them. You will oblige me greatly if you keep your promise and send me *Woe from Wit*. I don't understand why the Muscovites are angry at Griboyedov and his comedy: the title should be very comforting for them and the content, gratifying. What can I tell you about my life in Kyumen? Memories of Helsingfors fill its emptiness. I recall with pleasure certain candid hours spent with you and Mukhanov. I recall our mutual Alcina and sadly reflect on human fate. My friend, she herself is unhappy: this is a rose, this is the Tsarina of the flowers, but one damaged by the storm— her petals can barely hold on and are constantly dropping off. Bossuet said of a certain princess—I don't remember which—as he pointed to her dead body: "*La voilà telle que la mort nous l'a faite.*"* Of our Tsarina one might say: "*La voilà telle que les passions l'ont faite.*"† It is terrible! I saw her up close, and she will never leave my memory. I joked and laughed with her, but a deeply despondent feeling was in my heart at the time. Imagine some ornate marble tomb, under a happy southern sky, surrounded by myrtle and lilac: the scene is enchanting, the air fragrant, but a tomb is still a tomb, and with the sweetness, sadness pours into the soul. This is the feeling I had as I drew close to this woman, whom you know even better than I do.

I have been rambling on, which is easy enough to do. Farewell, dear friend! Keep circling in the whirlwind of Moscow's high society, but do not forget your lonely friend, to whom your memory is very dear. You neglected to send me your address. I am asking Mukhanov to send this letter on to you. Farewell; I embrace you with all my soul.

Ye. Boratynsky

---

* This is what death has made her for us.

† This is what the passions have made her.

Baratynsky began writing his new narrative poem *The Ball* not long after leaving Helsingfors. Although the poem is set in Moscow, its heroine, Princess Nina, was modeled on Agrafena Zakrevskaya and much of the plot (Nina's affair with a younger man who eventually leaves her for another woman) was drawn from what Baratynsky had seen in Helsingfors.

[Late March or early April, 1825, Kyumen]

He is risen indeed, worthy and kind Ivan Ivanovich, and there are rumors of it even among us, lots of them, believe it or not. Of course, where you are, in the enlightened capital, people know this better than in our benighted wilds. I thank you for your kind letter; I am very glad that, by having begun to write to me in Russian, you allow me to do the same. You and I have mostly spoken French together, which is why I began my correspondence with you in a language whose orthography and even turns of phrase I have forgotten from long disuse. I am now returning, with you, to the soil of our homeland.

Our regiment will be in Petersburg this summer. My heart beats with joy when I think that I will soon be within the circle of my true friends and will embrace you, my dear brother-poet. Your "Venetian Night" is, without flattery, delightful! In it, an exuberant reverie blends skillfully with dark reverie. The description of Venice is filled with a kind of southern sweetness, and the passage where the beautiful girl heads out to sea in her gondola is probably the best in the entire piece. So it seems to me, and I tell you my opinion without mincing words, since you yourself invited me to do so. I can hardly wait for *The Monk*, and I thank you for your praise of the excerpt from *Eda*. In the third section I took your advice and tried to put more lyrical movements in it than in the first two sections.

"Elysian Fields" was written four years ago; it is a French jest that's only good for an almanac. I'm halfway through a new narrative poem. Something will come of it! The main character is tricky but God rules the bold. This is what people in Moscow say about my heroine:

Whom does she lure into her house? / Are they not confirmed womanizers, / are they not sweet-faced novices? / Are not people tired of hearing / gossip about her shameless conquests / and seductive liaisons?

And this is what I add:

> Flee her: no heart is in her! / Fear her insidious speeches' / be-
> witching bait; / do not catch her amorous glances: / in her is the
> heat of a drunken bacchante, / the heat of fever, not the heat of love!

You speak of our journalists, but thank God, we don't get a single journal here and there's no one to interfere with my love of poetry. I only saw Polevoy once, before his departure for Moscow: he struck me as an enthusiast in the style of Küchelbecker. If he raves, then it's from a good heart and at least he's conscientious. Vyazemsky is the most irritating of them all. He was formed in the restless days of the internecine battles between Karamzin and Shishkov, and the militant spirit has not left him even now:

> In journalistic war he dishonors without reason / his gifts: / is this
> not like the famous leader and Catherine's friend / Orlov, who also
> loved fistfights?

This is an impromptu, as I think you can tell from the verses. Farewell.

Your devoted Boratynsky

24. TO NIKOLAY PUTYATA, IN MOSCOW.

[April, after the 5th, 1825, Kyumen]

I received your second letter from Moscow, dear Putyata; thank you. I read its first lines with lively interest. If my comparison was apt, then your extension of it was moving—but the coldness of the tomb has not yet completely numbed your soul: it is alive for friendship and for all that is good and beautiful. Errors are inseparable from humanity, and some of them do our hearts more honor than a premature understanding of certain truths.

> We need our passions and our dreams; they are
> the condition and the food of our existence:
> never will you subject to the same law
> the noise of the world and the graveyard's silence.

Why repent a strong emotion which, if it strongly shook your soul, perhaps also developed many capabilities in it that had previously been dormant? Don't you want to see things from a new point of view and, instead of our tomb, think of Shakespeare's plow, which tears up the soil and makes it fruitful?

But there's no end when it comes to comparisons. Your fairy has already returned to Helsingfors. Prince Lvov accompanied her. In Fredrikshamn she signed the post station book as follows: *"Le prince Chou-Chéri, héritier présomptif du royaume de la Lune, avec une partie de sa cour et la moitié de son sérail."** A certain merriment, innate or convulsive, never leaves her. I met with the general when he was passing through F—hamn. It seems I have little hope for a promotion—but so be it! Mukhanov has resigned his aide-de-camp position, and the corps lodgings have lost half their attraction for me. You are the only one I have now at the Helsingfors court. The other persons there are more than foreign to me. Why don't you drop by Kyumen to visit me? I live in the house of the regimental commander and have my own room. You would make me so happy!

I am writing a new narrative poem. Here's an excerpt from the description of a ball in Moscow:

> Brilliant with a thousand lights / is the vast hall; from high galleries, / violin bows are humming; a throng of guests; / with decorous importance in their eyes, / in patterned bonnets left unbuttoned, / a row of colorful elderly squiresses / are sitting. From boredom these eccentric dames / now adjust their garments, / now, crossing their arms, look / at the throng with dim attention. / Young ladies are whirling, / their eyes ablaze with pleasure; / with the fire of precious gems / their headpieces gleam. / Over their half-naked shoulders / golden curls are flying; / their dresses, light as smoke / outline their light figures. / Around some captivating Graces / a crowd of jealous admirers / bustles and churns; / anxiously, they catch every look: / the sorceresses, in jest, / turn them into unhappy or happy men. / All is in motion. Burning to win / the flattering attention of a beauty, / a cavalryman twirls his mustache, / a civilian dandy primly makes witty remarks.

---

* Prince Sweetie-Pie, heir presumptive of the Kingdom of the Moon, with a party from his court and half his seraglio.

25. TO NIKOLAY PUTYATA, IN MOSCOW.

"The Storm" and "Leda" were two of the poems Putyata had brought to Moscow for Küchelbecker's *Mnemosyne*. The Moscow censor had initially refused to allow "The Storm" to be published because of its diabolic allusion to "that spiteful spirit, the ruler of Gehenna," while approving the playfully erotic "Leda" despite its rather explicit depiction of the swan ravishing the nymph.

[April, after the 5th, 1825, Kyumen]

I was slandering you in my heart, dear Putyata, thinking you'd already arrived in Helsingfors without stopping to see me. Your letter gave me great joy: please come, please come, I will embrace you with the most tender friendship.

How is it that you are waiting for a letter from the general in order to return to the corps lodgings? Don't tell me you want to leave Finland, too? Who will you leave me with? How many changes have happened in two months!

Thank you for your praise of my excerpt. In the poem itself you will recognize certain impressions from Helsingfors. She is my heroine. I have already written around 200 verses. Come, you will look and you will judge, and I won't find a better or more legitimate critic.

The Moscow censor is either as innocent as a five-year-old girl or as merry as a drunken procuress: is it really possible to allow such an indecent poem as "Leda" to be published? Did Odoyevsky really print my name under it? God forbid! I won't be able to look lady readers in the eye! Try to write anything after this! My Leda publicly kisses her Swan, but a storm is not allowed to roar. How unsearchable are thy judgments, O Russian censor!

There is much that is laughable in Rus, but I am not disposed to laughter; in me merriment is the effort of a proud mind, not the child of the heart. Ever since childhood I have felt the burden of dependence and was sullen, unhappy. In my youth, fate took me in its hands. All of this serves as nourishment for genius, but here's the problem: I'm not a genius. Why did it all have to be like this, and not otherwise? At this question, all the devils would burst out laughing.

And this laughter would serve as an answer for the freethinker, but not for me and not for you: we believe in something. We believe in the beautiful and in virtue. Whatever has developed in my understanding for a better appreciation of the good, whatever has improved in my very self—these are treasures that cannot be bought by the rich man for money, or by the happy man with happiness, or by genius itself if it is wrongly aimed.

Farewell, dear Putyata; I embrace you with all my soul.

Boratynsky

On April 21, 1825, Emperor Alexander I, then in Warsaw, issued the order for Baratynsky's promotion to ensign, but the announcement did not reach St. Petersburg until May 3. The following day, Aleksandr Turgenev wrote to Pyotr Vyazemsky in Moscow: "Baratynsky is an officer: yesterday I received the decree from Warsaw, dated April 21. I have not been so happy in a long time." Nikolay Putyata presumably heard about the promotion in St. Petersburg, on his way back to Helsingfors from Moscow. He stopped in Kyumen on May 7 or 8 to deliver the news. A few days later, he described the poet's reaction in a letter to Aleksandr Mukhanov: "I cannot express to you Baratynsky's exhilaration when I told him about his promotion, his bliss at that moment, the genuine joy everyone felt at the change in his fate, which showed me how much they loved him, the candid conversations about the past and the future—it all gave me some of the most pleasant hours of my life."

26. TO ALEKSANDR TURGENEV, IN ST. PETERSBURG.

May 9, 1825, Kyumen-Town

Your Excellency,
    Gracious Sir,
        Aleksandr Ivanovich!

At last I am free, and it is to you I owe my freedom. Your magnanimous, persistent intercession has returned me to society, to my family, to life! Please accept, Your Excellency, this feeble compensation for the great good you have done me; accept these few words of gratitude, which perhaps you do not need but which are indispensable to my heart. It has now been a few days since everything around me has been breathing with joy; my good comrades have been congratulating me from their hearts, and it is to you that their congratulations belong! Soon I will return to my family; there tears of joy will flow, and it is you who will draw them forth! May God reward you and your heart.

With the deepest respect and complete devotion I have the honor to be your most obedient servant

Yevgeny Boratynsky

27. TO NIKOLAY PUTYATA, IN HELSINGFORS.

Here the names "Magdalina" (i.e. Mary Magdalene) and "Mephistopheles" refer to Agrafena Zakrevskaya and her former lover, Alexander Armfelt, a friend of Putyata's and, like him, an aide-de-camp to Count Zakrevsky. A few days after writing this, Baratynsky's regiment left Kyumen for St. Petersburg, where they would spend the summer.

May 15 [1825, Kyumen]

Thank you, Putyatushka, for the forwarded letters and especially for your own. You said in it almost everything that could be interesting to me—how can I repay you? Only with a lively gratitude. I received a short letter from Mukhanov: he is staying in Petersburg until July 20th, and I hope to see him there. You will be with us in spirit. We will rejoice and grieve together. In the meantime, let me tell you that I am already sporting the coat of a Neyshlotsky officer: this is rather nice, but what isn't to my liking is that I go to training every day and in two days I go on guard duty. I wasn't born for the tsar's service. Whenever I think about Petersburg, I shake with fever. There's no evil without some good and there's no good without some evil. If you can, tell Magdalina that I am sincerely grateful for her expressing her happiness for me. She does not leave my imagination. Write me what role Mephistopheles is playing and how it is with you. I often transport myself in my thoughts to your circle—but maybe it is no longer like the circle I once knew. We will soon be marching out [to St. Petersburg]: address your letters to me either in care of Mukhanov or in care of Baron Delvig at the Imperial Library. Farewell, dear friend. I embrace you with my whole heart.

Ye. Boratynsky

28. TO NIKOLAY PUTYATA, IN HELSINGFORS.

Agrafena Zakrevskaya, accompanied by her English companion (referred to only as "Miss" or "Misinka" ["Missy"]) and Karolina Levander, a young Swedish-Finnish woman from Helsingfors, had arrived in St. Petersburg in July.

[Early August, 1825, St. Petersburg]

I am at fault, dear Putyata; I am at fault—not in my heart, which is truly attached to you, but in my character, which is carefree and lazy. It's been a long time since I wrote you, but I have not stopped thinking of you, have not stopped thinking about our life in Helsingfors and the friendly way you showed up in Kyumen.

You can imagine how surprised and delighted I was by my unexpected meeting with Agr. Fyod., Misinka, and, finally, Karolina Levander, who had completely escaped my memory. I have seen them twice already. Agrafena Fyodorovna is very sweet to me and although I know it's dangerous even to look at her and listen to her, I seek and crave this tormenting pleasure. I am thinking of visiting Helsingfors in September, so I can thank the general for resurrecting me and so I can spend time with you.

I am leaving many details until the first post. Agrafena Fyodorovna will deliver this letter to you. She very kindly volunteered to do this. She can tell you why I haven't been able to write to you, why I did not come to Pargolovo, etc., etc.

I saw Mukhanov off to Moscow: he was nervous and sad when he left and he will be like that anywhere. What an unhappy gift—an imagination that too far exceeds one's reason! What unhappy fruit of premature experience—a heart thirsting for happiness but incapable of surrender to a single constant passion and losing itself in a multitude of limitless desires! That is Mukhanov's situation, and mine, and the situation of the greater part of the young men of our time.

In a few days we will be returning to Finland; I am almost glad about this: I've had my fill of baseless dissipation; I need to rise into myself, and having risen into myself, I'm sure I'll meet you and start writing you more often. I expect you can tell from the style of this letter what disorder my thoughts are in. Farewell, dear Putyata, till I have free time, till I'm sane, and finally, till I see you again. I hasten to her: you will suspect that I'm a bit infatuated. A bit, that's true—but I hope that the first hours of solitude will restore my reason to me. I'll write a few elegies and fall peacefully asleep. Poetry is a wondrous talisman: enchanting in itself, it makes other, harmful enchantments powerless. Farewell, I embrace you.

Boratynsky

The enclosed letter I originally thought I would entrust to Magdalina, but then I realized I had included certain dangerous details in it. I am sending this by post, and will give her a blank sheet of paper in a sealed envelope. What punishment for her curiosity if she unseals my letter! Farewell.

29. TO HIS MOTHER, IN MARA (IN FRENCH).

> Baratynsky, returning with the regiment to Finland, here writes from the town of Vyborg, about halfway between St. Petersburg and Rochensalm.

August 16 [1825, Vyborg]

I write you from Vyborg, my good Maman. Thank God, our troop inspections are over and we are on the road to that same Finland which so recently was an exile for me and which I now envisage only as a sweet and tranquil retreat. The exhausting and dissipated life I led in Petersburg has made me neglect our correspondence; I'm going to return to it, and at the same time I'm going to collect my mind to see a little what kind of fate I should arrange for myself now that I can do what I want. This task is a bit new for me: up to now I have lived without thinking about the future because more or less I didn't have one. At long last free, I would like to take all possible advantage of what I have seen and thought up to now, of my knowledge of myself and of others: I do not want the days that have passed to be days that are lost.

I hope to come to see you for at least six months. Only I don't know if I will set out on the road in the month of October or wait for the first winter road. I would like to know what you have decided with regard to Serge [*his brother Sergey*]. It is essential that he come to Petersburg with his certificate of nobility—without it we'll have a story that never ends. As soon as he presents himself, he will be accepted at the college I told you about, and I am almost certain that through his own ability and with the help of people who can intercede for him, he will remain in the general staff [of the army]. Zakrevsky will be spending winters in Petersburg, and I believe he will not refuse to employ himself on my brother's behalf, and he only has to say two words. I will be spending a few days in Helsingfors in order to thank the general for all he has done for me, and also to renew my relations with him a little. I saw Mme Zakrevsky in Petersburg: she had gone there to see the festival at Peterhof, bringing along a young Finnish girl so she could show her the wonders of the capital. We ran around the city together. My trip to Helsingfors will be a pleasure outing and a parting shot at the same time. Farewell, my good Maman; may God return you to full health and keep you safe. Tomorrow we leave Vyborg and on the 30th we'll be in Rochensalm.

III.
MOSCOW AND MARRIAGE
(FALL 1825–SPRING 1831)

Baratynsky spent most of September 1825 in Helsingfors. At the end of the month he was given a four-month leave and left for Moscow, where his mother and other family members were spending the winter. He had very likely requested the leave on the grounds of his mother's poor health, which seems to have been largely of a psychological nature. Baratynsky's biographer Geir Kjetsaa describes Aleksandra Baratynskaya's condition as "profound hypochondria", while Denis Davydov was certainly exaggerating when, in a letter to Count Zakrevsky dated December 10, 1825, he called her "half-mad."

30. TO NIKOLAY PUTYATA, IN HELSINGFORS.

[November, 1825, Moscow]

If I have not written to you since coming to Moscow, the fault lies not in my soul but in my mortal body, which took ill a week after I arrived. I am still not going out on visits, but in those first days I did manage to see your father, Ryleyev, and Mukhanov. It's strange that, although I have been living in Moscow almost two months, I have to write you as if I were in Kyumen, since I know nothing new, have been unable to observe anything, have met almost nobody new, and sit alone in my room with my old heart and its old memories. I delivered your letter to Mukhanov. What can I tell you about him? He spends most of his time at home, reads a lot, complains of being depressed, and is brought to life only by memories of Finland; he admits, however, that his passion for Aurora has very much subsided. Everything passes!

Since I have no more interesting topic, I will speak of myself. My family was already in Moscow when I arrived. Our meeting was joyful and sad. I found my mother in the most pitiful state, although my coming here has revived her a little. Brother Putyata, fate has not become any kinder towards me. Believe it or not, but it is now that the most difficult period of my life begins. I can't conceal from my conscience that I am indispensable to my mother, because of some diseased tenderness she has for me, and I am obliged (almost to save her life) not to be separated from her. But what do I see before me? What sort of existence? It's impossible to describe it. I told you in the past about certain details; now everything is the same, only worse. Living at home, for me, means living in a kind of noxious atmosphere, which infuses its poison not only into the heart, but even into the bones. I have made up my mind, but, I confess, not without effort. What can I do? To do the opposite would be monstrous egoism... Farewell, freedom! Farewell, poetry! Forgive me, dear friend, for imposing my sorrow on your soul, but I really needed to pour my heart out a little.

I am thinking of asking for a transfer to one of the regiments quartered in Moscow. For the time being, don't tell the general about this: someone will write to him from here. I heard you'll soon be coming to see us in our white-stoned town. Do come, dear Putyata, we will talk more about Finland, where I experienced everything that was alive in my heart. Its scenic, if gloomy, mountains resembled my former fate, which was no less gloomy, but at least it was fairly abundant in distinctive colors. The fate I now foresee will be like the monotonous Russian plains, covered, as now, in snow and presenting but a single eternally dreary picture. Farewell, my dear friend. I sent your letter to Oznobishin, but I haven't seen him yet due to my poor health. Your devoted

Ye. Boratynsky

31. TO ALEKSANDR PUSHKIN, ON HIS MIKHAYLOVSKOYE ESTATE NEAR PSKOV.

Although only three letters have survived from Baratynsky to Pushkin, and none from Pushkin to Baratynsky, the two poets had a close and complex relationship, marked by profound mutual respect and affection going back to when they first became friends in 1819. In the fall of 1820, Pushkin's ode "Liberty" and other poems against Alexander's regime had led to his banishment to the south of the empire—the Caucasus, Moldavia, and Odessa. A few years later, in 1824, he was exiled to his Mikhaylovskoye estate, in Pskov Province in western Russia, ostensibly because of his atheistic views. Pushkin followed Baratynsky's case closely, and more than once, in both poems and letters, drew parallels between his own fate and Baratynsky's "exile" in Finland. As late as May or June of 1825, Pushkin wrote to Aleksandr Bestuzhev: "[You write:]

'There is no encouragement in our country—and thank God!'
What makes you think there isn't? Derzhavin, Dmitriyev were
made ministers in *encouragement*. The age of Catherine was an
age of encouragements; this didn't make it worse than any other.
Karamzin, it seems, is encouraged; Zhukovsky can't complain,
nor can Krylov. ... Of the unencouraged I see only myself and
Baratynsky—and I don't say 'thank God'!"

In the letter to which Baratynsky is responding, Pushkin had ap-
parently teased him about being a "marquis"—that is, too influ-
enced by eighteenth-century French neoclassicism to appreciate a
Shakespearean-style "romantic tragedy" such as *Boris Godunov*,
which he had just completed. Baratynsky's Francophile tastes
often came in for criticism, sometimes in jest, sometimes in ear-
nest, among the writers of Pushkin's circle.

[First half of December, 1825, Moscow]

I thank you for your letter, dear Pushkin; it made me very happy, for
I greatly cherish your memory of me. The attention you give my rhymed
trifles would make me think a great deal about their worth if I did not
know that you are as kind in your letters as you are sublime and moving
in your works of poetry.

Do not imagine I am such a "marquis" that I would be unable to feel
the beauties of your romantic tragedy! I love Shakespeare's heroes, who
are almost always natural, always interesting, in the genuine dress of their
time and with strongly delineated characters. I prefer them to Racine's
heroes, but I give justice to the great talent of the French tragedian. I
will say more: I am almost certain the French are unable to have any
true romantic tragedy. Aristotle's rules are not what shackles them—one
can easily be free of those—but they lack the most important means to
success: an elegant vernacular. I respect the French classical authors; they
knew their own language, were interested in those poetic genres which
suited it, and produced much that is beautiful. I find their new romantics
a sorry sight: it's as if they have bitten off more than they can chew.

I long to have some idea about your *Godunov*. Our marvelous lan-
guage is capable of everything—I feel this although I am unable to bring
it to fruition. It is created for Pushkin, and Pushkin for it. I am sure your
tragedy is filled with extraordinary beauties. Go, complete what you have

begun, you, in whom genius resides! Raise Russian poetry to that same level among the poetries of all nations to which Peter the Great raised Russia among the world's powers. Accomplish alone what he accomplished alone—and our task is gratitude and amazement.

Vyazemsky is not in Moscow, but I will be visiting him in a few days in Ostafyevo and will carry out your commission. I read Küchelbecker's "Ghosts"—it's not bad, but it's not good either. His merriment is not merry and the poetry is feeble and stilted. I am not copying out *Eda* for you because it will be printed in a few days. Delvig, who is overseeing the publication in Petersburg, will get a copy to you right away, and indeed, two copies if you'll not be lazy and do for me what you did for Ryleyev. It is my most fervent wish to visit you, but God knows when I'll be able to. But I certainly will not miss the chance. In the meantime, let's exchange letters. Write me, dear Pushkin, and I will not be in your debt, although I write you with the same reticence with which one usually writes to elders.

Farewell, I embrace you. Why do refer to Lyovushka as Lev Sergeyevich? He loves you sincerely, and if in his flightiness he is somehow at fault before you—it's up to you to be gracious. I know you have been angry with him for a long time, but being angry for a long time isn't good. I'm interfering in what's none of my business, but you will forgive me because of my affection for you and your brother.

Your devoted

Boratynsky

My address: Moscow, by Khariton's in Ogorodniki, the Myasoyedov house.

On November 19, 1825, Alexander I died suddenly in the town of Taganrog, in southern Russia, with the news reaching Moscow and St. Petersburg only a week later. Because the childless Alexander's next-oldest brother, Constantine, had secretly renounced his right to the throne in favor of their brother Nicholas, a general confusion ensued about who would be the next tsar. Russia's revolutionary secret societies took advantage of this and staged an uprising of some 3,000 troops in Senate Square in St. Petersburg on

December 14, the day the army swore its allegiance to Emperor Nicholas I. After a standoff of several hours, and the killing of St. Petersburg's governor-general, the insurgents were dispersed with cannon fire. In the weeks that followed, the leaders of the uprising were arrested and interrogated. These were men from Russia's leading noble families and intellectual elite, and included Kondraty Ryleyev (one of the five who were executed the following summer), Aleksandr Bestuzhev, Wilhelm Küchelbecker, and a number of other friends of Baratynsky's.

32. TO NIKOLAY PUTYATA, IN HELSINGFORS.

Less than enthusiastic about a military career and feeling obliged to take care of his mother, Baratynsky had decided to ask for permission to retire from the army. He justified his request on the grounds of poor health; he had, after all, been ill since October (see Letter 30).

[Early January 1826, Moscow]

Dear Putyata, here is the letter to Zakrevsky about my retirement; I ask you, dear friend, either to simply give my letter to A. A. [Arseny Andreyevich] or explain to him why I am so late in asking for his help in gaining my release from service. I sent my request to the regiment before the disturbances in Petersburg. When they were happening, somewhat alarmed, I wrote to Lutk. [Lutkovsky] and asked him to hold back my request. When everything calmed down, I again asked him to forward my request along the chain of command. Now I simply do not know (I have received no news from Lutkovsky) whether he was able to intercept it or not. If he wasn't, then my request would have already reached you; if he was, then you'll be getting it in a few days. Please do me this favor, and another one, too. I actually don't know whether or not my Lutkovsky is alive: he doesn't answer me. Forgive me for troubling you with my errands, but you can feel that all my hopes are on you alone.

I see Aleksandr Mukhanov fairly often. It seems his love for Aurora has abated quite a bit. A few days ago I met Tolstoy the American. A very interesting man. He has the look of a good-natured fellow, and anyone who hasn't heard about him would get the wrong idea.

Verses somehow won't come, and I'm barely occupied by anything. When my fate is decided, and my spirit calmer, I will take up the pen again. In the meantime, here's an epigram for you on poets of the fair sex:

> Do not touch the Parnassian pen, / do not touch it, pretty tomboys! / There's not much good in it for beautiful girls, / and Cupid has given them other toys. / Is love to be abandoned by you, forgotten / for the sake of sorry rhymes? People laugh at rhymes, / the Lethean currents carry them off: / the ink remains on little fingers.

I embrace you.

33. TO NIKOLAY PUTYATA, IN HELSINGFORS OR ST. PETERSBURG.

This letter has survived only as a fragment.

[January or February 1826, Moscow]

… There's been a strange rumor going around Moscow: they're saying Magdalina is pregnant? I was stunned by this news. I don't know why, but for some reason her pregnancy seems indecent. Even so, I am very happy for Magdalina: a child will acquaint her with natural feelings and give her existence a kind of moral goal. To this day, this woman still pursues my imagination; I love her and would like to see her happy…

34. TO ALEKSANDR PUSHKIN, IN MIKHAYLOVSKOYE.

[January, after the 7th, 1826, Moscow.]

I am sending you *Urania*, dear Pushkin; it's no great treasure, but blessed is he who is content even with a small one. We are much in need of philosophy. Let me draw your attention, however, to a piece entitled "I Am." The author is a boy about seventeen years old and, it seems, offers hope. The style is not always exact, but poetry is there, especially at the beginning. At the end there's metaphysics, too obscure for verse. I should tell you that the Moscow youth are besotted with transcendental philosophy; I don't know if that's good or bad; I haven't read Kant and I confess I don't understand the new aestheticists very well. Galich has published a poetics in the German style. In it, Plato's discoveries are updated and, with certain additions, brought into a system. Since I don't know German, I was very glad to have the chance to learn about German aesthetics. What I like in it is its particular poetry, but it seems to me its principles can be refuted philosophically. But why am I going on about this, especially to you. Create the beautiful, and let others wrack their brains over it. You really let the elegists have it in your epigram. I come in for my share too here, and serves me right. I came to my senses before you did and, in one unpublished piece, say that "the simpering whining of the poets of our times" has become very cloying.

I heard you are starting a new narrative poem about Yermak. A truly poetic subject, one worthy of you. They say that when the news reached Parnassus, even Camoens's eyes popped out. May God bless you and give your muscles strength for the great deed.

I see a lot of Vyazemsky. A few days ago we were reading your shorter poems; we thought we'd skim through a few pieces and ended up reading the whole book. What are you planning to do with *Godunov*? Publish it or first try it out in the theater? I'm dying to know the play. Farewell, dear Pushkin; don't forget me.

35. TO NIKOLAY PUTYATA.

[January, before the 19th, 1826, Moscow]

Thank you, dear Putyata, for your letters. One of them brought a double benefit: it gave me great pleasure and calmed your mother, who had not had any news of you for some time and was a little worried.

It's no surprise you don't remember reading the description of Finland you found in the *Telegraph*. It wasn't written in Helsingfors, but in Moscow. My *Eda* will be coming out in a few days and I'll send you a copy right away. I thank kind Butkov, that tender admirer of F. V. Bulgarin, for his comment, but I will add my own. In poetry one does not say what is, but what seems. On the edge of the horizon the cliffs touch the sky; consequently, they rise to the skies. In prose I am at fault, but in verse, I am certainly right. Meanwhile, to comfort him, here's a little epistlet for his friend:

> In your pages you play the hypocrite, / distort both opinions and legends, / amiably burn incense to foolishness, / enviously slander talents; / your foul nature brings forth foul fruit: / "Shameful man! Shameful man!" everyone whispers. "Now that's news!" / —"Oh, don't whine! This is what I'm counting on: / subscribers pay me for dishonor."

I am thinking of sending a well-bound copy of *Eda* to the general. I forgot to wish him a happy new year, and now it's too late. I feel very bad about it. I wouldn't want him to think I've forgotten my benefactor. Worthless poetic carelessness!

I am bored in Moscow. I find my new acquaintances unbearable. My heart demands friendship, not politeness, and the affectation of amiability produces a heavy feeling in me. I look at the people around me with cold irony. I pay their greetings with greetings and am suffering.

I often think of my well-tested friends, the former comrades of my life—they are all far away! And when will we see each other again? Moscow for me is a new exile. Why are we sad in a foreign country? Nothing in it speaks of our past life. Isn't Moscow that same foreign country for me? Excuse my low spirits, but in boring Finland, maybe, it will give you a certain pleasure to know that even in Moscow good people are bored. Farewell, my dear; I embrace you. I thank Aleksandr [*Putyata's brother*] for not forgetting me; I remember you and him very much.

Boratynsky

Baratynsky's retirement from the army was approved by Nicholas I on January 31, 1826. In February or March, Denis Davydov introduced the poet to the retired Major General Lev Nikolayevich Engelhardt, and sometime in early April, Baratynsky became engaged to Engelhardt's eldest daughter, the twenty-one-year-old Nastasya. It was very short engagement; they were married in Moscow on June 9.

36. TO NASTASYA ENGELHARDT (IN FRENCH).

This, it seems, is the earliest letter (or note) we have from Baratynsky to the woman who would become his wife. We know nothing of its circumstances. Aleksey Peskov argues that it must be from the early part of the poet's courtship, since he still addresses Nastasya with the formal pronoun "vous" (even though he calls her, affectionately, "Nastinka"), whereas in the letters he writes to her after their marriage, he uses the intimate "tu."

[February (?) or March, 1826, Moscow]

I feel quite well, my dear Nastinka; I thank you for all your concern yesterday. I will preserve it as a sweet memory: it is a mark of your affection, and nothing in the world is dearer to me.

37. TO ALEKSANDR MUKHANOV, IN TULCHIN.

Mukhanov, now aide-de-camp to Field Marshal Peter Wittgenstein, based in Tulchin (in southwestern Ukraine), and Nikolay Putyata, as aide-de-camp to Count Zakrevsky, had both been in Moscow for the coronation of the new emperor on August 22. Pushkin, too, released from his exile in Mikhaylovskoye, had arrived in the city in early September.

[October, around the 20th, 1826, Moscow]

My dear Mukhanov. My brother Irakly has brought me word-of-mouth news about you; allow me to regret that he didn't bring me any written news. I feel bad that we saw so little of each other in Moscow, but I'm not at fault here: I was in the first throes of marriage and had certain obligations which, though perhaps more pleasant than the obligations of service, were none the less definite ones. I did get to spend time with Putyata and a few days ago saw him off to Petersburg, or rather, to Finland. He is headed to deathly boredom. He will not have a single comrade there, which is to say, not even one. I advised him to immerse himself in writing to keep from going mad. I saw A. F. [Zakrevskaya] after her delivery of a burden. What's there to say about her? She's lighter! The court has left. Moscow is stupid and disgusting, but this makes little difference to me because I am happy at home. I've started writing poetry again; I'm bringing "Ladies' Night" [i.e. *The Ball*] to a close. Pushkin is here; he read me *Godunov*: a marvelous work, which will mark an epoch in our literature. Farewell, dear friend. I embrace you warmly and just as warmly beg you not to condemn me to being forgotten. Your

Boratynsky

38. TO NIKOLAY PUTYATA, IN ST. PETERSBURG.

[November, 1826, Moscow]

How sorry I am that I didn't have a chance to say good-bye to you at your departure from Moscow, and since then I haven't had any news from you at all. What's going on with you? I found out from your mother that you are still in Petersburg and, according to the rumors in Moscow, you won't be going any farther. People here are saying that Zakrevsky will be the minister of justice. May God grant it! I think that both of you are equally fed up with Finland. One of my brothers arrived from Tulchin and brought news of Mukhanov: he's as bored as ever in his new post. It's even more boring in Tulchin than Helsingfors. My brother was telling me the details of life there. Wittgenstein lives on his estate and looks after his vineyards, but his headquarters is in town. He's a good German, happy in his family life, economical, not at all like our duke. With him, there are no women to chase after, nothing to fuss over, no one to make peace with or quarrel with—in a word, no court. Did you deliver my letter to Delvig? I haven't had a line from him. Do me a favor: pester him a little and find out if my works are being printed or not. Tell Delvig I am very angry with him. Three of my letters to him have gone unanswered. Writing to a person who doesn't answer is no different from raging at a cloud like some character in a fable. Be kinder than Delvig, kind Putyata; don't forget me and write.

I lead a quiet life, as befits a married man, and am very glad to have traded the restless dreams of the passions for the quiet dream of quiet happiness. I have changed from actor to spectator and, sheltered from the storm in my corner, I look out from time to time to see what the weather's like in the world. Farewell, my dear friend; love me if you don't want to be in debt to me, and know that my heart is ready to share your joys and sorrows.

[December 14, 1826, Moscow]

How happy I was to get your unexpected letter, dear Konshin! I had nearly lost track of you, but I still remembered you: it's impossible to forget so many years spent together, so many extraordinary events, so much genuine comradeship, so much genuine friendship! Yes, dear friend, your regiment has increased: I am married and happy. You know that my heart always longed for a quiet and moral life. My previous existence, disorderly and wayward, always contradicted both my traits of character and my opinions. I am finally breathing the air I need, but I will not start ascribing [*a word has been crossed out*] happiness to my philosophical rules; no, my friend, the main thing is that God has given me a good wife, that I desired happiness and found it. I was like a sick man who, wishing to visit a beautiful faraway land, knows the best road to it but cannot rise from his bed. The doctor comes and restores his health; he gets on his horse and sets off. [*One and a half lines have been crossed out.*] The faraway land is happiness; the road—philosophy; the doctor— my Nastinka. How's that for an allegory? And don't you recognize your Finnish friend in this passion for metaphysics? You and I, indeed, will be related. The Saratov governor is the brother of my aunt's husband. I will not be in your part of the country, but will spend at least another year in Moscow. If you fulfill your kind intention of visiting your old comrade, he will pour you a soup bowl of champagne and write you an Ode. I commend my wife to your good wishes. Please give my respects to your father and tell him that I vividly remember his Finnish hospitality. Where is Pyotr Andreyevich? Write to me directly in my own name in Moscow, the Nativity Stoleshnikov Parish, house of Professor Malov. Farewell, my dear; I embrace you with my whole heart and thank you for remembering me, which has brought me real joy. Your

Boratynsky.

40. TO NIKOLAY POLEVOY, IN MOSCOW.

The Poems of Yevgeny Baratynsky, the poet's first collection of lyric verse, finally appeared in the fall of 1827 after much delay and a change of publisher (see Letters 11 and 38). Nikolay Polevoy, the editor of the journal *The Moscow Telegraph*, had helped with the last stages of the book's publication and was handling its distribution in Moscow. In mid-November, he sent copies to Baratynsky, who was visiting his mother in Mara. Polevoy also included the recently published third chapter of Pushkin's *Eugene Onegin*, the narrative poem *The Div and the Peri* by the young poet Andrey Podolinsky, and several issues of the *Telegraph*.

[November, before the 25th, 1827, Mara]

I have received, kind Nikolay Alekseyevich, *The Div*, *Onegin*, and my poems. *The Div*, it seems to me, received an unbiased review from you in the *Telegraph*. Podolinsky, of course, has talent. As for *Onegin*, what is there to say! What a delight! What brilliant style—exact and free! This is a Raphael drawing, the vivid and unaffected brush of the painter of painters. As for me, I cannot tell you how obliged I am to you. The edition is delightful. Without you I would never have been able to appear in society in such beautiful attire. Many, many thanks. Complete your favor to me by fulfilling yet another most humble request. Please send 600 copies to Baron Anton Antonovich Delvig—Bolshaya Millionnaya Street, the house of Mme Ebeling. He and I have our own separate accounts and understandings. As for the rest, please do with them as you think best. Shipping such a large amount naturally requires money. It may well be that you do not now have the money at hand, so I am writing to my father-in-law to ask him to send you 100 [rubles]. Even without this, I am very much in your debt. Allow me to assure you that, if the edition does not pay for itself, I will, in any case, be a conscientious debtor. When the edition comes out, please do me the favor of sending my father-in-law 12 cop., including one on Alexandria paper. These are for my Moscow relatives. And you, kind Nikolay Alekseyevich, I would ask to give a copy each to Prince Vyazemsky, Dmitriyev, Pogodin, and ask your brother to accept my trifles as a souvenir from me, and as for your own feudal copy, do me the honor of placing it in your library between Batyushkov and V. L. Pushkin. Please send me another 8 copies. So many commissions!

It's no good doing business with a verse-maker. Forgive me all this in Lord Phoebus' name.

Farewell; I embrace you with all my heart.

Ye. Boratynsky

P.S. It occurs to me that it will be much too expensive to send 300 copies by post. Would it be possible to find someone who could take them?

41. TO ALEKSANDR PUSHKIN, IN ST. PETERSBURG.

[February, around the 23rd, 1828, Moscow]

I would have written to you a long time ago, dear Pushkin, had I known your address and if the simplest idea hadn't come to me too late, to write: *To Pushkin in Petersburg.* I certainly would have done this if Vyazemsky's departure had not given me the chance to write to you—a reliable opportunity. In my Tambov seclusion, I was very worried about you. There was a rumor that you had been carted off somewhere, and as you are a rather cart-off-able person, I believed it. Some time later I learned with joy that it was you who had been doing the carting, not you being carted. I am now back in Moscow, feeling orphaned. To me, at least, your absence is very much felt. Delvig was here with me for a short time. He talked a lot about you; among other things, he passed on something you had said, and it made me a little sad. You had told him: "Baratynsky and I aren't writing each other these days, or else I would have let him know," and so on.

Is it really true, Pushkin, that after becoming even closer friends in Moscow than we were before, we have since grown more distant to each other?

I, at least, love in you, as of old, both the man and the poet.

Two more *Onegin* cantos have been published here. Everyone talks about them, each in his own way: some praise them, others berate them, and everyone reads them. I very much love the vast plan of your *Onegin*, but most people don't understand it. They're looking for a romantic plot, looking for the usual thing, and naturally they don't find it. The high poetic simplicity of your creation seems to them poverty of invention; they do not notice that Russia old and new, life in all its changes, is passing right before their eyes—*mais que le diable les emporte et que Dieu les bénisse!*[*] I think that here in Russia a poet can hope for great success only in his first, immature attempts. He has the support of all the young people, who find almost their own feelings in him, almost their own thoughts, dressed in brilliant colors. The poet develops, writes with greater deliberation, with greater depth of thought—he is boring to officers, while brigadiers aren't happy with him because his verse, after all, isn't prose. Please do not take these reflections personally; they are general ones. Your portrait in *Northern Flowers* is a remarkable likeness and beautifully engraved. Delvig gave me a separate print of it. It is now hanging in my study, in a respectable frame. Vasily Lvovich is writing a romantic narrative poem. Ask Vyazemsky about it. It's a completely balladic composition. I imagine Vasily Lvovich as a kind of Parnassian Thunderclap who has given his soul to his romantic demon. Is it wrong to parody Zhukovsky's ballad? In the meantime, farewell, dear Pushkin! Please don't think badly of me.

42. TO NIKOLAY PUTYATA, IN ST. PETERSBURG.

[April (?), 1828, Moscow]

I am mortally at fault before you, my dear Putyata: it's taken me three centuries to answer your letter, but better late than never. But don't think I have an ungrateful heart: I cherish and value your friendship, but what can you do with innate carelessness?

> Forgive me, dear friend, this is the way / the Lord's power knew to make me: / I love putting off until tomorrow / what must be done today!

I am not fit for any civil service job, although I recently entered the Land Survey Office, but thank God, I don't have much to do; otherwise, things would be bad for my boss.

---

[*] But may the devil take them and God bless them!

Thank you for your friendly criticism. Your comments are fair in the particular, but if we were together, I might be able to prove to you that some of my changes are good for the whole. But in fact, I never vouch for the fairness of my own opinion. Poets are for the most part poor judges of their own works. The reason is the extraordinarily complex relationship they have with their works. The pride of the mind and the rights of the heart are in constant battle. One poem you love because you remember the emotion with which it was written. You are proud of your revision because you have conquered the heart's emotion with your mind. Which should you trust? There is one thing I'm not happy with in your letter: it's not thoroughly friendly. You write to me as if to a stranger you're afraid of boring; you talk a lot about me and not a word about yourself. How is your Alcina? Does she still hold you captive as before? By the way, I heard that A. A. [Zakrevsky] has been made minister of internal affairs. Are you staying with him? Do you think about living in beautiful Moscow? I am now a permanent Moscow resident. I live quietly and peacefully, am happy in my family life, but I confess, Moscow is not to my liking. Just imagine: I don't have a single comrade here, not a single person to whom I can say, "Remember?"—no one I can talk to freely and easily. This is very hard. I wait for you as for the May rain. The atmosphere here is dry, incredibly dusty. Married people need friendship even more than bachelors. Chasing after women gives a man who's young and free a little diversion almost everywhere: he kills time with some pretty fool of a girl and has few regrets. But a family man is no longer capable of this childish entertainment; he needs better food; for him a good natured comrade is indispensable, someone equal in strength to his own mind and heart, who is loved for himself, and not for the petty relations of petty vanity. Come visit us, my dear Putyata, and you will give me some truly happy minutes. Farewell; be magnanimous and forgive my laziness and other failings. Love me for the fact that I love you in my soul. Your

Ye. Boratynsky

My address: Nikitskaya Street, by Little Ascension Parish, the Engelhardt house.

I will send Magdalina a copy—but isn't it too late? Did Delvig give you the copy I signed for you?

Delvig, it seems, had asked Baratynsky for permission to publish two poems in the literary almanac *Northern Flowers*. Baratynsky did not want them published at all, while Delvig had proposed printing them anonymously.

[December, before the 4th, 1828, Moscow]

No, my darling Delvig, leaving out the name and leaving out the poems are not the same thing. I read them to several people and probably so did you; consequently, the author will be known and everyone will be asking the natural question: "Why did you conceal your name? It must have been for this or that reason." Humor me, my angel, destroy these two pieces entirely. In exchange I will send you a new poem next week entitled "The Little Demon": if the work itself is not clever, at least the title is impish. Your *Northern Flowers* will be magnificent. Will you include my portrait as you intended? I confess this would please my vanity. What works of your own are you putting in the *Flowers*? "The Last Epoch of the Golden Age" or something else? I hope the former. I received a letter from Pushkin in which he has a few words to say about my *Ball*. Like you, he didn't like the nurse's speech. I'm not defending it, but I would like to know why this speech in particular isn't good, because in order to fix it I have to know what's wrong with it. You explained the comic effect of my poem to me very well and made me feel better. I would be very upset if people saw in *The Ball* merely a joke, but this definitely must be the first impression. Works of this sort are like puns: the only difference is that they play with emotions, not words. Whoever guesses the author's true intention has the whole book in his hands. And speaking of hands: from the bottom of my soul I kiss the little hand of the sweet Sofya Mikhaylovna and sincerely thank her for taking care of my Nastinka [*illegible word*]. I love her like my own sister—but why even say this and make such a comparison? No one is dearer to me than the two of you. Sergey's packing [?] didn't cost him anything, so don't worry about it. Shiryayev delivered *The Double* and I got a receipt from him. Farewell, my dear Delvig: please give Gnedich my warm regards. I keep meaning to write him but somehow never get around to it. I embrace you.

Ye. Boratynsky

P.S. Do me a favor: don't be stubborn—throw away the poems I'm talking about. This doesn't cost you anything, but it's very important to me.

44. TO PRINCE PYOTR VYAZEMSKY, IN MESHCHERSKOYE, HIS ESTATE NEAR PENZA.

[Early April, 1829, Moscow]

You beat me to it, dear prince, but only in the deed, not the intention. I was planning to write you a long time ago, although, as I have little intercourse with either the literate or illiterate world, I could inform you of nothing interesting. But I did want to tell you how much I value your good wishes and, if you permit me to say so, your friendship. You cannot imagine how deserted Moscow is for me without you! When you were here, I saw lots of people I don't see now because I no longer have the hope of meeting you among them. You were the ribbon that tied the bundle together, and without you it has fallen apart. Pushkin is here, and I gave him your regards. He is waiting for spring to come so he can go to Georgia. I see him often, but we feel your absence very much. Somehow nothing comes from the two of us; we're like two mathematical lines. A third line is essential to compose any sort of figure, and you were it. You very flatteringly advise me to take up prose and, I confess, I find your encouragement very tempting. Your conversation has already had its effect on me, and I am already planning a novel, which I will write if I have enough patience and, especially, talent. Speaking of novels, Bulgarin's *Vyzhigin* has been published. What incredible banality! Four volumes, in which not only you will not find a single thought, a single opinion, a single picture, but it lacks even that dignity one might expect from Bulgarin, i.e., that special knowledge about a certain type of people with whom decent people do not consort—the originality of a spy's observations, if not literary ones; no, Bulgarin's soul is the kind of soil no manure can fertilize. His novel, *soi disant*, in the style of *Gil Blas*, includes only one characteristic feature: the dedication to the Ministry of Justice. I have nothing against the idea of publishing something with you: I have a few poems that have piled up and a thing or two in prose too. Write something on your side and if,

336

God grant it, we see each other in May, then we'll also see what use can be made of our materials. I told Polevoy about the *Telegraph*. I haven't seen Raich yet. I haven't said anything yet to Nadinka Ozerova, because she is now preparing for confession and your commission would not be conducive to her spiritual salvation. I will exchange the kiss of Christ with her as your compliment. Farewell, dear prince. Please convey my warm regards to the princess. I am very grateful to her for remembering me. Sverbeyeva asked me to greet you on her behalf whenever I write to you. She is going to foreign lands this spring and, it seems, she needs this. My wife thanks you and the princess for your remembrance. With true affection for you,

Ye. Boratynsky

45. TO PYOTR VYAZEMSKY, IN MESHCHERSKOYE.

[May, 1829, Moscow]

Vasily Lvovich [Pushkin] gave me your gift—a copy of "The Station." I offer you my warmest appreciation for this sign of your remembrance. You promised to put together a complete collection of your works—do not put this off: it will bring you profit in all possible senses and we will have something to read and talk about. [Aleksandr] Pushkin has left for Georgia. By the time I got your letter where you ask him for *Poltava*, he was no longer in Moscow. Generally speaking, I like *Poltava* less than Pushkin's other narrative poems: people are criticizing it backwards and forwards. Which is strange! I say this not because I overly respect the judgment of the public and was surprised that on this occasion it turned out to be wrong, but because *Poltava*, independent of its genuine worth, has, it seems, the things that bring success: a venerable title, interesting content, and a new and needed subject. I really don't know anymore what our public wants. *Vyzhigins*, apparently! Do you know that 2,000 copies of that nonsense have been sold? Either the public will turn completely stupid or it will finally come to its senses and ask, with noble indignation: "What do you take us for?" I have a favor to ask you. If you still have some extra copies of your portrait, could you give me one? D. Davydov cunningly cajoled me out of the one you already gave me; he wanted to make a

337

copy of it but instead of doing so, he has kept the original and now tells me directly, "I'm not giving it back." You can rightfully say: *on se m'arrache.*[*] Farewell, dear prince; I hope all your family is well and you are now more at ease in your heart. I extend my warm regards to the princess.

Ye. Boratynsky

46. TO PYOTR VYAZEMSKY, IN MESHCHERSKOYE.

Before Pushkin left for Georgia, he made comments on a copy of Vyazemsky's poem "To Them," which he left with Baratynsky, who in turn sent it on to the author with a brief note promising to add his own comments later, which he does here. Baratynsky also discusses Vyazemsky's translation of Benjamin Constant's novel *Adolphe* (it would be published in 1831). He writes from his father-in-law's estate Muranovo, some thirty-five miles north of Moscow.

[Late May or early June, 1829, Muranovo]

I am anxious, dear prince, to hear your opinion about Pushkin's comments on your poem "To Them." It seems we are of different minds about lyric irony. In my view, lyric poetry excludes anything that resembles wit, because the archness of wit is of a completely opposite nature to the enthusiasm of lyric poetry. Be angry, but don't make jokes. Let the irony be bitter, but not clever. That is why I do not like: "*dar na zubok byl nuzhen.*"[†] This line is too merry. I haven't said anything to you yet about your stanzas. One may criticize them as a whole and as parts. As a whole, one might wish for greater concision; as parts, one might pick on this or that expression—but this variety of feelings is beautiful in its profusion: why demand of it the beauty of moderation? If somebody finds your poem too long, or if this idea occurs to you yourself in a cold moment, then, truly, do not believe either those others or yourself: leave the whole untouched, and correct only this or that particular stanza. I think that in works of poetry, as in the creations of nature, there must definitely be, near beauty, some flaw that brings the beauty to life. I don't know if I am expressing

---

[*] People are fighting over me.

[†] A tooth-gift was needed [i.e. a gift for a newborn's first tooth].

myself clearly: my thought is that in every author certain flaws are indispensable for him to exist in a given genre, and if you destroy them, you destroy as well the measure of life in his works, and implacable taste will be, for creations of art, exactly what death is for the creations of nature. Let's assume it is possible to remake ourselves, but in such a case, you will be a different being, with different virtues and different imperfections. I feel how difficult it must be to translate the high-society *Adolphe* into a language that is not spoken in high society, but you must remember that one day it will be spoken [there] and that expressions which now seem exotic to us will sooner or later be ordinary. It seems to me you shouldn't be afraid of the fact that certain expressions are not in use and should try to make their root meaning correspond perfectly to the thought you want to express. With time they will be accepted and enter the everyday language. We should remember that those of us who speak Russian speak the language of Zhukovsky, Pushkin, and Vyazemsky—the language of poets—from which it follows that it is not the public who teach us but that it is up to us to teach the public. I do not agree, however, about the word *vytorguyem* [*we will strike a bargain (on something)*]. It belongs to a certain trade, and so does not befit a lady of society. Wouldn't *vygadayem* [*we will save (on something)*] be better as the more general word? I was delighted by your epigram on Bulgarin. I'm sending it to Delvig this very day.

Farewell, dear prince. Love your loving

Ye. Boratynsky

47. TO HIS WIFE, NASTASYA BARATYNSKAYA, IN MURANOVO (IN FRENCH).

The Baratynskys had gone to the Engelhardts' country home at the end of May, leaving their sick infant daughter Yekaterina (Katinka) in Moscow under a doctor's care. Baratynsky then returned to the city, while his wife and two-year-old daughter Aleksandra (Sashinka) remained in Muranovo.

[June, 1829, Moscow]

I have arrived safe and sound, my sweet friend. I find Katinka asleep, but they say she is all right, is coughing less, and is more cheerful. I cannot judge this for myself, since I write you having just now arrived. My heart aches from being separated from you: this test of absence is true agony. I feel completely disoriented. I saw your hat and some of your dresses in our bedroom with a pang of such melancholy it frightened me. I did not kiss you enough when I was leaving; everyone's presence there made me uncomfortable, and as soon as the carriage set off I felt the lack of a parting kiss. The sadness of my heart was asking for it. How strange I find it to be writing to you. It's as if I were starting an epistolary acquaintance with you quite different from the real one. Writing is such a little thing, and the person who said it is a comfort in absence was a very cold-hearted creature. I would like to tell you so many things I can't express. I will never say [in a letter] what I must say and will always be afraid that those turns of phrases found in every letter might make you think I am writing to you as I would to anyone else. I remember telling you about how Marya Andreyevna's husband used to end the letters he wrote to her—with a list of endearments and pet names; we both found that amusing, but you know, it now seems to me that this man loved his wife very much and was not being at all ridiculous. Right now, when I would like to say to you everything that is most tender, I can't find anything better than to call you *Popinka*, as if you were here beside me. My darling Popinka, may God keep you safe; you should have explained your errands to me before I left. Now I don't know if what you need is 1½ *arshins* or a half-*arshin* of calico for Sashinka. I will do what I can tomorrow; the rest I will leave for next time. Farewell, my Popinka; stay well and write to me. I am ending this letter; if in the course of the evening I have anything of interest to communicate, I will add to it. I kiss you with all my heart. Dvyatkovsky came to see Katinka yesterday and today. I kiss my dear Sophie; tell her to write me and not forget that it was you who taught her to spell, so I too have some right to her letters. I kiss you, my sweet friend, and wait impatiently for news from you.

48. TO PYOTR VYAZEMSKY, IN MESHCHERSKOYE.

[Between June 15 and July 18, 1829, Moscow or Muranovo]

I have not yet answered your last letter, dear prince, but I did do what you asked. Your letter to Pletnyov has been delivered to him. I read it, with your permission, and with true pleasure saw that you are planning an edition of your works. Your literary fame is already established, so I won't tell you that your book will have splendid success in that regard—that goes without saying—but I guarantee you success in book sales, which is also not unimportant and, as you yourself have said, it's more decent to take a quit-rent from the public than from peasants. Do not conclude from my long silence that you have been at all out of my thoughts. The reason for my silence was the loss of my younger daughter, which for a time threw me into total depression. The loss of an infant is not a great loss, but it vividly reminds us of the possibility of more important ones, and this death, which so suddenly, so irretrievably robs us of what we love, does not leave our memory for a long time. Death is like despotic power. It usually seems to doze, but from time to time certain victims betray its existence and fill the heart with prolonged horror. I recently saw Korsakov, who's planning to visit you in Penza. Where will you be spending the winter this year? If you'll be on your estate, then I will be in your neighborhood. I will try to see you. There's been no news at all of Pushkin. I would know nothing about him if I had not read in the Tiflis newspapers that he had arrived there.

Farewell, dear prince; I embrace you with all the fervor of my soul and commend myself to your remembrance.

Ye. Boratynsky

49. TO IVAN KIREYEVSKY, IN MOSCOW.

In late September, Baratynsky went with his family to Mara to spend the winter with his mother. His friend, the young philosopher and literary critic Ivan Kireyevsky, was planning a trip to Western Europe around the same time, although he later had to postpone it. Kireyevsky's mother, Avdotya Yelagina, was the hostess of one of the most important literary and philosophical salons in Moscow.

[First half of October, 1829, Mara]

I do not know if my letter will find you in Russia, but even so I write to let you know that I have arrived safely in my Tatar homeland and, mainly, to prove to you that, for you, I am not completely illiterate nor as lazy at letter writing as you imagine. Your departure from Moscow will console me in my own departure, but it saddens me to think that when I return I will not find you by the Red Gate, in the house of the former Myortvy. I hope, however, that we have spent enough time together, argued enough together, dreamed enough together so as not to forget each other. We are comrades in intellectual service, in intellectual campaigns, and our bond must be at least as reliable as it could ever be between comrades in the service of His Imperial Majesty or in the campaigns of Count Paskevich of Erivan. Write me from enlightened Paris, and I will answer you from barbaric Kirsanov. If my letters do not seem detailed enough to you, do not be angry: I am, in fact, not an avid writer, and this only serves as beautiful proof that we should not be apart. There is almost nothing for me to tell you about my life at the moment. I haven't yet managed to get my bearings in the new place. I hope that in rural seclusion my poetic energies will revive. It's high time for me to pick up my pen; it's been resting too long. Besides, the more I reflect on it, the more firmly I believe that nothing in the world is more practical than poetry.

Farewell, dear Kireyevsky; love and remember me, and I will surely not stop loving you and will not forget you. I send your dear mother my warm respects. She is kind to everyone, but if my feelings do not deceive me, she treated me as a friend and I remember this with the most tender gratitude. I embrace you.

Ye. Boratynsky

My wife sends her regards to your mother and to you.

50. TO IVAN KIREYEVSKY, IN MOSCOW.

[Second half of October or November (?), 1829, Mara]

Your kind, warm, and intelligent letter interested and gladdened and touched me. Do not think I want to write you madrigals; no, my dear Kireyevsky, but I am glad to find you just as you are, glad that my intuition did not deceive me about you, glad too of one other thing—that you, with your ardent and multifaceted sensitivity have grown to love me, and not some other person. I find enough warmth in my heart to never make yours grow cold, to share all dreams and to respond, one soul-felt word to another. Cherish this fire of the soul in yourself, this capacity for attachment, the pure, rich source of all that is beautiful, of all poetry, and, indeed, of profound thought. People who are made cold by the experience of vain activity display not penetration but a debility of the heart. To bring the heart fresh out of the experiences of life, not to let it be troubled by them—it is to this we must direct all our moral capabilities. The beautiful is more practical than the useful; it belongs to us in greater ownership; it penetrates all our essence, whereas everything else is barely felt by us. I write these lines with true elation; I know that your heart has no need of such encouragements, but for me, at the age I am now, having through certain circumstances experienced more than some, reflecting on things no less than others, it is sweet for me to offer, with deep conviction, this testimony on behalf of the first pure inspirations of the heart, forgivable and, in the opinion of egoism, good only for one period of life, but in my opinion, sacred and precious at any time.

I've let myself get carried away, my dear friend, but from a good heart. My desire is that you might return from your distant wanderings just as you were when you left and might embrace me with the same fervor as of old. Tell Maksimovich I will send him the first poem that gets itself written. If the Muses are not merciful to me, then he shouldn't berate me and must love me as before. Farewell, dear friend, regards from me and my wife to your dear mother. The next time you write to Sobolevsky, give him a few good friendly words from me. Write me exactly when it is you will be leaving Moscow.

My wife is very grateful to you for your friendly remembrance and loves you as much as I do.

51. TO NIKOLAY KONSHIN, IN TSARSKOYE SELO.

> Baratynsky's old friend from Finland had recently been appointed to a civil service post in Tsarskoye Selo, the imperial residence near St. Petersburg. There he published the literary almanac *Tsarskoye Selo*, to which Baratynsky had promised to contribute.

[Late October (?), 1829, Mara]

I am sending you, dear Konshin, the poems I promised. You will excuse their lack of weight and believe me when I say that my contribution is insubstantial not from stinginess but from poverty. I received your letter, addressed to me in Kirsanov. I warmly congratulate you on becoming a father and wish your dear Olinka all that you wish for her. I can imagine your joy and very, very much wish I could join Delvig at your house for the christening. May God bring us together one day! My life, it seems, will always be divided between Moscow and Tambov; you have settled in Tsarskoye Selo, but who knows what the future will bring! Maybe we will see each other, but may God grant only that it will not be through difficult upheavals that we are taken out of our present cycle. My wife warmly thanks dear Avdotya Yakovlevna for her good wishes and would be very sad if you think of her as a stranger. Farewell, dear Konshin; I embrace you with all my soul. Thank you for the news of Lutkovsky; I had not heard a word about him for a long time. Where has he gone, and was he given any command post? I know some of his relations and can't think which uncle it would be that he got his inheritance from.

Ye. Boratynsky

P.S. The year is stated under my poem "The Fairy": do not forget to print it in your almanac; that's essential to me.

[December, before the 20th, 1829, Mara]

Every day since my arrival in the countryside I have been meaning to remind you of myself, dear prince, but for some reason I never managed to and got no further than the good intention. But I can assure you that your letter would not have anticipated mine had it arrived one post later. Thank you for sending me your manuscript; I won't do it any great help, but it holds extraordinary interest for me as a translation of the worldly, metaphysical, subtly sensual *Adolphe* into our unrefined language, and as a translation from your hand. I have not yet had a chance to look it over. A raid by an entire horde of neighbors has robbed me of time for work. But I am sure of your success, and this success should be epoch-making for our literature. I sincerely rejoice over your preface to F.-Vizin. You alone, in the arena of our literature, have acted as a true writer; you convey your opinion about everything and, in the end, it is clear to us what you think about things, whereas all other Russian writers, even those with talent, are entirely without any form of thought. Delvig writes me that you and he are publishing the *Literary Gazette* together—is this true? And what good news if it is! Whatever you might publish, I ask you to consider me your collaborator, one of little strength, but diligent. Krivtsov I have seen only once, due to my poor health. He is an interesting man in his originality and in our parts he serves as the object of a great deal of gossip. I am taking advantage of the seclusion of the countryside, but not entirely in the way you advise. Prose does not lend itself to me, and my frivolous heart still draws me to rhymes. I am writing a narrative poem. You will find an excerpt from it in Maksimovich's almanac. I am afraid it might be excessively romantic. I offer my sincere regards to the princess and ask that you continue your friendship, so precious to me in every respect. I am truly fond of you, which I think you have guessed, and nothing could make me happier. Your devoted

Ye. Boratynsky

53. TO NIKOLAY PUTYATA.

In late August 1829, Putyata had written to Baratynsky from Adrianople in the Balkans (present-day Edirne, Turkey), where he was serving with the Russian army in the Russo-Turkish War of 1828–1829. His letter had included a detailed description of the town.

[Between late January and the fall, 1830]

Our correspondence, dear Putyata, was interrupted for the simple reason that you left for the army and I did not know where to address my letters. I thank you for your friendly remembrance. It brought me real joy. Your letter shows me that there are still people with whom I can recall the old days and breathe that atmosphere. I too have not stopped remembering you and loving you. My dear Putyata, you and I are rare people! How I wish I could see you and talk with you to my soul's content. I know your present sufferings and feel the keenest sympathy for what you are going through. There is nothing to comfort you, but we could grieve together. You have shown me Adrianople. Your letter is vivid and engaging: you should submit it to the *Literary Gazette*. Since we parted, there has been no change at all in my life, and thank God! You are still with Arseny Andreyevich [Zakrevsky]. Write me what is happening with you all; I am, after all, *de la famille.** How vividly I remember life in Helsingfors! You are obliged to go often to Finland. Can you believe I would now visit it with great pleasure? I think about Finland with gratitude: in that country I found many good people, better than those I have gotten to know in the fatherland; I found you; this land was the nurturer of my poetry. The finest dream of my poetic pride would be that future poets visit Finland in memory of me. Farewell, dear Putyata; write to me: I will not be lazy in answering. I embrace you with all my soul.

---

* One of the family.

54. TO PYOTR VYAZEMSKY, IN MOSCOW.

[January, before the 24th, 1830, Mara]

I am returning *Adolphe* to you with gratitude and ask you to excuse me for holding on to it for so long. This can in some way be explained by a family event in which it has been difficult to maintain the free flow of thought needed for literary work. My sister's engagement was announced and in the general domestic commotion I couldn't remain calm. You overcame great difficulties in your translation, but, if you permit me to offer my opinion, you were so vividly struck by the beauty of the original, like any good translator, that you imposed on yourself too strict a fidelity of translation. I know that circumlocutions possess little dignity, but one must yield to necessity, and in those places where you—an experienced connoisseur of Russian—find it impossible to preserve the precise expressions of the original, that is very likely where necessity exists. I have burdened your notebook with comments. I don't stand by any single one of them, but I offer them all as a group for your consideration. You yourself will decide which are useful and which are not. Maybe one or another will give you the inspiration for some happy correction. Contradiction rouses us, and hints force us to make guesses. If this is true, then I have done you a genuine favor by scrawling mercilessly over your manuscript.

I haven't had any communication from the new literary society you talk about. We should act against factions with factions. Let's form our own society, call together people with talent, and publish its papers—annually, monthly, however it works out. We are losing because we're lazy and our opponents are active. What influences the public is not the quality but the quantity of works. All the opinions of the public are like religious opinions. They are instilled by repetition, not persuasion. In a word, we must act. You will say, *"C'est bon à dire,"** and I understand you, but it's not all that *c'est bon à dire.* Let's give it a try. If it doesn't work out, we must not succumb to indifference.

I commend myself to your good favor. Will you be in Moscow for the winter?

Ye. Boratynsky

---

* Easy to say.

55. TO PYOTR VYAZEMSKY, IN OSTAFYEVO, SOME TWENTY MILES SOUTH OF MOSCOW.

> The Russian cholera epidemic of 1829–1831 reached Moscow in early September and the city and its environs were cordoned off by the army until early December. It was not until March 1831 that Moscow was officially declared free of cholera. The epidemic resulted in some 4,500 deaths in the city. Baratynsky's assurances here are premature, as he admits in his next letter to Vyazemsky.

[November, before the 23rd, 1830, Moscow]

Won't you soon decide, dear prince, to leave Astafyevo [*sic*] and have a look at Moscow's resurrection? If you still think the city is dangerous, you are mistaken. One can definitely say that there is no more cholera here. Those who have recently taken ill are, first of all, few in number, and, second, their illness is no longer what it was and they almost all recover. I have been in Moscow the whole terrible time and, although I didn't find it enjoyable, it was also not as sickening as I had expected. We shut ourselves in our house, not going out anywhere and not receiving anyone. Now we have all revived, but for my full revival I need your presence. I heard that the princess is in Astafyevo. Please convey my respects to her. Your devoted

Ye. Boratynsky

56. TO PYOTR VYAZEMSKY, IN OSTAFYEVO.

[Late November, 1830, Moscow]

I can't argue with you, dear prince, no matter how much I might want to. Staying in Astafyevo is, for now, wiser than coming to Moscow. My invitation was a bit impulsive, but it was inspired by my strong desire to see you. Thank you for your friendly and flattering letter, but believe me, I was touched by your concern even more than by your approving response to my work, although I highly value your approval. I have already sent your steppeland horse ride on to Delvig and, to judge by his well-known lack of promptness, I think your poem will arrive in time. It is filled with color and feeling. Such poetry is better than chlorine for purifying the air. You have freshened my soul with it and I am very grateful to you for sending it to *Northern Flowers* through me.

I don't know how to respond to your proposal about publishing Russia's classical authors or the old fellows. I haven't written very much prose and, as often as I've taken it up, it has always come to nothing. I run out of patience on the second page. In good conscience, I can't guarantee you anything. I'll get to work and see what I can do. Let me have Lomonosov. Since I don't have a lot of cleverness in my mind, I think I'd do better writing an important article than something playful. As for Tredyakovsky, I don't want to deprive either myself or the public of what you would say about him. Reading your letter, I think I can see how you smiled when you wrote his name. How much news there is in Moscow! Including an item of the greatest importance. Warsaw has risen up and the Grand Duke [Constantine Pavlovich] has been forced to leave town. And that's just the beginning. With a small number of troops he has positioned himself at the city's back door. The Vistula, which is behind him, doesn't allow him to retreat into Lithuania. Add to this the fact that Lithuania, too, is unreliable. The Lithuanian Corps is made up entirely of Poles. It's too much, far too much, to expect that even half of them will remain on the side of the Russians. Now is the moment of decisive battle, an outcome that will have countless consequences. What we need now is the greatest possible speed and energy. After this news, everything else is of little importance. Even so, I will tell you something (which you probably know already): the *Literary Gazette* has been banned, probably through Bulgarin's efforts, because of a four-line poem by Casimir Delavigne.

Farewell, dear prince. How sad that you're not close by, but there's nothing to be done about it. My wife thanks you and the princess for your very flattering remembrance of her.

Your devoted Ye. Boratynsky

Dmitry Sverbeyev and his wife, Yekaterina, hosted a literary-philosophical salon in Moscow, which was attended by Pushkin, Vyazemsky, Pavel Chaadayev, Ivan Kireyevsky, the poet Nikolay Yazykov, and Baratynsky, among others.

[Mid-December, 1830, Moscow]

I offer you my most heartfelt gratitude, worthy Dmitry Nikolayevich, for your friendly letter. I am truly touched by your remembrance of me. Believe me when I say that our, unfortunately, not lengthy acquaintance has left an indelible impression on me as well: I continue to hope that I will one day get to know you better and avail myself more fully of an acquaintance that even in its newness has been so pleasant. I did not lose track of you for long. I knew that you had been unable to take your trip to foreign lands and hoped to see you soon in Moscow, where, at the present time, it is perhaps safer than anywhere else. The cholera is now leaving us, and its effect was not as dreadful as we had expected. We spent the entire time in Moscow shut in our house, and I admit that the first weeks, when the disease was developing and it was impossible to predict what it would develop into, were indeed dreadful. Now we are coming back to life, just as other Moscow residents are. On the streets you see the same movement as before; in the houses, the same balls as before. Those who sought refuge on their suburban estates are returning to the city. Prince Vyazemsky is still in Astafyevo, but we expect him any day. His seclusion in the countryside was useful to him; he has written a great deal, and the same is true of Pushkin, who spent this terrible time on his estate near Nizhny Novgorod. He is here now and has brought with him four tragedies, a narrative poem, the last two chapters of *Onegin*, and an entire folder of prose. His industriousness is beyond belief.

I write you all these details knowing that you will find them interesting. Kireyevsky has returned from Germany. He has come back with an incredible hatred for Germans; in fact, he has brought many new philosophical ideas from there. You know the political news from the papers. The most recent is particularly important and interesting. You and I had many political debates; I would very much like to renew them, all the more so because, after thinking things over on my own, I have given up many of my opinions in favor of yours. I commend myself to your friendly remembrance and remain your truly devoted

Ye. Boratynsky

On January 14, 1831, Anton Delvig died suddenly after contracting what first appeared to be an ordinary cold; a few days later, however, he fell into "the unconsciousness of a fever," as Pyotr Pletnyov described it in a letter to Pushkin. "And so in three days an obvious illness destroyed him," Pletnyov wrote. "My dear, what sort of a thing is life?"

In mid-April, Baratynsky's narrative poem *The Concubine* was published in book form. Its subject, the relationship between a man and the gypsy woman who lives with him openly as his mistress in Moscow, was, to say the least, controversial. For many, the very name of the work was shocking. *The Ladies' Journal*, for example, "reviewed" the work by saying they could not print the title and certainly had not read the poem. Hoping to forestall such accusations of indecency, Baratynsky had published *The Concubine* with a long preface in which he attempted to define what constituted morality and immorality in a work of literature.

58. TO PYOTR PLETNYOV, IN ST. PETERSBURG.

Pletnyov had been part of the circle of poets around Pushkin when Baratynsky returned to St. Petersburg after his expulsion from the Corps des Pages. He had since become a literary critic, an editor, and a teacher at various elite schools—including the Corps des Pages. About a year after this letter was written, he would be appointed as a professor of Russian literature at St. Petersburg University.

[Late April–early May, 1831, Moscow]

I am sending you, dear Pletnyov, a copy of *The Concubine* in the hope that it will remind you of one of your old friends. I don't know if our late Delvig gave you my letter, where there was a lot of the kind of thing to which, knowing your heart, I might have expected a response. I didn't receive one and, I confess, that caused me great pain. However you might have changed over the course of our five-year separation, I can assure you that I have remained the same as I was before it. I have the misfortune to be too little known to those who know me or, to put it better, I do not stir in them enough interest for them to try to get to know me. What can I do? The worse for them! They are rejecting a heart capable of devotion. Farewell. I embrace you.

Ye. Boratynsky

IV.
KAZAN, KIREYEVSKY, AND *THE EUROPEAN*
SPRING 1831–SPRING 1832

Baratynsky's connection with Ivan Kireyevsky was (as he would later write to Nastasya) "at its full intensity" in the years 1831 to 1833, after the latter's return from Berlin and Munich, where he had attended the lectures of, among others, Hegel and Schelling (both of whom he met personally). Baratynsky's letters to Kireyevsky from Muranovo and, especially, from Kazan and Kaymary, clearly show the warmth of his friendship for the younger man and his profound regard for his intellectual abilities—in this he was joined, notably, by Pushkin, Vyazemsky, and Zhukovsky, all of whom saw in Kireyevsky the great hope for a Russian literary criticism founded on solid principles. For Baratynsky, however, Kireyevsky meant something more as well: he was one of the few people he could speak to openly and freely about literature, society, and life in general.

59. TO IVAN KIREYEVSKY, IN MOSCOW.

As the cholera epidemic retreated from Moscow, Baratynsky and his family left the city in early May to spend the summer at the Engelhardts' Muranovo estate.

[May or June, 1831, Muranovo]

How are you, my dear Kireyevsky, and what are you doing? Is solitude proving beneficial for you? Is your novel progressing? By the way, about the novel: I've been giving it a lot of thought recently and here's what I think about it. All previous novelists are unsatisfactory for our age for this reason: they all adhere to some system. Some novelists are spiritualists; others, materialists. Some express only the physical phenomena of human nature; others see only its spirituality. We need to unite the two types into one. We need to write an eclectic novel, where man would be expressed in both manners. Although everything has been said, it has all been said separately. By bringing the phenomena closer together, we present them in a new order, in a new light. There in a nutshell, and in Masonic language, you have my thinking. For the time being, I do nothing. For the time being, trees and vegetation entertain me in the countryside just as much as people do in the city. I go horseback riding every day; in a word, I lead the kind of life that only Ramikh could be happy with.

Farewell, my dear. I embrace you, and you must embrace Yazykov for me. Don't forget about the almanac.

Your Ye. Boratynsky

I read a quite flattering and quite undetailed review of *The Concubine* in the *Literary Gazette*. This was a friendly response. Is there something our enemies are saying? If you have anything, do me a favor and send it. I intend to respond to criticism. My wife greets you.

60. TO IVAN KIREYEVSKY, IN MOSCOW.

[May or June, 1831, Muranovo]

I won't thank you for your trouble: it's time to abandon such dry formulas between you and me; they speak of a certain mistrustfulness, and I have none towards you. I hope our feelings are mutual in this regard. Don't send me the money, but keep it until we see each other. I'll be in Moscow in July and definitely in September. I need to clarify my thoughts to you about the novel: I presented them too categorically. As an ideal example of finiteness, take *L'Âne mort* and *La Confession*; as an ideal example of spirituality—take all sentimental novels: you will see all the one-sidedness of each type of depiction and their mutual insufficiency. Fielding and Walter Scott are closer to my ideal, especially the former, but they guessed the demands of their own time through a kind of instinct, and for this reason, whenever they happened on the true path, they constantly strayed from it. A writer who is accustomed to thinking eclectically will, I believe, go further; that is, he will be even clearer. Don't think that I require a systematic novel: no, I am only saying that the old ones cannot serve as models. Every writer thinks; it follows then that every writer, even if he's not aware of it, is a philosopher. So it is his own philosophy, and not someone else's, that must be reflected in his works. We were born into an eclectic age: if we are true to our feeling, an eclectic philosophy must be reflected in our works; but the old models can throw us off the track, and I point to contemporary philosophy for contemporary works as a magnetic needle that can serve as a compass in our literary quests.

What's wrong with your mother? I hope her illness isn't serious. Kiss her hands for me and tell her she shouldn't rely solely on will power to get well and should at least for once do something to help herself, just as she helps other people every day. My wife sends you her warm greetings and thanks Yazykov for remembering her. My sister-in-law has also charged me with sending you greetings. The thing is that we all love you very much. I am sending you Salayev's receipt. If Loginov and the others buy *The Concubine*, then his copies will probably go quickly and we can ask him for money. Take it and hold on to it. Yazykov, why isn't your health improving? That really is sad. Farewell, brothers, until we next see each other. I embrace you.

61. TO IVAN KIREYEVSKY, IN MOSCOW.

[May or June, 1831, Muranovo]

I am answering you quite hastily, so I ask you to consider this document a note and not a letter. Thank you for the good news of your mother's health. I hope she will soon be strong again. About commercial matters, I could give you a very brief answer: I could say "do as you wish" and be at ease, but I know you're an extremely conscientious man, and if something went wrong, you'd be more upset than I would be. That's why I will say that, as far as Shiryayev goes, I agree with you. As for Kolygin, I am thinking of giving him a price of less than 8 rubles a copy; if someone takes a hundred copies, then 7 rubles 50 kopeks apiece, or even 7.

About the novel, it seems to me we're both right: every viewpoint is good, so long as it is clear and strong. I was writing to you more about the novel in general than about your own novel; I think, meanwhile, that my thoughts might inspire you with some idea, maybe the details for some scene. I know very well that it's impossible to re-create something once it's been created. Let me know how you find Gnedich. I confess I'm very sorry I won't see him. I loved him, and this feeling has not yet grown cold. Maybe today I'd find something ridiculous in him: how strange! It's pleasant to look at the bell tower in the village you were born in, although it no longer seems as high as it did when you were a child. For the time being, I'm not doing anything: I go horseback riding and, like you, I'm reading Rousseau. I will write to you about him in a few days: he has awakened many thoughts and feelings in me. An exceptionally remarkable man and more sincere than I first thought. Everything he says about himself undoubtedly happened, only not entirely in the same order he tells it. His *Confessions* is a tremendous gift to humanity. I embrace you.

Ye. Boratynsky

P.S. I received the money.

62. TO IVAN KIREYEVSKY, IN MOSCOW.

[May or June, 1831, Muranovo]

Your friendship, dear Kireyevsky, belongs to my domestic happiness; its picture would be quite incomplete if I left out our conversations about you, the pleasure with which we read your letters, the sincerity with which we love you and rejoice that you pay us the same feelings. We both see you as a dear brother and in our thoughts attach you to our family life. You do not leave it and, in our dreams of the future, when we arrange it to our heart's desire, you are always in our neighborhood, always under our roof. You are the first person, of all the people I know, with whom I unburden myself without shyness: this means that no one else has ever inspired in me such trust in his soul and in his character. I would make a description for you of our country life, but I'm not in the mood right now. I will tell you, briefly, that we drink tea, dine, and have supper an hour earlier than in Moscow. This is the frame of our existence. In it put strolls, horseback riding, conversations; put in something that has no name: that general feeling, that sum total of all our impressions, which makes us wake up cheerful, stroll around cheerful, that grace of family happiness, and you will get a fairly accurate idea of my life. My *Concubine* I leave completely in your care. I can hardly wait for your review. Send it to me when you finish. The shortcomings in *Boris* [*Godunov*] you can allude to briefly and write about its merits at length. In this way you will do justice to yourself and to your relationships. I don't fully agree with you that the style of *Joan* served as the model for the style of *Boris*. Zhukovsky could only teach Pushkin to master unrhymed [*indecipherable word*] verse, and not even that, since Pushkin has not followed the methods of Zhukovsky, always observing the caesura. The style of *Joan* is good in itself; so is the style of *Boris*. In *Boris*'s style we see a faithful feeling for the olden days, a feeling that constitutes the poetry of Pushkin's tragedy, whereas in *Joan*, the style is beautiful without any particular relation.

Farewell, my dear. I embrace you warmly. Write to us. My wife is very grateful to you for your friendly regards. In fact, I always write to you on behalf of the both of us. Embrace Yazykov for me; I am very glad he is on the mend. I very much want to see you both and maybe I'll come for a day or two to Moscow if my health allows it. Don't forget to pay my respects to Gnedich.

Ye. Boratynsky

63. TO IVAN KIREYEVSKY, IN MOSCOW.

[June 1831, Muranovo]

Imagine, dear Kireyevsky, we have quite suddenly decided to go to Kazan and it may be that I won't have the chance to say goodbye to you, since we have heard rumors that there is cholera in Moscow again and my family won't let me go under any circumstances. I write to you in the midst of the bustle that's an inseparable part of travel preparations. I am sending you my own Sismondi and Villemain. They were unable to get a copy in Petersburg and you can't imagine how bad I feel to disappoint you. Urbain told me he would have it in July. If so, then buy the whole work from him and, substituting the one volume, send it to me in Kazan. Get the money from Salayev. The copies of *The Concubine* we gave him have probably all been sold. By the way, I sent you his receipt but you don't say if you got it. So that's how it is, my dear: right when I was thinking of settling down in Moscow, I'm leaving it. But I would definitely have had to make this trip in a year or two and be separated from my family. Now we are going together and, if I stay there until next spring, there won't be any need for me to go back again. In spite of this, I leave with a heavy heart and the future frightens me, all the more since I love the present. God grant that I won't find any change in Moscow and that I find you all as I left you. Farewell, my dear, there's no time to write more. There's a ton of things to do. I embrace you. Yazykov too. Convey my respects to all your family, whom I'm ready to call my own.

Ye. Boratynsky

64. TO IVAN KIREYEVSKY, IN MOSCOW.

> Baratynsky writes from the Engelhardt house in Kazan. He and his family had gone there with Nastasya's father and sister.
>
> *[Late June or early July, 1831, Kazan]*

I write you from Kazan, dear Kireyevsky. I couldn't write on the road because we were avoiding the towns, where cholera has reappeared. As a traveler I have the right to speak of my impressions. I will name the main one: boredom. You can go from one end of Russia to the other without seeing anything different from the place you set out from. It's all flat. The Volga alone brought me joy and made me think of Yazykov, who in fact I was thinking about anyway. When we arrived in Kazan, I started reading the Moscow papers and saw an announcement in them for the brochure "On Boris Godunov." This isn't yours, is it? Probably not; first, because you're too lazy to write and publish something so swiftly, and second, because you promised to send me your article before it went to print. I hope to do some proper writing in my rural seclusion. If I didn't notice anything of interest on the road, at least I did a lot of thinking. Traveling through our homeland is good in that it doesn't interfere with reflection. It is traveling through a limitless space measured only by time: that's why it brings forth its own fruit, just as time does. By the way, it wouldn't be a bad idea to mark distance in Russia by hours, not versts, the way it's done in some countries for reasons not so indisputable. Farewell, my dear. I write nonsense to you because I'm tired, because it's hot. I'll write you a more decent letter from the village. Convey my regards to your family. My wife doesn't write because she's running errands. She's buying the different things we need for the village and isn't at home right now. I embrace you with all my soul.

Ye. Boratynsky

65. TO NIKOLAY PUTYATA, IN ST. PETERSBURG.

[Late June or early July, 1831, Kazan]

I am late in answering your letter, dear Putyata, but you will forgive me when you learn that I received it quite recently and that it was forwarded to me from Moscow to Kazan, where I now am with my entire family. I thank you for delivering *The Concubine* to the intended recipient and for your comments. I don't dispute the fact that there are a few careless, and even bad, verses in *The Concubine*, but believe me that, in general, the author of *Eda* has made greater achievements in his most recent narrative poem. I'm not even talking about the difficulties that were overcome, about the very genre of the poem, which is full of action, like a prose novel. Compare impartially the dramatic parts and the descriptive parts: you will see that the conversation in *The Concubine* is more uncontrived, more natural; the descriptions more precise, simpler. As a matter of fact, there are far more bad places in *Eda* than in *Sara*. In the latter, you can criticize a particular verse, a turn of phrase, but in *Eda* you can criticize whole passages, for example, the hussar's entire conversation with Eda in the first canto. Usually, I think my latest work is worse than my earlier ones, but when I reread *The Concubine* I'm always struck by the lightness and fidelity of the style in comparison with my earlier long poems. If a certain carelessness is visible in *The Concubine*, there is no sign whatsoever of labor—and this is precisely what is needed in a poem filled with difficult details, from which one must emerge the total victor or else not attempt the matter at all. But now I'm rambling, my dear. Excuse me for arguing with you. You know that I will gladly agree with criticism when I think it justified, but I don't agree with yours. I wish I could tell you something interesting, but I live in complete seclusion and have nothing to share with you apart from my thoughts. I see from the newspapers that the cholera is coming to an end where you are, but I know from experience that moderation in diet and trying not to catch cold are sure ways to escape it.

I hope that you will not be one of its victims and that God will allow us to embrace each other once more. Farewell. My address: my name, in Kazan.

Ye. Boratynsky

In early July, the Baratynskys went to the Engelhardt estate of Kaymary, some thirteen miles north of Kazan. There were, it seems, certain legal issues that needed to be dealt with. Vyazemsky wrote to Pushkin on August 24, 1831: "I recently received a letter from Baratynsky in Kazan, where they have all gone, that is, the Engelhardts, as he writes, for reasons of business, but I have been told that it was to get away from the cholera. 'I am writing,' he says, 'not for posterity, as you might too amiably assume, but for the lower district court.'"

66. TO PYOTR PLETNYOV, IN ST. PETERSBURG.

[Mid- to late July, 1831, Kaymary]

When I received your letter, dear Pletnyov, I was packing for a long trip, which is why I didn't answer you at the time. Now I write you not from Moscow but from a village 20 versts from Kazan. I have become farther from you in distance, but not in my heart. Your letter has distressed my soul. It breathes disillusionment and dejection. With bitter remorse I think that I myself have in some way contributed to your sad disposition of spirit. Content in my soul with a vivid friendly memory of you, I took no care to assure you of it and, it seems, forgot about my old friend. It horrifies me to think that, when you thought of me, you said to yourself: see how unfeeling, how ungrateful people are! Meanwhile, I was guilty of only laziness, of putting off till tomorrow what needed to be done today. Delvig's loss is irreplaceable for us. If we ever do see each other again, if one Saturday we sit down together at your table—my God!—how lonely we will be! My dear, the loss of Delvig has shown us what the irretrievable past is, which we intuited through sorrowful inspiration; what the desolate world is, which we talked about without knowing the full significance of what we were saying. I haven't yet started on Delvig's life. His death is still too fresh in my heart. Laments alone are not enough; thoughts are needed, and I haven't yet been able to bring them into order. Let's talk about you. Have you really left literature completely? I know that poetry isn't contained in the dead letter, that it's possible to be a poet in silence, but I am sorry that you have left an art which, better than any philosophy, consoles us in the sorrows of life. To express a feeling means to resolve it, to master it. This is why the gloomiest of poets can maintain a cheerfulness of spirit. Take up your pen again, my dear Pletnyov; do not betray your calling. Let us complete our life's task with fortitude. A gift is a commission. We must fulfill it despite all obstacles, and the main one is despondency.

Farewell, my dear. I've become a preacher. Listen to my exhortations and I will listen to yours. Thank you for your praise of *The Concubine*: it consoled me amid the ill will of my other critics. I embrace you with all my soul. Write me when you find the time. Give my regards to Pushkin. My address: my name, in Kazan.

Ye. Boratynsky

67. TO PYOTR VYAZEMSKY, IN MOSCOW.

[August or September, 1831, Kaymary]

Thank you for sending me *Adolphe* and for the introduction to Kazarsky, whom, however, I was only able to see for half an hour. I was at his house just before his departure from Kazan. There is much kindness in him: he is extremely grateful to you for the introductions you provided for him in Moscow, and he can't praise enough his flattering reception by the Pashkovs, Kindyakovs, and in general Moscow's merriments [?—*the word is unclear*]. I reread *Adolphe* at leisure. You have chosen the best system of translation, namely, the one most beneficial for the language. When you sent me your manuscript, I didn't understand your intention—that's why my comments were truly senseless. I reread your intelligent and witty preface, which so well explains and augments [?—*the word is unclear*] Benjamin-Constant's work. You have forced me to completely rethink all the ideas that my first reading of *Adolphe* had given me. You allude to an illness of the soul peculiar to our age, which the author of *Adolphe* very slightly delineates: he touches on it throughout, while you—more than he does—force us to see it. This illness, which remains not fully examined by him, could be the subject for a new novel. Give it some thought: perhaps you will write it. Another thing: is it really true that there is no cure for the emotional depravity we see in our age? And are we actually worse than our predecessors? I am not entirely given to the contemporary dreams of improvement, but I am inclined to think that no epoch is better or worse than another. In our time, it seems to me, the successes of morality, the exalted detailed enlightenment of the conscience very much balance out those caprices of the heart, the habits of egoism unknown to the previous age. In the old days, Adolphe would either leave Ellénore without a second thought or would inwardly view his leaving her as an effort of virtue, and his conscience wouldn't torment him in the least. His sufferings show that he belongs to a time in which it is not permissible to toy with the attachments of the heart, to an age in which infatuation is rare but fickleness unforgivable.

Farewell, dear prince. I lost track of the time talking with you, as if I were sitting in your study by the fireplace. Please convey to the princess my warm regards and remember me to Aleksandr Ivanovich Turgenev, if he's still in Moscow.

[August, before the 6th, 1831, Kaymary]

Why are you silent, dear Kireyevsky? Your silence worries me. I know you too well to ascribe it to indifference, nor do I have the right to ascribe it to laziness. Are you well? Is everyone in your family well? I really don't know what to think. I'm in the most hypochondriacal frame of spirit, and there's but one question spinning around stubbornly in my mind: why you don't write? I need to have a letter from you. I don't know what to talk to you about. I've been in my Kazan village for a month now. At first I was dealing with all the estate business and talking to managers and village leaders. There's a legal matter I'm involved in, so I was talking to judges and secretaries. You can imagine how much fun this is. Now I'm done with all that and still don't know how to use my free time. Ideas come one after the other, but I can't settle on any one of them. My imagination is primed, my reveries are vivid but capricious, and my lazy mind can't bring them into order. So here you have my psychological confession.

On the road and partly at home I reread Rousseau's *Héloise*. How is it that this novel once seemed passionate? It's amazingly cold. I could barely find two genuinely touching passages and only two or three expressions straight from the heart. Saint-Preux's letters are better than Julie's—there is more naturalness in them; but in general these are moral treatises, not the letters of two lovers. In Rousseau's novel there is no dramatic truth whatsoever, nor the least dramatic talent. You'll say it's not needed in a novel that makes not a single pretension to these things, a novel that's purely analytical. But this novel is in letters, and the voice of the letter-writer should be heard in the letter's style: in a way, it's the same as conversation—and look what an advantage the creator of *Clarissa* has over Rousseau. It's obvious that Rousseau's object was neither the expression of character nor even the expression of passion; rather, he chose the form of his novel in order to give an account of his views on religion, to analyze certain subtle moral questions. It's obvious that he wrote *Héloise* in his old age: he knows what feelings are and delineates them accurately, but in his heroes this same self-knowledge is cold, for it doesn't belong to their years. The novel is bad, but Rousseau is good as a moralist, as a dialectician, as a metaphysician, but... hardly as a creator. His characters have no physiognomy and although he says in his *Confessions* that they appeared vividly to his imagination, I don't believe it. Rousseau knew—understood—only himself; he observed only himself, and all his characters are Jean-Jacques, whether they're in trousers or skirts.

Farewell, my dear. I share with you what I can: my thoughts. For the love of God, write. Give my regards to all your family and Yazykov. I hope I will soon stop worrying about you and be only a little bit angry.

69. TO IVAN KIREYEVSKY, IN MOSCOW.

[August, before the 13th, 1831, Kaymary]

I am seriously grieving for you, dear Kireyevsky. Here's another post come and not a word from you. You are surely ill, or something quite extraordinary has happened to you. This latter conjecture does not console me. You'd keep silent about your sorrow but would surely share your happiness. The more I think about possible reasons for your silence, the more alarmed I become. I would like to ascribe it to laziness, but I know that, unfortunately, you don't have that fault when it comes to friendship. I'm angry at your relatives. They know that our connection is not one of simple acquaintance. And that they should tell me what's happening if you yourself are unable to write. Today I thought about asking your mother if you are all right, but then abandoned the idea out of superstition. I write you with anxiety and sadness. Farewell, my dear; God grant that my fears are unfounded. If you have been sick (which I almost do not doubt) and are still not recovered enough to write, ask your mother or brother or sister to let me know about you. All my family send their regards to you and share my anxiety. I embrace you.

Ye. Boratynsky

70. TO IVAN KIREYEVSKY, IN MOSCOW.

> We do not know what sadness Kireyevsky was struggling with at the time, but Baratynsky's comment about the "bashful secret" demanded by an emotion other than friendship suggests that he thought his friend was depressed over a love affair.

[Second half of August (?), 1831, Kaymary]

At long last I have news from you, dear Kireyevsky, but it is not consoling. There are many sad things in your letter. Thank you for your confidence in my friendship. It is demonstrated in your candid allusions. I feel, I share, your position, although I don't completely know what it is. Your dark fate lies on my heart. If in certain instances the advice and even the comfort of friendship are useless, its concern is always gratifying. I do not want to compel your trust; I know it is in your heart, although it is not expressed in words; I understand this shyness of feeling; I do not ask you to go into any details, but please let me know, if only in general terms, how you are and what is troubling you. In this way you will satisfy both the curiosity of friendship and that bashful secret which is demanded by a different emotion. Whatever is troubling you, you at least know that there is no one who would rejoice in your joy or be grieved by your sorrow more than I. This faith is where the true comfort of friendship is found. I think of you with the very same faith, and it augments my domestic happiness. Farewell, dear Kireyevsky, I embrace you with all my soul. How is poor Yazykov—ill and stricken with grief from his mother's death? Tell me about him. How much sorrow for you all at one time! I cannot recover from the effect of your mournful letter and without sadness imagine your home, so recently loud with merriment and now filled with such deep despondency. Don't be lazy about writing me, because I need your letters. When your soul gets brighter, and when I know that, then you can put off writing from post to post, but for the present this would be unforgivable of you.

Your Boratynsky

Kireyevsky, who was overseeing the distribution and sales of *The Concubine* in Moscow, was also keeping Baratynsky informed of the critics' reactions. Of these, the most significant was that of Nikolay Nadezhdin, who wrote a lengthy review in his journal, *The Telescope*, where he attacked both the poet's ideas about morality in literature (as expressed in the preface) and the poem itself.

[September, before the 21st, 1831, Kaymary]

I'm answering two of your letters at once, dear Kireyevsky, because they arrived at the same time. Don't be surprised: the Moscow post comes to Kazan twice a week, but we send to the city for it from our village only once a week. Thank you for your efforts on behalf of *The Concubine*. Let's hope it sells out this winter. In fact, its success or failure is all the same to me these days. I've somehow grown cold to its fate. I am truly delighted by your intention to publish a journal. My only fear is that it might be just another of the thousand plans we have that remain—plans. If things do get going, I will be your indispensable and diligent collaborator, all the more as everything inclines me to prose. I hope to provide you with two or three stories a year and assist you in some lively debates. I haven't been reading criticism of *The Concubine*; I don't get journals here. If you could send me the issue of *The Telescope* where the objections to my preface were published, I will definitely respond—and do so to the point and at length. I have given even more thought to my subject since *The Concubine* came out, thinking about all the questions that touch on it, and I hope to resolve them without in any way contradicting my initial positions. My article would be suitable for your journal. I will keep your issue of *The Telescope* safe and send it back to you as soon as my article is ready.

You are wrong to consider me an implacable critic of Rousseau; on the contrary, I am thoroughly fascinated by him. In *Héloise*, I criticize only the novel, just as one might criticize what is created in Byron's narrative poems. People used to compare Byron and Rousseau, and I find this comparison entirely just. In the works of both authors, one shouldn't look for independent fantasy, but only the expression of their individuality. Both are poets of the self, but Byron surrenders unconditionally to the contemplation of himself; Rousseau, born with a more analytical soul, needs to deceive himself; he moralizes and in his morality expresses the demands of his own, suspicious and tender, soul. In *Héloise*, the desire to show his elevated conception of moral perfection in man, to brilliantly resolve certain difficult problems of conscience, constantly forces him to forget dramatic verisimilitude. Love, by its very nature, is an exclusive emotion that bears no admixture whatsoever; that is why *Héloise*, in which Rousseau more often surrenders to an inspiration more moralizing than passionate, leaves such a strange and unsatisfying impression. We see in the *Confessions* that it was his love for Mme Houdtot which gave him the inspiration for *Héloise*, but from the disproportionate space in the novel occupied by morality and philosophy (which is in Rousseau's blood), we feel that the ideal of Saint-Lambert's mistress [*i.e.* *Mme Houdtot*] was always yielding in his imagination to the ideal of Jean-Jacques. The shortcomings of the latter are found even more in the composition of Rousseau's soul than in the composition of his novel. I like *Héloise* less than Rousseau's other works. The novel—and I stand by this—is a work totally at odds with his genius. While in *Héloise* every page makes me angry, and even its beauties irritate me, all his other works captivate me irresistibly. The warmth of his words permeates my soul; his sincere love of the good touches me; his easily offended sensibility speaks to my heart. You see how I let myself get carried away chatting with you. My wife, who loves you very much, sends her regards. I embrace you.

Ye. Boratynsky

72. TO NIKOLAY YAZYKOV, IN MOSCOW.

> In January 1828, Baratynsky had been officially registered as a civil servant in the Land Survey Office (see Letter 42). This was done entirely for bureaucratic reasons; he never actually worked there. In July 1831, he requested, and was given, permission to resign, and his friend Yazykov then "filled" the vacated position. The accommodating director of the Land Survey Office was a man named Bogdan Germes, whose surname is identical to the Russian name for the Greek god Hermes.

> *[September, before the 21st, 1831, Kaymary]*

Thank you, dear Yazykov, for your postscript to me [*on one of Kireyevsky's letters*]. This is, alas, a great achievement for your laziness and genuine proof of your friendship. Now that you have taken over my position in Germes's department, you are obliged to replace me in full. I served two years with outstanding zeal, for which I was found worthy of being promoted in rank. Ask Kireyevsky to tell you about my service achievements: I'm sure this will inflame you with a grateful spirit of competition. It seems that the god of poets is now not Apollo, but Hermes: besides you and me, Vyazemsky too used to serve under him. How about writing some verses for him where you offer him fine praise for the fact that under his leadership even the Land Survey Office has been transformed into Mount Helicon. By the way, speaking of verses: I've somehow gone off them and have only prosaic plans in my mind. This is very sad.

[*Here follows the poem "A child, I would the forest echo."*[*]]

This is the only poem I've written since we said goodbye; I was trying to express my sorrow. What are you doing, and will you be writing any poems soon? Send me what you write. That will wake up the inspiration in me.

Kireyevsky's starting a journal. This news has brought me great joy. Let's help him with all our strength: the thing will definitely take off.

Farewell, I embrace you very fondly.

Ye. Boratynsky

73. TO IVAN KIREYEVSKY.

[*Between September 21 and October 5, 1831, Kaymary*]

Thank you for your note. This is truly the attention of a friend, and if you knew what satisfaction a hermit receives from even the briefest lines from a lively place (not to mention how pleasant it is to see that we are remembered by those we love), you would always do as you have done now. We're not always in the mood to write, we don't always have ideas, we don't always have time for a long letter, but we can always say hello and goodbye, which mean more in a letter than they do in an upstairs room. I will follow your example, but don't stop giving it. This will free

---

* See p. 117.

our correspondence of any affectation, any calculation; and besides, when you sit down in front of a piece of paper to write just two words, you will always write more, and there will be true inspiration in this added part. Today my head is rather empty and I will end my letter with the news that I am alive and healthy, but so the letter won't be completely empty, I will copy out two little poems for you, which I recently wrote. [*Here follow the poems "My Elysium" (without the title) and "In days of limitless distractions."*] These poems, like the one I sent Yazykov, are for you and yours. Don't show them, and don't give them, to outsiders. I embrace you with all my soul.

Ye. Boratynsky

74. TO IVAN KIREYEVSKY, IN MOSCOW.

[October, before the 8th, 1831, Kaymary]

Thank you for Pushkin's and Zhukovsky's verses. I had wanted to copy them out, but you anticipated me. I read Zhukovsky's verses, unsigned, in the *Northern Bee*, and couldn't for the life of me guess the author. I was struck by the unusual rhymes and exemplary firmness of style, but the casual tone put all thought of Zhukovsky out of my mind. Pushkin's first poem I like better than the second. It lays things out and shows us the real vantage point from which we should view our war with Poland. You underlined the verse: "*Stal'noy shchetinoyu sverkaya.*"[†] You probably find it overdone. You may be right, but it's strong and vivid.

I've already answered you about the journal. Set to work and God speed. As far as the name is concerned, I think it would be best to choose something that doesn't actually mean anything and wouldn't display any pretensions. "The European," which the public won't understand at all, will be understood by journalists in an offensive way—and why should you give them ammunition in advance? Can't you call the journal "The Northern Messenger," "Orion," or something arbitrary but at the same

---

[*] See pp. 115 and 119.

[†] Glistening with steel bristles.

time meaningless, like *Le Nain jaune*,[*] which was published by the Bonapartists under Louis XVIII? You expect too much from me, and I doubt I will fulfill even half your expectations. I can assure you of one thing: my diligence. Your journal has very much inspired me to action: I have written a few more small poems, besides the ones I sent you. Now I am writing a short drama—my first attempt in this genre—which, no matter how bad it might be, will still do for a journal. I will probably finish it this week and send it to you. Don't tell anyone about it, but read it and let me know your opinion. I'll publish it in the journal without my name. I'm not telling you about my longer-range ideas out of superstition. You never write anything if you boast about it beforehand. I'm very curious to know what you will say about Zagoskin's novels. All his works taken together show both talent and foolishness. Zagoskin is a truly curious psychological phenomenon. Send me your article when you write it. When I return to Moscow, I'll help you in a real way. I have to write in a rush in order to write a lot. I need to surrender myself to journalism, the way I do to conversation, with all the vivacity of questions and answers; otherwise, I am too demanding of myself, and this attitude often makes me lose interest even in my good ideas. In the meantime, everything I manage to write in my seclusion will belong to your journal. Farewell, give my regards to your family.

Ye. Boratynsky

Tell Yazykov that Rozen is angry at him because not only did he not send the poems from last year, but he didn't even answer his letter. He complains about this a lot and quite touchingly too.

75. TO IVAN KIREYEVSKY, IN MOSCOW.

[October, between the 8th and the 26th, 1831, Kaymary]

I am writing you just a few words, dear Kireyevsky; as for the reason, you'll see from my letter to your mother. I received a notification about money; I expect this is from your efforts. There's probably a letter with the

---

[*] The Yellow Dwarf.

money, but I haven't yet had a chance to send to the city for it. Farewell, my dear. I finished the drama I wrote you about and am very moderately happy with it. I ask you again: don't tell anybody I'm writing anything. My answer to all the almanac folks is that I have no poems, and in a few days I'll say the same thing to Pushkin. I embrace you.

Ye. Boratynsky

76. TO IVAN KIREYEVSKY, IN MOSCOW.

[October, before the 26th, 1831, Kaymary]

This dimwittedness you're talking about has happened to me a hundred times at social gatherings. I would get angry at myself but, I admit, with a good opinion of myself: I didn't reproach myself for being stupid, especially in comparison with those who excelled at this skill I lacked. To console you even more in your grief (I say "grief" in jest), I'll tell you that no mortal has ever shone as much at *petits jeux,** and especially at *secrétaire*, as Vasily Lvovich Pushkin or even his brother, Sergey Lvovich. The latter, when asked, *"Quelle différence y a-t-il entre m-r Pouchkine et le soleil?"* answered: *"Tous les deux font faire le grimace."*† Indeed, what's there to say? Although we might peek in on society from time to time, we are not society people. Our mind is formed differently, its habits are different. Polite conversation is, for us, an acquired effort, a theatrical invention, for we are alien to the present life, the present passions of fashionable society. I'll say one thing more: that *laisser aller*‡ which makes us nimble at social gatherings is a natural quality of limited people. They get it from their self-importance, which is always inseparable from stupidity. People of a different sort acquire it through experience. Comparing their own abilities with those of others over a long period, they finally notice their own advantage and give themselves freedom, not so much from a sense

---

* Party games.

† "What is the difference between Monsieur Pushkin and the sun?"— "They both make you grimace."

‡ Letting oneself go; effortlessness.

of their own worth as from their certainty of the worthlessness of the greater part of their rivals.

I am not yet sending you my attempt at drama because it must still be copied, and my copyist is still in bed. Thank you for the money and for Villemain. My soul felt lighter when I saw this scribbled-over volume, which had well and truly tormented me. I've already read two parts: there is much that is good and well said, but Villemain often portrays as new and as his own idea things that have long been known to the Germans and were discovered by them. Much of it is merely for the success of the moment and the applause of a faction. One more observation: in Villemain one often detects an affectation of refinement, an affectation of the best tone. His modest reservations are, for one thing, monotonous, and for another, somewhat overdone. You feel that he is admiring his own worldly-aesthetical humility. This does not keep his work from being very engaging. As for the Guizot I will tell you that right now I don't have the money. If you can lend me the necessary amount until January, then buy it; if you can't, then tell Urbain that I don't need the Guizot, or ask him to wait for the money.

Farewell; all my family send you regards. I will write to Yazykov in the next post and in the meantime I embrace him.

Ye. Boratynsky

77. TO IVAN KIREYEVSKY, IN MOSCOW.

In his review of *The Concubine*, Nadezhdin lambasted Baratynsky's assertion (in the preface) that literature should be viewed as "a science like other sciences" and we should "seek in it *knowledge*, and nothing else." The critic countered that literature was an art, and "art and science are completely different things!" For Nadezhdin, true literature was distinguished by "beauty": "Mad is the artist who brings to life the image of a snail on the canvas or translates the croaking of a frog into musical notes: even madder is the poet who squanders his creative efforts on the representation of vices and crimes, whose loathsomeness is much more abhorrent."

Thank you for your friendly congratulations and kind jests. In fact, I am holding you to your word: *The European* must definitely be published in the year of my Mashenka's birth, and then, when she's twelve, if she's capable of listening to your lectures, I really do ask that you see to her education.

It's not a problem that my poem was passed around. I sent Pushkin another one too: "Deluded Orpheus, do not sing," but I assure you there is nothing more in my soul. I'm not giving up writing, but I want to stop publishing for a while, even for a long while. Poetry, for me, is not some conceited pleasure. I have no need of praise (from the rabble, obviously), but I don't see why I should be obliged to subject myself to their abuses.

I read Nadezhdin's critique. I don't know if I will respond to it—and what would I say? He agrees with me in everything and only reproaches me because I, supposedly, believe that refinement is unnecessary in refined literature; meanwhile, I said very clearly that I would not speak about the beautiful because only a few would understand me. This critique delighted me; it showed me that I had fully attained my goal: I had convincingly refuted a universal prejudice, and any reader with even half a mind, who could see that the morality of a literary work should be sought neither in the choice of the subject nor in injunctions, neither in the one nor in the other, would conclude with me that it must be sought in truth alone or in the beautiful, which is nothing other than the highest truth. A fine thing it would have been if I had spoken in Nadezhdin's language. Of his thousand subscribers, I doubt if one could be found who understood anything on the page where he tries to explain the beautiful. And what's most amusing is that the translation is found precisely in the preface he is criticizing. If I do answer him, it is only because I would feel guilty about making you hunt down and send me the journal to no purpose. I am writing, but I'm not writing anything decent. I'm very unhappy with myself. "*Ne pas perdre du temps c'est en gagner,*"* said Voltaire. I console myself with this maxim. I am now writing the life of Delvig. This is only for you. You remind me about the Sverbeyevs, whom, in fact, I

---

* Time not wasted is time gained.

haven't forgotten. Send them my regards and say that if they'll be staying in Moscow next winter, I hope to spend many pleasant hours at their home. I embrace you.

Ye. B.

78. TO IVAN KIREYEVSKY, IN MOSCOW.

[November 29, 1831, Kaymary]

November 29th—there you have the date. I missed one post because in my deep seclusion

I forgot to call by name / all the days of the week.

I thought it was Monday when it was Wednesday. During this time, however, I've been laboring for your journal. I answered Nadezhdin. My article, I think, is twice as long as my preface. I myself am amazed that I could write so much prose. The fair copy of my drama is almost done. I am now at work on a story, which you remember: "The Ring." You will get it all in the next parcel post. It's all mediocre, but it will do for a journal. Thank you for your promise to send me the stories by the Little Russian author. As soon as I read them, I'll write about them. The idea of writing about Zagoskin is really frightening. I am hardly one of his ardent admirers. His *Miloslavsky* is rubbish, and *Roslavlev* may be even worse. In *Roslavlev* the novel is worthless and the historical viewpoint both silly and inaccurate. But how do you say these cruel truths to an author who, after all, has written the best novels we have?

I'm very sorry Zhukovsky doesn't like the title of my poem [*The Concubine*]. I try to justify it in my response to Nadezhdin. I cannot understand why intelligent, enlightened people are so offended by a word whose full meaning is allowed in all conversations. Tell me what he thinks about the poem itself, what he praises and what he condemns. Don't be afraid of upsetting me. Zhukovsky's opinion is especially important to me, and his criticisms will be useful to me. I have the plan for a new long poem thought out from every angle. Whether it will be good or not, God knows. I'll start writing in a few days. I won't give you an account of my plan because that would deaden it. By the way, the epistle to Yazykov and the elegy you call European belong to *The European*. I will send you two or three other short poems in the next post.

Farewell, give my regards to your dear mother, who I won't manage to write to today. Remember me to Aleksey Andreyevich [Yelagin— *Kireyevsky's step-father*]. How is his health, and has he completely calmed down about the cholera?

Ye. Boratynsky

My wife has gone to a veneration at a nearby hermitage and will answer your mother's letter in the next post.

79. TO IVAN KIREYEVSKY, IN MOSCOW.

[Early December, 1831, Kaymary]

Here are the things for *The European*. Excuse it all being so badly over-written: you know my passion for corrections. I couldn't resist making them even as I send this to you. I feel particularly bad about my drama, which isn't worth the corrections. And I wouldn't send it to you at all if I didn't think that in a journal even something mediocre is good for taking up a few pages. Look over my response to the critic, and if anything seems superfluous to you, throw it out. I'm very much afraid that in it I don't keep to the German orthodoxy, and a few heresies have crept in. Print the drama without my name and don't read it to anyone as my work. But do put the author's name under the tale. I read your announcement: it could not have been better written, and I knew right away it was yours. Your explanation of the journal's title was both intelligent and modest. But in our country people don't understand modesty, and my fear is that your announcement didn't have enough charlatanry to get subscribers. But so be it. I'll be subscribing to some of the Russian journals next year and will respond to any attacks on you when necessary. Besides the plan for my narrative poem, I also have plenty of bile in reserve: I'll welcome the chance to release it. This is entirely a business letter. I need to give you a commission—not a literary one, of course, but also not completely foreign to it, since it has to do with my stomach. I am sending you 50 rubles. Please do me the favor of having someone buy me half a *pood* of cocoa and send it to me by the parcel post. They sell it in Hunter's Row: ask someone, maybe even Einbrod, how to tell fresh cocoa from stale. Farewell; I embrace you very warmly. Anything else I manage to write I'll send. We are moving from the village to the city. I will recommend *The European* to everyone I know in Kazan.

Ye. Boratynsky

80. TO IVAN KIREYEVSKY.

[Mid-December, 1831, Kazan]

If you've already received permission to publish the journal under the name *The European*, then let it stay *The European*. The name is not the point. You embarrass me with your too high opinion of my drama. I should tell you right away that it is merely an attempt at drama: a few scenes with the lightest possible story line. The only reason I'm not in despair about it is that I hope eventually to write something a bit more serious. If I followed my inclination, I would do with it what you do with some of your works, namely, throw it in the stove. By the way, I don't think that's particularly wise of you. For one thing, it's not for me to be the judge of my own work; for another, anyone who picks up the pen is struck by some sort of beauty, so no matter how much their work may be open to criticism, there's sure to be something good in it. As for perfection, this, it seems, is not given to mankind, and thinking about it is more likely to cool down than inflame the writer. Zhukovsky thinks the same thing; he advises us to be wary

> of the talent-killing / arrogant thought of perfection.

So Zhukovsky will be in Moscow. How sad that I'm in Kazan. Give him my very warmest greetings. I saw an announcement in the papers about his new ballads coming out. I can't wait to read them. I'm familiar with *The Tales of Belkin*. Pushkin read them to me in manuscript. Write me what you think of them. Thanks for not being lazy about writing. With every letter you write I feel even more attached to you, if that's possible. My respects to your dear mother. What was wrong with her? Needless to say, I'm truly glad to hear she's better. Embrace Yazykov for me, and send me his new poems.

Ye. B.

You write me about the portraits of famous people. But just think a moment: such people are very few in our country, and these portraits would have to be panegyrics, which means no one would be interested in them. You'll say we don't have to call them all by name, but two or three signs are enough to easily recognize a person you know, especially an author, and even the shadow of non-elation will be taken as an insult, and a personal one at that. Let's put our compatriots aside, but that shouldn't keep you from putting on paper everything you know about Schelling and the other eminent people of Germany. There's no need to make them into a riddle, for we have to know who they are in order to value them—and are there many people who know them, not only personally but also from their works? There you have my opinion: judge for yourself whether or not it's fair.

81. TO IVAN KIREYEVSKY.

[Late December, 1831, Kazan]

Thank you for your germane criticism. At the end of my response to Nadezhdin I got carried away at quite the wrong moment. Here's the correction for you: "The first lines we are willing to accept as irony, that is to say, as a careless joke on the not-well-intentioned allegiance of *The Moscow Telegraph.* We will not dispute the feelings of self-superiority which inspired them; we will only note that they are out of place and can be taken as an incautious admission. Let us do justice to the critic: it is clear in his biased review that..." etc.

Replace "lack of logic" with "lack of reflection"; if any other expression seems too harsh to you, you have my permission to soften it.

The first issue of your journal is splendid. There can be no doubt of its success. It seems to me we have to prod journalists so that in their replies they inform people about the existence of the opposing journal. Your announcement was too modest. Tell me: do you have many subscribers? In the Moscow papers, print that such-and-such articles are included in the first issue of *The European*. This will be very helpful to you.

My family and I send you and your family our warmest greetings for the holidays and the new year. God grant that next year finds us together.

We have moved from the village to the city: I am tortured by boring visits. I'm getting to know the local society, with little hope of finding any pleasure in it at all. There's nothing to be done about it: one must submit to custom, all the more because for the most part custom is sensible. I look at myself as a traveler who is riding through the boring, monotonous steppes. Once he has crossed them, he can say with pleasure: I saw them. Farewell until next week.

Ye. B.

Thank you for the cocoa. I expect it cost about 15 rubles to send; with the remaining money, if possible, send me Zhukovsky's new ballads.

82. TO IVAN KIREYEVSKY.

[Early (?) January, 1832, Kazan]

I just received the unexpected and delightful new book you sent: the Guizot, which I very much wished to have. Thank you. I notice that I have to repeat these words in every one of my letters to you. Write me: do I owe you very much? I have money now.

I've gotten to know the city here a little better. I came down with a bad cold the first day I arrived and couldn't go out. But you know, in my view, a provincial city is livelier than a capital. When I say "livelier," I don't mean more enjoyable, but there is something here that Moscow doesn't have: action. I have found the conversation of some of our guests very interesting. Everyone talks about their own affairs, or about the affairs of the province, whether with disapproval or praise. Everyone, as much as you can tell, is actively striving for some practical goal and, because of this, has a physiognomy. I can't develop my whole idea for you; I will say only that in the provinces there is not a trace of that indifference to everything, which characterizes most of our Moscow acquaintances. In the provinces there is a greater sense of civic duty, more enthusiasm, more political and poetic elements. When I am able to examine this society more closely, perhaps I will write something about it for your journal, but I have seen enough already to always choose a provincial city over a capital as the setting for a novel. I am praising your *European* here, but I don't know if my praises will make anyone subscribe to it. Only two or three houses here subscribe to books and journals, and then they lend them out to their acquaintances. The terrible Artsybashev lives here: I spoke to him without knowing it was him. I will try to get to know him better so I can examine his nature. When Kachenovsky was first pointed out to me, I looked at him with genuine curiosity; my imagination, however, deceived me: *Je le vis, son aspect n'avait rien de farouche.*[*]

I embrace you, and you must embrace Yazykov for me. My respects to all your family.

83. TO NIKOLAY YAZYKOV, IN MOSCOW.

> Baratynsky had received a letter from Yazykov with, presumably, the poem "To I. V. Kireyevsky (In His Album)," which includes the lines: "The time is near: the hangover dreams / of my brave Muse / will pass; to a new road / she will bring her voice / and reverently sing / a hymn to the God of our fatherland…" Baratynsky opens his letter with his own poem to Yazykov.
>
> *[January, before the 7th, 1832, Kazan]*

Crowning with ivy and grapes / her high forehead, / the young muse used to sing / with you of wild living / and brave joy, / and the mad and blind crowd, / now forgetting itself, / would burn with crude love for her; / now raging in idiotic sanctimony / at the free melodies, / would swear at the wondrous maiden / by a deity it could not understand. / The blaze of inspiration in her gaze, / the fire of rapture on her cheeks / was drunken fever in her eyes / and the crimson of desire. / She is high-born; / great fame becomes her; / only for her lover does she / adorn the garb of a Maenad. /

---

[*] I saw him, but there was nothing savage in his appearance.

Present her, present her soon, / singer, in worthy brilliance to the world: / give your soul's bosom-friend / a diadem and royal robes; / reveal her sovereign status: / Let her astonish with her beauty! / Let her majestic gaze confound / her evil-tongued judge / so that with shame he recognizes in her / his Empress and mine!

This is what your epistle [to Kireyevsky], executed with freshness and beauty and sadness and rapture, inspired in me. Talent alone is not enough to be able to write in your own way; you need to be inspired by your heart and the life at hand. Your poetry is all that is stirring my soul. Your student elegies will live into posterity; but you are right to want to choose a different road. As a poet grows into manhood, his poetry too must mature; otherwise, there will be no truth or genuine inspiration. I wait anxiously for the first issue of *The European* [*indecipherable word*] I very much want to see what sort of success it can expect. The announcement was too modest. You are wrong to be afraid of its weightiness. Our public loves that. It has little capacity for being carried away and does not understand the beautiful. But it respects learnedness and always buys ready knowledge with ready cash. Farewell, my dear Yazykov. I love you with all my soul.

Ye. Boratynsky

84. TO IVAN KIREYEVSKY, IN MOSCOW.

[January, before the 18th, 1832, Kazan]

It's been a long time since I had any letters from you, dear Kireyevsky, and I'm not complaining, since I know you have a lot to do. I do have a request to ask you: if my first epistle to Yazykov hasn't been printed yet, don't print it: it seems rather weak to me. Print the second one instead, which I'm happier with. I lead the most foolish life here, distracted but without pleasure, and I can't wait to return to our village. We move the first Sunday of Lent. There I hope to put the time to good use for myself and for *The European*, but that is completely impossible here. Imagine who I found in Kazan: young Pertsov, who is famous for his jokes in verse; Pushkin was praising him to us. Not only is he a very smart man, he's also well educated, with definite talent. He read me excerpts from his comedy in verse which were full of energy and wit. I'll try to get him to give them to us for *The European*. He's the only one here I speak to in my natural language. So there you have the bulletin of my day-to-day life. Why aren't you sending me *The European*? I received Zhukovsky's ballads. A number of them show a remarkable perfection of style and a simplicity that Zhukovsky didn't have in his earlier works. He's even making me want to rhyme some legends myself. Farewell, I embrace you.

Ye. Boratynsky

85. TO AVDOTYA YELAGINA, IN MOSCOW.

Kireyevsky's mother, Avdotya Yelagina, was the niece of Vasily Zhukovsky, who had tutored her when she was a child and remained her close friend.

[Mid-January, 1832, Kazan]

Your letter, dear Avdotya Petrovna, made me sadly count the months I must still spend far away from you, in my Kazan exile. Truly, no one could be kinder than you, and whoever does not love you must have a poor heart. Shall I tell you that mine is boundlessly devoted to you? You must not doubt this, otherwise you would do a great injustice to both yourself and me. Moscow is dear to me because of you, and I would feel sorry for the city if so many people I know and love were not gathered there. Zhukovsky's verses have been entertaining me all week. Who would have thought they were written by a melancholic and a member of the court! I especially love Zhukovsky when he's up to his pranks: it's so comforting to see such childlike simple-heartedness in a man with a superb mind, which confirms that the power of thought is no obstacle to the heart's happiness. If in Zhukovsky's other works I love the poet, then I love the man himself in his jests—but, it seems, there's no need for me to praise Zhukovsky to you. Aleksey Andreyevich is already angry at you; I'm afraid I might come in for it too. I will, however, tell you (and now I'm being serious) that I understand the magic of your seeing each other again, all the happiness and all the sadness of it. You spent your childhood and youth together, and the impressions of the past, linked imperceptibly one to another, all came alive and started speaking at once. This holiday, like all great holidays, has passed, leaving us bewildered and alarmed, and for a long time afterwards we cannot adapt ourselves to our ordinary life. I understand the emptiness you felt after Zhukovsky's departure. I am working diligently for *The European*, and in a few days you will receive enough material for an entire issue. I have a long narrative poem in my head, but I haven't started writing it yet: protracted labor frightens my laziness. Farewell, my dear, my good Avdotya Petrovna. Be healthy: someday so many years will have passed that our friendship, too, will have its memories.

Ye. Boratynsky

86. TO IVAN KIREYEVSKY, IN MOSCOW.

> The first issue of *The European* appeared on January 7, 1832. Baratynsky received it some two weeks later. This issue included Kireyevsky's programmatic essay "The Nineteenth Century" and the first installment of his "Survey of Russian Literature for 1831," devoted to Pushkin's play *Boris Godunov*, as well as two unsigned articles by Kireyevsky—a note on the writing style of the French historian Abel-François Villemain and a review of Aleksandr Griboyedov's play *Woe from Wit*. Also included in this first issue was Baratynsky's poem "In days of limitless distractions," published under the title "Elegy."

[Late January or early (?) February, 1832, Kazan]

Your *European* is unrivaled. The ideas, the manner of expression, the choice of articles—there's been nothing like it in our journals since the time of Karamzin's *Messenger of Europe*, and I think it will have just as much success, for it has, for our present age, all the merits Karamzin's journal had for its age. Only do not abandon your own work. All the articles written by you are particularly good. Your discussion of the 19th century is rich in ideas, but if we were together I'd take issue with you on certain points. This is not a criticism. The subject is so vast it may be viewed from a multitude of different perspectives, and my comment shows only that you have awakened my mental activity. The article on

Villemain's style is splendid. It's impossible to say more in fewer words with such clarity, such taste, such truth. Both Villemain and Balzac are appraised fully and with remarkable justice. Your review of *Godunov* is distinguished by just the same fidelity, the same simplicity of view. You cannot imagine the thrill I felt as I read your journal's enlightened pages; I could hardly believe I was reading Russian prose—I'm so used to getting similar impressions only from foreign books. I am sending you a short poem by Pertsov, which I'm very unhappy with. He has read me a lot of things that are better and I don't know why he chose this piece for *The European*. I will talk to him about it. He read me a comedy written in beautiful verse filled with wit, and its many characters are faithfully and vividly depicted. He has definite talent, but clearly not all genres come to him with equal ease.

Is your mother well? We haven't had anything from her in a long time. Kiss her hands for me and remember me to Aleksey Andreyevich.

Please tell me if you have sent me my cocoa? I haven't yet received it.

To end, here's an epigram for you, which has to be printed without my name:

> Who is my inevitable scolder? / My indispensable betrayer? / My inevitable envier? / Nothing to think about here—he's one of my own. / An enemy is more often useful to us than a friend; / thus the sublunary world is constructed. / Oh, how dear, how beloved / is an enemy given by nature herself!

87. TO IVAN KIREYEVSKY, IN MOSCOW.

The second issue of *The European* appeared on January 29 (Baratynsky had not yet received it). The two issues elicited an enthusiastic response from Pushkin, who wrote Kireyevsky: "Up to now, our journals have been dry and worthless, or useful but dry; *The European*, it seems, joins usefulness with allure." He did, however, offer a few words of practical advice: do not include too much high-quality poetry in a single issue but save something for a rainy day, and, with regard to Kireyevsky's reviews, which Pushkin praised ("at long last, we have genuine criticism"): "avoid scholarly expressions, and try to translate them, that is, use circumlocutions: this will be both pleasing to the uneducated and useful for our infant language." He ended his letter with appreciation for Kireyevsky's assessment of Baratynsky's work (in the second issue), adding, "I hope *The European* will wake up his idleness."

[Around February 17, 1832, Kazan]

I understand, brother Kireyevsky, that the care-filled life of the journalist and, especially, dissenting comments and idle judgments are distressing you most unpleasantly. I suspected you would be in this position and I'm sorry I'm not there with you, because there's a similarity in the shape of our views and we would strengthen each other in them. The opinion of Zhukovsky, Pushkin, and Vyazemsky seems wrong to me. When we try to accommodate the public, we do not move people forward. Writers teach the public, and if people find in writers something they don't understand, it instills in them even more respect for the knowledge they don't possess; embarrassed by their ignorance, they are forced to seek this knowledge out. I hope that Polevoy is less clear than you; nevertheless, his journal sells out and, undoubtedly, does a great service, for even if he doesn't provide any ideas, he awakens them, while you both provide them and awaken them. Everyone has the right to scold the public, and the public never gets angry at this since no individual takes personally what is said about the collective body. Vyazemsky made a witty remark—and that's all. If you don't have many subscribers, the reason is: 1. the announcement was too modest; 2. you're not well known in literature; 3. you've excluded fashion pages. But have the patience to publish into next year and I guarantee you success. After reading *The European*'s first issue here in Kazan, we subscribed to it. In general we liked the journal very much. We found it intelligent, erudite, and diverse. Believe me, Russians have a special ability—and a special need—to think. Give them nourishment: they will say thank you. But don't lose sight of variety and novelties, which are what make a journal a journal and not a book. Your article on the 19th century is incomprehensible to the public only where you go into philosophy, and, indeed, your findings are understandable only to those who have been initiated into the mysteries of the latest metaphysics. On the other hand, your literary conclusions, the application of this philosophy to reality, are remarkably clear also to those who know this philosophy through feeling though it might not yet be fully comprehensible to the mind. I don't know if you will understand me, but such is the progression of the human mind: we believe before we investigate, or rather, we investigate only so as to prove to ourselves that we are right in our belief. This is why I find it useful to do as you do, that is, to acquaint our readers with the results of science so that, by making them love it, we force them to get interested in it. I will try to send you something for the third issue. You're right: Kazan has not been very inspiring for me. But I hope that some of the impressions and observations I've acquired will not be wasted. Farewell; don't give in to despondency. Literary work is its own reward; in our country, thank God, the degree of respect we acquire as writers is not proportional to commercial success. I know this to be true also from experience. Bulgarin, despite his successes in this genre, is despised even in the provinces. I have never yet met the people he writes for.

Ye. Boratynsky

88. TO IVAN KIREYEVSKY, IN MOSCOW.

Baratynsky must have received the second issue of *The European* just a day or so after sending Kireyevsky the previous letter. This issue included the second installment of Kireyevsky's "Survey of Russian Literature for 1831," devoted to *The Concubine*, as well as Baratynsky's Hoffmannesque prose tale "The Ring" and the "Response to Criticism," where he answers Nadezhdin's attacks on his narrative poem.

[February, before the 22nd, 1832, Kazan]

I begin my letter with complaints against you, and a fair number have piled up. First, you don't write how much I owe you for the Guizot and the other small items. There's no need for us to stand on ceremony, especially in this matter. Second, allow me to take you to task for not telling me your opinion of my drama. You probably don't like it, but do you really know me so little as to be afraid of offending my writerly pride by telling me frankly that I have written nonsense? I'll be more delighted by your praises when I see you don't coddle me. I received the 2nd issue of *The European*. The review of *The Concubine* is, for me, a genuine service. It's a shame there is so little writing in our country, especially so little that's good; otherwise, you would make a name for yourself with your aesthetic criticism. You have understood me perfectly; you entered the poet's soul and captured the poetry I was imagining as I wrote. Your sentence, "He transports us into a musical and pensively spacious atmosphere," made me tremble with joy, for this is the very virtue I have suspected in myself in moments of writerly pride, though I never expressed it so well. I cannot help but believe your sincerity: there is no poetry without conviction, and your sentence belongs to a poet. I am not the least bit angry that you berate the genre I chose. I think the same about it and want to leave it behind. The 2nd issue of *The European* is in general as good as the first.

We are moving from the city back to the village. I hope I will write; at least I have the firm intention of not indulging my laziness. If verses prove stubborn, I'll take up prose. Farewell, I embrace you.

Ye. Boratynsky

I got the cocoa.

89. TO IVAN KIREYEVSKY, IN MOSCOW.

[Early March, 1832, Kaymary]

You analyze my attempt at drama more seriously than it deserves. I was studying the form and my idea was more about putting anecdotes into scenes rather than writing an actual play. I chose a trivial subject so as not to spoil a good one with my pupil's pen. If there's something interesting in the movement, something natural in the dialogue, I am satisfied with myself, since I wasn't thinking about beauties of a higher sort.

Have you read the 8th chapter of *Onegin* and what do you think about it, and about *Onegin* in general now that Pushkin has finished it? At different times I have thought different things about it. Sometimes *Onegin* seemed to me to be Pushkin's best work; sometimes the opposite. If everything in *Onegin* were Pushkin's own, it would undoubtedly attest to the writer's genius. But the form belongs to Byron; the tone, too. A multitude of poetic details have been borrowed from one writer or another. What belongs to Pushkin in *Onegin* are the characters of his heroes and the local descriptions of Russia. The characters are pale. Onegin is not deeply developed. Tatyana has no distinctive quality. Lensky is trivial. The local descriptions are beautiful, but only where they are purely sculptural. There is nothing that might definitively characterize our Russian life. In general, this work bears the mark of a first attempt, although one by a person with great talent. It is brilliant, but it is almost all like student work because it is almost all imitative. This is how people usually write in their first youth, more from a love for poetic forms than from a genuine need to express themselves. Here you have my current opinion about *Onegin*. I entrust it to you as a secret and I hope it remains between us, for it is quite wrong of me to criticize Pushkin severely. But I feel bad about concealing the true shape of my thoughts from you.

As I was getting this letter ready, I received a second letter from you. Pertsov lied to you: I will definitely be spending next winter in Moscow, but I don't expect to remain its permanent resident and in any case I am building a house in the countryside. I already told you that we will be living on our own. This will cause us expenses that we can't calculate until we make the attempt. It goes without saying that living in Moscow will be beyond our means, and then, whether we want to or not, we will have to settle in the countryside. Your plans have been the same as mine more than once, so you will easily believe that if I see any way to stay in your Moscow, I won't leave it. It seems you did not like my acquaintance Pertsov very much. I confess that he's not quite to my liking either. It may well be that he is a man of intelligence and even good moral qualities, but somehow his essence does not harmonize with mine. I feel awkward and sullen with him. Is it true that Gorskina is marrying Shcherbatov? She used to correspond rather frequently with my sister[-in-law] Sonichka, but now, for some three months, she has stopped writing her. When you see her, reproach her on my sister's behalf for this unamiable change.

The university here has received a document from the minister of education which recommends strict monitoring to ensure that students read neither the *Telegraph* nor the *Telescope* as these journals spread harmful ideas. People are saying their publication has been suspended. Is this true? Farewell, my dear, I embrace you with my whole soul. I am sincerely glad to hear of your mother's improved health and warmly kiss her hands.

Ye. Boratynsky

On February 22, 1832, Nicholas I issued an order banning all further publication of *The European*. He had become convinced that Kireyevsky was "a not right-minded and not trustworthy person" who was secretly promoting revolution (especially in the essay "The Nineteenth Century"). As Kireyevsky wrote to Zhukovsky a day or so later: "I have finally received the official prohibition. They are accusing me in the most preposterous way, saying that by the word 'enlightenment' I mean 'freedom,' by 'the obligation of reason' I mean 'revolution,' and so on. How can one justify oneself? If I simply say, 'That's not what I meant,' they won't believe it; if I try to prove the absurdity of the accusation through the sense of the article itself, they won't understand it and won't read it. And what tone does one take when entering into polemics with the sovereign himself, whose name appears in every line of the wordy prohibition?" It was only thanks to Zhukovsky's intervention that Kireyevsky was not arrested and sent into exile.

90. TO IVAN KIREYEVSKY, IN MOSCOW.

[March, before the 14th, 1832, Kaymary]

I had been attributing your silence to a lack of time and didn't conceive that anything unpleasant had happened; you can imagine how shocked I was by your letter in which you inform me of so many domestic sorrows and then, at the end, tell me that your journal has been banned! Your mother's illness (and it's not the first since we left you) has distressed us extremely, even though you say in your letter that she's feeling better. As to the banning of your journal, I am still stunned. No doubt some secret, vile, and unjust informer has been at work here, but what's the comfort in knowing that? Where is judgment to be found against him? After this, what can possibly be attempted in literature? Like you, I too have lost any strong incentive for literary labors. The banning of your journal simply fills me with gloom, and, judging by your letter, it has filled you with melancholy. What's to be done! Let us think in silence and leave the field of literature to the Polevoys and Bulgarins. Let us thank Providence that it made us friends and that we each have found in the other a person who understands him, and that there are also a few other people akin to us in mind and heart. Let us enclose ourselves in our own circle, like the first Christian brethren, possessors of a light that was persecuted in its own time but is now triumphant. Let us write without publishing. Perhaps a more propitious time will come. Farewell, my dear; I embrace you. Write to me. I need your letters. This persuasion you will find compelling.

Ye. Boratynsky

My wife fervently asks that you keep us informed about your mother's recovery.

91. TO IVAN KIREYEVSKY, IN MOSCOW.

[April, before the 12th, 1832, Kaymary]

You spent your birthday rather sadly. I hope the old adage won't come true and this day won't serve you as a pattern for all subsequent days this year. There are many moments in life when we are struck by its senselessness: in these moments some people draw conclusions similar to yours, others find hope for a different, better existence. I am among the latter. I won't argue now about a subject that could fill volumes, but I am happy to let my thoughts transport me to the time when we resume our endless debates. *Evenings at Dikanka* without a doubt shows a man with talent. I had been ascribing the tales to Perovsky, though I didn't recognize him at all in them. In general there is less sense in them and more life and originality than in Perovsky's works. Yanovsky's youth is sufficient excuse for what is incomplete and superficial in his tales. I would be very glad to meet him. We'll talk about Skaryatin's wedding when we see each other. Maybe I will prove to you that our assumptions were not particularly unreasonable. Farewell; my wife and I wish you and your family all the best for the holiday.

Your Ye. Boratynsky

[Late April or early May, 1832, Kaymary]

I haven't written you in such a long time that I feel quite guilty about it. My silence was not from laziness, not from a lack of time, that's *just the way it was*. This *just the way it was* is a Russian absolute, but it's impossible to explain it. Today I genuinely have no time to write letters because I'm writing verse, and yet here I am writing to you. How can this be if not that it's *just the way it is*? I am very grateful to Yanovsky for his gift. I would very much like to meet him. We have never yet had an author with such jovial joviality; this is a great rarity for a northern land. Yanovsky is a man with definite talent. His style is lively, original, filled with colors and often taste. In many places the observer is evident in him, and in his tale "A Terrible Vengeance," he was more than once a poet. Our ranks have increased: this conclusion might be a little immodest, but it expresses well my feeling towards Yanovsky.

The only thing you wrote me about Khomyakov's tragedy is that it's finished. Tell me about it in more detail. My brother in Petersburg, to whom Khomyakov read it, writes me that it far surpasses Pushkin's *Boris*, but he doesn't say anything that might allow me to form some idea about it. I am relying on you for this.

Please convey my thanks to dear Karolina for translating my *Transmigration of Souls*. I have never been so annoyed with myself for not knowing German. I am sure she has translated me beautifully and I would find it more delightful to read myself in her translation than in my original: just as a person is more eager to recognize himself in a flattering portrait than in the mirror.

My sister[-in-law] Sonichka is angry that you suspect Gorskina of being somewhat coquettish. That's not the issue, however; rather, it's that she has heard rumors that you find a great resemblance between the two of them, from which it follows that you have the same opinion about her, and she does not admit its justice.

Farewell, my dear. Do me a favor and tell me what your rank is. I need it so I can address the receipt for you from the Trustees' Council. This won't cause you any trouble: they'll just deliver it to you and that's that. How are the Sverbeyevs? Give them my regards, and the same to all your family.

Your Boratynsky

Write me as soon as possible about your rank. I leave here on May 25th.

93. TO IVAN KIREYEVSKY, IN MOSCOW.

[May, before the 16th, 1832, Kaymary]

I will make it a rule not to miss a single post and write you every week, if only a couple of words. Writing to you is already something my heart requires, and it will be easy for me to keep to this rule. What you say about a fable for the new world I find very just. I don't know anyone richer than you in truly critical thoughts. I have written only one work in this genre and therefore cannot lay claim to the honor you ascribe me. The invention of this genre will belong to both of us together, for your comment has made an impression on me and I will certainly try to write a couple dozen epigrams along these lines. Writing them isn't hard; what's hard is finding ideas worth expressing. We are on the eve of our departure from here. My father-in-law is going to Moscow, my wife and I to my mother in Tambov Province. But even so, still write to me in Kazan until you get a letter in which I tell you definitely about my departure. We will see each other at the end of August and, if God grant it, we will live together [in the same city] for a long time. Farewell, I embrace you.

Ye. Boratynsky

What is Yazykov up to? Is this lazybones of a lazybones writing anything? I ask that he feel sorry for me: one of the ladies here, a woman of advanced years who has not yet lost pretensions to beauty, has written me an epistle in verses without meter to which I am obliged to reply.

94. TO IVAN KIREYEVSKY, IN MOSCOW.

[May, before the 30th, 1832, Kaymary]

My father-in-law has left for Moscow. I was supposed to leave at the same time for Tambov, to my mother's, where I intended to spend the summer, but my wife's poor health has kept me here. Write to me as before in Kazan. I cannot imagine what Khomyakov's tragedy must be like. Dmitry the Impostor is a distinctly historical figure; our imagination cannot help but give him a physiognomy that corresponds with the writings of the chroniclers. To idealize him is the height of art. Byron's Sardanapalus is a hazy figure to whom the poet can give whatever expression he likes. There's no one to say: "That's not what he looks like." But we have all, as it were, seen Dmitry and we judge the poet as a portrait painter. The genre Khomyakov chose is distinctly fascinating: it presents a wide frame for poetry. But I think it's better suited to Yermak than Dmitry. Will he be publishing his tragedy soon? I can't wait to read it, all the more because its publication contradicts all my conceptions and I hope to draw some completely new poetic impressions from it. During this time I've written only short poems. I've got five of them now, including one on Goethe's death which I'm happier with than the others. I'm not sending you any of them so I'll have something to read you when we see each other. Forgive me this Khvostov-like sentiment. Farewell. Our relatives will spend some three days in Moscow. Try to see them: they will tell you about our adventures in Kazan.

95. TO IVAN KIREYEVSKY, IN MOSCOW.

[First half (?) of June, 1832, Kazan]

You developed your idea about the fable to me with remarkable clarity. I wish you would write an article about it. Your idea is new and, as I see it, just: it's worth an article. I am keeping your letters, and when we see each other in Moscow, I'll find those two in which you talk about the fable. You can put what you said in them into your article, since it would be hard to express it better. You're an extraordinary critic and the banning of *The European* is a great loss for you. Have you really not been writing anything since then? What about your novel? Wieland, I think, once said that if he lived on an uninhabited island he would be perfecting his poems with the same zeal as among a circle of literature-lovers. We must prove that Wieland was speaking from the heart. Russia is for us uninhabited, and our disinterested labor will prove the high morality of our thought. I read *Tsar Saltan here*. This is a completely Russian fairy tale, and, I think, that is where its shortcoming lies. What sort of poetry is it to put Yeruslan Lazarevich or the Firebird into rhyme word for word? And what does this add to our literary riches? Let's leave the materials of folk poetry in their original form, or collect them into a single whole, which would surpass them just as much as a good history surpasses contemporary diaries. The only way to collect poetic materials into a single whole is through a poetic invention that corresponds to their spirit and, as much as possible, encompasses all of them. There is none of this whatsoever in Pushkin. His fairy tale is equal in merit to one of our old fairy tales—and that's all. One might even say it is not the best among them. How far removed is this imitation of Russian fairy tales from Delvig's imitation of Russian songs! In a word, I was not at all satisfied with Pushkin's fairy tale. Farewell, greet Sverbeyev and his wife for me. Write to me as before in Kazan. I don't know if I will be here long. I will try to be in Moscow in July so I can see Zhukovsky and embrace you all the sooner, but whether this is possible I don't know yet.

96. TO SOFYA ENGELHARDT, IN MOSCOW (IN FRENCH).

Nastasya Baratynskaya's younger sister Sofya was one of the poet's closest friends. There are few people to whom Baratynsky writes as openly about the tensions between him, his mother, and his siblings.

[June, before the 19th, 1832, Kazan]

We are going to Mara, my good Sophie, and I am happy enough about it, since the trip was inevitable this year or the next, and the longer we put it off, the more disagreeable it would be. You cannot imagine the rage I feel at times from my mother's conduct towards me and how indignation and the feeling of respect owed my mother battle inside me. My mother's letter, which you will read, at least subtracts from our relations that Radcliffian, Melmothian and, above all, indecent coloration which they are able to assume, which means there will be an honest civility between us. We should leave here on the 19th. We will travel by post-coach and on the 26th or 27th already be in the midst of our excellent family. Farewell, my angel. As things have worked out, we will see each other a fortnight later [than expected], but we can console ourselves that we will be free next year and a few more as well. Add to this the fact that our letters will become noticeably interesting. I kiss you, my dear, good friend, from the depths of my heart. Kiss little Sonichka for me, if you have the courage. Keep well, and write us as often as you have till now.

97. TO IVAN KIREYEVSKY, IN MOSCOW.

[June, before the 19th, 1832, Kazan]

I am writing you for the last time from Kazan; on the 19th I go to Tambov. From now on address my letters: Tambov Province, City of Kirsanov. What you tell me about Hugo and Barbier makes me, if possible, even more impatient to return to Moscow. What has been lacking for the creation of a new poetry are, indeed, new convictions of the heart, an enlightened fanaticism—this, as I see it, has appeared in Barbier. But it's unlikely he'll find a response in us. The poetry of belief is not for us. We are so far from the sphere of new activity that we understand it quite imperfectly and feel it even less. We look at the European enthusiasts almost the way sober people look at drunks, and if their outpourings are sometimes comprehensible to our mind, they have almost no effect on our heart. What is a reality for them is an abstraction for us. Individual poetry alone is natural for us. Egoism is our lawful deity, for we have thrown down the old idols and do not yet believe in new ones. A person who finds nothing outside himself for adoration must sink deeper within himself. For the time being, this is our assignment. Possibly, we might even think of imitating, but there will be no life in these systematic attempts and the force of things will bring us back to a road more natural to us. Farewell, give my regards to your family. One day I'll ask you to rent a house for me in Moscow! One day you and I will sit with our philosophical reveries from 8 o'clock in the evening to 3 or 4 in the morning, not noticing how the time flies! Once I'm in Moscow I hope not to be parted from you for a long time and to give my life the settledness I've long desired.

V.
MOSCOW SOCIETY AND THE MINUTIAE OF LIFE
SUMMER 1832–FALL 1839

The Baratynskys left Kazan in mid-June intending to visit the po-
et's mother in Mara. They stopped on the way in Penza, where they
happened to meet Denis Davydov, and then, for reasons we do not
know, they suddenly changed their plans and returned to Moscow,
or possibly to Muranovo, the Engelhardts' suburban estate.

98. TO IVAN KIREYEVSKY, IN MOSCOW.

[July or August (?), 1832, Muranovo (?)]

Here's *Lapidaire* for you, which I keep forgetting to send. My sister-in-
law will tell you why I didn't send you a letter with her. My justification is
eminently persuasive and it's what I use, or the kind of thing I use, when
corresponding with relatives. Speaking practically, I haven't written you
till now not because I forgot you, not because I didn't have anything to say
to you, but because I prefer conversations to letters and hope to see you
soon. I've started writing my novel, but it's slow going. I've lost the habit
of work, of long concentration. There's something of the wanderer in my
thoughts—a response to the life I've led up to now. I long for a more settled
life, for my Moscow apartment, from which I won't move a step before 3
o'clock every day and will force my mind to again love consistency and
constancy in its thoughts. Farewell, give my regards to Odoyevsky, whom
I like very much. I embrace you. Excuse my previous [laziness] and don't
attribute the infrequency of my letters to anything else.

Ye. Boratynsky

Prince Vyazemsky had moved to St. Petersburg about a year earlier.

[Second half of August (?), 1832, Muranovo]

Without ever reaching our Tambov village, which was my destination, circumstances forced me to suddenly change course to Moscow, so I went in the opposite direction to your package, which is now in the hands of my brother, who will bring it to me himself but not until winter. I was truly touched by this sign of your remembrance. I saw it as attention to a bond that may be distant but where, as you rightly assume, there is much of the soul. I spent a few days in Penza, where D. Davydov had arrived before me. This was right at the time of the fair. As we strolled along the same rows where you had strolled a couple of years earlier, we talked a lot about everything, and I was annoyed at fate for choosing the wrong time and bringing me to Penza two years too late, or you two years too early. Of your many acquaintances, it seems the pretty Zolotaryova girl has the most vivid memories of you. I paid a visit to the "little bare head" whose praises you sang: she lives up to your poem and to her fame. I have nothing to tell you about Moscow. I live outside the city and go into town rarely and as need arises. On my last trip I met Princess Odoyevskaya, who showed me your poem to Aurora Stjernvall, who once inspired me as well. To judge by your poem, she still deserves her name and is as rosy and brilliant as ever. When will I see you? And since [*female name crossed out*] spent the winter in Petersburg, it follows you won't be leaving soon either. At least be in Moscow in your thoughts. You can pass the time wherever you want and where it pleases fate, but to live you must be at home. Farewell, dear prince; again I thank you for remembering me. Belief in your friendship is one of my necessities.

Ye. Boratynsky

100. TO PYOTR VYAZEMSKY, IN ST. PETERSBURG.

[Second half of December 1832 or January 1833 (?), Muranovo]

My brother will give you this letter, and I ask you, dear prince, to receive him with all cordiality. Literary connections are sometimes worth as much as those of blood, and I commend him to you, fully trusting in this thought.

It has taken me a long time to answer your kind, friendly letter, but I am deeply grateful to you for it. You are missed in Moscow. There is no social gathering in which you are not remembered and your absence not regretted. I met your old acquaintance M. Orlov and his extremely kind wife. In what was once your usual circle, your absence is felt even more strongly. D. Davydov sent me the opening of your epistle to him, in which you poetically refashion yourself to his style. He is thinking of galloping over to Moscow for a week or two. Won't you decide to follow his example and ask Pushkin to come with you? Then the word will become deed; then

All the boys will be on hand / from the friendly guild.

I haven't written anything new and am immersed in my old things. I sold Smirdin the complete collection of my poems. It seems this will indeed be the last one and I won't add anything to it. The time of individual poetry has passed and another has not yet ripened.

Please give my respects to the princess and believe in my constant devotion to you.

Ye. Boratynsky

101. TO PYOTR VYAZEMSKY, IN ST. PETERSBURG.

[February, before the 3rd, 1833, Moscow]

Our Muscovite literary brotherhood has come up with the idea of publishing an almanac by Easter, and I, dear prince, have been given the task of requesting your support. Offer us a helping hand in the name of your beloved Moscow. The contributors here are Kireyevsky, Yazykov, Chadayev (in translation), myself, and a few other young men whom you don't know but who perhaps would profit from knowing you. Ask Pushkin not to abandon us but at least to give us some trifle as a sign of his comradeship. I expect that Gogol, the author of *Evenings in Dikanka*, visits you and I'm sure he often sees Pushkin. He's got a lot in reserve. Ask him from all of us for anything he can contribute. Don't forget Kozlov either. In a word, ask around for us with friendly generosity. I am counting on your love for Moscow, for literature, and I am also relying a little on your good will towards certain of the participants. Please give my regards to Pushkin. I am very grateful to him for the part he played in selling my collected poems. I owe it to him that I sold them for seven thousand instead of five.

Farewell, dear prince, I sincerely wish you all the best. My address: by the Arbat gate, the Zagryazhsky house.

Ye. Boratynsky

102. TO SOFYA ENGELHARDT, IN SKURATOVO (IN FRENCH).

In May, the Baratynsky family left Moscow for Mara, where they would stay until the following March. Sofya Engelhardt, meanwhile, took care of their infant son Dmitry (Mitinka) on the Engelhardt estate in Skuratovo, near the town of Chern in Tula Province. We do not know what happened between Sofya and Kireyevsky ("the silly business this winter"). It is likely that the family hoped Kireyevsky would propose to her. In any case, no letter survives where Baratynsky chides Kireyevsky over his treatment of Sofya.

[Second half of June, 1833, Mara]

We have only just now started receiving your letters—that's how unreliable the horrible Chern post office is. Thank you, my dear angel, for everything you write us. Your heart, so good and tender, breathes in every line. Do not preach to me of moderation in my conduct here. I feel magnificent indifference towards everything that happens. *The measure is full* and relations that were once so muddled and difficult have become perfectly simple. Having decided to be neither hot nor cold to anyone, I no longer get upset no matter who it is. I am perfectly polite, completely friendly, and never bring up the past, as if it has been forgotten to the benefit of all. The funny thing is that nobody notices the revolution that has occurred in me, and they still direct at me some of the same juvenile antics of which I've been the dupe for so long. Still, it's quite sad, after thirty years of tenderness, to find yourself being so cold towards those who were the objects of it. The fault lies not with me [*one line is crossed out*]—that is what consoles me. When you cease to love, even with legitimate reason, you always feel a little worse off than before, and you yourself regret it. Where will this letter find you, my dear friend? I would like you to already be in Moscow; if that is so, it will reach you later. Once you are back in Moscow, our correspondence will be entirely regular. And speaking of the great city: I have not yet written to K. [Kireyevsky]; I intend to write him next Friday and now, when I think of it, memories of the silly business this winter are awakened in me and stir my indignation. If I do write to this man, it is only to take him to task for his ill will towards you. Thank you for the good news you give us about Mitinka. You have no idea how delighted I am by your attachment to him. I kiss you tenderly, my angel, be well. God willing, we will see each other again this winter and the time will pass quickly until then. Kiss Mitinka for me.

103. TO IVAN KIREYEVSKY, IN MOSCOW.

As Baratynsky mentioned to Vyazemsky (Letter 100), he had sold the rights to publish his complete poems to the St. Petersburg bookseller A. F. Smirdin. In the spring of 1833, however, the Moscow dealer A. S. Shiryayev took over the publication of the poems; it is not clear why. Perhaps Baratynsky wished to have the book produced in Moscow so Kireyevsky could oversee things while he was in Mara.

[August, before the 4th, 1833, Mara]

What are you doing and why don't you write me? Could it really be because you haven't been able to memorize my address? Admit it: this is a bit of stubbornness on your part, which you can't justify with any sort of dialectics. So you have no excuse, here's my address: *Tambov Province, Kirsanov.* It's quite uncomplicated. I haven't written you before now because of the incredible heat we've been having this year, which has robbed me of all activity, both mental and physical. I keep putting off writing from one post to the next, and so a fair amount of time has passed. I came to our village expecting to find there leisure and freedom from care, but I was wrong. I have been forced to take part in estate management issues: the village became the patrimony, and there's a world of difference between the two. The worst of it is that the business activity is fascinating in itself; you get completely immersed in it whether you want to or not. I haven't thought about literature once since I've been here. I am leaving all my poetic plans until the fall, after the grain has been harvested. Are you doing anything? You wanted to work diligently with the pen, and you don't have my excuses. I hope you didn't give your word to Khomyakov and me in vain. You were recently seen at Berger's. That's very kind of you. Is your portrait a good likeness and will you send it to me soon? Farewell, my respects to all your family. If you see Shiryayev, please tell him that I am receiving the proofs quite irregularly. A sheet should be returned in three weeks and he is returning them in five. If things keep on like this, I won't get printed until next year.

E. Boratynsky

104. TO IVAN KIREYEVSKY, IN MOSCOW.

[October, before the 27th, 1833, Mara]

I thank you for your gift with all my heart. I received your portrait. It is a good likeness, even a very good one, but like all portraits and all translations it is unsatisfactory. It's strange that painters who deal exclusively with the portrait do not know how to catch on the wing, during a conversation, the genuine physiognomy of the original, and copy merely the patient. I remember Berger's soulless system, which he himself once explained to me. In his opinion, the portrait painter must not give free rein to his imagination, must not interpret the copied face arbitrarily but must meticulously follow all material lines and trust the resemblance to this precision. Here too he was true to his system, which is why your portrait is able to thrill anyone who does not know you as particularly as I do, while it leaves me quite happy with what you sent me but unhappy with the painter. About myself I have almost nothing to tell you. I am completely embroiled in the estate accounts. And no wonder: there is total famine here. To supply the peasants with food we need to buy 2,000 quarters of rye. At current prices, this comes to 40,000. Such circumstances can make you wonder. As the oldest in the family, all logistical measures rest on my shoulders. Farewell, my warm regards to all your family.

Ye. Boratynsky

105. TO IVAN KIREYEVSKY, IN MOSCOW.

[November, before the 28th, 1833, Mara]

A few days ago I received from Smirdin the program for his journal with a letter inviting me to participate. I don't know if he will succeed in this venture. Our writers are no match for the French, but there is nothing poorer and paler than Ladvocat's *Cent et un.* Even so we have to help him. His boldness and industry deserve every encouragement. Are you preparing anything for him? Do you know you have a ready, and wonderful, article for a journal? It's your theory of grooming, which you could publish as a fragment. I remembered it recently when I was reading Balzac's theory of walking. Comparing both articles, I found a great resemblance between the two of you in your turn of mind and even in your style, but with this difference: you still have a wide-open field in front of you and can avoid his shortcomings. You have what he had at the start: a conscientious refinement of expression. He noticed its effectiveness and became less conscientious and even more refined. You will remain conscientious and avoid affectation. Like him, you have a need to generalize ideas, the desire to point out how every object and every fact are in sympathy with and correspond to an entire world system, but he errs, I think, in his excessive flaunting of erudition, in the theatrical way he borrows shop expressions from every science. Success has made him spoiled. I also dislike his too-general, too-frivolous sentilism. His constant pretensions to profundity do not entirely conceal his French frivolity. How can a thinker admit he has not reached a single conviction? And what is more, isn't it ridiculous to boast about this! You can be a

Balzac with two or three opinions that give you the foundation he lacks, with a language more direct and quick-witted, and just as clear. Farewell, I send my regards to your family.

Ye. Boratynsky

Do me a favor: find out Pushkin's countryside and town addresses; I need to write to him. I have unsealed the letter specifically to add this.

106. TO IVAN KIREYEVSKY, IN MOSCOW.

[December, before the 22nd, 1833, Mara]

You sadden me with your bad news. What's the problem with your eyes? I hope this letter finds you sighted. I have had occasion to praise seclusion, but not the kind blindness brings. And speaking of seclusion. You raise again the question of which is preferable: a life in society or a reclusive life? Both are essential for our development. We need to receive impressions and we also need to draw conclusions from them. Just as we need sleep and waking, food and digestion. What remains to be determined is the ratio of the one to the other. That will depend on each person's temperament. As for me, I say of society what Famusov says of dining: *You eat for three hours, and in three days it's not digested.*

You belong to the new generation, which thirsts for excitements; I to the old, which prays to God to be delivered from them. You call blazing activity happiness; it frightens me, and I prefer to see happiness in tranquility. Each of us draws these opinions from his own era. But these are not only opinions; they are feelings. Our organs have developed in correlation with the ideas that have nourished our mind. If we each accepted the other's system theoretically, we still would not essentially change. The needs of our souls would remain the same. I do not understand seclusion to mean being alone; I envision

A haven from worldly visits, / locked behind a sturdy door, / but, with a grateful soul, / open to friendship and the maidens of inspiration.

Such will I build for myself sooner or later, and I hope you will visit me there. I embrace you.

Ye. Boratynsky

107. TO IVAN KIREYEVSKY, IN MOSCOW.

[February (?), 1834, Mara]

I apologize for not writing you in such a long time, dear Kireyevsky. The reason for this is, first, the headaches to which I'm susceptible and which have come on me as if on purpose two post days in succession; then, I live amid such worries and find myself under the influence of such impressions (I have told you a little about the calamitous state of my mother's health) that I do not always have the strength to pick up the pen. You wish me to give you topics for literary articles? I long ago lost sight of general questions for the sake of exclusively existing. But why not give you, for example, the very subject I'm speaking of: the social life and the individual life. How much should a person, by the laws of his given conscience, allot to the former and how much can he give the latter? Are solitary needs lawful? What are the proportions and preponderance (*balance*) of the external and internal life in the most enlightened regimes, and what are they in Russia? I would like to see these questions contemplated and resolved by you. I need your help in my relations with Shiryayev. It's been two months already, and I haven't received the proofs. I assume that, for the sake of speed, he has decided to print from my manuscript, without worrying about whether I might have corrections to make. In any case, I am sending you *Eda* and *Feasts*, which I corrected long ago but are only now ready for sending—evidence of that moral laziness which has possessed me for some time now. I am also sending you a preface in verse for the new edition and the title page with a musical epigraph. I hope Shiryayev will agree to an engraving or lithograph of this page. He can do me this favor in exchange for the extra poem I am sending him. I embrace you and greet all your family.

Ye. Boratynsky

I hope your mother and brother are now in good health. We too have been having terrible epidemics all winter and we've all been sick one after the other.

This letter, a postscript to one of Nastasya's, was written, atypically, in Russian.

Baratynsky's collected poems, originally planned for publication in the spring of 1833, had been delayed because of the poet's ten-month absence from Moscow (from May 1833 to March 1834) and, possibly, also because of Kireyevsky's marriage to Natalya Arbeneva in April 1834. In the fall of that year, Baratynsky again left Moscow, either for Mara or Kazan, and it was during this time that he made the final corrections to the proofs. The fact that he entrusted these now to Sofya Engelhardt and not Kireyevsky may suggest the beginning of the break with his friend. The epistle to Vyazemsky he mentions in his letter to Sofya did not make it into the book (Baratynsky would instead use it seven years later as the dedication to *Dusk*). Another five months would pass before *The Poems of Yevgeny Baratynsky*—in two volumes: the first with the lyric verse, the second with the narrative poems—was finally published, in April 1835.

[Early November, 1834, Mara or Kazan]

Here are the proofs for you, my darling. Take care of things for me. In the next post I will send you the epistle to Vyazemsky and an epigram. I completely forgot about my promise because I was dealing with estate business. Here is another task for you. In the 4th chapter of *The Concubine* I had gotten rid of the last passage beginning with the verse "Yeletsky, having seen his guests out." I am going to restore it and am writing about this to the printing house, but I'm afraid they won't understand me. Before you send me the proofs, look at them, and if my wish has not been carried out, send them back [to the printing house] and ask them to explain what the issue is. Farewell, I embrace you. Tell me what you think of my corrections.

In January 1835, Baratynsky bought a two-story stone house on Bolshaya Spiridonyevskaya Street (present-day Spiridonovka) in the Arbat district of Moscow.

[Between June and August, 1835, Moscow or Muranovo]

I spent this past month in great distress, my dear Maman. First, Sashinka fell dangerously ill and we had to take her to Moscow. We had barely returned to Muranovo when Lyovushka proved to be in an even more alarming state and we again left for the city; it was a long time before he was out of danger. Thank God, he is recovering now, but he's still very weak. He had nothing less than inflammation of the chest. I am currently busy with some needed repairs on the house I bought. It is costing me quite a lot, but at the same time I have been more fortunate than most who have made this sort of investment. There was nothing essential that needed renovating. The government has ordered a roadway to be built from Moscow to Yaroslavl which will go past the village we own in the Pereslavl District. This work is supposed to be finished in two years. It will double our revenues and, most of all, make it easy for me to transport to Moscow some magnificent construction timber, of which I own 150 *arpents*. Farewell, my dear Maman. I kiss your hands, as do my wife and your grandchildren.

E. Boratinsky

110. TO HIS WIFE, IN MURANOVO (IN FRENCH).

> June 9, 1836, was the Baratynskys' tenth wedding anniversary. Apparently, he had to make an urgent trip from Muranovo to Moscow to retrieve a wallet.

[June, around the 9th, 1836, Moscow]

I have found the wallet, so be calm. I'm fine, but I'm a little drunk. Strinyovsky and I do nothing but talk of you. He tells me things that make me more and more fond of him. He is a brother to us. I am having him write you himself, and I kiss you tenderly, my angel, as on the first day of my marriage. That's a bit of nonsense: I love you even more now, but one does not know how to say it. Do you know, it's been ten years since our wedding—this is a solemn event! Is this a lease I renew for another ten years? It is the law with no statute of limitations. Farewell, my dear friend, my dear child. Do not badger me over the silliness of my letter. At heart, I am a little sad not to have you here beside me, even though I am in a good mood. God bless you.

111. TO PYOTR VYAZEMSKY, IN ST. PETERSBURG.

> Pushkin died in St. Petersburg on January 29, 1837, from wounds received two days earlier in a duel with Baron Georges d'Anthès over his wife's honor. Baratynsky, in Moscow, would have heard the news no earlier than February 2. Significantly, and unusually for him, Baratynsky recorded the full date of his letter.

February 5, 1837

I write you under the thunderous impression produced in me, and not in me alone, by the horrific news of Pushkin's death. As a Russian, as a comrade, as a family man, I grieve and rage. We have lost a talent of the first degree, one who perhaps had not yet attained his full development, who would have accomplished the unforeseen if the nets set out for him by circumstance had been untangled, if in his last, desperate struggle with them, fate had tipped its scales in his favor. I cannot express what I am feeling; I know only that I am profoundly shaken, and with tears, protest, and bewilderment I ask: why is it so, and not different? Is it natural that a great man, in his mature years, should perish in a duel like some reckless boy? How much does the fault here lie with him, or with someone else, or with an unhappy predestination? In what sudden disfavor towards the emerging voice of Russia did Providence take his eye off the poet who had long been her glory and who (no matter what malice and envy might say) was still her great hope? I was visiting his father at the very moment he was told of the terrible event. Like one gone mad, he refused for a long time to believe it. Finally, in response to everyone's quite unconvincing exhortations, he said, "Only one thing is left to me: to ask God not to take away my memory, so I won't forget him." This was uttered with heart-rending tenderness.

There are people in Moscow who learned of the public calamity with abhorrent indifference, but the sympathetic, shocked majority will soon force them into decent hypocrisy.

If I have not answered your letter until now, it is the fault of circumstances which, perhaps, you already know. I lost my father-in-law and his death has placed many material worries on my shoulders. Also, I wanted to enclose something for your literary anthology with my letter and have been waiting for a minute of free time and inspiration but so far in vain.

Ye. Boratynsky

112. TO PYOTR VYAZEMSKY, IN ST. PETERSBURG.

Pushkin's friends, led by Vyazemsky, were preparing a memorial issue of *The Contemporary*—the journal Pushkin had launched in April 1836—with the proceeds going to the poet's family. Baratynsky would be represented by the masterful meditative elegy "Autumn."

[March (?), 1837, Moscow]

I send you my contribution for *The Contemporary*. The news of Pushkin's death found me on the last stanzas of this poem. Everyone works in his own way. With a lyric poem, I always start by tossing it down with something more than carelessness, in verses sometimes without meter, sometimes without rhyme, thinking only about its development, and only after that do I start refining the details. Thrown onto paper but far from finished, I had put my elegy aside for a long time. Even now there is much in it that I'm unhappy with, but I decided to be kind to myself, all the more because the careless elements I have retained seem pleasing to fate. I commend myself to your friendly remembrance.

Ye. Boratynsky

With the death of Lev Engelhardt in November 1836, Muranovo, Kaymary, and the other Engelhardt properties passed to Nastasya, Sofya, and their brother, Pyotr. The brother, who was mentally ill, was committed to a hospital not long after his father's death, and his sisters became his official guardians and trustees. Most of the business responsibilities for these properties (as well as the Mara estate) fell on Baratynsky's shoulders and took up more and more of his time. Meanwhile, his involvement with literature and, especially, with the Moscow literary world was diminishing. From 1837 on, he wrote only a few poems a year, all of which were published in St. Petersburg (mostly in *The Contemporary*).

It was also around this time that the Baratynskys ended their friendship with Kireyevsky and his mother and even began viewing them as "enemies" (as far as we can tell, the hostility was not publicly expressed and may not have been mutual). The reasons for the break cannot be established with certainty. There were rumors going around that Baratynsky had started drinking heavily, and it seems likely that the poet and his wife believed Kireyevsky or Avdotya Yelagina to be their source (and possibly the source of other rumors as well—see Letter 125). Although there is no firm evidence that Baratynsky was an alcoholic, it is clear that after Pushkin's death and with his own increasing sense of alienation from the literary world, he experienced bouts of depression—as he admits to Pyotr Pletnyov (Letter 116).

There may also have been lingering resentment that Kireyevsky had rejected or in some other way offended Sofya Engelhardt. But this could hardly have remained a potent reason for the animosity after November 1837, when Sofya married Baratynsky's good friend Nikolay Putyata.

113. TO HIS MOTHER, IN MARA (IN FRENCH).

In the spring of 1838, Baratynsky began renovations on his Moscow house. Curiously perhaps, at the same time he planned a trip abroad, to "the German Athens"—a destination that suggests the influence of Kireyevsky and his circle. But the "main goal" of the trip would be Italy, which presumably reflects the poet's deeper yearnings.

[May or June, 1838, Moscow]

I write you from Moscow, my dear Maman, where I am completely occupied by my building work. I am trying to hurry it along as quickly as possible because I have to have everything completed soon. Nothing has more need of the master's eye, and I have plans to be away this fall for a fairly long time. I want to take a look at foreign lands. I'm thinking of traveling around Germany and stopping in Munich—which at present is the German Athens, for it is the home of Schelling, Heyne, Menzel, and nearly all the eminent minds of our time—and then going on to Italy, the main goal of my trip. It will be very hard for me to be separated from my family, but this is a moral duty I owe myself, for there may well come a day when I regret not having done it in time. On September 1st, I hope to be in a stagecoach. I will take the main European road through Livonia and Courland, but will return through Kiev and, God willing, pay you a visit, my dear Maman, with all the defects of the traveler. I tenderly kiss your hand.

E. Boratinsky

114. TO HIS MOTHER IN MARA (IN FRENCH).

> It was possibly the illness and death of his four-year-old daughter Sofya (Sophie) that caused Baratynsky to postpone his travel plans.
>
> *[September, before the 24th, 1838, Moscow]*

You already know, my good Maman, that we have had the sadness of losing our little Sophie. I despaired of her recovery a long time ago, but my poor wife could not consent to abandon all hope and the fateful moment found her still nurturing illusions. We have both suffered greatly. Thank God, we are at present enjoying a certain calm. I have spent the entire summer in worries connected with the building work. I am finally in my own home, but this has cost me a great of deal of pain, and I have promised myself never to do anything of the sort again. You cannot imagine what it's like to deal with Moscow laborers and how far they take their knavery and insolence. I am completely exhausted and believe that if I ever have to renovate a house again, I will fall ill from it. The city is almost completely deserted at the moment. We see no one, or almost no one. This is a time of rest, which I am very much enjoying. Farewell, my dear and good Maman, I kiss your hands with all my heart.

115. TO NIKOLAY PUTYATA, IN ST. PETERSBURG.

> Instead of Germany and Italy, Baratynsky now began planning a trip to the Crimea on the Black Sea—for the sake of his and his wife's health, as he explained to Putyata. As his letter also makes clear, Putyata was now not just a friend and brother-in-law, but also a partner in all business relating to the Engelhardt properties.

[Late February or March (?), 1839, Moscow]

You were probably surprised, just as Sonichka was, by our intention to travel to the Crimea. This has long been a desire of mine, and besides, sea baths are indispensable for my wife and myself. If we are going for any reason, it's for our health. Our trip makes necessary various changes in our shared finances, and I ask you, dear friend, to assume the management of the property that is under trusteeship. You were planning to go this year to Kazan. If you were to do this at the end of April or beginning of May, then we would spend the month of May together in Moscow—except for the ten days or so you would spend in Kazan—and would be able to make all the arrangements.

Concerning Skuratovo, which will also be under your supervision, Ivan has found a manager, a literate sub-officer, to fill his position. I will bring him to Muranovo, so he'll have the right to examine the manager he himself has chosen and, if there should be any matters at all to deal with, he can ride over and take care of them on the spot. The manager gets a salary of 300 and a very modest allowance.

Write whether you will be in Moscow or not. I very much need to see you (now I am speaking solely in a business sense). I need to give you all the papers. Everything would go easily if I could speak to you, but explaining it in writing is almost impossible. If we do not see each other, then I will send you a full power of attorney from my wife for both Kaymary and Skuratovo. I will put the papers in order and send them to you. What's hardest is dealing with the trusteeship. I am thinking of letting your [brother] Ivan Vasilyevich in on their way of doing things; in difficult cases he could handle matters for us. I embrace you, Sonichka, and Nastya, as I look forward to your answer.

Ye. Boratynsky

Do me a favor and deliver the enclosed letter to Pletnyov.

> After Pushkin's death, Pletnyov assumed responsibility for *The Contemporary*. His "anger" would have been caused by one of Baratynsky's poems appearing in a rival publication.

[Late February or March (?), 1839, Moscow]

My dear friend, my always as ever dear Pletnyov! My relative [Sofya] Putyata writes me that you are angry with me. Thank you for this. Someone who is angry remembers and, it may be, loves. The poem published in *Notes of the Fatherland* was torn from beneath my pen by my brother Sergey, whom you may have met, since he's now in Petersburg— that's why it's a little weak in style. For a long, long time there has been no contact at all between us, but for a long, long time I have not been writing verse and that world where we once met and grew close I have abandoned. But can you think I have forgotten the past? If that were true, what would there be to remember? But fate, which in my youth took me away from people, from their customs, from the conditions of worldly life, and rewarded me with friends like you, afterwards cast me, inexperienced and long deluded, into both society and the minutiae of ordinary life. As a husband, I had to learn the things children learn, had to understand relationships, acquire habits, guess at things that others knew as certainties. These past ten years of an existence that, at first glance, has nothing at all unusual about it have been harder for me than all the years of my Finnish imprisonment. I have become weary, have succumbed to gloom. I did not place you on the same level as the people I later came to know, but given these new impressions, whose gradual development and connection are unknown to you—given this long and complicated tale, which has so profoundly changed me—where to begin? How to express myself to a friendship from many years ago, but I don't want to send cold and incomplete lines. Isn't this the reason old people are so taciturn? In the end, what all this rambling means is this: you, your friendship, the memory of the past are precious to me, and if at any moment it has seemed otherwise to you, you were deceived by appearances.

I am sending you a few small poems I tossed off this past week.

I am now busy with all the things that come from preparing for a big trip. My family and I are going to the south shore of the Crimea, where I will spend about a year and a half. I want sunshine and leisure, completely uninterrupted solitude and, if possible, unlimited quiet. I am thinking about taking up the pen again, and if all that has accumulated in my mind and laid itself on my heart finds release and expression, I hope to be a good servant to *The Contemporary*.

Farewell. I embrace you tenderly. Preserve for me your old friendship.

Ye. Boratynsky

117. TO HIS MOTHER, IN MARA (IN FRENCH).

Zinaida, born August 28, 1839, was the Baratynskys' ninth, and last, child. Two children had died—Yekaterina in infancy (see Letter 47) and Sofya at age four (see Letter 114). Their other children were Aleksandra ("Sasha" or "Sashinka," born 1827), Lev ("Lyovushka," born 1829), Mariya ("Masha," born 1831), Dmitry ("Mitya" or "Mitinka," born 1832), Nikolay ("Nikolinka," born 1835), and Yuliya ("Yulinka," born 1837).

[End of August or early September, 1839, Muranovo (?)]

I have good news to tell you, my dear Maman: my wife has given birth. We have a new daughter. She will have the name Zenéide [Zinaida] and promises to be not bad-looking. Nastinka is recovering little by little, though more slowly than she has previously. The timing of the trip we intend to make depended on when she gave birth. We are planning to go to Odessa this fall. My wife's frequent confinements have affected her nerves, and everyone is advising her to take sea baths in the south. The climate should also be good for the children, who are disposed to catching colds, and the city offers everything we need for their education.

I would very much desire it, dear Maman, if you would permit Natalie to come with us. Her discomforts, as the doctors call them, can be cured completely only by sea baths. We would like to spend the winter in Odessa, visit the south shore of the Crimea in the spring, and in early fall hope to have the happiness of seeing you in Mara. This trip is a joy to my imagination, which has long been living in the south and trying to divine it. The ancient coast, it is said, unites the beauties of Switzerland with those of Italy. By chance I found in my father-in-law's library an excellent work by Sestenzevitch on the antiquities of Taurida. It will be our guide in our excursions. Farewell, dear Maman, I ask your blessing for our newborn child and for all the older ones as well, including my wife and myself.

E. Boratinsky

Nastinka is not writing you herself because she is still quite weak.

118. TO HIS MOTHER, IN MARA (IN FRENCH).

[December, before the 18th, 1839, Moscow]

A thousand thanks, dear and good Maman, for the pains you took in negotiating on my behalf, and doing it so well. I am following your advice to the letter and will translate your lines word for word when I write an official response to the excellent Lapat. How happy I am to know that you have been occupied at home by some agreeable cares: I am referring to your refined and stylish rooms, your reupholstered furniture. I very much wish you could cast a glance over the accommodations we have at the moment. They are on the second floor; the rooms are not large, but are arranged almost with luxury and made elegant by virtue of some well-chosen furniture. This was the starting point for my investments. I told myself: in our country, people do not comprehend the poverty that results from the profusion of furniture demanded by fashion today. This is luxury on a small scale, in place of another that is no longer within reach of the wealthy. In other countries, this elegance is now accessible to the majority; with us, it is a source of poverty. Given this fact, I am leasing the main floor of my house to some conceited types and enjoy adding each day to the comforts and charms of my humble retreat, as the money from the rent makes me rich enough to do this. There are others in Moscow who are following my example—a certain family named Koloshin, who got the idea after seeing the good result from our apartments. This has all been quite sudden, and one might say to me: *You are a jeweler, Monsieur Josse.* But do you know what can be said in response? That abuses have shifted, and today a person is only too happy to be able to recall that ego proscribed by education and so often subjected to ridicule, whose total absence has banished all naïveté in social relations and given them an arrogance, an insipidness, a coldness without equal. I am certain that those who are obliged to go into society will be struck by the justice of this remark. Our little society is in good health at the moment. We are fairly happy with the people we have looking after the children. This will come together "little by little," as we say. Gogol, the author of *The Inspector General*, has written a large novel entitled *Dead Souls*. He is supposed to come to Moscow in a few days and I hope he will read us some pages. Farewell, my dear, my good Maman; I kiss your hands with all my heart.

E. Boratinsky

VI.
THE PULL OF ST. PETERSBURG
1840

The Baratynskys' plans to spend the winter in Odessa were never realized. Instead, perhaps because of his more regular involvement with Pletnyov's journal, *The Contemporary*, and very likely encouraged by Pletnyov himself, Baratynsky was now thinking more and more about the city where he first became a poet.

119. TO HIS MOTHER, IN MARA (IN FRENCH).

[Mid-January, 1840, Moscow]

With my Aunt Sofya Ivanovna's convoy we received so many signs of your remembrance, dear Maman, that I truly do not know how to thank you. The dress for the little one is charming; we could not wait to put it on her and thus she took her first promenade through rooms other than her own. Your excellent preserves lend a wonderful atmosphere to the little soirées we often have, and what is more, my wife and Natalie like to indulge in some solitary gourmandizing from time to time. I write you on the eve of my departure for Petersburg. A whim came on me to take advantage of the comfort of stagecoach travel and spend a fortnight with my brother, my sisters-in-law, and my old friends. There is also a practical reason: I am on the point of making an advantageous sale to Smirdin, the only one of our publishers who has capital, of the rights to a third edition of my rhymes, adding the sin of one more volume. The money I receive from this will be of great help to me for my trip to the Crimea. It's been 15 years since I have been in Petersburg, and 15 years, too, since I have seen many of those with whom I once had intimate ties. I will find much that has changed. Perhaps the impression will be sad, perhaps it will be among those that place the final stamp on middle age. One must be willing to accept this. Farewell, my dear and good Maman, I and your grandchildren tenderly kiss your hand.

E. Boratinsky

On February 2, 1840, after a three-day journey, Baratynsky arrived in St. Petersburg. This was his first visit since leaving the city fifteen years earlier. He stayed with Nikolay and Sofya Putyata. His brother Irakly, now a distinguished army officer (he would eventually rise to lieutenant general) and aide-de-camp to the emperor, was also living there with his wife, Princess Anna Davydovna Abamelek-Baratynskaya ("Annette").

[February 3, 1840, St. Petersburg]

I arrived in Petersburg Friday evening by the most beautiful road in the world, in the most comfortable manner, without even suffering from boredom thanks to my traveling companion, who turned out to be a man of sense with the kind of practical knowledge our Russian merchants possess. There's no need to tell you how happy Sophie and her husband were to see me arrive so quickly; the only ones at home were Sophie and Anna Vasilyevna [*Putyata's sister*]. It was she who saw me first, letting out a little cry of joy—entirely natural—and quite ready to throw herself in my arms. There was not a hint of that hostility I had seen in Moscow; she was completely cordial, but even so I tried to bring the past into the open. As for Nikolay Vasilyevich, he received me with such tenderness that I was quite touched; all in all, my first impressions from Petersburg have been more than satisfactory. Upon my arrival, I had word sent to Irakly that I would be staying with the Putyatas. He sent back word that he was ill, and I went to see him straightaway. Indeed, I found him in bed. It was nothing of consequence—just spasms. Annette ran to embrace me. To what degree her embraces came from the heart, who knows. Here I found Lazareva-Biron and her husband, and Prince Abamelek, who was about to take his sister Catherine to the ball. I gave him Natalie's letter. Neither Annette nor Irakly asked for any news about her. What do you think of that? Farewell, my Popinka. I am writing you on Saturday morning. Before dinner, I am going to visit Pletnyov and Irakly, and will dine at his place or at home, depending on whether or not they're celebrating Annette's name day. I kiss you and the children. Nastinka is utterly sweet and seems to have recognized me. Tomorrow, I will give you new details, but right now my head is spinning and I can't put my thoughts in any order at all. I kiss Natalie.

[On the first page of the letter, the following note is written in Russian:]

Having folded the letter, I suddenly remembered a business matter. I forgot to send the receipts with the trustee accounts, and they are always enclosed with them. These receipts are in the middle drawer of my bureau, but the key to it is in the uppermost drawer, where I keep the passports. There are three receipts—two from 1839 and one from 1840: for the mortgage on Kaymary in the amount of 80,000; for Natasha's part of Atamysh, it seems, 40,000; for Muranovo, 16,000. Find them, my darling, and give them to Ivan. Write me if you were able to find them. This omission is worrying me.

121. TO HIS WIFE, IN MOSCOW.

This and the following letters to Nastasya from St. Petersburg were all written in Russian.

[February 4, 1840, St. Petersburg]

I received your little letter, my darling Nastya, and was overjoyed by it. Thank you for writing right after my departure. I continue my Petersburg journal and, for the sake of order, begin with what concerns Moscow. I had a comical clearing of the air with Anna Vasilyevna. She had indeed been angry and this is why: at our party I had been teasing her about Korsakov in the presence of Liza Chirkova: "You completely sacrificed me," she told me, "and it was very awkward for me. And then I had worries of my own and wasn't in good spirits." Now she and I are great friends. On Saturday morning I went out on visits. I went to Pletnyov's, Zhukovsky's, Vyazemsky's. Nobody was at home. My good, my kind Pletnyov came to see me at around 7 after dinner. He hasn't changed in any respect: neither in his friendship for me nor in his general saintly simple-heartedness. He asked me to have dinner with him on Tuesday, "just the two of us." Don't you agree that this invitation is in itself a complete description of the man? He talked to me about his daughter. [*The next line is indecipherable.*] loves and, it seems, is very sorry for [them]. He misses his old comrades: "Now, after many long labors I have independence and, even more, everything is what I wished for, only there is no one to share this prosperity with."

418

He urged me to live in Petersburg. Vyazemsky, in reply to my calling card, wrote me a few kind words, suggesting that he come see me. It was already late and we agreed to meet at the Odoyevskys'. [*Twelve lines are crossed out.*] there I was also introduced to Myatlev, whose comical verses you know: "A roach falls / In a glass" etc. I had expected to find a young rake. But guess what: this man is a dignified court humorist, 45 years old. Zhukovsky began asking me about *his relations*. I answered as best I could. I was introduced to Lermontov, who read a splendid new poem; he is without doubt a man of great talent, but morally he didn't appeal to me. There's something uncongenial, something Muscovite about him. Myatlev read his "Travels of Mme Kurdyukova in Foreign Lands," in verses that alternated between Russian and French. It was great fun and he reads superbly. After this, he entertained everyone with all sorts of anecdotes, but me less than the others, because he reminded me of my brother Lev, who definitely surpasses him especially in taste but also in a feeling for decorum even in this genre. Myatlev closed the evening. I am writing you on Sunday morning. Tomorrow I'll add something new.

122. TO HIS WIFE, IN MOSCOW.

[February 5, 1840, St. Petersburg]

Today, my darling, I have no time to write much. I rose later than usual and am rushing to Zhukovsky, who can only be found at home before 12 o'clock. Yesterday we all dined at Irakly's. In the evening I was at the Karamzins'. I embrace you and the children.

123. TO HIS WIFE, IN MOSCOW.

Although Baratynsky does not mention it here, among the things he discovered at Zhukovsky's were the unfinished articles Pushkin had written about him. As Putyata later recalled: "V. A. Zhukovsky, to whom the sovereign had assigned the task of going through Pushkin's papers, gave Baratynsky one of his hard-bound manuscript notebooks in folio. In it was Pushkin's then-unpublished fragment about Baratynsky. The notebook remained with the latter for a very short time; he was already about to leave and asked me to return it immediately to Zhukovsky, which I did."

[February 6, 1840, St. Petersburg]

I just now received your third letter, my sweet friend, and I see how right you were to ask me to write to you every day. Your little letters are a necessity for me, and this morning I was already waiting with longing for the postman. I read a few passages from your letter to Nikolay Vasilyevich (Sonichka had not yet risen) and he laughed a lot. Here nobody says a word about our enemies, not even Odoyevsky. The princess [Odoyevskaya] told me about the terrible memory she was left with after staying with the Yelagins. She hates Kireyevsky and, it seems, Avdotya Petrovna even more. But I need to tell you everything in order: Sophie K. [Karamzina] is extremely charming; she and I established a certain rapport right away; people say that I was very kind too. The Karamzins have a *salon* in the full sense of the word. In the course of the two hours I spent there, some twenty people appeared and vanished. Vyazemsky was there. Then Bludov arrived. Vyazemsky reminded him of his old acquaintance with me. He very kindly pretended he hadn't forgotten it, saying that we had listened together for the first time to *Boris Godunov*. This isn't true, but of course I didn't contradict him. I forgot to tell you that, after Irakly's, and before the Karamzins, we listened at Odoyevsky's to Sologub's tale "The Tarantass," decorated with vignettes full of art and imagination by a certain Prince Gagarin. The vignettes are delightful, but the tale is mediocre. Everyone was criticizing it. I too joined the critics, but was more moderate than the others. The debate begun at Odoyevsky's continued at the Karamzins' and was the main topic of conversation. The next day (yesterday), I visited Zhukovsky. I spent some three hours at his place, sorting through the unpublished new poems of Pushkin. They are of an astonishing beauty, entirely new in both spirit and form. All his last pieces are distinguished by—what, do you think?—power and depth! He was just now coming into his maturity. *What have we done, Russians, and whom have we buried!*—as Feofan said at the funeral of Peter the Great. More than once my eyes filled with tears of artistic enthusiasm and bitter regret. I dined at Pletnyov's. He is kind and good. We went to the French theater and sat in Princess Abamelek's box. They were presenting *La Lectrice*, with Mme Allan performing. She is pretty, but not extraordinarily so. They say she wasn't in a good mood and somebody had offended her backstage. Princess Odoyevskaya was sitting alone in her box; when her eyes met mine, she motioned for me to join her and I sat with her through the entire first act. That's where we talked about Yelagina and Kireyevsky. I spent the late evening with our relatives. So here you have not a letter, but a journal. Don't tell anyone my comments about [*two words are crossed out*]. I embrace you, my sweet friend, together with the children. Already I long to be home, although I pass the time very pleasantly.

124. TO HIS WIFE, IN MOSCOW.

The references to "Ararat" and the Orient refer to the fact that Annette Baratynskaya's relatives, the Abameleks and Lazarevs, were of Armenian descent. (Russians thought of the entire Caucasus region as belonging to "the Orient.")

[February 7, 1840, St. Petersburg]

Here, my darling Nastya, is a note for Mikhey concerning Chicherin. Send it to his address. I am writing Chicherin directly from here. Tell Sofya Mikhaylovna that the matter is settled. Yesterday was not especially noteworthy. In the morning I was at Vyazemsky's and saw all of Ararat. I was well received everywhere. I was introduced to Khristofor [Lazarev]'s wife, who bears on her face the mark of her Oriental descent, not at all captivating, and who dresses in a way that lets you see for a fact whether or not her breasts are nice-looking. I dined at Sobolevsky's but spent the evening with our relatives. Sonichka asked me to tell you that as long as I'm here and writing you every day, she won't be writing to you. And that's that. Sonichka, thank God, has very much recovered. She and her husband have a very nice life together. It's obvious they love each other very much and have almost the same tone with each other as we do. At home Putyata is a lot more animated than you might think. Every day I value him more. Nastinka has not grown very much, but she is beginning to talk, and she has various *gentillesses.*[*] She's teething now and is a little restless. Today we are all dining at Irakly's. Farewell, my sweet friend. I embrace you a thousand times. I kiss the children. I am having a very good time here. Just imagine: not once have I managed to have a nap after dinner, and I don't even feel the need for it.

125. TO HIS WIFE, IN MOSCOW.

[February 8, 1840, St. Petersburg]

I spent yesterday morning at Vyazemsky's. We spoke about Pushkin. V. went into the details of the social relations that forced Pushkin into the duel. He didn't say anything new. He suggested that I go with him to see Pushkin's widow, saying she is very grateful when her husband's old friends visit her. I intend to go. She lives an extremely solitary life. She goes only to the Karamzins', and that very rarely. I don't know how, but the conversation turned to health. "*Vous êtes un peu malade imaginaire,*"[†] Vyazemsky said to me. I laughed and asked him how he knew this. "That's what people were saying during the cholera. In fact, I'm inclined that way myself." And on this note the conversation, for me a very curious one, came to an end. I told him, however, that I was not at all capable of exaggerating in my imagination any sort of ailment; on the contrary, I'm perhaps too careless and don't like medical treatments. You can see that our friend Kireyevsky—even back then, when our connection was at full intensity—that he or his mother were antagonistic to both of us. From Vyazemsky's I went to visit Vielgorsky, Sologub, and finally Vyazmitinova. She had already heard about my arrival in Petersburg from her maids. She appeared delighted to see me. Then she started complaining that everyone has abandoned her. "*Les Benkendorff ne m'écrivent plus depuis deux ans. Je ne sais pas ce qu'ils font.*"[‡] She had aged, but not

---

[*] Kindnesses.

[†] You're a bit of a hypochondriac.

[‡] The Benkendorffs haven't written me in more than two years. I don't know what they're doing.

a lot. She's still quite youthful. From her place I went to [*two and a half lines erased*]. She was surprised at my being in Petersburg. Altogether I wasn't at their houses for more than half an hour. I spent the rest of the morning at Irakly's, who has completely recovered. Neither he nor she breathed a syllable about Natasha. *On dirait c'est un parti pris.*[*] I find that this in itself is not very decent. I dined with our relatives and in the evening went to the Assembly. I saw the heir, the Grand Duke Michael, and the Duke of Leuchtenberg, who is not as handsome as his portraits but who is nevertheless very handsome and seems even more so when you look at him closely than at first glance. The sovereign, to my regret, was not there. I had gone to the assembly particularly to see the tsar's family. I met a Moscow acquaintance, Brusilov. He was delighted to see me. He was missing Moscow. I met [*one line erased*]. He plays an important role here, not because of his verse of course but in his service, and he tries to make sure you take note of it through the noble unhurriedness of his manners. Tell Pavlov that here, thank God, people are even less concerned about domestic literature than in Moscow. I gave his letter to Odoyevsky last Saturday, but I didn't manage to exchange two words with him at his reception. The Odoyevskys are dining with us tomorrow. Perhaps I'll manage to bring the voice of the Moscow brethren to his ear. Farewell, my darling. I kiss you tenderly. I miss you very much. I embrace the children.

126. TO HIS WIFE, IN MOSCOW.

[February 9, 1840, St. Petersburg]

Yesterday I spent the day quite uselessly. I made a few visits in the morning, but didn't find anyone at home, then dined at Dumé's with the young people, whose number, however, also included Vyazemsky. There were gypsies singing. We all got good and tipsy. They drank to my health. I was touched by this. By the way, the dinner was vile and we paid too much: 65 a person. I'm not spending much money here. Even with this 65, I've still spent less than 1,000. The cabs here are cheaper than in Moscow.

---

[*] One would say they have made up their mind.

Taking cabs from morning to night, I've never yet had to spend more than 60 kopeks, and I haven't been haggling the price. Vyazemsky sat down next to me at dinner and was very kind. I saw the old Vyazemsky in him. In general, he's more cheerful than he was the last time I saw him in Moscow. He was chiding the younger generation for not knowing how to drink and have fun. Then his nephew Karamzin, a bit tight, threw a shot glass on the floor, but it didn't break. "You see," Vyazemsky said, "he could drop it, but he doesn't have the strength to shatter it." Today is Taglioni's benefit. Irakly promised to get me a ticket. I'm starting to feel bored. I'm not used to this uninterrupted ordeal in which I'm spinning. It would be nice to live permanently in Petersburg, having at least one day of rest between two of dissipation. I want to go home, my darling, and I would be ready to leave this very day. Petersburg is pleasant in its lack of unpleasant impressions, and I, of course, would be thrilled to exchange Moscow for it. But here you have fun because it's Petersburg [*one line is crossed out*]; it's too young. I paid a visit to my Uncle Pyotr Andreyevich, who bathed me in tears. He complained terribly about my brother Sergey and the trick he played. Imagine where I saw him later: at the Assembly. I gave him the slip. Farewell, my darling Nastya; I embrace you and the children.

Ye. Boratynsky

127. TO HIS WIFE, IN MOSCOW.

[February 10, 1840, St. Petersburg]

I wanted to write you a long letter, but I won't be able to. Irakly is sitting here with me and it's time to go to the post office. I saw Taglioni. Amazing. I spent the evening at the Karamzins'. I embrace you and the children.

I received your letter where you talk about Timiryazeva. I see her husband almost every day. He will soon be leaving Petersburg.

Irakly has left and I can continue my letter. Yesterday our relatives gave a dinner. The Odoyevskys, husband and wife, and Annette and her husband were there. I have gotten to know the prince and princess well. I'm on the friendliest terms with both of them. We were all together at the theater, where she introduced me to Countess Laval. I won't begin to talk about Taglioni. Everything exceeded all expectation. A blend of passion and grace that cannot be described but must be seen. The unexpectedness, the charm, the truth of the poses: it takes your breath away. At the Karamzins', I saw nearly all of Petersburg's polite society. I met Pushkin's widow. Vyazemsky led me over to her and we renewed our acquaintance. She is as charming as ever and has gained much from being accustomed to society. She speaks neither cleverly nor foolishly, but freely. The general tone of society [here] truly satisfies the ideal one forms in youth, from books, about the height of elegance—complete naturalness and courtesy transformed into moral feeling. People in Moscow don't have the slightest idea of this. Sofya Karamzina and I are in full friendship. Yesterday Zhukovsky teased her to the point of tears. This little scene was very sweet and amusing. She possesses genuine vivacity and unfeigned playfulness, gracefully moderated by a certain respect for decorum. This sets her apart from Annette Blokhina, with whom she shares a great similarity. I have just now received the children's letters and yours, my sweet friend. I myself won't have time to ask around about a governess. I'll pass the commissions on to Annette and Sonichka. I thank the children for their letters. Kiss them for me, each in turn. Farewell, I'm sealing this quickly and then to the post.

128. TO HIS WIFE, IN MOSCOW.

[February 12, 1840, St. Petersburg]

On Saturday I was at the Academy of Arts and saw Bryulov's *Last Day of Pompeii*. All previous art pales before this work—but only art, not the essence of painting. The colors, the perspective, the roundness of the bodies, figures that seem to be coming out of the canvas—everything is beyond description—but I think that someone who studies Raphael, Michel Angelo, or Titian will find in them more thought, more beauty. Bryulov's faces bear a uniform expression of horror and not a single figure is ideally beautiful. I was also in his studio. I saw a beautiful portrait of Zhukovsky, one of Krylov, and a few paintings he had only started. I didn't see Bryulov himself; he is ill. I dined at Khristofor Lazarev's, on Ararat, as Irakly said. It was dreadfully boring, although I was sitting next to Annette. Khristofor hounded me with literary questions and, among other things, tried to get me to tell him candidly who has the greater talent: Nikolay or Ksenofont Polevoy. From the Lazarevs I went to the French theater, to our relatives' box. Princess Odoyevskaya was with them. They were presenting *Le Gamin de Paris*, a play I didn't like at all in Moscow and which I found here to be very clever and sweet. I spent the evening at the Odoyevskys'. This time it was like an evening at the Sverbeyevs'. The pedant Salomirsky started a philosophical debate, and my blood started boiling. On Sunday I dined at my uncle's with my brother Irakly. At 4 o'clock we were finally free and I went to my brother's, where for the first time since I've been in Petersburg I managed to fall asleep for an hour after dinner. At 8 o'clock I was at the home of a certain eccentric named Shishmaryov, who Vyazemsky had introduced me to at Dumé's. He is a very rich man, doesn't know any language but Russian, and is smart and shrewd. He plays the simpleton. He receives his guests (guests from the highest circle) in a chekmen coat and likes to do a bit of drinking and carousing. There were gypsies singing and dancing there, and he was singing and dancing with them. *En résumé*, it was boring. I spent the evening very pleasantly at the Karamzins'. I feel the good will of the whole social world here, and you know what a wonderful effect this has. All of it is making me tired. The life I lead here is too much for me. Farewell, my sweet friend, I kiss you a thousand times. I embrace the children. Tell them I don't have time to write them each separately, but they ask about this so adorably that I wouldn't otherwise refuse to amuse them. I embrace Natasha.

129. TO HIS WIFE, IN MOSCOW.

[February 13, 1840, St. Petersburg]

You haven't written to me in two days, my sweet Nastya, and I was starting to worry when Stremoukhova arrived and told me she had seen you before she left and you are [well], thank God. Countess Laval let me know through my brother Irakly that she would like to get better acquainted with me and would be at home at such-and-such a time. I went to see her yesterday. She is very talkative, and consequently amiable. [*Four lines are crossed out.*] I dined at my brother Irakly's. It was his birthday. Of the Russians there was only me. The Armenians are unbearable. Khristofor Lazarev again ambushed me with literary questions. This time he brought up Professor Davydov and wanted to know what made his course on literature more tedious than Villemain's! In the evening everyone was at our place. Farewell. Sobolevsky has arrived and is distracting me. I embrace you and the children.

130. TO HIS MOTHER, IN MARA (IN FRENCH).

Baratynsky returned to Moscow around February 20.

[Late February (?), 1840, Moscow]

I returned from Petersburg, my dear Maman, with better impressions than I ever expected. I found my old friends as well disposed to me as in the past and made some very agreeable new acquaintances. The Karamzin family are among them. I would have liked to stay another fortnight to solidify my new ties a little, but I was anxious to see my family again. I left Irakly and Annette in good health. When I was leaving Petersburg, people were worried about a corps of 12,000 men, under the command of Perovsky, who were marching on Khiva but of whom there had been no news. Today, we learned that they were forced to retreat, having found the desert covered in deep snow, 30 degrees below freezing, which caused the death of many camels and many people. Seven thousand troops stationed outside Moscow have been ordered to march to Perovsky's aid. This corps will pass through Tambov Province, because it is headed to Astrakhan. This movement of troops will make the price of grain rise again, and that is the main reason why I'm telling you this. My little, or rather, my large family are in good health. We are very happy with the tutor we have. He is an excellent man and thanks to him the children are making noticeable progress. Sashinka has improved remarkably in music. I was very sorry to learn that my dear aunt has been so gravely ill. I wish her a quick and complete recovery. I kiss my sister and fondly kiss your hands.

E. Boratinsky

[As she usually did when Baratynsky wrote to his mother, Nastasya added a postscript. Her note in this case is of particular interest:]

I was very happy with Eugène's trip, my dearest Maman, because of the pleasure he found there and the more than flattering welcome made to him in general, and since news of this kind travels quickly, several people came to see us on the very day of his return, not yet knowing of it, in order to inform me of the effect produced by his arrival and visit [in Petersburg]. He was greeted like a famous celebrity and, according to what several ladies write, he had wild success, or to use the literal expression, he had the colossal success of an amiable man. In writing you this, my dear Maman, I do not fear being ridiculous by repeating such nonsense, since I am certain it will give you a moment of pleasure. I fondly kiss your hands and commend myself to your blessing as do your grandchildren, my dear Maman. Be so kind as to convey my respects to my dear aunt; I hope that her health will be completely restored with the springtime, and that Sophie's health is good. I kiss her with all my heart.

Your respectful daughter,

Nastasie Boratinsky

131. TO HIS WIFE, IN ST. PETERSBURG.

In early May, a few months after Baratynsky's trip, Nastasya herself went to St. Petersburg to arrange boarding schools for two of their children, Mariya (Masha), age 8, and Dmitry (Mitya), age 7. At this point the Baratynskys were planning a trip to Paris in the summer or fall and, probably, a move to St. Petersburg when they returned.

[May 10, 1840, Moscow]

You can't imagine how sad I am that we quarreled when we were saying goodbye. Especially when I'm alone with myself, it's very hard for me. Also, Masha and Mitya's absence is very much felt in the house. Sasha and Lyovushka are sad, and the rooms feel empty. The Englishwoman has arrived. She seems quite decent. I dined at Gogol's; I found the whole brotherhood there except—who do you think?—Kireyevsky and Pavlov. I again found myself on very friendly terms with Orlov. In general, I didn't have a single unpleasant impression. I embrace you with my whole heart. I am rushing to get these lines off to the post office. [*Three lines are crossed out.*] This has taken me time but the letter still isn't ready, and I will leave it till tomorrow. [*Four lines are crossed out.*] Farewell, Nastya. I kiss the children.

132. TO HIS WIFE, IN ST. PETERSBURG.

In this letter, Baratynsky mixes a fair amount of French in with the Russian and even coins a couple of Russian-French hybrid words. Here the French sentences are translated in the body of the letter (in italics), with the original provided in footnotes.

[May 10–11, 1840, Moscow]

My sweet Nastya, I am now writing you at leisure. I feel very much in the wrong before you, but did you really not understand that I felt not the least bit of malice towards you? I was simply making a lot of noise, as if I weren't saying goodbye to you and there would still be time to exchange a few heartfelt words. In this case I forgot about the clock, just as you do sometimes. The point is I'd be feeling sad without you anyway, but this little quarrel adds an unbelievably heavy feeling into the mix. I sit alone with the Demon of a diseased imagination and, maybe, an equally diseased conscience. You know me through yourself. I wait for a few words from you that could calm me, and my best faith lies in the fact that you will certainly write them; well, enough of this: I could go on about it forever. [*Four lines are crossed out.*] I feel the absence of Masha and Mitya so strongly that I no longer think of asking you to leave Nikolinka and Yulinka behind when we go abroad. No, we'll take them with us. Now I make judgments about you through myself. I received the money from Kazan—19,600 and I don't remember how many rubles. Tell Sonichka that I am not using it to settle any accounts until they come to Moscow. In Muranovo everything is ready, as much as possible: today I settled accounts with the plasterer and painter. The house and the wing where Sonichka used to live are finished, as much as possible, for 120+.

Koloshina wrote a very sweet note to Sashinka, which I answered on her behalf. That seemed more tactful to me. At Gogol's dinner, Orlov was drunk and you can't imagine how particularly friendly he was to me. All the *commèring** I did with Vyazemsky has borne the best possible fruit. Orlov and I left Gogol's together. I told him, "Our life is divided into two halves: how should you be with the people you love, and how should you be with indifferent people? Maybe I'll find out in foreign lands. *It's been very hard for me here.*† He mumbled something approvingly. We parted on good terms. At Gogol's, Chadayev also started to *explicate himself with me*‡ and invited me to his Mondays. "Vyazemsky," he said, *"shared some friendly gossip with me, but some unfriendly gossip had to precede it,"* and *(in front of everyone)* I replied to him: *"The best thing to do is follow the precept of Mme Genlis: confine yourself to personal relationships and do not listen to idle chatter."*§ I didn't mean to be witty and spoke from the heart, but later people told me I was very wicked. Apparently, there's nothing more wicked than the truth. *You realize that quoting Mme Genlis to* Chadayev *put him immediately in the category of old men.*¶ I hadn't considered that. I am writing to you Friday evening. Tomorrow I'll add a few more words. I kiss you from afar as I usually kiss you good night.

I continue on Saturday morning. We are all well, thank God. Sashinka somewhere found a letter Lyovushka was intending to send Aleksandra Grigoryevna Koloshina. Here it is: "Madame. I have the honor to inform you that I am no longer occupied with these silly thoughts. I write you so I will not have to blush every day when I am at your house. Lev Boratynsky."

---

* Baratynsky uses a hybrid word (*nakomeril*) formed from the French *commère*: "a gossip."

† *J'ai eu ici bien du fil à retordre.*

‡ Another Russian-French hybrid (*eksplikovat'sya*), from the French *s'expliquer avec quelqu'un*: "to clear the air with someone."

§ "Vyazemsky," he said, *"m'a fait un commèrage amical; mais la commèrage in-amical a du le précéder,"* et *(au milieu de toute societé)* I replied to him, *"Ce qu'il y a de mieux à faire, c'est de suivre le précepte de Mme Genlis, de s'en tenir aux relations personnelles et ne pas écouter les cancans."*

¶ *Tu conçois que Mme Genlis citée à Chadayev le mettait tout de suite au nombre des vieillards.*

I have copied it word for word. Isn't it hilarious! Farewell, my sweet friend. I kiss you, the children, Sonichka and her Nastya. I embrace her husband.

Ye. Boratynsky

133. TO PYOTR PLETNYOV, IN ST. PETERSBURG.

> Nastasya returned to Moscow in late May or early June, having left Masha and Mitya in St. Petersburg boarding schools. In 1840, Pletnyov became the rector of St. Petersburg University and so was in an excellent position to advise Nastasya about the children's education.

[Early June, 1840, Moscow]

I thank you, old friend, for all the trouble you took on behalf of my children, for the good advice you gave to my wife, etc. etc. I am very glad she finally had the chance to meet you. She returned from Petersburg filled with gratitude to you for your friendship. Our relatives the Putyatas have come for a visit. Sophie told me you invited my Masha to visit you on Sunday, not fearing the childish scampering so unusual in your secluded study. I thank you, but my fatherly heart trembles when I think of her pranks. Farewell; be well. God grant we see each other soon.

Ye. Boratynsky

134. TO HIS MOTHER, IN MARA (IN FRENCH).

[July (?), 1840, Muranovo]

Dear and good Maman, must I again be writing to you instead of kissing your hands in Mara? My departure has been delayed by a thousand unforeseen things. Business I could not complete without my sister-in-law [Sofya] Putyata being present, and for which I needed to take advantage of her stay here, has taken longer than I expected. Then there were rumors about danger on the roads due to the desperation of the people dying of hunger—all of this made us decide to delay our trip until just before the new harvest. I hope soon to have the happiness of seeing you again, but our trip abroad is now out of the question. We have just had a number of considerable losses. One of our Kazan villages, 34 peasant houses, burned down, and the grain we had planned to sell had to be used to feed the victims of the fire; we will have to buy seeds in Kazan and Tula to sow on the peasants' lands. Both they and we have, strictly speaking, nothing but orache. No one expected a good harvest, but who could have foreseen that we wouldn't even have enough for seeds! So our wonderful plans have gone up in smoke. At one point, we were afraid the endless rains would end up destroying the spring crops, but, thank God, we now have good weather. People are merrily mowing the lovely grass. Farewell, dear and good Maman; I can hardly wait to be on the road and, with God's help, this will happen soon. My wife and your grandchildren fondly kiss your hands.

E. Boratinsky

135. TO SERGEY SOBOLEVSKY, IN ST. PETERSBURG.

> With the postponement of their travel plans, the Baratynskys decided to move to St. Petersburg at once. A day or so after Baratynsky wrote to Sobolevsky asking for his help, Nikolay Putyata wrote to a mutual friend, Sergey Poltoratsky: "Instead of Paris [Baratynsky] has left for Tambov, but he will be spending the winter in Petersburg. It's closer to Europe and going abroad is more convenient from there. Now is no time to think about traveling, which costs a lot of money."

> *[August, before the 6th, 1840, Moscow or Muranovo]*

Do not refuse my request, my dear friend Sergey Aleksandrovich, although I give you a troublesome task. I am moving with my family to Petersburg and need an apartment by the 1st of September or even a few days sooner. Please take this work upon yourself and find one for me, and if any deposit is required, pay it and I will reimburse you when we see each other in the near future. The apartment I need is, in general, something economical, and here are the main conditions:

— As I don't intend to keep horses, it should be, as much as possible, in the center of town between Irakly and the Putyatas.

— It should come with one servant's room, a kitchen, a carriage shed for one 4-seat carriage, and a cellar.

— Three separate, that is, not communicating, rooms for the children, as well as the usual sitting room, bedroom, and study.

— There's no need for it to be on the 3rd floor, or for the rooms to have high ceilings; in a word, even something the size of Prince Odoyevsky's former apartment.

I assume that such an apartment can be had for some three thousand a year, especially since I was thinking of an apartment for this price in [*illegible name of owner*]'s house by the Horse Guard barracks, which is precisely what I need, but maybe this place is already occupied. In fact, I am so much in need of a prearranged shelter that I don't want to hem you in with any precise conditions. But it's been a difficult year, I'm a man with a family, and from all that I write, you can see that I require the strictest economy.

Do me this important favor and, with your English precision, reply to me at the address: Tambov Province, City of Kirsanov. The sooner I can be certain of an apartment, the better. The moment you can assure me of one, my prepared convoy of carriages in Moscow will start moving.

I am leasing it for a year. Farewell; I write you in the midst of all the bustle of packing. Today I leave for about ten days to Tambov Province to visit my mother, and from there I would like to go straight on to Petersburg.

Ye. Boratynsky

136. TO SERGEY SOBOLEVSKY, IN ST. PETERSBURG.

[Mid-August, 1840, Mara]

Thank you, friend Sobolevsky, for not being too angry at my tedious commission. For this God rewards you without delay. Rejoice and be glad: I found my estate here in such a condition, and received such news from the other properties, that I cannot think of going to Petersburg. I am staying in the village [Mara] for a year; I am surrounded by beautiful steppeland views, but more distant ones are not allowed me. Please thank Dmitry Putyata for me; he was also asking around on my behalf. I am very obliged to you for the interest you've taken in my situation, and I regret that it will still be a long time before I see you. My brother Sergey has gotten a thirst to write you so I yield my place to him.

Ye. Boratynsky

137. TO NIKOLAY PUTYATA.

> Only the opening of Baratynsky's letter is included here. The remainder concerns various detailed financial matters relating to the Engelhardt properties.

[Mid-August, 1840, Mara]

There is such bad news from every side and the coming year is so terrible in its poverty of income and impending expenses that we have decided to give up Petersburg and spend the present year in the village. I am sending a reliable man, my former tutor Mikhey, to get the children. Send them with him, dear friends, in my brown carriage. I hope to see you all in Moscow...

Ye. Boratynsky

VII.
MURANOVO, *DUSK*, AND PLANTING TREES
FALL 1841–SUMMER 1843

> After being forced yet again to change his plans, Baratynsky began
> looking for ways to secure a regular income that would enable him
> both to travel to Western Europe and to move to St. Petersburg.
> So not long after his return from Mara in the spring of 1841, he
> plunged into a number of building projects on the Muranovo es-
> tate—a sawmill, brick works, and the reconstruction of the manor
> house—all with the intention of making his properties as profit-
> able as possible.

138. TO NIKOLAY PUTYATA, IN ST. PETERSBURG.

[Between September and November, 1841, Muranovo]

I have been thinking a long time about the sale of our Muranovo
timber, about why it's not selling even at the average price, and I found
two main reasons: first, buyers so often have the chance to buy timber lots
for next to nothing from the disorganized gentry that the purchase does
them very little honor, representing only 20 percent ordinary interest;
second, we ourselves are afraid of making a mistake in the actual value
of timber that is uneven, incorrectly felled, etc. I initially concluded from
this that a few *desyatinas* at least should be felled by the owner himself
and he should try to sell them as logs and firewood. Then I remembered
a sawmill I had seen in Finland. But first I should tell you that, when I
was thinking about felling our timber lots myself and since I don't know
how to prevent abuses and facilitate sales, I turned my attention to our
Becker, who has a great deal of economic knowledge and as a merchant's
son has maintained various commercial contacts in Moscow to this day.
I proposed that he take it on himself to supervise the timber felling and
the sale of materials in exchange for 10 percent when the takings exceed
600+ per *desyatina*, and he accepted my proposal. I started talking to him

about the sawmill. It turns out they are very common in Courland and quite inexpensive. Once I calculated the unbelievable profit we would get from building a similar mill, I seized on the idea and started working on it right away.

Here is, briefly, my calculation: I measured the most average *desyatina* and calculated 400 stumps on it.

— 400 stumps yields 800 logs (and a little more, since the best trees yield 3 logs).

— Each log yields 4 planks, for a total of 3,200 planks.

— In Moscow, planks of the very worst sort sell for 200 per hundred.

— If we assume a price of just one ruble a plank, then one *desyatina* would yield 3,200.

In addition there remains: the third thin log, which is sawn into boards, and the aspen and birch timber, as well as the flitches, which are sawn into firewood, and the tops, which would be used in household heating and in the brick works I want to build at the same time. On the whole, with the most moderate luck, a *desyatina* should yield up to 5,000+. I found a mechanic, a Mr. Pragst, who built a similar mill at the Narva Falls. He came to see me in Muranovo because at first I was thinking of replacing our gristmill with the sawmill, but it turned out there wasn't enough water. Our mill would be powered by 8 horses.

The outlay:

Machinery	7,000
Exterior structure	1,500
10 saws, sufficient reserves for approx. 10 yrs	2,500
16 horses	1,600
	12,600

The mill will yield 500 planks a day; it is possible to fell up to 25 *desyatinas* in a year. In five years, the whole operation will be finished. If sales are successful, then I will install another mill, which Pragst promises to build me for 5,500, and then I can fell the timber in 2½ years.

You see what meager capital is needed for the most splendid results! I hope you won't hesitate to go half and half on the losses against the profits of the enterprise, but I ask 10 percent for my idea and for my trouble when a *desyatina* brings in more than 1,000.

The contract with Pragst is already done. I am about to work on the exterior structure.

The main annual expense will be the feed for the horses, but part of this will be offset by better fertilization for the fields. My hope is that all the yearly expenses will be covered by the income from the brick works alone.

Farewell, this long business letter has made me dead tired.

The main thing is this: we need to sell goods whose price is not defined by standing timber. When it is turned into planks, into firewood, you sell it cheaply but you sell it like grain, and timber is people's first necessity after grain.

Don't be surprised at the enormous profit I'm hoping for. Sawing 400 stumps into planks by the usual method costs the buyer up to 3,000. On top of that, he pays for it to be stacked and sawn into logs, which with me will be done by our own people. Add to this the price of the timber itself and you won't have any doubt left at all.

The brick works will start operating with hired labor. They take 7+ per thousand… Scrap wood, which would have been wasted anyway, will be used for baking the bricks.

Obviously, we're no longer going to Kazan. We're leasing a house from Mme Palchikova, in Artyomovo. Sonichka knows this village; it's three versts from us and at the same distance from the forest as Muranovo.

Concerning the management of the Kazan estates, I seem to have found a reliable method for introducing the quit-rent system there while avoiding its inconvenience: nonpayment of rent. I'll tell you my idea another time.

I hope this year to arrange all our economic affairs, including the trusteeship, in such a way that they won't give me too much bother in the future and I'll be able to get back to my previous occupations, which I'm more accustomed to.

We are all well, thank God. I, by the way, am as cheerful and happy as a sailor in sight of the harbor. God grant I don't make a mistake.

139. TO HIS MOTHER, IN MARA (IN FRENCH).

In the fall, the Baratynskys began renting a house on the nearby estate of Artyomovo. They would live there for nearly a year, with Baratynsky overseeing the construction of the sawmill, brick works, and a new manor house in Muranovo, just a few miles away.

[Second half of November or early December, 1841, Artyomovo]

We live in such profound solitude, dear Maman, that the only news I can relate to you concerns our health, which, thank God, is good. A suburban Moscow estate in winter is a retreat of a peace more profound, a silence more absolute, than the countryside in the Russian interior. I must tell you that winter here is in full swing: the ground is covered in snow and the sleigh paths are established. We had wanted to repair a four-seat *vozok** to use for our occasional trips to Moscow, but we have given up the idea because of the side roads, which in this heavily wooded region are so narrow it is impossible to reach the main road in a large carriage. These side roads are nothing more than the barely visible tracks of the peasant's sled on the rare visits he makes to a neighboring village. All the manor houses are empty. We have so little expectation of visits that in the house we have leased—a large house built in the old manner, which is to say, with a very inconvenient layout—we have left only one entrance open, the servants' entrance, both to protect ourselves from drafts and to have room for our entire household, which now includes a French governess who also gives music and drawing lessons and a teacher of Latin, Russian, and mathematics. The vestibule, whose door onto the front steps is sealed shut, is the French lady's refuge. Our time passes in the most complete uniformity. The hours take their color from the children's different lessons and are marked especially by the different pieces of music they are learning, which tell us where we are in the day. Sashinka, it seems, has a true talent for drawing. After only a few lessons from her teacher, she

---

* A type of covered sleigh (Baratynsky uses the Russian word).

has made astonishing progress, and the teacher is quite mediocre. One can hope she will one day be able to perfect her abilities to an uncommon degree.

As for me, I have been occupied this whole time with my [saw]mill. The exterior construction is finished, and in 15 days I will have the machinery operating as well.

I hope, dear Maman, that this letter finds you in good health. I kiss your hands with all my heart as well as those of my dear aunt.

E. Boratinsky

140. TO HIS MOTHER, IN MARA (IN FRENCH).
[December (?) 1841 or January (?), 1842, Artyomovo]

The news Aleksandr Antonovich brought me from Mara, and from you, my dear Maman, was most agreeable. It was a happy accident that took me to Moscow on the very day of his arrival. We chatted for a long time. Ever since I've been busy with the venture I told you about, I have often been in Moscow. It has required a small loan, which, however, has not been easy to arrange, since money is scarce. I hope to succeed; I have all I need for success. I am going to turn my timber into planks, which are easy to transport and have a set price, by a method that is much less expensive than the usual method. I was given 400 [rubles] per *arpent*. I can now get more than 5,000. I have got our Becker interested in this business. As soon as the machinery is ready, he will quit his post as tutor and begin supervising the works. As the son of a merchant, he has maintained some commercial ties in Moscow. He will help with the turnover. I hope to be free this spring and have all the means I need to move to Petersburg. I fondly kiss your hands, my dear Maman, and commend myself to the memory of all my relations.

E. Boratynsky

[March 8, 1842, Artyomovo]

Yesterday, March 7th, my name day, I sawed the first log at my sawmill. The planks are excellent in their cleanness and regularity. It is almost impossible for the saws to break, as the precautions taken in this latest invention are so satisfactory. The machinery is powered, not by 8 horses, but by 4.

Twenty *desyatinas* of forest have been felled. Altogether, including all expenses, a *desyatina* yields more than 1,000+, apart from knotty wood and the remaining standing young forest, of which more than half will be good wood in about two years, so that when the operation is complete, it will be possible to get another 300 or so rubles from each of the already-felled *desyatinas.*

In a few days I will send you 3,000+ from the Skuratovo revenues. The remainder you will have to receive in installments over the course of the entire year, since we are selling almost our entire spring crop to the peasants, and the money for this we hold back every three months from the amount issued by the treasury for the post-horse system. I embrace you both and the little ones.

Ye. Boratynsky

142. TO NIKOLAY AND SOFYA PUTYATA, IN ST. PETERSBURG.

On April 2, Emperor Nicholas I issued a "Decree on Obligated Peasants," which allowed landowners to make binding contractual agreements with their peasants regarding land allotments, labor, and rents. The decree provoked fears among the nobility that riots would ensue. In his note to the first publication of the following letter, in 1867, Nikolay Putyata wrote: "[Baratynsky's words] testify to the sympathy he nurtured for the emancipation of the peasants and his hopes for this. The eradication of serfdom constantly occupied his thoughts. In his conversations with me on this subject, he expressed the opinion that the only way for emancipation to happen should be by allotting land as the peasants' own property while compensating landowners through a financial operation, but what sort of operation, he would add, 'this I won't attempt to suggest: finances aren't my business.'"

Christ is risen! I wish you a happy holiday, which we, for our part, have begun satisfactorily. At 3 in the morning we were at mass in the neighboring village, broke our fast, and slept. I am writing you on Easter day itself.

After a moment of hesitation we decided to stay where we are, since if something happens (which, certainly, can be expected) we have a refuge in Moscow and, even closer, in Trinity, where, by the way, our police station is also located, as is our local government, which undoubtedly has been given the necessary assistance in the present circumstances. The wording [of the decree] is excellent. It would be impossible to approach the matter more intelligently, more cautiously! Blessed is he who comes in the name of Lord! I have sunshine in my heart when I think of the future. I see, I sense the possibility of completing a great work both quickly and peacefully. Farewell, I embrace you and your little ones with all my soul.

Ye. Boratynsky

143. TO NATALYA BARATYNSKAYA, HIS SISTER, IN MARA (IN FRENCH).

[April, before the 25th, 1842, Moscow]

I learned, dear Natalie, from one of Sophie's letters that you were indisposed, but since she was speaking in general about illnesses going around, I assumed it wasn't serious. I see that you were more ill than I had believed; like you, I am very grateful you are feeling better and have a good appetite. Thank you for all the details you give me. I am happy that Lise has finally made a decision. It was long overdue, and she has still come out of it cheaply.

You receive the Moscow newspaper. You are familiar, then, with the remarkable decree, so admirable in its restraint, in its foresight, which, without seeming to, resolves the greatest of difficulties. [*Indecipherable.*] All my prayers are for the one who has not feared to attempt this most difficult and most beautiful work. The respective rights [of landowners and peasants] are, to some degree, already defined and here is the touchstone. I have published a little volume of verses [*Dusk*] and, although you already familiar with almost the entire contents, I will send you a copy. Adieu, dear Natalie, I kiss you tenderly and wish you a happy holiday [*Easter*].

E. Boratinsky

Nastinka kisses you and offers you her best wishes for the holiday. She does not write you herself because she is very tired.

> In May 1842, Baratynsky's collection of verse, *Dusk*, was published in Moscow by the book dealer Auguste Semen. Unlike Baratynsky's previous poetry collections (in 1827 and 1835), this was a slim volume of only twenty-six poems (including the dedicatory poem to Vyazemsky) and was subtitled as a single "work" (*sochineniye*). Also unusually, the spelling of the author's surname was the one the poet used regularly in his private correspondence but never before for his published verse: *Boratynsky*.

144. TO PYOTR PLETNYOV, IN ST. PETERSBURG.

[May, before the 26th, 1842, Moscow]

I am sending you, dear friend Pyotr Andreyevich, a copy of my *Dusk*, and with it more than ten other copies to be delivered to various people. I know I am giving you a very tedious task, but for the sake of our old ties I'm not letting myself feel too ashamed about it. Some copies here are addressed to old comrades with whom perhaps you're no longer in touch. Give them to Lev Pushkin; these are mutual acquaintances of ours. Don't refuse to write me a few lines with your opinion of my little book, although almost all the poems have been published already—collected together, they should more vividly express the poet's general direction, his general tone. I embrace you with all the feeling of our now more than twenty years of friendship.

Ye. Boratynsky

My address: Moscow, Spiridonyevskaya Street, in my own house. And let me know yours: I heard you bought a house on Vasilyevsky Island.

In mid-May, Nikolay and Sofya Putyata, with their eldest child, Nastya, left on a trip to Germany and Italy. Their two other children, Olga (Olinka) and Yekaterina (Katinka) were left in the Baratynskys' care.

[Late May, 1842, Artyomovo or Moscow]

Your children, thank God, are well. All will be done exactly as you write in your letter, dear friend. The revenues, as much as they are coming in, will be deposited in the Trustees' Council. Tell me: is the grain left in the Treasury meant to be sold when the prices are high or as a reserve for the peasants? Then I'll know how to arrange things. Your letters, dear Sonichka, did us much good. We read them with heartfelt gratitude, with complete affection towards you for your efforts to cheer us up and dispel the diseased dreams of our imagination, which, however, have proven to be not entirely dreams. Our suppositions are now being strangely justified. We are now no longer the only ones who suspect the existence of an organized coterie. It is being railed against by its new victims in Moscow. Nastinka, who doesn't have time to write you today, will tell you the whole thing in detail. Annette Blakhina is not going to the Caucasus but to Staraya Russa to hunt for bridegrooms, which she does not conceal from anyone. I feel very sorry for her poor daughters. We saw her when we were in Moscow yet again on our own endless affairs and some tasks we were given. We finally found a German woman for [*indecipherable*], and found a drawing teacher for ourselves for 100 rubles a year—a genuine artist who was living in such poverty that before we could take him into our house we had to help him find some suitable clothes. What's remarkable is that he's German. We are all well, thank God. I'm at work on estate business. The house is going up; the wood is being sold. In the fall I will be planting trees. On your way back, come to Moscow and visit us and our new home. I'll enjoy bragging about the fruits of my activity, if God blesses it. Farewell, I embrace you on behalf of myself, Nastya, your children, and my children. Drink good health in the waters of Marienbad and enjoy making good use of the European air.

Ye. B.

146. TO PYOTR VYAZEMSKY.

The epistle to Vyazemsky that opens *Dusk* as a dedication had originally been intended for the 1835 edition of Baratynsky's collected poems (see Letter 107).

[Between late May and July (?), 1842, Moscow]

This small collection of poems [*Dusk*] was consigned to printing almost if not solely to take advantage of your permission to publish the dedication. Accept them both with your usual good will towards the author. Please deliver the enclosed copy to Princess Vera Fyodorovna [*Vyazemsky's wife*]. I will consider myself happy if my offering is even a little pleasing to her.

Ye. Boratynsky

147. TO HIS MOTHER, IN MARA (IN FRENCH).

[July (?) 1842, Artyomovo]

The praises you give my book, dear and good Maman, are for me the sweetest and most flattering I could have received. So I have let myself savor them with all that naïveté, all that good sense of pleasure, to which I am susceptible. At present, I am quite far from being in a literary mood, but I greet from afar the time when my building work will be finished, when I will have fewer practical concerns (a point of rest that is perhaps imaginary), but which smiles on me with the idea of resuming my former occupations. You think I am settling in the countryside for a long time. My great activity is, at heart, nothing but a great need for peace and tranquility. Our house at present has all the atmosphere of a little university. We have five foreigners living with us, among whom chance has brought us an excellent drawing teacher. Our inexpensive mode of life and the profits we expect to reap from the exploitation of our forest allow us to do a great deal for the children's education; meanwhile, they and their teachers enliven our solitude. This fall, I will have a pleasure new for me, that of planting trees. We have a fine elderly gardener who loves his work, and I am relying on his good advice. Farewell, dear Maman. I tenderly kiss your hands, as do all your grandchildren.

E. Boratinsky

[First half of August, 1842, Artyomovo]

It's been an infinity since I last wrote you, dear and good Maman; in the agitated, restless life I've had this summer, I kept waiting for a good moment to write a letter, but it never came. I have thrown myself into enterprises that brought me more trouble than I could have foreseen, in particular, formalities about the trusteeship, which I didn't expect and which have given me many problems. Thank God, everything has been ironed out little by little, and all I have left now are common worries, which cannot help being very complicated. In the course of the year I've spent here [*in Artyomovo*], I have set up a sawmill, turned 25 *arpents* of forest into planks and firewood, and almost finished building a house. The new house in Muranovo already has a roof and is plastered on the inside. What remains to be done are the floors, doors, and window frames. It is a very pretty thing: a little improvised Lyubichi. I hope to be able to live in it by the end of August. I've had a lot of disappointments: of the six men I brought from various villages to work on the mill, who during the summer had to help on the construction of the house, three have been constantly sick and are at this moment in the hospital. Nevertheless, things are going rather well. I got more than 50 rubles a quarter for the millet I had delivered from Vyazhlya, and 28 rubles for the wheat from Skuratovo. Throughout this time I've always had as many as fifty workmen to feed, and at the moment I have thirty of them. The capital represented by 25 *arpents* of timber at current prices proves that I was not mistaken in my calculations. I am looking forward to September, which is when there are buyers for this type of merchandise, and with a little luck, I will be able to congratulate myself on my activity. I'm writing you pure Balzac here, and indeed, I think this winter I will attempt a novel in his genre. I kiss your hands tenderly and promise you not to undertake anything from now on that could make me unlearn writing.

E. Boratinsky

149. TO PYOTR PLETNYOV, IN ST. PETERSBURG.

[August 10, 1842, Moscow or Artyomovo]

I am late in replying to you, my old and good friend, but do not reproach me with ingratitude. Your letter found me in the midst of material worries, which have been absorbing all my time and thoughts—all the more because, accustomed as I am to an abstract and meditative life, I am less capable of the labors demanded by reality. To lead the quiet life of the thinker in actual fact requires a deep and submissive inner acquiescence to certain everyday commotions. I don't have this, but I hope it will come. How little we saw of each other in Petersburg! How much I would like to meet with you not just for a minute, but to live for a while in the same place, to share, as before, our poetic dreams, the diverse revelations of the mature life! Between us are 16 years of distance spent apart, but our brief time together proved that we spent it thinking alike. The physiognomy of our souls has not changed, and if thoughts have taken on the severe coloring of severe years, the heart has preserved almost all of its youthful gaiety, a treasure safeguarded by fidelity to first attachments and the constant purity of our strivings. Circumstances now keep me in a little village where I am building things, planting trees, sowing, not without satisfaction, not without love for these peaceful occupations and the beautiful nature that surrounds me—but my better, if distant, hope is Petersburg, where I will find you and our shared memories. The goal of my current activity is to acquire the means to live permanently in Petersburg, and I almost do not doubt I will achieve it. Beginning this fall I will have a good deal of leisure and, if God grant it, I will again set to work on rhymes. I have many ideas and forms in readiness, and although the complete indifference to my labors on the part of the Mssrs journalists hardly spurs me to literary activity, I am, by God's grace, even more indifferent to them than they are to me. Farewell, I embrace you tenderly. My friendly regards to Grot.

P.S. The delivery of my *Dusk* to different places entailed certain expenses. Permit me, as a favor, to settle accounts with you. Unseal the package to Lev Pushkin: there is a copy for Natalya Nikolayevna [*Aleksandr Pushkin's widow*]. I had assumed he was definitely in Petersburg and wanted to lessen your trouble by entrusting him with the copies for his relations and circle of acquaintances.

150. TO HIS MOTHER, IN MARA (IN FRENCH).

In the fall of 1842, the Baratynskys moved from Artyomovo to the new house in Muranovo.

[Mid-December, 1842, Muranovo]

If I have any excuse for not writing to you in such a long time, my dear Maman, it is extreme fatigue and nervous collapse caused by our countryside move, which, strictly speaking, was not finished until now. Every day there is something to be done and the noise of the hammer has not yet stopped ringing in the house. The house is attractive and comfortable, but I am still not used to it and am far from enjoying that pleasure of possession, of the fruit of one's labors, of satisfaction in a work accomplished, of which I have heard people speak. That's fine when you have put six days into it, but six months is something else, and you reach the summit a little bit jaded. Our way of life is always the same: the children's lessons follow in succession with punctuality and in a way mark the distribution of our hours. Our older ones delight us with their progress. The youngest have not yet reached the age when they enjoy learning, but they too are advancing little by little. My timber trade is going rather well. This is a completely new activity for me and so to a certain degree it is fascinating. Judging from the news I've received, we've had an altogether good harvest, but I expect that the prices, except for the rye, will be rather low. My living in the countryside and a little success in industry are what allow me to hold back from selling the low-priced seeds and so create a reserve, which I have wanted to do for a long time. With God's help, this will bring me large profits in the future, a regular and sufficient source of revenue. Here we are almost at Christmas. I wish you a happy holiday, dear Maman, and the same to my aunt, my sisters, and my brothers. May God keep you all in good health. I kiss your hands with all my heart.

E. Boratinsky

[Between January and March, 1843, Muranovo]

Dear Maman, I have been slow in responding to one of your kindest letters. Natalie and Sophie's arrival gave me delightful distractions, which, in keeping with the eternal injustice that governs the world, have been felt by the Kirsanov mail. My letter will probably anticipate Sophie's arrival by a few days. She is bringing you a few literary novelties. There have been only a few this year. *Consuelo* and *Zanoni* are among the more remarkable ones. The European mind is turning towards mysticism. The material revolution is over. God grant that this moment of fatigue is the sleep that precedes a new activity for poetry, whose presence alone testifies to the happiness of nations and their true life. Annette came to see us in the countryside and at the moment we have some gentlemen from Yaroslavl staying with us who bring us news from the city and from Irakly. They say that he and Annette are extremely well liked in their city. They speak of my brother's tactful leniency and the sociability that Annette's character lends the city. Nobody feels sorry for the Poltoratskys. I said that my brother's fortune does not allow him to do everything that his predecessor did for the pleasures of society. They answered that only now, thanks to Irakly's and his wife's style, has the social scene come to life. In all they have said to me, I see real enthusiasm. I hurry to pass these details on to you since I know how much they will please you. I kiss your hands, dear Maman, and return to our guests.

E. Boratinsky

[April, around the 11th, 1843, Muranovo]

The great holiday [*Easter*] is upon us, dear Maman. Accept my felicitations and good wishes of every kind, which I have for you. I send felicitations also to my good aunt, my sisters, and my brothers, and the rosy scamps of the new generation. Your name day is coming and I wish you much sunshine so the trees and flowers in your garden come to life and your grandchildren can run around at their ease. We are having passable weather; the sky is blue, but it's still cold out. A fair bit of snow remains on the ground and it freezes at night. The children's great pleasure is horseback riding between three and four o'clock. Taking walks on foot is still impracticable. Springtime will bring me distractions in the form of new labors. I have a few building projects to finish and many excavations. After this comes work in the fields, which I also take part in, since I can't leave the house without finding laborers at their work—our little land can be encompassed in a glance. I enjoy giving a few orders for them to make mistakes, to give the foreman the satisfaction of pointing them out to me and thus teaching me. Do you know, this is the only way to get these people to tell you what they know? The total revenue we can make here is so small that you don't lose much if you make a mistake. As for the forest venture, the felling this year has brought in results even more satisfying than the first year. I am now almost certain I did the right thing. All I fear now is a drop in prices, which is not likely. The children's studies are going splendidly. They have profited greatly by the regular lessons they get thanks to our staying in the countryside. For music, we now have Mme Field, who does not play as well as her husband but who knows his method and those little tricks of the artist, which are often his great resource and which conjugal love confided to her. I tenderly kiss your hands, dear Maman, and ask your blessing for all of us.

E. Boratinsky

153. TO HIS MOTHER, IN MARA (IN FRENCH).

[June (?), 1843, Muranovo]

Our unchanging life, which, thank God, is devoid of events, has until now been the reason for the rarity of my letters, my dear Maman, but for some time the complete opposite has been true. I've been on the move for a month now. I made one trip to Tula Province to survey our property there and another to Vladimir Province for the same purpose. I was fortunate enough to come to terms with my neighbors without making many sacrifices. But as luck would have it, I was obliged to race around the country right when Varinka and Natalie were in Moscow, which meant I did not have more than a few moments to give them. I heard Liszt perform and was not as happy with him as I had hoped to be. The rapidity of his playing was beyond all imagination and at the same time beyond the means of the piano. The notes follow each other so closely that, to the ear, they merge together in a confused drone that does not please. This rapidity takes the wind out of the instrument. What is more, I do not find in him a true feeling for music. He spoils the most beautiful motifs by adding embellishments that are without point and without ideas. His *fortes*, his *piano pianissimos*, while marvelous in themselves, are without effect because they never serve to express a true musical intention. He intersperses improvisations but is merely playing scales. One constantly feels as if he's testing the piano in order to buy it. I much prefer Thalberg. Here Liszt was the object of ovations that were doubly ridiculous: first, it was an enthusiasm of imitation so as not to lag behind Berlin, and then, even if it was genuine, it went beyond all measure: one could not have done more for the savior of the country. It was reason enough to be disgusted by fame. Farewell, dear and good Maman. Your grandchildren are well and tenderly kiss your hands.

E. Boratinsky

With sufficient revenues now coming in from his timber business, Baratynsky was finally able to embark on his long-awaited and twice-postponed trip to Western Europe. In early September 1843, he and his family arrived in St. Petersburg, from where they would leave for Germany. They stayed, naturally, with the Putyatas.

154. TO VYAZEMSKY, IN ST. PETERSBURG.

[September 10, 1843, St. Petersburg]

I am very sorry I didn't think to give you the address of Putyata's new apartment, thus depriving myself of the pleasure of seeing you today. Tomorrow I'll be running errands the whole morning and so I, along with my hosts, come to you with a most humble request: do not refuse to dine with us. You will see, among others, the Odoyevskys. We are gathering at 5 o'clock. In any case, I will not leave Petersburg without seeing you again and receiving your blessing for my European pilgrimage.

Ye. Boratynsky

155. TO HIS MOTHER, IN MARA (IN FRENCH).

Baratynsky was traveling with his wife and three of their children, Aleksandra (age 16), Lev (age 14), and Nikolay (age 8); their other children stayed behind with the Putyatas.

[October, around the 22nd (NS) / 10th (OS), 1843, Dresden]

It's now been nearly eighteen days since we've been on the road, my dear Maman. A six-seat stagecoach, which we arranged in Petersburg, took us to the border, or rather, to the first Prussian post-house. Since then, we have been taking coupés, where our family is separate, even though in the stagecoach there are still four seats almost always occupied. This manner of traveling is very lively: you see each other when the horses are changed and at mealtimes, and exchange a few words. The roads are superb and the post-horse service operates with admirable regularity. We spent two days in Königsberg and eleven in Berlin. I had a letter of recommendation for the secretary of our embassy, which I made use of. I was introduced to our ambassador, Baron Meindorff, a very courteous and amiable man. He invited me to dine at his home with Count Bludov, whom I have known a long time. He has been traveling with his daughter and is now returning to Petersburg. I spent an evening with them.

We took our first trip by railway when we went to Potsdam. We saw the house where Voltaire stayed and the little apartments of the Great Frederick—indisputably very great as it was he, essentially, who created Prussia and laid the groundwork for its administration today. Berlin is a charming city, not as beautiful as Petersburg but better proportioned. Life there displays the most extreme orderliness. All relations are foreseen and fixed—commercial ones by time immemorial, social ones by customs never broken. There, without suspecting it, the citizen submits to the same discipline as the soldier. After a few days, in fact, you adopt the city's way of life and find yourself enjoying the extreme security that comes from this complete absence of the unforeseen. We are now in Dresden. Needless to say, we have seen the famous gallery. Raphael's *Madonna* is a triumph of the Christian idea and one never tires of admiring it. It is best to say nothing about it and simply let the generations come, one after the other, to prostrate themselves before this divine masterpiece. I cannot help mentioning another work, less celebrated but perhaps just as great in its sublime sorrow: this is the so-called *Christ of the Money* by Titian. We have been to see one of the prettiest sites in the area around Dresden, the Tarente Valley. Despite the advanced season, it is still delightful. I have been taking great pleasure in my impressions of our trip and at least as much in those of the children, who receive their impressions with all the vivacity and freshness of their age and so complement and enhance our own. We are returning to Leipzig, where we will take the stagecoach to Frankfurt; from there we will go on to Mainz, then travel down the

Rhine to Cologne, from where the railway will take us to Brussels, then on to Paris. I have been telling you only about the pleasant things abroad, but I must absolutely inform you of one horrible impression. This is the tunnel between Leipzig and Dresden. Imagine an underground passage that takes more than three minutes to go through and where the darkness makes you fear you are running out of air. My wife, who is susceptible to feelings of suffocation, made me so alarmed for her that I was quite pale the moment we saw light. She kisses your hands, my dear Maman, and your grandchildren ask you for your blessing so they can understand the arts, whose manifestation surrounds them, and the remnants of nature that modern civilization embalms like the mummies of Egypt, believing they will preserve them and yet unable to do so.

156. TO NIKOLAY AND SOFYA PUTYATA, IN ST. PETERSBURG.

[Mid-October, 1843, Leipzig]

Nastinka was writing to you in Dresden, and I am now adding this in Leipzig, which we have returned to, following your advice. We spent the night here and now are going to Frankfurt on the German "longs," i.e. by long-distance coach. We'll be stopping nights and should be there on the fifth day. I am finding great pleasure in traveling and in the quick succession of impressions. The railways are a wonderful thing. They are the apotheosis of distraction. When they finally encircle the entire earth, there will be no more melancholy in the world. I embrace you, Sonichka, and the children, both yours and ours. When we arrive, I will perhaps relate to you some of the impressions and observations traveling has given me. Farewell until Frankfurt.

157. TO NIKOLAY AND SOFYA PUTYATA, IN ST. PETERSBURG.

The Baratynskys arrived in Paris in early or mid-November.

[Second half of November, 1843, Paris]

My friends, my sisters, I'm in Paris! And thanks to Sobolevsky—to whom I will soon write separately—thanks to his useful friendship, I am seeing more than just the buildings and boulevards here, although the first material look at Paris rewards in abundance a long journey's labors. I already had a look at the Faubourg St-Germain and saw some of the literary men but, in my view, the most remarkable thing in France are the ordinary people themselves, who are welcoming, intelligent, cheerful, and filled with an obedience to the law—they understand all its importance, all its social benefit. I was surprised in Berlin by the civic order, precision, and unquestionable nature of relationships. How amazed I was to find the same thing, but to a higher degree, in populous Paris, on its crowded streets, in its numberless transactions. In Germany it was still possible to sense a certain discontent with the laws of the social order that everyone obeys: here people from the lowest ranks of the rabble are proud of them. A few clear ideas about community have become the birthright of every person and constitute such a mass of sanity that it is difficult to think the common people could be led astray from the path of their true well-being. Meanwhile, the [political] parties are in a ferment. I do a lot of listening and a lot of reading. The people who came from the ranks and fill the newspapers and salons are not firm in their opinions. Here the defectors are less base than it seems at first glance, and many of them, when taking an opinion opposite to what they previously expressed, do so with a completely sincere inconstancy. These days everyone is occupied by the question of education: who should be in charge of it—the clergy or the university? An eminently important question, involving aspects of legitimism... Lamartine has published a ridiculous diatribe, which I was forced to praise among the company with whom I had begun an acquaintance. The opposing party's responses, deferential to the poet's talent, are very amusing. The professors have begun their courses and, no matter what they speak about, whether anatomy or chemistry, they find a way to touch on the question everyone is interested in. We are living in the very center of town. Our address: *Rue Duphot, près le boulevard de la Madeleine, no. 8.* Today I will be at Mme Aguesseau's, tomorrow at Nodier's, and the day after that at Thierry's. For all these acquaintances I am indebted to the Circourts. Farewell, I embrace you and the children. My very best regards to Sobolevsky and Pletnyov. I see A. I. Turgenev almost every day; he's been a little unwell. He reproaches Vyazemsky for not writing to him: "Remind him of me." I see Balabin, a very intelligent, very knowledgeable man, and every time we meet I feel closer to him.

158. TO HIS MOTHER, IN MARA (IN FRENCH).

[First half of December, 1843, Paris]

Dear Maman, I wrote you as soon as I arrived in Paris, but a letter from Petersburg, where they say you sent me a letter that never reached me, makes me fear that mine has been lost in the same way. It contained only my first impressions of the great city, mere repetitions of what other travelers have felt but which are impossible to refrain from expressing, like exclamations that arise upon seeing some striking object, despite the fact that they are the same as everyone else's. Well, we are now settled in, so let me start by giving you our address: *Paris, rue Duphot, près le boulevard de la Madeleine, no. 8.*

We began by putting our house in order, finding teachers for our children, and then I made use of my letters of recommendation. I now have connections with a number of literary people and, especially, with the entire Faubourg St-Germain. I was sent to people from various parties, so little by little I have made acquaintances in the most diverse parts of Paris. The Faubourg St-Germain is generally poor in material means, but it is excessively valued by the fortunate of the day, and everyone knocks on its doors, which are rarely carriage gates. No one has their own townhouse anymore. They all have little apartments, perhaps like the one in which Mme Scarron once received good company. At the home of the Duchess de R., a valet without livery, in suspenders, half-opened the door and announced me, among a circle of aristocrats from the *ancien régime*. This world is prudish to excess, and makes the traditions and polite manners of the past resound like sacerdotal ceremonies whose secrets are known only to the priest. Failing to dominate politics, this world has thrown itself into a puritanism not of morals but of forms. It does not feel restrictive to a Russian who lives in Petersburg or Moscow—in almost the same circumstances—but it is annoying and hateful to the new Frenchman. The ladies of the Faubourg St-Germain read neither Hugo, nor Sue, nor Balzac, but they work in concert with the priests of ultramontanism. This weak party has allied itself with the last efforts of papal Rome. The great question of the moment is to obtain for the clergy the prerogative of educating the youth—to the detriment of the university. The Faubourg lends a hand here, in consideration of the principle of legitimism, equating it entirely with that of the sovereignty of the church, and everything is in movement. Here I visit the Countess de T., the Marquise d'A., the granddaughter of the famous president, connected with the house of the Mortemarts, which ends with her, the Duchess de R., whom I mentioned, the Countess de F., the daughter of the Academician, the Countess de B., the wife of Napoleon's ambassador first to Sweden, then to Spain. She receives the nobility of the empire, and I had the pleasure of seeing Marshal Soult at her home. Finally, there's a Russian woman, Mme Svetchine, who, they say, has the finest salon in Europe since it is the finest in Paris. It is quite true that there is no celebrated person of any sort who might not be seen here, and even today, having become extremely religious, she submits her guests to an overly severe selection. Next come the authors: Alfred de Vigny, Mérimée, the two Thierrys, Michel Chevalier, Lamartine, and Charles Nodier—whom I have seen in his last days, for he is at this very moment near death, but I had a moment of pleasant conversation with him on the day before he became dangerously ill—and there are a few Russians I see—but what should I tell you of the whole thing, of Paris and its inhabitants? Let me start with the city itself, with Paris. I do not want to repeat myself about how it first appeared to me, about the bustle of the streets, because perhaps you did receive my first letter, but I will note that there are some inaccuracies in what most travelers tell us. First of all, the bustle of the streets is owing mainly to the pedestrians, who don't create any congestion, and when this does happen, they don't form the kind of mob we see on our boulevards on festival days. The carriages, and there are not very many, move at a very small trot and for the most part are only hackneys and omnibuses. On rare occasions you may see a carriage belonging to the truly rich, with two mouse-dun horses and a coachman in scarlet trousers, and they are all very respectful towards the sovereign who, a new Proteus, walks the sidewalks under a thousand different forms: in a blouse, a frock coat, etc. When you're in a carriage you neither enter nor leave through the carriage gate of a house, you stop in front of it and ring to be let into the courtyard, which is very clean and which you walk through on foot to the home of the people you want to see—a custom sometimes broken in the Faubourg St-Germain, but this neighborhood is somewhat isolated and this manner of doing things, from a fear of accidents, is not strictly required. Paris is one big store, since the first floors of the houses are all stores; also, no matter where you live, almost everything is close at hand—not only necessities, but luxuries too—although for the most part it's all mediocre. Paris is magnificent as a whole; the details are prettified miseries. Contemplating the city from this point of view, I thought of these two lines from Voltaire:

> *Et vous composerez, dans ce chaos fatal,*
> *Du malheur de chaque être le bien général.*[*]

But to sense the fallacy of this application, remember that the more equal distribution of the goods of the land has contributed powerfully to the happiness of France by making a large number of people reasonably happy and reasonably content. The general physiognomy of a people who walk upright, to the totally fresh eyes of the traveler, is not deceptive. There is in the French a kind of satisfaction I have not noticed anywhere else. A politeness, a benevolence, a cordiality, even among the lowest ranks of the people, which proves that their habits of temperament do not include the kind of bitterness I have seen everywhere but in France—proof of a superior order of things. But to return to material concerns, you can find anything you want at the Palais-Royal, which is Paris's *Gostiny Dvor*, but far more magnificent than the one in Petersburg or even the "City" in Moscow; it is illuminated by gas every evening, as our cities have been only once: on the day when everyone celebrated our army's entrance into the very city from which I write you—but no shop owner has even twenty thousand francs in capital. The luxury items are scattered around; the rich must take the trouble of searching for what they want in twenty different

---

[*] And you will compose, in this fatal chaos, / the general good from each being's misfortune.

places. Life is so well-ordered here you might suspect that there are very strict morals; that is not yet the case, but the framework is definitely in place. You have to warn the doorman if you think you will be returning home past midnight—and generally speaking, you don't see anyone on the Paris streets at that hour; they become as silent as a village.

159. TO NIKOLAY AND SOFYA PUTYATA, IN ST. PETERSBURG.

[First half of December, 1843, Paris]

It's a good thing I'm only spending one winter in Paris; otherwise I'd change from a person with some sense into a total layabout, or what's worse—a man of society. Not only me, but all Parisians are on their feet from eleven in the morning to twelve at night and spend the hours in visits. For actual Parisians, who have their own concerns, whether of business or politics, and visit every person with a certain goal in mind, this life is not completely overwhelming, but for someone who's here for just a short time, it's exhausting to the extreme, even if one is curious about it. Despite people's cordiality and the novelty of what you are seeing, you feel the lack of direct relationships, and if I were in Paris without my family, I don't know if I'd endure a similar existence. My first acquaintances took me into the Faubourg St-Germain—to Mme Fantone, Mme Aguesseau, and Princess Golitsyna—the old passion of our D. Davydov, when her name was still Zolotnitskaya. Here you can find academicians and Catholic proselytes of both sexes. They're all toiling in the vineyard of the Lord, meaning of the abbots. On the rather isolated streets of the famous suburb, Latin priests with concerned looks run back and forth in such great numbers that if, in keeping with the Russian custom, you spat away to protect yourself from them all, a person might contract consumption. Through Circourt I met Vigny, the two Thierrys, Nodier, and Sainte-Beuve; through Sobolevsky, Mérimée and Mme Ancelot; through chance, the former publisher of one of the extreme republican journals, through whom I hope to meet G. Sand. I have also met, or renewed my acquaintance with, a number of our countrymen. Russians look for other Russians in Paris, as they generally do in foreign lands. Even the most frivolous of them can guess what we have in our hearts and are prepared for sentimentality. The different social circles, from a political point of view, present the saddest possible reality. The legitimists—intelligent without hope, reckless by incorrigible habit—pursue the ideas of their party and held a requiem mass for it in London that was both ridiculous and touching. The republicans lose themselves in theories without a single practical idea. The conservative party more or less hates its true representative, the king who was chosen by it. Everywhere there are elements of dissension. There is movement among the priests, who have been resurrected for disastrous hopes, for under the guise of mysticism they pursue the idea of a return to their former domination. And there you have France! Meanwhile, in the salons of Paris the constitution of French politeness quietly brings together intelligent, strong, and passionate representatives of all these diverse strivings. I embrace you both and all the little children, both yours and ours. In my next letter I will tell you details about all the people I have named.

160. TO NIKOLAY AND SOFYA PUTYATA, IN ST. PETERSBURG.

[Late December, 1843, Paris]

I congratulate you on the new year, dear friends! I embrace you, your children and ours, and wish you a better new year than the Parisian one, which is nothing but a specter of the past, in wrinkles and holiday garb. I congratulate you on the future, for ours is larger than anywhere else; I congratulate you on our steppes, for this is a vastness for which the sciences here have no substitute; I congratulate you on our winter, for it is robust and brilliant and the eloquence of its frost calls us to action better than any orator here; I congratulate you on the fact that we are, indeed, twelve days younger than other nations and so perhaps will outlive them by twelve centuries. I can prove the truth of each of these statements in scholarly fashion, but now is not the time; let's leave it till the day we'll be together again, for of all Russian writers there is not a single one who less enjoys writing than he who loves you so tenderly. My regards to Sobolevsky and Pletnyov, to whom I am planning to write—about which of a multiplicity of topics I don't know, but I will try to express something with all the truth that depends on me.

Ye. Boratynsky

161. TO NIKOLAY AND SOFYA PUTYATA, IN ST. PETERSBURG.

[January, 1844, Paris]

Sonichka's last letter brought us news of your shared great loss. You cannot doubt the fullness of the feeling we share with you. The memory of your worthy father belongs not only to your filial grief, but to all who knew and valued him; it belongs to history, to the civic history of 1812. You are having a difficult winter: so many emotional upheavals and so many material worries. My life here, too, is not exhilarating. I'll be happy with Paris when I leave it. For the foreigner who feels no passionate concern in anything, for the cold observer, social obligations, which nourish only a curiosity often deceived in its expectations, are distinctly burdensome. I go everywhere I am expected to go, like a schoolboy to his classes. I am, of course, rewarded for my labor by a mass of information and impressions, but it is nevertheless labor and only very, very rarely pleasure. In one of Vyazemsky's letters to Turgenev he included a few lines that are, for me, especially gracious. Tell him, if you get the chance, that I was very touched by them and that they are preserved in that feeling which has been so well called the heart's memory. Poor Turgenev has been ill almost since my arrival in Paris: he has sciatica in his arm and rheumatism in his sides. He says he owes these ailments to the fact that somewhere in Germany, when he was trying to find Zhukovsky, he fell into a stream and was chilled to the bone, and hasn't been able since to fully recover. He doesn't leave his armchair, which, for a man as active as he is, is worse than the sickness itself. We go out in the evenings to the Faubourg St-Germain, though for the time being we are still faithful to the Orthodox Greco-Russian church. The Catholic proselytism here is unbearable. I am being forced to read a pile of boring books, and right now I have on my table *Institut des Jésuites* by Father Ravignan. What sort of book do you think this is? An explanation of the statutes of the order, written with the simplicity of an infant—or the innocence of a dotard who has lost his memory—by a man of some forty years who is remarkable for his erudition and talents. Here is my description of this work: *livre niais, écrit pour les niais par un homme qui n'est pas niais.*[*] I see almost all the writers here. Tomorrow I'll be at Lamartine's. Thierry has promised to introduce me to Guizot. Since he became a government minister, it's been rather hard to get access to him. I have letters to Sobolevsky and Pletnyov which I have begun but not finished because of the Parisian hustle and bustle. Yesterday, Nastinka and I attended a ball of the *ancienne liste civile*[†] and saw the whole French aristocracy in full splendor. Be well; I embrace you and the children.

162. TO NIKOLAY AND SOFYA PUTYATA, IN ST. PETERSBURG.

[Early April (NS) / late March (OS), 1844, Paris]

Thank you for your wish to have my portrait. Unfortunately, I received your letter right before our departure for Italy, but even so I will try to satisfy your friendly whim here in Paris, where, as you advise, it's possible to have a few copies lithographed. If I don't manage it (for time is pressing), I'll leave it till Rome. We leave Paris with the most agreeable impressions. Our acquaintances here have shown us so much good will, so much friendship, they have healed old wounds. Here we have been given letters of recommendation for Naples, Rome, and Florence. We can, if we wish, get to know the society there, as we have here, but I expect we won't find the time for it. There are people in Paris whom, indeed, we are sad to leave behind. A traveler should be a traveler: it's best he not stay anywhere too long if in fact he wants to enjoy his misanthropic happiness. We are going to Marseilles; from there, by sea, directly to Naples, and then by land to Rome, etc., and are returning to Russia via Vienna. When I see you, I will be rich in memories of every sort. I was tiring of Parisian life, but now, as I say goodbye to it, I am satisfied with what I have experienced. I

---

[*] A foolish book written for the foolish by a man who is not foolish.

[†] The old civil list (i.e. the upper nobility).

stopped writing you about Paris itself because my opinion was changing every day. Besides, you have to be born in Paris to be able to find, among its demands and distractions, leisure for thought and written expression. The Russian sees and can't believe that this very same life is led by local scholars who are constantly making advances in science and every year publish some sort of book. I embrace you, my dears, as I do your children and ours. Although it is good to be abroad, I long to return to my homeland. I want to see you and chat in Russian about foreigners. Balabin sends you regards. He's a smart, good, enlightened, and kind man.

163. TO HIS MOTHER, IN MARA (IN FRENCH).

[Around April 10 (NS) / March 29 (OS), 1844, Marseilles]

It is from Marseilles that I write you, dear Maman, after a trip by stagecoach of four days and five nights. We are about to go by sea to Naples, from where we will travel up Italy bit by bit through Rome and Florence and then return to Russia through Vienna. After staying five months in Paris, we realized two things: that we had seen there almost everything of note, that we had been out [in society] enough to have a fairly good idea of what it offered that was different from ours, and second, that we had spent less money than we presumed. And here we are on the shores of the Mediterranean after crossing a pleasant and picturesque country that is now all blossoms and verdure. Even so, I have left Paris with regrets; despite the exhausting life I led there, I found a thoroughly warm welcome for the two of us from a number of people (persons of true sympathy). The children spent the winter at their studies and made great progress of every kind. Now we are about to greet beautiful and classical Italy, but I will make one comment: living in foreign lands has, above all, the benefit of making you like your own country better; the advantages of a gentler climate are not as great as you imagine, while the advances of civilization are not as salient as you expect. The peoples I have seen so far are not equal to Russians, neither in heart nor in mind. They are dull-minded in Germany and lawless in France; add to this that if a Frenchman combines being foolish and stupid, he's a past master at it. I will return to my country cured of many biases and filled with indulgence for a number of the genuine faults we possess and which we delight in exaggerating. Farewell until Naples, dear and good Maman. I kiss my sisters and brothers and kiss the hands of my dear aunt. I hope at some point in Italy to put my memories of Paris in order, but this was impossible to do in the city itself: impressions kept multiplying and life was too tumultuous.

164. TO NIKOLAY AND SOFYA PUTYATA, IN ST. PETERSBURG.

> The Baratynskys had not intended to stay long in Naples. From Marseilles, Nastasya wrote her sister-in-law Sofya Mikhaylovna Baratynskaya (Sergey's wife): "Now we are going directly to Naples, but we will be there a very short time, only long enough to receive letters."

[Late April or early May, 1844, Naples]

It's been fifteen days since we've been in Naples, but from the fullness of the uniform and eternally new impressions it feels as if we've been living here a long time. In three days, as if on wings, we were transported from the complicated social life of Europe to the lushly vegetative life of Italy— Italy, which given all its merits should be marked on the map as a separate part of the world, for in fact it is neither Africa nor Asia nor Europe. Our three-day sea voyage will stay with me as one of my most pleasant memories. I managed to escape sea sickness. In the leisure of good health, I didn't leave the deck but watched the waves day and night. There was no storm, but rather what our French sailors called *très gros temps**—in other words, excitement without danger. In our section, the non-sufferers were one very nice Englishman, two or three unremarkable people, a Neapolitan *maestro* in music, Nikolinka, and myself. We entertained ourselves in the casual way of military comrades. At sea the fear of something horrible happening, although not an everyday occurrence, and shared sufferings, or being in their presence, for a moment connect people as if Moscow society, let alone that of Paris, did not exist. On the ship, at night, I wrote a few verses which I will send to you, once I've corrected them a little, with the request that you pass them on to Pletnyov for his journal.

---

* Very foul weather.

Here is Naples! I get up early. I hurry to open the window and drink in the revitalizing air. We live in the Villa Reale, above the bay, between two gardens. You know that Italy is not rich in trees, but where there are trees, they are incredibly beautiful. Just as our trees, in their romantic beauty, their pensive swaying, express all possible shades of melancholy, so the bright-green, sharply defined leaf of the trees here portrays all degrees of happiness. And now the city has awakened: on a donkey, in the fresh green of Italian hay speckled with raspberry-colored flowers, the Neapolitan rides at a walk, half-naked but in a red hat: this is not a horseman but one of the blessed. His face is merry and proud. He believes in his sunshine, which will always watch over him and never leave him.

Every day, twice a day—in the morning and late evening—we walk down to the wondrous bay, look at it and can't stop looking. On the Chiaja, a boulevard whose imitation we can see in our own boulevard in Moscow, there are a few statues, which now the Italian moon, now the Italian sun, illuminate for us. I understand the artists who need Italy. This illumination, which brings out all nuances, the whole rendering of the human face, without the harshness of lamplight and in all the precision and softness an artist dreams of—this illumination can be found only here, beneath this miraculous sky. Here and only here can the draftsman and the painter be formed.

We have inspected some of the local surroundings. We saw what was possible to see in Herculaneum, we were in Puzzoli and saw the Temple of Serapis, but what is intoxicating here is that inner existence bestowed by the sky and the air. If the sky beneath which Philemon and Baucis were changed into trees is as wonderful as the sky is here, then Jupiter was bountifully good and they are blessed for all eternity.

We will be staying in Naples two or three months. During our sea voyage, Nastinka's nervous rheumatisms came back with a constant pain in the stomach. One of the best doctors here, recommended to us by Princess Volkonskaya, has firmly prescribed her sea-water baths and the local ferrous water. We have all of this just across the street and it's very cheap. I had assumed that Khlyustin would bring me a business letter from you, but he was held back in Königsberg by sudden illness. Please write me again all your details so I can organize my affairs. Naples is not included in my letter of credit. Do me the favor of sending me another letter of credit, for about five thousand, for Naples and the other cities we'll need to go through, assuming we return to Russia through Vienna. I embrace you both tenderly, just as I do all of your and our little children.

165. TO NIKOLAY AND SOFYA PUTYATA, IN ST. PETERSBURG.

The first lines of this letter apparently refer to an illness suffered by the Putyatas' eldest daughter, Nastasya (Nastya). It is not known exactly when this and the following letter were written, or which was written first, but they are the last of Baratynsky's letters that have been preserved.

[May–June, 1844, Naples]

We wait impatiently for a letter from you that is even more reassuring with regard to Nastya and the two of you. Despite the worst being over for you, we could not read your last letter without shuddering as we thought of what you have been through. Like you, we too are relieved, trusting in the grace of God, which is already so evident. We live in Naples as in a village: the days are uniform—but the sky, the air, the south in general give no time for either boredom or brooding. Every day I delight in one and the same thing, and always with new intoxication. The heat is unbearable, but in Russia it is sometimes more stifling. The cheerful temperament of the Neapolitans, their extraordinary vitality, their ceaseless movement, processions, parish holidays with fireworks—it's all so carnival-like, so unconditionally merry, it's impossible not to be carried away by it, to surrender like a child to this most silly, most happy distraction. This life is definitely to my liking: we stroll, go bathing, sweat, and don't think about a thing, or at least don't dwell for long on any one thought—that's not in the local climate. I embrace the two of you, darling Nastya, and the other little children, yours and ours. Next time I will write in more detail, but now I'm in a hurry not to miss the post. May God keep you all safe and sound!

166. TO NIKOLAY AND SOFYA PUTYATA, IN ST. PETERSBURG.

[May–June, 1844, Naples]

We received a number of your letters all at once, because we had the good sense to write to Rome and Florence and have them forwarded to us in Naples. Circumstances are forcing us to stay here much longer than we expected, and instead of returning to Russia at the end of August, we'll be lucky if we can return by the end of November. Please manage things on my behalf. The deadlines for the payments to the Trustees' Council for my Tambov estate are in June and July, if I remember correctly, and I have left two of last year's receipts for you, friend Putyata. Half of each of them needs to be paid. The receipts for Nastya's property are with Dmitry: they are all due in October; for each of them a third needs to be paid, which by my calculation he can do from the income at home, but I don't know how the rents are coming in so you need to take it on yourself to make sure everything is in order. Last and most important: as I was getting ready to go abroad, I borrowed money from a lady in Moscow—I don't remember her name but Becker knows her and her address—it was 32 thou. at 9 percent, which she took in advance. It is essential I pay this debt of honor, for which I need to use all our revenue from this year, excluding what we owe you and the five thousand I asked you to send us in Naples. Whatever amount is lacking take from the timber funds: this amount will go towards paying your debt to me for the Muranovo house and the timber operation. If, as is likely, all of this together still does not come to 32 thou., then pay her what is possible; for this you have to use Becker. I am sending you two poems. Give them to Pletnyov for his journal. In a few days I will send you letters addressed to him, Sobolevsky, and Vyazemsky. Please send them on. We are leading the sweetest possible life in Naples. We have already seen all the wondrous places in the vicinity: Puzzoli, Baiae, Castellammare, Sorrento, Amalfi, Salerno, Paestum, Herculaneum, Pompeii. Now our week passes in lessons for the children, and every Sunday we have *une partie de plaisir** and look at the local churches, palaces, and castles, or we

---

* A pleasure outing.

simply go for a drive out of town to some little village. I tenderly embrace you both, and your and our children.

Ye. Boratynsky

Baratynsky's death came not long after. As he had written to the Putyatas (Letter 164), Nastasya's poor health ("nervous rheumatisms" and "a constant pain in the stomach") was keeping them in Naples much longer than they had intended. On July 10 (NS) / June 29 (OS), his wife felt so ill that a doctor was called. He advised bloodletting. As Nastasya wrote the next day to the Putyatas: "As we found this repugnant, [the doctor] said he was afraid of a cerebral fever; this frightened Eugène so much that, even after being reassured, he had something like an attack of nerves; later in the night he had a violent headache and attacks of bile; the purgatives he took did not work; he vomited bile instead of purging, and as if on purpose I was not anxious; we were expecting the doctor for me at seven in the morning; at six and a quarter it was over."

Baratynsky died on the morning of July 11 (NS) / June 29 (OS), 1844. Nastasya, "completely destroyed by grief" (as an acquaintance described her), moved with the children to the home of the Russian painter Aleksandr Ivanov, then living in the city, until they could return to Russia. Ivanov also saw to the necessary arrangements. The poet's body was kept for a year at the British Cemetery in Naples, until it could be transported by sea to St. Petersburg, where, on September 12 (NS) / August 31 (OS), 1845, Yevgeny Baratynsky was buried at the Alexander Nevsky Monastery, in what is today the Tikhvin Cemetery. Pyotr Pletnyov wrote to his friend Yakov Grot: "On Friday (August 31) I was at the funeral of the poet Baratynsky, who died exactly a year and two months ago. He was buried at the Nevsky Monastery next to Krylov, Gnedich, and Karamzin. Apart from the family, relatives (the Putyatas and their wives), and members of the household, there were the following literary men: Prince Vyazemsky, Prince Odoyevsky (with his wife), Count Vladimir Sologub—and no one else."

Not long afterwards, Nastasya and the children moved permanently to Kazan, and the Putyatas settled in the house Baratynsky had built in Muranovo.

NOTES

INTRODUCTION TO THE NOTES

THE POEMS

The first task of the translator is to decide what to translate. When it comes to Baratynsky's lyric works, this is not just about deciding which poems to translate but also which versions of the poems. "Excuse it all being so badly overwritten," the poet wrote to Ivan Kireyevsky when he mailed him a few works for *The European*, "you know my passion for corrections. I couldn't resist making them even as I send this to you" (Letter 79). A few years earlier, writing to Nikolay Putyata, he tried to explain "the extraordinarily complex relationship [poets] have with their works": "The pride of the mind and the rights of the heart are in constant battle. One poem you love because you remember the emotion with which it was written. You are proud of your revision because you have conquered the heart's emotion with your mind." (Letter 42.) Baratynsky, indeed, did not merely make "corrections" to his works before sending them to be published; a great many of his poems, after they appeared in journals and almanacs, he revised further, sometimes drastically, before including them in his collections. In a number of significant cases he made even later revisions, which never appeared during his lifetime but are reflected in the volume edited by his son, Lev Baratynsky, in 1869. This edition, titled *Sochineniya* [*Works*], was republished with few changes by another son, Nikolay, in 1884.

Complicating matters further, all the poems published during Baratynsky's lifetime were subjected to the strict censorship of the regimes of Alexander I and Nicholas I. Later editors of Baratynsky's works, beginning with his son, have understandably sought to undo the changes ordered by the censor and present the poems as intended by the poet.

The first modern scholarly edition of Baratynsky's works—one that incorporated careful textological research—was the two-volume *Polnoye sobraniye stikhotvoreniy* [*Complete Collected Poems*] edited by M. L. Gofman and published by the Imperial Academy of Sciences in 1914 and 1915. Gofman took the unusual approach of using the first publications of the poems as his main texts, while providing later versions of thirteen poems in a separate section and variants for all the poems in his commentary. As he explained, "In the basic text of the present publication, we have accepted the initial reading because we think that it alone can acquaint the reader with the full scope of Boratynsky's work, while in all other publications, the literary physiognomy of the Boratynsky of the Alexandrine era [i.e. to the end of 1825] (when he was especially popular, and much more so than in the 1830s) has remained in shadow" ("Ot redaktora," in *CCP 1914*, 1: xiii).

The next important editions of the collected poems (both published in the prestigious series *Biblioteka poeta* ["The Poet's Library"] by the Leningrad publishing house Sovetskiy pisatel') appeared in 1936, in two volumes jointly edited by I. Medvedeva and Ye. N. Kupreyanova, and in 1957, in a single volume edited by Kupreyanova alone. Both bore the same title as Gofman's edition: *Complete Collected Poems*.

Unlike Gofman, however, the editors attempted to present the "final" versions of the poems and, for the most part, incorporated the late changes that had appeared in the 1869 edition. They also tried to preserve, to some degree, the structures of Baratynsky's books, with both editions printing the poems of the collection *Sumerki* [*Dusk*] (1842) as a separate group; the 1936 edition also presented the poems of the 1827 collection separately, arranging them, as in that collection, in genre-defined sections: three books of "Elegies," followed by "Miscellany" and "Epistles."

The single-volume *Stikhotvoreniya; Poemy* [*Poems; Narrative Poems*], compiled in 1982 by L. G. Frizman and published in the series *Literaturnyye pamyatniki* ["Literary Monuments"] by the USSR Academy of Sciences, also followed the principle of reproducing the structures of Baratynsky's books: here Frizman chose to replicate not only *Dusk*, but also the 1835 edition. In the early 1830s, when Baratynsky was preparing his lyric poems for this edition, he made some peculiar choices: he stripped most of the works (but not all) of the titles they had previously borne, either in the 1827 collection or in journals and almanacs, and arranged them in a somewhat cryptic order, mixing early and later poems and numbering them with Roman numerals. Frizman, therefore, did same in the first section of his 1982 edition: the poems are mostly untitled and are ordered and numbered as in the 1835 edition. At the same time, as his predecessors had done, he corrected whatever he believed was the result of censorship, but unlike Medvedeva and Kupreyanova he did not incorporate most of the changes from the 1869 edition. He did, however, include the late revisions in "The Last Poet" and, partly, in "On the Planting of a Wood."

In 1989, yet a third edition of Baratynsky's poems appeared in "The Poet's Library" series—again as *Complete Collected Poems*—this time compiled by V. M. Sergeyev. Unlike his Soviet predecessors, Sergeyev presented the poems in strict chronological order (as could best be determined), ignoring the structures of Baratynsky's books altogether, even that of *Dusk*. He followed Frizman, however, in the removal of the titles as well as in most textological decisions, including the rejection of the majority of the late changes (although, as in Frizman's edition, these were included as "variants"). It should be noted that all the Soviet editions, from Medvedeva and Kupreyanova's to Sergeyev's, modernized Baratynsky's spelling and punctuation and lowercased references to God. Although this was a standard practice, the modernization was sometimes excessive and often inconsistent.

In 2000, a new edition of Baratynsky's *Complete Collected Poems* appeared, in the series *Novaya biblioteka poeta* ["The New Poet's Library"], published by Akademicheskiy proyekt in St. Petersburg; it was edited by L. G. Frizman and followed the same basic principles as his "Literary Monuments" edition in 1982.

I have not had the opportunity to examine the 2000 edition myself, but it has, in any case, been superseded by the multi-volume *Polnoye sobraniye sochineniy i pisem* [*Complete Collected Works and Letters*], which began publication in 2002 under the supervision of A. M. Peskov and a team of editors (A. R. Zaretsky,

I. A. Pilshchikov, and O. V. Golubyova). Two books came out that year: volume 1, containing all the poems written from 1818 to 1822, and the first part of volume 2, with all the poems from 1822 to 1834. Production then stalled. Peskov died in 2009, at the age of fifty-seven, but the edition was able to resume in 2012 with the first part of volume 3, edited by A. S. Bodrova and N. N. Mazur. This book included all of *Dusk* and the remaining lyric poems, as well as juvenilia, collectively written lyrics, and poems ascribed to Baratynsky. The still-missing second parts of volumes 2 and 3 are expected to present detailed literary-historical commentary to the poems in those volumes, but the published first parts already contain meticulous textological notes. We can only hope that the editors will be able to publish the missing parts in due course, as well as the other planned volumes with Baratynsky's narrative poems, prose, and letters.

The editors of *CCWL* have made some genuinely bold decisions. As a rule, they take as their main text the last finished version known to have been intended by Baratynsky, restoring, where possible, deletions or changes that were clearly ordered by the censor (as, for example, in "The Storm" and "What good are fantasies of freedom to the prisoner?"). In some cases, when it cannot be clearly established that a change was the result of censorship (as with the ten-line deletion in "Rhyme"), their "basic" text may be one that previous editors have rejected as censored. But whenever there are competing versions of a poem—as when the version published in a collection is substantially different from the poem's earlier publication in a journal, or when later revisions cannot be authenticated as the poet's intended "final" version—the different redactions are published together, in full, with the last indisputable "authorial version" placed first. In addition, in an effort to be as faithful as possible to the manuscripts and printed texts they are working from, the editors present the poems in nineteenth-century orthography, including characters dropped from the Russian alphabet in the reforms of 1918.

While this latest edition of Baratynsky's works makes the options available to the translator as clear as they can ever be, it does not absolve him of having to decide which version of a text should be presented to the English-speaking reader (if, indeed, he has decided to present only a single version of a poem). For the present selection, I have in most cases followed the traditional principle of choosing what would, after due consideration, appear to be the poet's intended "final version"—essentially, the same principle used in the 1936 and 1957 "Poet's Library" editions. Thus, I find no reason to believe that the great majority of the later revisions presented in the 1869 edition published by Baratynsky's son did not originate with the poet and represent his intentions, although there is no way of knowing, of course, if he would have kept these changes had he lived to oversee the publication of yet another edition of his works. Despite my respect for Frizman's 1982 edition, and even more for the extraordinary textological research that underlies the *CCWL* edition, I find it a little sad to treat as mere "variants" or "later redactions" such passages as the brilliant opening of "Death" or the verse in "Arbitrary was the pet name" where the poet calls into the bottomless depths of eternity; in most cases, the later revisions enrich the poems in ways that are unmistakably Baratynskian. The one poem in the present selection where I do follow the "basic text" in *CCWL* is "On the Planting of a Wood," a work with an exceptionally complex textological background.

In the publication here of the Russian texts of the poems, although I have not returned to the pre-revolutionary orthography, I have compared the modernized spelling and punctuation of the twentieth-century editions against the collections published in Baratynsky's lifetime, as well as the 1869 edition. In many instances (but far from all), I have restored the earlier punctuation and some of the earlier spellings.

For both the translations and the Russian texts, I use the titles that Baratynsky had removed for the 1835 edition of his *Poems*. My reasoning is that he did this with the aim of creating a particular emotional and thematic "flow" in that specific collection, as is reflected in the ordering of the poems, but since here we present the translations in more or less chronological order with no attempt to reflect the arrangement of the 1835 edition, it makes sense to restore the poems' earlier titles, which can be both meaningful and helpful to the reader. Moreover, they have become well established through their use in all major editions of Baratynsky's works before 1982, a point that holds true even for the title "On the Planting of a Wood," which was most likely supplied not by Baratynsky himself but by his widow (hence, the title is bracketed in the selection).

In my notes to the poems, I first give the date of the work's initial publication and note its inclusion (or non-inclusion) in the collections of 1827 and 1835 (for the earlier poems) or *Dusk* (for the later poems), indicating as well the nature of any revisions (minor or significant) and censorship issues. Usually, I do no more than point out that revisions occurred—time has not allowed me to provide full translations even of, for instance, the beautiful earlier versions of "Finland" and "Confession." I do, however, occasionally discuss certain specific changes, especially where competing "established" versions exist.

The notes also seek to present a useful historical, literary, and biographical context for the poems, providing basic information about their addressees (or targets) and, where pertinent, drawing connections with ideas expressed in Baratynsky's letters. I have also glossed names and terms that are likely to be unfamiliar to present-day readers, but better-known classical names (e.g. *Apollo, Aphrodite, Tantalus*) I have left unexplained; they can, after all, be found in most English dictionaries. In all these things, I have often, and often silently, relied on the commentaries found in the editions I have mentioned, providing sources only for more salient points.

Let me add a note about the dates that are placed beneath the translations of the poems. Unbracketed dates are used when there is reasonable certainty about the year the poem was written; dates in angled brackets (e.g. *<1822>*) refer to the last possible year the poem could have been written, based, in most cases, on its date of publication. When a question mark appears with a date, it indicates a reasonable conjecture. When more than one date is given, they refer to substantially different versions of the poem.

In contrast to the poems, the letters present few textological issues. The main problems relate to dating them, but these questions have largely been resolved by A. M. Peskov in his *Letopis' zhizni i tvorchestvo Ye. A. Boratynskogo* [*A Chronicle of the Life and Work of Ye. A. Boratynsky*] (1998), where all the existing letters have been published, either in the original Russian or in Russian translation from the French, and dated as precisely as possible (the one exception is Baratynsky's first letter to Ivan Kozlov [Letter 18], which Peskov believed to be a fabrication). Peskov's *Chronicle* also provides an enormous amount of indispensable, scrupulously researched biographical information, as well as countless excerpts from letters and memoirs by Baratynsky's relatives, friends, and acquaintances, contemporary reviews and articles about the poet, and many other relevant documents. In addition, the *Chronicle* gives us concise information about the poet's family and ancestors (going back thirteen generations) as well as the various places he lived. As a result we get a very full picture of Baratynsky's life.

The overall goal of the notes is to give the reader the necessary information to appreciate the context in which the letters were written and, as much as possible, clear up questions that might arise. There are, in fact, two sets of commentary: the biographical notes that appear alongside the translations and aim to create as coherent a narrative as possible, and the explanatory notes (below) that try to clarify obscure references and provide sources for quotations and other specific data.

To a large extent, the information I provide is based on Peskov's *Chronicle*, but many references are not explained there, or not explained with the kind of context a non-Russian reader might need. Among the other works I have consulted, the most important is the biography *Yevgeniy Baratynskiy: Zhizn' i tvorchestvo* [*Yevgeny Baratynsky: Life and Work*] (1973), by the Norwegian scholar Geir Kjetsaa (who is also responsible for the first publication of many of Baratynsky's letters), as well as T. J. Binyon's 2004 biography of Aleksandr Pushkin, which contains a wealth of information about the period. To track down some of the names Baratynsky mentions in his letters, I have also relied on various biographical and literary encyclopedias and other reference works that are readily available on the Internet. Thus I discovered, for instance, information about the "hermitage" near Kaymary (mentioned in Letter 78) and that "Khlyustin" (in Letter 164), who was supposed to deliver a letter from Nikolay Putyata but died en route, was the brother of Countess Anastasie de Circourt, who had introduced Baratynsky to a number of his Paris acquaintances. While in itself fairly trivial, this latter fact (surprisingly, not mentioned in the *Chronicle*) helps us to better appreciate the connections that existed for a Russian of Baratynsky's stature who was traveling in Western Europe. Here I should stress that, although I made use of the sometimes less than reliable *Wikipedia* (in its English, Russian, French, and German versions), especially for basic background information, I always tried to confirm what I found there with more established scholarly sources.

Throughout the notes, both to the poems and to the letters, I use abbreviations and short-form titles in English, or simply the author's name, when referring to editions of Baratynsky's collected poems and other frequently cited works (e.g. *Poems 1827, CCP 1936, Kjetsaa*). When referring to Russian journals and almanacs of Baratynsky's day, I use English translations of their titles (e.g. *The Contemporary* instead of *Sovremennik*). With both decisions, my goal is to make the reading experience a little easier for those who have no Russian. Keys to both the cited works and the Russian periodical names are found in the References section that follows.

— R. G.

REFERENCES

COLLECTIONS OF BARATYNSKY'S POEMS PUBLISHED DURING HIS LIFETIME

Poems 1827 — *Stikhotvoreniya Yevgeniya Baratynskago* [*The Poems of Yevgeny Baratynsky*]. Moscow: Tipografiya Avgusta Semena pri Imp. Mediko-Khirurgicheskoy Akademii, 1827.

Poems 1835 — *Stikhotvoreniya Yevgeniya Baratynskago* [*The Poems of Yevgeny Baratynsky*]. 2 parts. Moscow: Tipografiya Avgusta Semena pri Imp. Mediko-Khirurgicheskoy Akademii, 1835. Part 1 consists of the lyric poems, numbered I to CXXXI; part 2 consists of the long poems (*poemy*) *Eda, Piry* [*Feasts*], *Bal* [*The Ball*], *Telema i Makar* [*Thelema and Macarius*], *Pereseleniye dush* [*The Transmigration of Souls*], and *Tsyganka* [*The Gypsy*].

Dusk — *Sumerki: Sochineniye Yevgeniya Boratynskago* [*Dusk. A Work by Yevgeny Boratynsky*]. Moscow: Tipografiya Avgusta Semena pri Imp. Mediko-Khirurgicheskoy Akademii, 1842.

FIRST BOOK PUBLICATIONS OF THE NARRATIVE POEMS

Eda — Published with the poem *Feasts* in *Eda: Finlyandskaya povest', i Piry: Opisatel'naya poema* [*Eda: A Finnish Tale, and Feasts: A Descriptive Poem*]. St. Petersburg: Tipografiya Departamenta Narodnago Prosveshcheniya, 1826.

The Ball — *Bal: Povest': Sochineniye Yevgeniya Baratynskago* [*The Ball: A Tale: A Work by Yevgeny Baratynsky*]. St. Petersburg: Tipografiya Departamenta Narodnago Prosveshcheniya, 1828; published under the same cover with A. S. Pushkin's long poem *Graf Nulin* [*Count Nulin*] as *Dve povesti v stikhakh* [*Two Tales in Verse*].

The Concubine — *Nalozhnitsa: Sochineniye Yevgeniya Baratynskago* [*The Concubine: A Work by Yevgeny Baratynsky*]. Moscow: Tipografiya Avgusta Semena pri Imp. Mediko-Khirurgicheskoy Akademii, 1831. The poem was retitled *Tsyganka* [*The Gypsy*], when it was republished in *Poems 1835* (part 2).

EDITIONS PUBLISHED BY BARATYNSKY'S FAMILY

Works 1869 — *Sochineniya Yevgeniya Abramovicha Baratynskago* [*The Works of Yevgeny Abramovich Baratynsky*]. [Compiled and edited by L. Ye. Baratynsky.] Moscow: Grachev and Co., 1869.

Works 1884 — *Sochineniya Yevgeniya Abramovicha Baratynskago* [*The Works of Yevgeny Abramovich Baratynsky*]. 4th ed. [Edited by N. Ye. Baratynsky.] Kazan: Universitetskaya tipografiya, 1884.

MODERN SCHOLARLY EDITIONS

CCP 1914 — *Polnoye sobraniye stikhotvoreniy Ye. A. Boratynskago* [*Complete Collected Poems of Ye. A. Boratynsky*]. Edited by M. L. Gofman. 2 vols. Vol. 1: St. Petersburg: Imperatorskaya Akademiya Nauk, 1914; vol. 2: Petrograd: Imperatorskaya Akademiya Nauk, 1915.

CCP 1936 — *Polnoye sobraniye stikhotvoreniy* [*Complete Collected Poems*]. Edited with commentary by Ye. N. Kupreyanova and I. Medvedeva. Biblioteka poeta, Bol'shaya seriya. 1st ed. 2 vols. Leningrad: Sovetskiy pisatel', 1936.

CCP 1957 — *Polnoye sobraniye stikhotvoreniy* [*Complete Collected Poems*]. Edited with commentary by Ye. N. Kupreyanova. Biblioteka poeta, Bol'shaya seriya. 2nd ed. Leningrad: Sovetskiy pisatel', 1957.

Poems 1982 — *Stikhotvoreniya; Poemy* [*Poems; Narrative Poems*]. Edited with commentary by L. G. Frizman. Literaturnyye pamyatniki. Moscow: Nauka, 1982.

CCP 1989 — *Polnoye sobraniye stikhotvoreniy* [*Complete Collected Poems*]. Edited with commentary by V. M. Sergeyev. Biblioteka poeta, Bol'shaya seriya. 3rd ed. Leningrad: Sovetskiy pisatel', 1989.

CCWL — *Polnoye sobraniye sochineniy i pisem* [*Complete Collected Works and Letters*]. Moscow: Yazyki slavyanskoy kul'tury, 2002–present. As of January 2015, the following volumes (or parts of volumes) have been published: Vol. 1: *Stikhotvoreniya 1818–1822 godov* [*Poems 1818–1822*]. Edited by A. M. Peskov, A. R. Zaretsky, and I. A. Pilshchikov. 2002. Vol. 2, part 1: *Stikhotvoreniya 1823–1834 godov* [*Poems 1823–1834*]. Edited by A. M. Peskov, A. R. Zaretsky, and O. V. Golubyova. 2002. Vol. 3, part 1: *"Sumerki"; Stikhotvoreniya 1835–1844 godov; Juvenilia; Kollektivnoye; Dubia* [*"Dusk"; Poems 1835–1844; Juvenilia; Collective Work; Dubia*]. Edited by A. S. Bodrova and N. N. Mazur. 2012.

FREQUENTLY CITED WORKS

Chronicle — *Letopis' zhizni i tvorchestva Ye. A. Boratynskogo* [*A Chronicle of the Life and Work of Ye. A. Boratynsky*]. Compiled by A. M. Peskov; edited by Ye. E. Lyamina and A. M. Peskov. Moscow: Novoye literaturnoye obozreniye, 1998.

Binyon — Binyon, T. J. *Pushkin: A Biography*. London: HarperCollins, 2004.

Handbook for Travellers — Blewitt, Octavian. *A Handbook for Travellers in Southern Italy, Being a Guide for the Continental Portion of the Kingdom of the Two Sicilies, Including the City of Naples and Its Suburbs...* London: John Murray, 1853.

Kjetsaa — Kjetsaa, Geir. *Yevgeniy Baratynskiy: Zhizn' i tvorchestvo* [*Yevgeny Baratynsky: Life and Work*]. Oslo: Universitetsforlaget, 1973.

Materials — Ye. A. *Boratynskiy: Materialy k yego biografii: Iz Tatevskogo arkhiva Rachinskikh* [*Ye. A. Boratynsky: Materials for His Biography: From the Tatevo Archive of the Rachinskys*]. Edited by Yu. N. Verkhovsky. Petrograd: Tipografiya Imperatorskoy akademii nauk, 1916.

Pushkin's Correspondence — Pushkin, A. S. *Perepiska A. S. Pushkina* [*Correspondence of A. S. Pushkin*]. 2 vols. Compiled with commentary by V. E. Vatsuro et al. Moscow: Khudozhestvennaya literatura, 1982.

Putyata — Nikolay Putyata, "Pis'ma Ye. A. Baratynskago k N. V. Putyate" ["The Letters of Ye. A. Baratynsky to N. V. Putyata"], *Russkiy arkhiv* 5, no. 2 (1867), cols. 263–299.

True Story — A. M. Peskov, *Boratynskiy: Istinnaya povest'* [*Boratynsky: A True Story*]. Moscow: Kniga, 1990. The predecessor to Peskov's *Chronicle*, this is a biography of Baratynsky's life up to his retirement from military service in February 1826, as told in letters and other documents.

Vatsuro and Gillelson — Vatsuro, V. E., and M. I. Gillelson. *Skvoz' "umstvennyye plotiny": Ocherki o knigakh i presse pushkinskoy pory* [*Across "Mental Dams": Essays on Books and the Press in the Pushkin Period*]. 2nd ed. Moscow: Kniga, 1986.

SOURCES FOR BARATYNSKY'S LETTERS IN FRENCH

Chronicle — Letters 96 and 102.

Lyamina, Ye. E., Ye. Ye. Pasternak, and A. Peskov, "Baratynskiye" ["The Baratynskys"], *Litsa: Biograficheskiy al'manakh* 2 (1993): 206–268. — Letters 47, 110, and 163.

Khomutov, A., "Iz bumag poeta I. I. Kozlova" ["From the Papers of I. I. Kozlov"], *Russkiy arkhiv* 24, no. 2 (1886): 177–202. — Letter 18.

Kjetsaa — Letters 2, 3, 7, 9, 14, 36, 118, and 120.

Materials — Letters 4, 6, 10, 29, 109, 113, 114, 117, 119, 130, 134, 139, 140, 143, 147, 148, 150, 151, 152, and 153.

Works 1869 — Letters 6, 14, 21, 155, and 158.

Alcyone — *Al'tsiona*, yearly almanac, published by Ye. F. Rozen, 1831–1833, Moscow.

The Contemporary — *Sovremennik*, monthly, founded and published by A. S. Pushkin, 1836; published by P. A. Vyazemsky and others, 1837; by P. A. Pletnyov, 1838–1846; by N. A. Nekrasov and I. I. Panayev, 1847–1866; St. Petersburg.

The Contender — *Sorevnovatel' prosveshcheniya i blagotvoreniya* (full title: *The Contender in Enlightenment and Philanthropy*), publication of the Free Society of Lovers of Russian Literature, monthly, 1818–1825, St. Petersburg.

Dawn — *Utrennyaya zarya*, yearly almanac, published and edited by V. A. Vladislavlev, 1839–1843, St. Petersburg.

The Day Star — *Dennitsa*, yearly almanac, published by M. A. Maksimovich, 1830–1834, Moscow.

The European — *Yevropeyets*, monthly (only two issues appeared), published by I. V. Kireyevsky, 1832, Moscow.

The Ladies' Journal — *Damski zhurnal*, twice-monthly, then weekly (1829–1833), published by P. I. Shalikov, 1823–1833, Moscow.

Library for Reading — *Biblioteka dlya chteniya*, monthly (in 1865, twice-monthly), founded and published by A. F. Smirdin and initially edited by O. I. Senkovsky (later with different publishers and editors), 1834–1865, St. Petersburg.

Literary Gazette — *Literaturnaya gazeta*, every five days, published and edited by A. A. Delvig and O. M. Somov, 1830–1831, St. Petersburg.

Literary Pages — *Literaturnyye listki*, monthly (1823), semi-monthly (1824), published by F. V. Bulgarin, 1823–1824.

Messenger of Europe — *Vestnik Yevropy*, twice-monthly, founded and published by N. M. Karamzin, 1802–1803; then by others, including V. A. Zhukovsky, 1808–1810; finally by M. T. Kachenovsky, 1815–1830; Moscow.

Mnemosyne — *Mnemozina*, semi-annual almanac, published by W. Küchelbecker and V. F. Odoyevsky, 1824–1825, Moscow.

Moscow Messenger — *Moskovskiy Vestnik*, twice-monthly, published and edited by M. P. Pogodin, 1827–1830, Moscow.

Moscow Observer — *Moskovskiy Nablyudatel'*, twice-monthly, edited by V. P. Androsov and S. P. Shevyryov (the literary section), 1835–1837; acquired by N. S. Stepanov in 1838; edited (unofficially) by V. G. Belinsky, 1838–1839.

Moscow Telegraph — Moskovskiy Telegraf, twice-monthly, published by N. A. Polevoy, 1825–1834, Moscow.

The Muscovite — Moskvityanin, monthly (twice-monthly, 1849–1856), published and edited by M. P. Pogodin and S. P. Shevyryov, 1841–1856, Moscow.

Northern Archive — Severnyy arkhiv, twice-monthly, published by F. V. Bulgarin, 1822–1828, merged with *Son of the Fatherland* in 1829, St. Petersburg.

Northern Bee — Severnaya pchela, thrice-weekly, daily beginning in 1831, published and edited by F. V. Bulgarin, 1825–1830, with N. I. Grech, 1831–1859; by P. S. Usov, 1860–1864.

Northern Flowers — Severnyye tsvety, yearly almanac, compiled by A. A. Delvig with the assistance (from 1827) of O. M. Somov, 1825–1832, St. Petersburg; the 1832 issue was compiled by A. S. Pushkin to benefit Delvig's family.

Notes of the Fatherland — Otechestvennye zapiski, monthly, P. P. Svinyin, 1820–1830; revived in 1839 by A. A. Krayevsky as publisher and editor, 1839–1859 (with V. G. Belinsky as literary critic, 1840–1846); then published by Krayevsky with various editors, 1860–1884.

The Pole Star — Polyarnaya zvezda, yearly almanac, published by K. F. Ryleyev and A. A. Bestuzhev, 1823–1825, St. Petersburg.

The Slav — Slavyanin, weekly (in 1830, twice-monthly), edited by A. F. Voyeykov, 1827–1830, St. Petersburg.

Son of the Fatherland — Syn otechestva, weekly, 1812–1825; then with different frequencies (twice-monthly, weekly, monthly), 1825–1844; founded and published by N. I. Grech, 1812–1828; merged with *Northern Archive* in 1829; published and edited by Grech and F. V. Bulgarin, as well as others, 1829–1852.

The Snowdrop — Podsnezhnik, yearly almanac, published by A. A. Delvig and O. M. Somov, 1829, and by Ye. V. Aladyin, 1830, St. Petersburg.

The Telescope — Teleskop, twice-monthly, published by N. I. Nadezhdin, 1831–1836, Moscow.

Tsarskoye Selo — almanac, published by N. M. Konshin and Ye. F. Rozen, 1829 ("for 1830"), St. Petersburg.

Urania — Uraniya, almanac, published by M. P. Pogodin, 1826, Moscow.

The Well-Intentioned — Blagonamerennyy, various frequencies (monthly, twice-monthly, weekly), published by A. Ye. Izmaylov, 1818–1826.

Source for periodical information: *Russkaya periodicheskaya pechat' (1702–1894): Spravochnik,* ed. A. G. Dementyev, A. V. Zapadov, and M. S. Cherepakhov (Moscow: Gos. izd. politicheskoy literatury, 1959).

NOTES TO THE POEMS

POEMS 1820–1834

COMPLAINT ("THE DAY COMES SOON!")

First published as "Elegiya" ["Elegy"], 1820; republished in a significantly revised and short-ened version as "Ropot" ["Complaint"] in *Poems 1827*, and again in *Poems 1835*, without the title, under numeral XXVI.

This was the first of Baratynsky's poems published with the genre label "elegy." According to a family tradition recorded by Baratynsky's nephew Sergey Rachinsky (*Materials*, vi [2nd pagination]), the poem was addressed to Varvara Nikolayevna Kuchina (born ca. 1800), a distant cousin Baratynsky is said to have fallen in love with when he was living on his uncle's Podvoyskoye estate from 1816 to 1818.

SEPARATION

First published as "Elegiya" ["Elegy"], 1820, with typographical mistakes, and again in 1821 with corrections; republished in a significantly revised and shortened version as "Razluka" ["Separation"] in *Poems 1827*, and again in *Poems 1835*, without the title, under numeral X.

As with "Complaint" (above), a family tradition held that this poem, too, was ad-dressed to Varvara Kuchina.

EPISTLE TO BARON DELVIG ("WHERE ARE YOU, CAREFREE FRIEND?")

First published as "Poslaniye k b. Del'vigu" ["Epistle to Baron Delvig"], 1820; republished in a significantly revised version as "K Deliyu. Oda (s latynskogo)" ["To Delius. An Ode (from the Latin)"] in *Poems 1827*, where the name *Delvig* is replaced by *Deliy* ["Delius"]; republished in *Poems 1835*, without a title but with the name Delvig restored in the text, under numeral XIX.

The poet Anton Antonovich *Delvig* first met Baratynsky in St. Petersburg in late 1818 or early 1819. The two became friends and, later in 1819, shared an apartment. They described their living arrangements in a jointly composed poem in a mock-heroic classical meter (unrhymed dactylic hexameters):

> By the Semyonovsky Guards, 5th Company, once there lived,
> cramped in a little house, Baratynsky and Delvig—two poets.
> They led a quiet life. They didn't pay much for the flat,
> owed the pub money, but still, they rarely would dine at home.
> Often at times when stormclouds darkened the autumn sky,
> they would go out in the drizzle wearing their thin cotton trousers,

and with their hands in their pockets (since they didn't own gloves!),
walking and laughing, would state: "What feeling we Russian folk have!"

Там, где Семеновский полк, в пятой роте, в домике низком,
Жил поэт Баратынский с Дельвигом, тоже поэтом.
Тихо жили они, за квартиру платили не много,
В лавочку были должны, дома обедали редко,
Часто, когда покрывалось небо осеннею тучей,
Шли они в дождик пешком, в панталонах трикотовых тонких,
Руки спрятав в карман (перчаток они не имели!),
Шли и твердили шутя: "Какое в россиянах чувство!"

wandering the shores of Finland — In January 1820, Baratynsky was transferred from the Jaeger Life Guards in St. Petersburg to the Neyshlotsky Infantry Regiment, based in Fredrikshamn (present-day Hamina) on the Finnish coast.

Lilette — A conventional name popular with such eighteenth-century French elegists as Évariste de Parny (1753–1814).

Mad crowd of murmurers, you criticize in vain! — In 1819 and 1820, Aleksandr Pushkin, Delvig, Baratynsky, and Wilhelm Küchelbecker (a group known as "the alliance of poets" [*soyuz poetov*]) scandalized the more conservative faction of the St. Petersburg literary world with their light-hearted verses celebrating sex, carousing, liberal ideas, and their own friendship.

on my feet the shackles bind me — Although his family had requested the transfer to the Neyshlotsky Regiment (the commander was a relative), and although the regiment was often posted in St. Petersburg, Baratynsky and his friends tended to portray his sojourn in Finland as an "exile." While he suffered from boredom and separation from his friends, the hardest part of Baratynsky's time in Finland was the lack of freedom deriving from "the contradictory nature of my position," as he wrote to Vasily Zhukovsky in 1823: "I do not belong to any social estate, although I do possess a kind of title. I have no proper right to the hopes, the pleasures, of any of the estates. I must wait in idleness, at least in psychological idleness, for a change in my fate." (Letter 12.)

FINLAND

First published as "Finlyandiya" ["Finland"], 1820; republished in a significantly revised version in *Poems 1827*, and again, still preserving its title, in *Poems 1835* under numeral I, as the opening poem of the collection.

Written in early 1820, not long after Baratynsky's arrival in Fredrikshamn, it was this poem, more than any other, that consolidated his fame. In his memoirs, Nikolay Konshin recalls the first time he heard Baratynsky read the poem: "I remember one winter evening. There was a storm outside. Attentive silence surrounded our Skald when he, enraptured, read to us in a solemn sing-song voice, in a manner learned from Gnedich, taken from the Greeks, accepted by Pushkin and all the famous poets of that time—when he sang to us his *hymn to Finland*. … One of us then remarked that the shades of Odin and his heroes had flown down to listen to this hymn and were knocking on our windows in greeting to the poet." (Quoted in *True Story*, 162–163.) The poem was first printed in the important literary journal *The Contender*, published by the Free Society of Lovers of Russian Literature.

So this is the homeland of Odin's sons — Like Russian poets before him (such as Derzhavin, Batyushkov, and Zhukovsky), Baratynsky mistakenly assumed that the Finns shared the same Nordic traditions and mythology as other Scandinavians.

Soundless now is the shield of summons, the skaldic voice / unheard, the blazing oak tree cold — All images associated with Viking culture.

THE WATERFALL

First published as "Vodopad" ["The Waterfall"], 1821; republished under the same title with minor revisions in *Poems 1827*, and again in *Poems 1835*, without the title, under numeral LIII.

According to the memoirs of Baratynsky's friend and company commander Nikolay Konshin, the two of them visited the Imatra Falls in Finland, on the Vuoksi River near Lake Saimaa, in early July 1820: "The poet stood for a long time above the deafening abyss, his arms crossed over his chest" (quoted in *Chronicle*, 100).

aquilon — A poetic name for the north wind.

IN AN ALBUM

First published as "V al'bom" ["In an Album"], 1821; republished under the same title with minor revisions in *Poems 1827*; not included in *Poems 1835*.

Most commentators today believe the poem was initially addressed to Sofya Dmitriyevna Ponomaryova, née Poznyak (1794–1824), the hostess of a literary salon attended by writers associated with the journal *The Well-Intentioned*. If so, it must have been written in February 1821, soon after Baratynsky first met Ponomaryova. Baratynsky's feelings for Ponomaryova intensified over the fall and winter of 1821–1822, when his regiment was posted in St. Petersburg, and he wrote a dozen or so poems—including "Disillusionment," "The Kiss," and "To…" ("The obvious infatuation")—that A. M. Peskov believes were addressed to her ("Vzglyad na zhizn' in sochineniya Boratynskogo," in *Chronicle*, 21–22).

The poem "In an Album" was also inscribed (though not in Baratynsky's hand) in the album of Anna Vasilyevna ("Annette") Lutkovskaya (ca. 1804–1879), whom Baratynsky "chased after" in 1824 (see Letter 15); she was the niece of Yegor Lutkovsky, the commander of the Neyshlotsky Regiment.

In the late eighteenth and early nineteenth centuries, albums were a widespread fashion among young Russian noblewomen, who collected poems, witticisms, and other writings in these scrapbooks.

DISILLUSIONMENT

First published as "Elegiya" ["Elegy"], 1821; republished with minor revisions as "Razuvereniye. Elegiya" ["Disillusionment. An Elegy"] 1822; republished as "Razuvereniye" ["Disillusionment"] in *Poems 1827*, and again in *Poems 1835*, with the same title, under numeral LXXXII.

This is perhaps Baratynsky's best-known poem. It was set to music by Mikhail Glinka in 1825 and is still regularly performed as an art song (known in English as "Do Not Tempt Me Needlessly"). The poem was possibly addressed to Sofya Ponomaryova (see note to the poem "In an Album").

THE KISS

First published as "Potseluy (Doride)" ["The Kiss (To Doris)"], 1822; republished with minor revisions as "Potseluy" ["The Kiss"] (with no dedication) in *Poems 1827*, and again in *Poems 1835*, without the title, under numeral LVII.

A. M. Peskov believes this poem reflects the "culmination" of Baratynsky's infatuation with Sofya Ponomaryova ("Vzglyad na zhizn' in sochineniya Boratynskogo," in *Chronicle*, 21).

TO DELVIG ("GIVE ME YOUR HAND")

First published as "K Del'vigu" ["To Delvig"], 1823; republished in a significantly revised version as "Del'vigu" ["To Delvig"] in *Poems 1827*, and again in *Poems 1835*, with the same title, under numeral LXXIV.

On Delvig's friendship with Baratynsky see the notes to "Epistle to Baron Delvig."

the fate with which I struggled — After being expelled from the Corps des Pages military academy in 1816 on grounds of theft, Baratynsky was forbidden by Emperor Alexander I from entering any civil or military service, unless he chose to enlist in the army as a rank-and-file soldier; essentially, he was stripped of his rights and privileges as a nobleman.

You brought me to the good Muses' family — It was Delvig who first encouraged Baratynsky to write poetry and, in early 1819, even had his juvenile verse published, without his knowledge, in the journal *The Well-Intentioned* (*Chronicle*, 90–91).

EPILOGUE

First published as "K ***" ["To ***"], 1823; republished with minor revisions as "Epilog" ["Epilogue"] in *Poems 1827*, and again in *Poems 1835*, without the title, under numeral LXIV. The title refers to the poem's placement in *Poems 1827*, at the end of the third, and last, group of "Elegies."

Helicon is now my past — In the classical Greek tradition, Mount Helicon was one of the homes of the Muses: the poet is leaving poetry behind.

CONFESSION

First published as "Priznaniye" ["Confession"], 1824; not included in *Poems 1827*; republished in a significantly revised version in *Poems 1835*, without the title, under numeral XCIII.

Baratynsky very likely did not include the work in *Poems 1827* because, having recently wed, he did not want people to think the poem's description of a loveless marriage (lines 23–33) related to his new wife. The addressee of the poem is unknown.

Aleksandr Pushkin was particularly impressed by this poem. In a letter to Aleksandr Bestuzhev, dated January 12, 1824, he wrote: "Baratynsky is a delight and marvel; his 'Confession,' perfection. After it, I will never again print my elegies." (*Pushkin's Correspondence*, 1: 463.)

HOPELESSNESS

First published as "Beznadezhnost'" ["Hopelessness"] 1823; republished under the same title with minor revisions in *Poems 1827*, and again in *Poems 1835*, without the title, under numeral XX.

I reached the midpoint of life's journey — A clear echo of the opening line of Dante's *Inferno*: "At the midpoint in the journey of our life..." The poem's title, too, has similar echoes; the portal to Dante's hell is inscribed with the words "Abandon all hope."

TRUTH

First published as "Istina. Oda" ["Truth. An Ode"] 1824; republished as "Istina" ["Truth"] in *Poems 1827*, and again in *Poems 1835*, without the title, under numeral VI.

TO... ("THE OBVIOUS INFATUATION")

First published as "K..." ["To..."], 1824; republished under the same title in a significantly revised version in *Poems 1827*, and again, with additional minor revisions in *Poems 1835*, without the title, under numeral XXI. Further minor revisions appear in *Works 1869*, with the title "G. Z.," probably meaning *Grafine Zakrevskoy*, i.e. "To Countess Zakrevskaya"—the poem, however, was first published in the summer of 1824, months before Baratynsky met the countess (see note to "How much you have in so few days," below).

A. M. Peskov is probably right in asserting that the poem was addressed to Sofya Ponomaryova (see note to the poem "In an Album") and therefore written in the fall of 1821 (*Chronicle*, 109).

There once was a philosopher — René Descartes, who famously wrote: "I think, therefore I am."

Iapetus' son — The Titan Prometheus, who stole fire from the gods and was punished by Zeus by being chained to a mountain in the Caucasus. In the classical Greek story, it was an eagle that fed on his liver, not *a raven pecking at his heart*, but in the Russian reception of the myth, the eagle was sometimes replaced by a hawk or raven, and Prometheus's liver by his breast or heart (*CCWL*, 1: 443–444).

TO A. A. V.

First published as "A. A. V—oy" ["To A. A. V."], 1827 (in two different literary almanacs!); republished under the same title in *Poems 1827*, and again in *Poems 1835*, without the title, under numeral XLVIII.

The poem is addressed to *Aleksandra Andreyevna Voyeykova*, née Protasova (1795–1829), Zhukovsky's goddaughter and the hostess of an important literary salon in St. Petersburg in the 1820s. Baratynsky seems to have come under her spell in the summer of 1824, when his regiment was posted in the capital.

SHE

First published as "Ona" ["She"], 1827, in the journal *The Slav*; it was not included in either *Poems 1827* or *Poems 1835*.

Although some commentators have speculated that the poem relates to Baratynsky's wife, Nastasya Lvovna Baratynskaya (e.g. *CCP 1936*, 2: 290), and was presumably written during their courtship in the spring of 1826, A. M. Peskov's suggestion that it was written for Aleksandra Voyeykova during Baratynsky's infatuation with her in the summer of 1824 is more plausible (*Chronicle*, 28, n. 1). Not only is it similar in tone to the poem "To A. A. V.," it was published in *The Slav*, the new journal edited by her husband, Aleksandr Voyeykov. The poem's exclusion from both *Poems 1827* and *Poems 1835* also suggests that it was not addressed to Nastasya Baratynskaya.

JUSTIFICATION

First published as "Opravdaniye" ["Justification"], 1825; republished under the same title in a significantly revised version in *Poems 1827*, and again, with minor revisions in *Poems 1835*, without the title, under numeral LXXII. Two further minor revisions appear in *Works 1869*.

first Delia, then Daphne, then Liletta — Conventional names derived from Latin (Tibullus, Ovid) and French (Parny) love poetry.

Paphian pilgrimesses — A euphemism for prostitutes: Paphos, on Cyprus, was the center of the cult of Aphrodite in antiquity (it was believed to be the place where the goddess of love rose from the sea).

THE SKULL

First published as "Cherep" ["The Skull"], 1825; republished in a somewhat revised version as "Mogila" ["The Grave"] in *Poems 1827*, and again, with further revisions in *Poems 1835*, with the title "The Skull" under numeral CVI.

THE STORM

First published as "Burya" ["The Storm"], 1825; republished under the same title in a somewhat revised version in *Poems 1827*, and again, in a censored version, in *Poems 1835*, without the title, under numeral III.

The poem was written during the poet's stay in Helsingfors (Helsinki) in the fall of 1824. In November, terrible storms in the Gulf of Finland caused flooding in both Helsingfors and St. Petersburg (the St. Petersburg flood would later serve as the background for Pushkin's narrative poem *The Bronze Horseman* [1833]).

In *Poems 1835*, lines 11–20 ("Is it not that spiteful spirit… by the power of his mutinous might") were deleted by the censor and replaced with rows of periods. These same lines had caused difficulties earlier, when the poem was first published in the journal *Mnemosyne* (see Letter 25).

that spiteful spirit, the ruler of Gehenna — Satan; in the Judeo-Christian tradition, Gehenna is the name of the place of the damned.

To die on raging billows… — The same romantic desire can be found in a letter Baratynsky wrote his mother when he was fourteen asking for permission to serve in the navy: "Imagine, my dear Maman, a furious tempest and me on the top deck, as if commanding the enraged sea, a wooden plank between me and death" (Letter 4).

"THE FATHERLAND'S FOE, THE TSAR'S VALET"

Not published until 1935, in the journal *Zven'ya*, from a copy of the poem made by Nikolay Putyata before leaving Helsingfors in February 1825.

The epigram is directed against Emperor Alexander's closest and most powerful adviser, Count Aleksey Andreyevich Arakcheyev (1769–1834), who was entrusted with organizing peasant villages into a system of brutal "military settlements"; in the 1820s, he essentially became the tsar's unofficial prime minister. As historian Anatole G. Mazour has noted, "In the history of the nineteenth century the name of Arakcheev stands as a symbol of the darkest reaction and the cruelest oppression. … Tactless, bigoted, and unsympathetic with suffering, he was hated by more people than was any other statesman of his time." (*The First Russian Revolution: The Decembrist Movement, Its Origins, Development, and Significance* [Stanford, Calif.: Stanford University Press, 1937], 41–42.) The governor-general of Finland, Count Arseny Andreyevich Zakrevsky, called Arakcheyev "the most dangerous man in Russia" (quoted in I. Medvedeva, "Ranniy Baratynskiy," in *CCP 1936*, 1: lv), so it is no surprise that Baratynsky wrote his epigram during his stay with the Zakrevskys in Helsingfors in the winter of 1824–1825.

he does his evil in the shadows — Possibly a reference to the fact that Arakcheyev's most ruthless brutalities towards the peasants took place outside St. Petersburg, on his estate of Gruzino in Novgorod Province.

"HOW MUCH YOU HAVE IN SO FEW DAYS"

First published in *Poems 1827*, with censor-ordered changes in the last two lines; republished in *Poems 1835*, under numeral XLIII, with the penultimate line replaced by a row of periods—the line was restored in *Works 1869*.

The poem is addressed to Countess Agrafena Fyodorovna Zakrevskaya, née Tolstaya (1799–1879), the wife of the governor-general of Finland. Beautiful and intelligent, Zakrevskaya was famous for her unconventional behavior and dramatic mood swings, as well as for her many flirtations and love affairs. Baratynsky got to know her during his stay in Helsingfors, from October 1824 to February 1825, and like many others, developed a fascination with her that is reflected in his poems and letters (see Letters 21, 22, 24, and, especially, 28). She was the model for Princess Nina, the passionate and promiscuous heroine of his narrative poem *The Ball* (1828). Pushkin, too, became her lover a few years later, when the Zakrevskys were living in St. Petersburg. He depicted her as appearing among the women of the north "like a lawless comet in the calculated circle of the stars" in the poem "Portrait" (1828), and commentators have identified her as the "resplendent Nina Voronskaya, that Cleopatra of the Neva," who sat next to Tatyana in Chapter 8, stanza 16, of *Eugene Onegin*.

weeping like the Magdalene — In the Western tradition, Mary Magdalene is commonly portrayed as a repentant prostitute; this is not the case in Eastern Orthodoxy, however, and the censor found Baratynsky's comparison unacceptable. We should note that "Magdalina" was also one of the names by which Baratynsky referred to Zakrevskaya in his letters to Nikolay Putyata (see Letters 27 and 28).

siren — The word translated here is *rusalka*—in Slavic mythology, a female water spirit who entices men into rivers to drown them.

INSCRIPTION

First published as "Nadpis'" ["Inscription"], 1826; republished under the same title in *Poems 1827*, and again in *Poems 1835*, without the title, under numeral LXII.

Until the mid-twentieth century, the poem was thought to be an epigram on the playwright Aleksandr Sergeyevich Griboyedov (1795–1829): in Nastasya Baratynskaya's copy, it bears the dedication "A. S. G.," and in *Works 1869*, it is subtitled "On a Portrait of Griboyedov." (For this reason, Yuri Tynyanov used Baratynsky's poem as the epigraph to his 1928 biographical novel about Griboyedov, *The Death of the Vazir-Mukhtar.*) Later scholars, however, beginning with Ye. N. Kupreyanova in *CCP 1957* (352), have generally held that the poem more likely alludes to Agrafena Zakrevskaya (see the note to the previous poem); compare Baratynsky's description of her as a marble tomb in Letter 22.

STANZAS ("HAPPY IS ONE IN THE FOREST WILDS")

First published as "Stansy" ["Stanzas"], 1825; republished under the same title in a significantly shorter version in *Poems 1827*, and again in *Poems 1835*, without the title, under numeral CII.

Epicurus or Epictetus — Here the Greek philosophers *Epicurus* (341–270 BCE) and *Epictetus* (55–135 CE) represent the opposing philosophical systems of Epicureanism (the active pursuit of pleasure and avoidance of suffering) and Stoicism (dispassionate acceptance of what we cannot control).

STANZAS ("THE CHAINS THAT FATE HAD LAID UPON ME")

First published as "Stansy" ["Stanzas"], 1828; republished in *Poems 1835*, without the title, under numeral CVIII. In the 1828 publication in the *Moscow Telegraph*, the sixth stanza ("I did know brothers...") was deleted by the censor; the stanza was restored in *Poems 1835*, with the verb in the third line appearing as *stranstvuyut* ("roam"). In *Works 1869*, the verb is *bedstvuyut* (translated as "languish in misery"). In an early draft, the poem is titled "Mara," the name of the Baratynsky estate in Tambov Province (Gofman uses this title in *CCP 1914*), while in *Works 1869* it appears under the title "Rodina" ["Motherland"].

The chains that fate had laid upon me / fell from my hands — A reference to the fact that on April 21, 1825, Baratynsky was promoted, by order of Emperor Alexander I, to the officer's rank of ensign, which restored all the rights of nobility that he had lost in 1816 after his expulsion from the Corps des Pages military academy. In an early version of the poem, the chains of the opening line were described more provocatively as coming not from fate but from the autocrat (*samovlastitel'nyye*).

I'm seeing you, my native steppeland — The description that follows in the next two stanzas relates to Mara, the estate near Kirsanov in Tambov Province, where the poet was born and spent most of his childhood.

I did know brothers... — Baratynsky was close to a number of the revolutionaries involved in the Decembrist uprising in St. Petersburg on December 14, 1825, especially the writers Wilhelm Küchelbecker, Kondraty Ryleyev, and Aleksandr Bestuzhev. In the aftermath of the failed revolution, Ryleyev, one of the leaders, was executed, while Küchelbecker was sent to prison and Bestuzhev to Siberia.

Some far away in misery languish; / others are in this world no more. — Baratynsky here repeats, and slightly modifies, a phrase Pushkin had used in his prose epigraph to the narrative poem *The Fountain of Bakhchisaray* [*Bakhchisarayskiy fontan*] (1824), which he attributed to the medieval Persian poet Saadi: "Many, like me, have visited this fountain—but some are no more; others roam far away." (In *Poems 1835*, Baratynsky used the same verb as Pushkin: *stranstvuyut* ["roam"].) After the Decembrist uprising, these words became a kind of code referring to those who were executed or banished. In early 1827, in the *Moscow Telegraph*, reviewing Russian literature from the two previous years, Nikolay Polevoy wrote: "I look at the circle of our friends, formerly so lively, merry, and often sadly repeat the words of Saadi, or Pushkin, who paraphrased Saadi's words: 'Some are no more; others roam far away.'" The effect of Polevoy's words is evident from a report to the secret police, almost certainly made by the rival journalist and informer Faddey Bulgarin: "The sorrow over perished friends... was understood by everyone and gave the journal a big boost. In the article they are all grieving over the past two years... and the exile of the insurgents." (Quoted by L. G. Frizman in *Poems 1982*, 620.) Pushkin himself used the formula again, in the final stanza of *Eugene Onegin* (1832): "But those, to whom, in a friendly meeting, / I read the first stanzas... / some are no more, and others far away, / as Saadi once said." For more on the phrase, and its possible source in Saadi, see Vladimir Nabokov's commentary to his translation of *Eugene Onegin*, rev. ed. (Princeton, N.J.: Princeton University Press, 1975), 3: 245–250.

she is my young wife... — Baratynsky married Nastasya Engelhardt in Moscow on June 9, 1826, and their daughter Aleksandra was born in March 1827. Baratynsky brought his wife and infant daughter to Mara for the first time in the summer of 1827.

THE LAST DEATH

First published as "Poslednyaya smert'" ["The Last Death"], 1827, and again in *Poems 1835*, with the same title, under numeral CXIV.

ASSURANCE

First published as "Uvereniye" ["Assurance"], 1829, with the date specified as "1824"; republished in *Poems 1835*, without the title, under numeral XL.

M. L. Gofman (*CCP 1914*, 1: 256) and most commentators after him have speculated that by specifying the poem's date as 1824, Baratynsky was attempting to conceal the fact that the poem was written after his marriage—probably in 1828 or 1829—and that it was addressed to Agrafena Zakrevskaya (see the note to "How much you have in so few days").

with an Old Believer's worry — The sect known as Old Believers broke from the official Russian Orthodox Church in the mid-seventeenth century over the liturgical reforms introduced by Patriarch Nikon. An Old Believer who prayed to new, post-reform icons might well worry that he was praying to a false god.

THE FAIRY

First published as "Feya" ["The Fairy"], 1830, with the date specified as "1824"; republished in *Poems 1835*, without the title, under numeral II.

Baratynsky insisted that Nikolay Konshin, the editor of the literary almanac *Tsarskoye Selo*, where the poem first appeared, print the date as 1824 (Letter 51). As with the poem "Assurance," this was most likely an attempt to conceal the fact that it was written after Baratynsky's marriage. The poem possibly alludes to Agrafena Zakrevskaya (see the note to "How much you have in so few days"); in 1825, writing to Nikolay Putyata, Baratynsky calls her "your fairy" (Letter 24).

"MY GIFT IS MEAGER AND MY VOICE NOT LOUD"

First published, with other poems, under the general title "Anthological Poems," 1829; republished in *Poems 1835*, without a title, under numeral CXII.

a reader in posterity — In the essay "On the Interlocutor" (1913), the poet Osip Mandelstam compares this poem to a message in a bottle tossed into the sea: "Reading Baratynsky's poem, I experience the very same feeling as if such a bottle had come into my hands. The ocean with all its enormous elemental force came to its aid, helped it fulfill its predestined purpose, and the one who has found it is seized by a sense of the providential. In the seafarer's tossing of the bottle into the waves and in Baratynsky's dispatch of the poem there are two equally distinct characteristics. The letter, exactly like the poem, is not addressed to anyone in particular. Nevertheless, they both have an addressee: for the letter, this is the person who happens to notice the bottle in the sand; for the poem, it is the 'reader in posterity.' I would like to know if there is anyone who encounters these lines by Baratynsky who does not tremble with the kind of joyful, terrible shudder you feel when someone unexpectedly calls out your name. ... Baratynsky's penetrating gaze is directed past his generation—though there are friends in his generation—in order to rest on the unknown but definite 'reader.' And everyone who happens upon Baratynsky's verses feels himself to be such a 'reader'—chosen, called by name." ("O sobesednike," in *Proza* [Ann Arbor, Mich.: Ardis, 1983], 17, 19.)

THE LITTLE DEMON

First published as "Besyonok" ["The Little Demon"], 1829; republished in *Poems 1835*, without the title, under numeral CXVI.

Sending the poem to Delvig for his almanac *Northern Flowers*, Baratynsky noted, "If the work itself is not clever, at least the title is impish" (Letter 30).

Thunderclap — In Zhukovsky's ballad "The Twelve Sleeping Maidens" ["Dvenadtsat' spyashchikh dev"] (1817), the character Thunderclap [*Gromoboy*] sells his soul to the devil for, among other things, a bag of gold that never runs out.

Gray Wolf... Sivka-Burka... magic beans... water of life... water of death... the cap of invisibility... flying carpet... the Firebird... the Maiden Tsar — All characters and motifs from Russian fairy tales (Sivka-Burka is the name of a magic horse). For Baratynsky's thoughts about literary works based on fairy-tale motifs, see Letter 95.

thrice-nine lands away — Russian fairy tales often begin with some variation of the formula "Beyond thrice-nine lands, in the thrice-ninth tsardom, in the thrice-tenth realm there lived..."

DEATH

First published as "Smert'" ["Death"], 1829; republished with significant revisions in *Poems 1835*, without the title, under numeral XLII. A few later revisions (notably in the first stanza) appeared in *Works 1869*.

The opening lines underwent some noteworthy changes. The version published in the *Moscow Messenger* in 1829 began: *O smert'! tvoyo imenovan'ye / Nam v suyevernuyu boyazn': / Ty v nashey mysli t'my sozdan'ye, / Paden'yem vyzvannaya kazn'!* ["O death! Naming you / sends us into superstitious fear: / in our thought you are a creature of darkness, / the punishment called forth by [our] fall!"]. The opening of the version in *Poems 1835* is much more concise: *Tebya iz t'my ne izvedu ya, / O smert'!...* ["I do not bring you forth from darkness, / O death!..."]. Finally, in the revision published in *Works 1869*, Baratynsky expresses the idea even more compactly: *Smert' dshcher'yu t'my ne nazovu ya...* ["Death I call not Daughter of Darkness..."]. But what is most striking here is the use of the archaic Church Slavonic (i.e. liturgical) word for daughter (*dshcher'*), which produces a kind of consonantal fanfare, a dense succession of echoing sounds that invoke the same ecclesiastical brimstone as earlier—*Smért' dshchér'yu t'mý...* (literally, "Death, [as] daughter of darkness")—but then, with the turn on the negative particle *ne*, the intensity dissolves in the phonic lightness of *ne nazovú ya* ("I will not call"). Here the translator must admit defeat, awed by the majesty of the poet's music.

Daughter — In Slavic folklore, Death is personified as female (the noun is feminine in Russian and other Slavic languages).

FRAGMENT (A SCENE FROM THE POEM *BELIEF AND UNBELIEF*)

First published as "Stsena iz poemy 'Vera i neveriye'" ["A Scene from the Poem *Belief and Unbelief*"], 1829; republished as "Otryvok" ["Fragment"] in *Poems 1835*, under numeral CXXX (the penultimate poem in the volume of lyrics). Since the title "Fragment" requires a certain context, I have restored the original title in parentheses. Other than this poem, there is no record of any narrative or dramatic work in verse (*poema*) titled *Belief and Unbelief*.

with humble hearts we must believe / and wait the end with quiet patience — These two lines (*V smiren'i serdtsa nado verit' / I terpelivo zhdat' kontsa*) form the epitaph on Baratynsky's tombstone in the Tikhvin Cemetery of the Alexander Nevsky Monastery in St. Petersburg.

MY MUSE

First published as "Muza" ["My Muse"], 1830; republished in *Poems 1835*, without the title, under numeral CV.

TO IMITATORS

First published as "Podrazhatelyam" ["To Imitators"], 1830; republished in *Poems 1835*, without the title, under numeral XXXIX.

"NOW AND THEN A WONDROUS CITY"

First published in 1830; republished in *Poems 1835*, under numeral XCV.

"WHERE'S THE SWEET WHISPER"

First published in *Poems 1835*, under numeral CXXII.

MY ELYSIUM

First published as "Moy Eliziy" ["My Elysium"], 1832; republished in *Poems 1835*, without the title, under numeral CXXI. Baratynsky included the poem in a letter to Ivan Kireyevsky in the fall of 1831, apparently intending it for Kireyevsky's journal, *The European* (Letter 73); around the same time, however, he also sent it to Pushkin, who published it in the special issue of *Northern Flowers* dedicated to the memory of Delvig (see note to Letter 75 and Letter 77).

Elysium — In classical mythology, the realm in the Underworld where the blessed go after death.

oblivion's water — Lethe, the river of oblivion, flowed past the fields of Elysium, as described by Virgil in Book 6 of *The Aeneid*.

You are alive there, Delvig — Baron Anton Delvig died on January 14, 1831, at the age of thirty-two, after a brief and at first seemingly benign illness (see the biographical note between Letters 57 and 58).

"A CHILD, I WOULD THE FOREST ECHO"

First published in *Poems 1835*, under numeral CXXXI (the concluding poem in the volume of lyrics). Baratynsky included the poem in a letter to Nikolay Yazykov written from the Kaymary estate in September 1831 (Letter 72).

"IN DAYS OF LIMITLESS DISTRACTIONS"

First published as "Elegiya" ["Elegy"], 1832; republished in *Poems 1835*, without a title, under numeral CXXIX. Baratynsky included the poem in a letter to Ivan Kireyevsky from Kaymary in the fall of 1831 (Letter 73).

a twisted genius lived beside me — The image recalls lines from Voltaire quoted by the sixteen-year-old Baratynsky in a letter to his mother from Podvoyskoye (Letter 6): *Chacun a son lutin qui toujours le promène / Des chagrins aux amusements* ["Everyone has his imp, who always leads him / from sorrows to amusements"] ("Jean qui pleure et qui ris" ["Jean Who Cries and Who Laughs"], 1772).

"MY ARTLESS PENCIL HAS SET DOWN"

First published in *Poems 1835*, under numeral CXIII.

my disfavored spring — This "spring" refers to the nine years following the Corps des Pages expulsion when Baratynsky was in disfavor with the emperor (1816–1825).

ON THE DEATH OF GOETHE

First published as "Na smert' Gete" ["On the Death of Goethe"], 1833; republished in *Poems 1835*, with the same title, under numeral CXIX.

In a letter to Ivan Kireyevsky written in May 1832, Baratynsky noted that of the few poems he wrote during the eleven months he spent in Kazan and Kaymary, this was the one he was happiest with (Letter 94).

The great German poet and novelist Johann Wolfgang von Goethe died on March 22, 1832, at the age of eighty-two.

She appeared — That is, death (see note to the poem "Death").

"WHAT GOOD ARE FANTASIES OF FREEDOM TO THE PRISONER?"

First published in *Poems 1835*, under numeral XI. In this version, the question, "And is not the voice / we hear in them *its* voice?" was removed by the censor, with misplaced ellipses resulting in distortions in lines 15–16. The full lines were not published until 1921, in Yu. G. Oksman's article –Stikhotvoreniya Yevgeniya Baratynskago' v tsenzure," in A. S. Nikolayev and Yu. G. Oksman, eds., *Literaturnyy muzeum: Tsenzurnye materialy 1-go otd. IV sektsii Gosudarstvennogo Arkhivnogo fonda*, vol. 1 (St. Petersburg [Petrograd]: Gosudarstvennyy arkhivnyy fond SSSR, 1921?), 16.

"WHEN WILL THE DARKNESS DISAPPEAR"

First published in *Poems 1835*, under numeral LXVI.

"CANTICLES HEAL THE SPIRIT IN AFFLICTION"

First published in *Poems 1835*, under numeral XCIX.

In a letter to Pyotr Pletnyov, written in July 1831 (Letter 66), Baratynsky expresses an idea similar to that found in the poem: "[Poetry is] an art which, better than any philosophy, consoles us in the sorrows of life. To express a feeling means to resolve it, to master it. This is why the gloomiest of poets can maintain a cheerfulness of spirit."

"O THOUGHT, THE FLOWER'S FATE"

First published in *Poems 1835*, under numeral CVII.

"BELIEVE ME, GENTLE ONE"

First published in *Poems 1835*, under numeral CXI. The poem is addressed to the poet's wife; in *Works 1869*, it appears under the title "To N. L. Baratynskaya."

"THERE IS A LOVELY COUNTRY"

First published in *Poems 1835*, under numeral CXVII.

Little is known about the omitted eight lines (11–18); possibly, Baratynsky inserted the ellipsis intentionally to create a pause between the general ideas of the opening lines and the personal recollections that follow. Considering that the last lines relate to the family's grief over the death of Natalya Engelhardt (see note below), the editors of *CCWL* believe that Baratynsky may have begun writing the poem as early as 1827 (*CCWL*, 2/1: 163).

Armida's gardens — In Tasso's *Jerusalem Delivered* (1581), set during the First Crusade, the Saracen sorceress Armida falls in love with the Christian soldier Rinaldo and imprisons him in her enchanted gardens.

I remember a pond... — This and the following lines describe the topography of Muranovo, the suburban Moscow estate of Baratynsky's father-in-law, the retired Major General Lev Engelhardt (1776–1836). The poet met the Engelhardt family in February or March of 1826, and in early April became engaged to Engelhardt's eldest daughter, the twenty-one-year-old Nastasya (*Chronicle*, 175, 179–180). In the years following their marriage, Baratynsky and his family often spent the summer in Muranovo.

She, with a sickly flush upon her cheek... — The apparition is Nastasya's sister Natalya Engelhardt, who died of consumption at the age of twenty-one in December 1826 (*Works 1884*, 217; *Chronicle*, 185).

"IT'S SPRING! IT'S SPRING! HOW CLEAN THE AIR"

First published in *Poems 1835*, under numeral CXXV.

"ARBITRARY WAS THE PET NAME"

First published in *Poems 1835*, under numeral CXXVI; in *Works 1869*, the poem appears under the title "N. L. Baratynskoy" ["To N. L. Baratynskaya"] with a revision of the third-to-last line (which previously read *Im k tebe voskliknu ya* ["with it I'll call out to you"]).

The poem is addressed to the poet's wife.

pet name — In a letter to his wife, from June 1829, Baratynsky writes: "I remember telling you about how Marya Andreyevna's husband used to end the letters he wrote to her—with a list of endearments and pet names; we both found that amusing, but you know, it now seems to me that this man loved his wife very much and was not being at all ridiculous. Right now, when I would like to say to you everything that is most tender, I can't find anything better than to call you *Popinka*, as if you were here beside me. My darling *Popinka*, may God keep you safe." (Letter 47.)

LEFT TO RUIN

First published as "Zapusteniye. Elegiya" ["Left to Ruin. An Elegy"], 1835; republished in *Poems 1835*, without the title, under numeral LXV. A few small later revisions appeared in *Works 1869*.

The poem was composed during Baratynsky's extended stay in Mara from June 1833 to March 1834. It was the last-written work to be included in *Poems 1835* (see note to Letter 107).

The poem's Russian title is sometimes translated as "Desolation," but this is misleading; the English word suggests a state of hopelessness that is not at all present in the poem. The Russian word *zapusteniye*, a deverbal noun from the intransitive *zapustet'* ("to be in a state of dereliction"), also related to the transitive *zapustit'* ("to abandon"), refers primarily to a physical condition. Although it uses a different part of speech, the title "Left to Ruin" seems to better capture the dilapidation denoted by the Russian word.

I paid my visit to you — Here and throughout the poem, Baratynsky describes the landscape park on the family estate of Mara, in Tambov Province, where he lived as a child.

a skillful artist laid them out... — The poet's father, Abram Baratynsky, designed the English-style park at Mara in the early years of the nineteenth century. A neighbor, the political philosopher Boris N. Chicherin, described the park in his memoirs: "Abram Andreyevich settled in the part of Vyazhlya that bears the name Mara, and here he began to live in grand squirely style. Not far from the house there is a ravine covered in woods with a gushing spring at the bottom of it. Here there were ponds, cascades, a stone grotto with a hidden walkway leading from the house, gazebos, little bridges, skillfully laid-out paths. The poet Baratynsky, in his poem 'Left to Ruin,' describes in touching detail this spot where the early days of his childhood were spent but which was more or less abandoned after his father's death in 1810. The widow no longer thought about maintaining the squire's old whims; she devoted herself wholly to the education of the children, and it must be said that she fully achieved this goal." ("Iz moikh vospominaniy: Po povodu dnevnika N. I. Krivtsova," *Russkiy arkhiv* 28, no. 4 [1890]: 508.)

my overgrown Elysium — See note to "My Elysium."

a distant grave has taken his dust — Baratynsky's father died in Moscow in 1810 and was buried there at the Andronnikov Monastery of the Savior.

"A FAITHFUL RECORD OF IMPRESSIONS"

Not published until 1936, in *CCP 1936* (1: 316), on the basis of an autograph manuscript belonging to Yu. N. Verkhovsky. The poem seems to have been intended as a "preface in verse" to *Poems 1835* (see Letter 107).

Lethe — In classical tradition, the river of oblivion in the Underworld.

DUSK

Published by the Moscow bookseller Auguste Semen in 1842, the book bears the subtitle *Sochineniye Yevgeniya Boratynskago* [*A Work by Yevgeny Boratynsky*]. On an existing fair copy submitted to the Moscow censor for review, an earlier title, "A Winter Night's Dream" ["Son zimney nochi"] has been crossed out and replaced by the title "Dusk" ["Sumerki"]. (Facsimiles of the published book and the censor's copy are printed in *CCWL*, 195–288, and 291–362, respectively).

The title of the book is often translated as *Twilight*, but the Russian word *sumerki*, related to the verb *smerkat'sya* ("to get dark"), is more connotative of thickening darkness (*mrak*) than dwindling light; hence, *Dusk* seems the more appropriate translation.

TO PRINCE PYOTR ANDREYEVICH VYAZEMSKY

First published, 1836; republished in *Dusk*, 1842. Baratynsky originally intended to include the poem in *Poems 1835* (see Letters 108 and 146). In *Dusk*, the poem, printed in italic, serves as the dedication.

The poet and literary critic *Pyotr Andreyevich Vyazemsky* (1792–1878) established himself as a writer in the first decade of the nineteenth century. His half-sister, Yekaterina Kolyvanova, had married the writer Nikolay Karamzin in 1801, which led to Vyazemsky's close personal and literary ties with the older generation of "Karamzinian" poets, dedicated to Europeanizing Russian writing: Zhukovsky, Konstantin Batyushkov, Vasily Pushkin (Aleksandr's uncle), and others who formed the "Arzamas" group. In the early 1820s, Vyazemsky and his wife, Princess Vera Fyodorovna, became part of Aleksandr Pushkin's circle of intimate friends. Vyazemsky and Baratynsky, however, did not really come to know each other until later in the decade, when they were both living in Moscow. In the early 1830s, Vyazemsky moved to St. Petersburg, where he was in government service. Among other things, by dedicating his book to Vyazemsky, Baratynsky signaled his renewed affinity to the older liberal and Western orientation of Russian letters, extending back through Pushkin to Zhukovsky and Karamzin.

May the hour of anguish quickly pass! — In the fall of 1834, when Baratynsky wrote the poem, the Vyazemskys had taken their daughter Polina to Italy to be treated for consumption; she died a few months later (*Chronicle*, 323–324).

Star from a Pleiad now dispersed! — The original *pleiad*, in Greek mythology, were the seven daughters of the sea nymph Pleione, who were immortalized as stars in the constellation Pleiades. The term was later used for several groups of poets—in Alexandria in the third century BCE and, most famously, for the circle around Pierre de Ronsard in sixteenth-century France ("La Pléiade"). Here, Baratynsky uses it for the poets who dominated Russian literature in the early 1820s: Pushkin, Vyazemsky, Delvig, Küchelbecker, Ryleyev, Yazykov, and himself, among others. By 1834, the Decembrist Ryleyev had been executed, Delvig was dead, Küchelbecker (another Decembrist) was in prison, and Baratynsky, in Moscow, was wondering if he would ever write verse again. In the twentieth century, literary scholars borrowed Baratynsky's phrase to refer to this same group as the "Pushkin Pleiad" (*Pushkinskaya pleyada*).

THE LAST POET

First published, 1835; republished with minor revisions in *Dusk*, 1842; later, relatively minor changes appeared in *Works 1869*; these reflected revisions made by Baratynsky on a published copy of *Dusk* (with an apparent misreading in stanza 6 of *bodrym* [here translated "eager"] as *gordym* ["proud"]). The version used in the translation is based on *Poems 1982*, which incorporates the later revisions and corrects the mistake in *Works 1869*. In the *Dusk* version, we find the following earlier readings (accepted by some editions, including *CCWL*, as authoritative): in stanza 2, line 6: "Luxury breathes, taste shines" (changed later to "Pontus bears commercial cargo"); in stanza 6, lines 3–4, the poet asks why we submit our "burning" hearts to "cold" schemes; in stanza 9, the poet hears the "voice" (not the "song") of the waves; and in the last stanza, it is the "voice of the sea" (not its waves) that causes man to feel embarrassed.

"The Last Poet" was first published in the first issue of the *Moscow Observer*, whose literary section was edited by Stepan Shevyryov with contributors drawn mainly from the circle around Ivan Kireyevsky. Baratynsky's poem complemented Shevyryov's programmatic opening essay, "Literature and Commerce" ("Slovesnost i torgovlya"), which set forth the journal's opposition to the commercialization of literature.

Hellas has returned to life — Greece, called here by the classical name "Hellas" (*Ellada* in Russian), won its independence from the Ottoman Empire in 1830, after nine years of war.

Pontus bears commercial cargo — "Pontus" was one of the classical names of the Black Sea. In 1828, Russia's support for Greek independence had led the Ottoman Empire to close the Straits of the Dardanelles, connecting the Black Sea with the Mediterranean, to all Russian ships. The Treaty of Adrianople, in 1829, reopened the Straits to certain forms of shipping, but it was not until 1833 that Black Sea commerce between Russia and Greece fully resumed.

Parnassus blooms!… a living stream beats from Castalia's spring — The Castalian Spring, in Delphi at the base of Mount Parnassus, was sacred to Apollo and the Muses. According to Greek tradition, the nymph Castalia was transformed into the spring by Apollo and her waters became a source of poetic inspiration.

cold Urania's acolytes — Urania, the muse of astronomy, is here understood as representing science in general.

Aeolus — The god of the winds.

the cliffs of Leucas... the shade of Sappho... Phaon's lover — According to legend, the poet Sappho flung herself from a cliff on the island of Leucas (Lefkada) after being rejected in love by the ferryman Phaon.

"SUPERSTITION—IT'S A FRAGMENT"

First published, 1841; republished with minor revisions in *Dusk*, 1842.

Superstition — The word rendered "superstition" is *predrassudok*, today more commonly translated as "prejudice." In the nineteenth century, however, the word did not primarily mean a bias against certain groups, but irrational opinions based on received ideas, especially in relation to religious belief.

NOVINSKOYE

First published in *Dusk*, 1842.

In an earlier version, copied in an album from the 1820s, the poem was addressed directly to the woman: *Kak vzory tomnyye svoi / Ty na pevtse ostanovila...* ["When your languorous eyes / you rested on the singer..."]. Commentators generally agree that Baratynsky is describing an encounter between Pushkin and a woman (possibly the poet Yekaterina Timasheva) that occurred not long after Pushkin's return to Moscow in the fall of 1826 from his Mikhaylovskoye exile. (A. M. Peskov argues that this must have happened in February or April 1827, during either the Shrovetide or Easter carnival and Baratynsky wrote the first version of the poem soon after—see *Chronicle*, 189.) As S. G. Bocharov notes in the commentary to his popular edition of Baratynsky's works, the change of address is significant: "In the revision of the poem—clearly made after Pushkin's death [in January 1837]—it was readdressed to the poet himself and thus, in a way, was dedicated to his memory" (Ye. A. Baratynsky, *Stikhotvoreniya* [Moscow: Sovetskaya Rossiya, 1976], 320–321). On Baratynsky's relationship to Pushkin, see Letters 31, 34, 41, and 111.

Novinskoye — Novinskoye Fairground (*Novinskoye gulyan'ye*) was the name of a thoroughfare in Moscow where carnivals were held in the first half of the nineteenth century (present-day Novinsky Boulevard, known as Tchaikovsky Street in Soviet times). Baratynsky provides a vivid description of a carnival on Novinskoye in Chapter 2 of his narrative poem *The Gypsy* (first published as *The Concubine*, 1831; revised 1835):

"It was Easter week / and to Novinskoye it called / Moscow's citizens. Everyone ran, / everyone hurried: old and young, / hovel-dwellers, mansion-dwellers, /

in a lively, confused throng, / to where, as if by itself, / for a short time, in a single moment, / shining with dappled palaces, / rustling with colored banners, / within the city a new city arose: / the light capital of idleness / and rankless merriment, / the idol of Russian leisure!"

> Неделя светлая была
> И под Новинское звала
> Граждан московских. Все бежало,
> Все торопилось: стар и млад,
> Жильцы лачуг, жильцы палат,
> Живою, смешанной толпою,
> Туда, где, словно сам собою,
> На краткий срок, в единый миг,
> Блистая пестрыми дворцами,
> Шумя цветными флюгерами,
> Средь града новый град возник:
> Столица легкая безделья
> И бесчиновного веселья,
> Досуга русского кумир!

SIGNS

First published, 1840; republished, with a somewhat revised third stanza, in *Dusk*, 1842.

"ALWAYS ARRAYED IN GOLD"

First published, 1840; republished, slightly revised, in *Dusk*, 1842. The addressee is unknown. Interestingly, when Baratynsky translated this poem into French prose during his stay in Paris in the winter of 1843–1844, he titled it "Le Crépuscule" ["Dusk"].

"AN AUTHOR PAST HIS PRIME!"

First published in *Dusk*, 1842.

The epigram is aimed at Ivan Lazhechnikov (1792–1869), the author of several historical novels, including the popular *House of Ice* [*Ledyanoy dom*] (1835). In a draft version of the epigram, the writer was accused of having exhausted his gift on novels, not articles.

tampering with the spelling rules — In *The Heretic* [*Basurman*] (1838), Lazhechnikov introduced a number of modifications to the standard Russian orthography in order to make spelling conform more closely to pronunciation.

Naples was once turned upside down / by a fisherman — On July 7, 1647, the fisherman Tomasso Aniello (known as Masianello) led a successful revolt in Naples against the rule of Spain. He was declared Captain-General of the city, a title confirmed by the Spanish viceroy, but nine days later (not twelve, as in the epigram), he went mad, denounced his fellow-citizens, and was assassinated. The story was well known in Russia in the 1830s from the popular opera by Daniel Auber, *La Muette de Portici* (1828), a highly romanticized retelling of the uprising.

THE STILLBORN

First published, 1835; republished, with significant revisions, in *Dusk*, 1842, where the last line reads *V tyagost' tvoy prostor, o vechnost'!* ["Heavy is your expanse, O eternity!"], a change apparently ordered by the censor. Beginning with M. L. Gofman in *CCP 1914*, editors have usually restored the line *O bessmyslennaya vechnost'!* ["O eternity so senseless!"], which was crossed out in the censor's copy of *Dusk*.

It is worth noting that when Baratynsky was eight years old his mother gave birth to a stillborn child. On March 6, 1808, his father wrote to relatives: "We haven't written you for as many as three post days, but to tell you the truth, I would like to erase this time forever from my memory. My Aleksandra Fyodorovna prematurely gave birth to a three-month-old child." (*Chronicle*, 54.)

ALCIBIADES

First published, 1835; republished, with minor revisions, in *Dusk*, 1842.

Alcibiades (450–404 BCE), the famous Athenian general and statesman, was celebrated by Plato, Thucydides, Plutarch, and others for his physical beauty and military courage, but also condemned for his arrogance and vanity.

COMPLAINT ("POISON OF GLORIOUS SUMMER")

First published, untitled, 1841; republished as "Ropot" ["Complaint"] in *Dusk*, 1842.

You turn the placid dreamer, the pupil of Europe's enticements, / into a Scythian brute — The contrast Europe/Scythia alludes to the emerging anti-Western (Slavophile) views of the circle around Ivan Kireyevsky (in a tradition dating from medieval times, Russians traced their roots to the Scythians of antiquity). The transformation may well be aimed at Kireyevsky himself, who, during the period of Baratynsky's closest friendship with him, had published the journal *The European* (1831–1832) but at the time the poem was written was involved in the launch of a new journal called *The Muscovite* (see the notes to "To a Coterie", below).

TO THE WISE MAN

First published, untitled, with the poem "Thought, always thought!" under the general title "Anthological Poems," 1840; republished as "Mudretsu" ["To the Wise Man"] in *Dusk*, 1842. The reference to "the unsettling word of creation" (line 3) proved unacceptable to the censor, so the line was rewritten for *Dusk* as "Cast by the will of Zeus into the turbulent world" (*Nam, izvolen'em Zevesa broshennym v mir kolovratnyy*). The earlier line was restored in *CCP 1914*.

"SWEET PHYLLIS WITH EACH WINTER'S SEASON"

First published in *Dusk*, 1842. Although it is assumed that Baratynsky's epigram is based on an actual woman, all speculations as to her identity have been refuted (see *Kjetsaa*, 215–216; *Chronicle*, 383).

Sweet Phyllis — The name *Phyllis* (in Russian, *Filida* or *Fillida*) is strongly associated with pastoral poetry and may have been chosen to suggest an innocent shepherdess, a popular image in the late eighteenth century, when "Phyllis" would have been a young woman.

THE GOBLET

First published, 1835; republished, slightly revised, in *Dusk*, 1842.

Aÿ — Here, champagne. The French town Aÿ is famous for its production of the sparkling wine.

"GUSTING WINDS AND VIOLENT WEATHER"

First published, 1839, with the poems "Blessed the man who holy things discloses!" and "I am not yet ancient as a Patriarch" under the general title "Anthological Poems"; republished, slightly revised, in *Dusk*, 1842, where, in line 5, instead of *Vol'noy pesn'yu* ["a free song"], we find *Boykoy pesn'yu* ["a vigorous song"], a change ordered by the censor.

"WHAT USE ARE YOU, DAYS?"

First published, 1840; republished, with minor revisions, in *Dusk*, 1842.

TO A COTERIE

Not published until 1882, in *Russkiy arkhiv* 22, no. 6 (1882): 252, without attribution, in a group of other unattributed poems (not by Baratynsky), under the general title "Iz stikhotvoreniy bylago vremeni" ["Some Poems of a Bygone Time"]; republished, and attributed to Baratynsky, in *Russkiy arkhiv* 28, no. 1 (1890): 326, under the title "Ob odnom literaturnom kruzhke" ["On a Certain Literary Circle"]. In both cases, what was lacking in the brotherhood was *zdravyy smysl* ["common sense"], instead of *dar pryamoy* ["true talent"] (line 3). The version used for the translation was first published in *CCP 1914*, with the title "Kotterii" ["To a Coterie"]; it is based on a text written in Nastasya Baratynskaya's hand on the censor's copy of *Dusk*, where it appears, without a title, after the poem "What use are you, days?" (reproduced in *CCWL*, 328)—hence its position in the present book (as in *CCP 1957* and *Poems 1982*, both of which otherwise preserve the order of the poems in *Dusk*). On a separate copy of the poem, also in Nastasya Baratynskaya's hand, it bears the title "To a Coterie" [*Kotteriye*]. Presumably, the censor excluded the poem because of what was perceived as a blasphemous use of the words of Jesus in lines 7–8, although it is also possible that the poem was never submitted to the censor and was intended to be included with the *Dusk* poems in a later publication of Baratynsky's works (see the full discussion in *CCWL*, 3/1: 106–109).

The *coterie* addressed in the poem was the circle of Moscow writers and thinkers associated with Ivan Kireyevsky and the salons hosted by his mother, Avdotya Yelagina, and the Sverbeyevs (see headnote to Letter 57); they included the poet and critic Stepan Shevyryov, the historian and journalist Mikhail Pogodin, the prose writer Nikolay Pavlov and his wife, the poet Karolina Pavlova (née Jänisch), the poet Nikolay Yazykov, and the poet and philosopher Aleksey Khomyakov. Although Baratynsky had once been close to this group, by the late 1830s he and his wife were convinced that Kireyevsky and Yelagina, and perhaps others in the circle, bore a personal animus towards them. In September 1838, for example, Nastasya wrote to her sister, "I don't remember if I told you that I somehow happened to find myself at the Sverbeyevs' Friday salon, and there I saw the whole enemy society, who have lost their power to send me into panicked horror" (*Chronicle*, 347). Baratynsky's letters to his wife in 1840 also make reference to "our enemies" and the Moscow "brotherhood" (Letters 123, 125, 131, and 132), and in May 1842, Baratynsky writes to the Putyatas, "Our suppositions are now being strangely justified. We are now no longer the only ones who suspect the existence of an organized coterie. It is being railed against by its new victims in Moscow." (Letter 145.) While the intensity of Baratynsky's comments in these letters suggests a personal grievance (see the biographical note between Letters 112 and 113), he was certainly also opposed philosophically to the group's Slavophilism, as it was expressed particularly in the journal *The Muscovite*, founded at the end of 1840 by Pogodin and Shevyryov with the support of Kireyevsky. Indeed, the journal's launch might well have been the occasion that led Baratynsky to compose his epigram (*Chronicle*, 354). Interestingly, although it was never published in his lifetime, this was one of the poems Baratynsky translated into French prose in Paris in the winter of 1843–1844.

"Amen, amen, where three of you are gathered,... I will not be in your midst." — The opposite of what Jesus tells his disciples: "For where two or three are gathered together in my name, there am I in the midst of them" (Matthew 18: 20).

ACHILLES

First published, untitled, 1841; republished, slightly revised, as "Achilles" ["Akhill"] in *Dusk*, 1842.

Styx's icy waters — According to Greek legend, Achilles' mother, the sea nymph Thetis, bathed him as a baby in the waters of the River Styx, in the Underworld, to make him invulnerable. But the water did not touch the heel by which she held him.

"AT FIRST, THE THOUGHT, WHEN IT'S MADE FLESH"

First published, under the title "Thought" ["Mysl'"], 1838; republished in *Dusk*, 1842.

"I AM NOT YET ANCIENT AS A PATRIARCH"

First published, 1839, with the poems "Gusting winds and violent weather" and "Blessed the man who holy things discloses!" under the general title "Anthological Poems"; republished, slightly revised, in *Dusk*, 1842. The addressee is unknown.

"CLAMOROUS DAY IS WELCOME TO THE CROWD"

First published, 1839; republished, with minor revisions, in *Dusk*, 1842.

"HAIL TO YOU, MY SWEET-VOICED CHILD!"

First published in *Dusk*, 1842. In *Works 1884*, the poem is accompanied by the footnote: "To his son Lev Yevg[enyevich] on the occasion of his first poetic attempt" (255). Lev Baratynsky (1829–1906) would have been eleven or twelve when the poem was written.

"WHAT SOUNDS ARE THESE?"

First published as "Vanitas vanitatum" (in Roman script), 1841; republished, without the title, in *Dusk*, 1842. The original Latin title refers to Ecclesiastes 1: 2: "Vanity of vanities, saith the Preacher; vanity of vanities, all is vanity."

Overturn your tripod — In ancient Greece, the tripod, a three-legged stand or stool, was sacred to Apollo; in particular, it was the seat from which the Delphic oracle issued her prophecies. In his poem "To the Poet" ["Poetu"] (1830), Pushkin tells the poet that, if he is satisfied with his own work, that should be enough: "Satisfied? So let the crowd attack it [your work] / and spit on the altar where your fire burns, / and in their childish playfulness shake your tripod." Baratynsky goes further, essentially telling the aged singer to renounce his prophetic role.

You're one of the chosen—no mere artist! — Commentators have tended to gloss this line as follows: "The word 'artist' [*khudozhnik*] is used here in the sense of a 'tradesman in art'" (L. G. Frizman's note in *Poems 1982*, 649–650). But Baratynsky is saying something more radical: that the poet's place is not on earth as an artist, but in heaven among the chosen—an interpretation consistent with the rejection of the poet's futile role as prophet.

"THOUGHT, ALWAYS THOUGHT!"

First published, with the poem "To the Wise Man" (untitled) under the general heading "Anthological Poems," 1840; republished, slightly revised, in *Dusk*, 1842.

THE SCULPTOR

First published, 1841; republished, somewhat revised, in *Dusk*, 1842.

While explicitly based on the Greek myth of the sculptor Pygmalion, whose passion for his statue was rewarded by Aphrodite bringing it to life, Baratynsky's formulation of the story seems to owe even more to the poems of Michelangelo, who described how, by removing the outer layers, the sculptor puts "into the hard mountain stone / a living figure / that emerges the more, the more the stone recedes" [*in pietra alpestra e dura / una viva figura, / che là più cresce u' più la pietra scema*] ("Sì come per levar, donna, si pone" [*Rime*, no. 152]).

AUTUMN

First published, 1837, in the issue of *The Contemporary* dedicated to the memory of Aleksandr Pushkin; republished, with numerous minor revisions, in *Dusk*, 1842.

Baratynsky sent the poem to Pyotr Vyazemsky in March 1837 with the note: "I send you my contribution for *The Contemporary*. The news of Pushkin's death found me on the last stanzas of this poem." (Letter 112.)

"BLESSED THE MAN WHO HOLY THINGS DISCLOSES"

First published, 1839, with the poems "Gusting winds and violent weather" and "I am not yet ancient as a Patriarch" under the general title "Anthological Poems"; republished, slightly revised, in *Dusk*, 1842.

The theme of the poem is closely related to views Baratynsky expressed in the preface to *The Concubine* (1831), where he argued that rather than demanding practical moral teachings from literature, we should "see in it a science like other sciences, should seek in it *knowledge*, and nothing else" (*Poems 1982*, p.

463). He explains his point further in a letter to Ivan Kireyevsky: "Any reader [of the preface] with even half a mind, who could see that the morality of a literary work should be sought neither in the choice of the subject nor in injunctions, neither in the one nor in the other, would conclude with me that it must be sought in truth alone or in the beautiful, which is nothing other than the highest truth" (Letter 77).

The fruit falls from the apple tree, and heaven's / law is apprehended... — An allusion to the famous story of how Isaac Newton discovered the law of gravity.

RHYME

First published, 1841, without lines 14–23 ("When the orator mounted the podium... who governed his majestic word"); republished, slightly revised but still missing the same lines, in *Dusk*, 1842. The missing lines were inscribed by Nastasya Baratynskaya on an edition of *Dusk*, with the note "(lines omitted by the censor)." They were finally included in *Works 1869* and appeared in the basic text of the poem in all later editions of Baratynsky's works until *CCWL*. But the version in *Works 1869* contained other significant changes as well, specifically in lines 24–33 ("But no agora for our thought... Resolve this unresolvable question"). Scholars are divided as to which version should be considered "basic": M. L. Gofman (*CCP 1914*), L. G. Frizman (*Poems 1982*), and V. M. Sergeyev (*CCP 1989*) use the version published in *Dusk* as their main text (while adding the missing ten lines), whereas Ye. N. Kupreyanova (with I. Medvedeva in *CCP 1936* and alone in *CCP 1957*) uses the later version. A. S. Bodrova and N. Mazur, the editors of *CCWL*, vol. 3/1, present the version published in *Dusk* as the basic text (without restoring the omitted lines), while providing as well the full text of the redaction in *Works 1869*. I have decided to use the later version as the main text for the translation, but I also offer a translation below of lines 24–33 from the *Dusk* version.

the dove of the ark — In Genesis, Chapter 8, Noah sent out a dove from the ark after the rain ended. It was not until the dove returned with an olive leaf that he knew the waters had receded.

Variant of lines 24–23 (published in *Dusk*, 1842):

> But who today inquires of
> our lyres for their benevolent secrets?
> Who follows us to the world above
> upon their now-disfavored music?
> The poet in our age knows not
> whether he truly sails the heights!
> Both judge and under judgment, let him
> say what the singer's fever is:
> A gift sublime? An absurd disease?
> Let him solve the unresolvable question.

> А ныне кто у наших лир
> Их дружелюбной тайны просит?
> Кого за нами в горний мир

Опальный голос их уносит?

Меж нас не ведает поэт

Его полет высок иль нет!

Сам судия и подсудимый,

Пусть молвит: песнопевца жар

Смешной недуг иль высший дар?

Решит вопрос неразрешимый!

POEMS 1839–1844

"MY STAR I KNOW, I KNOW MY STAR"

First published as "Zvyozdy" ["Stars"], 1840, in the almanac *Dawn*. The poem was initially intended for the book *Dusk*: it appears in the existing censor's copy, without the title and in a slightly revised version, between the poems "Novinskoye" and "Signs" (reproduced in *CCWL*, 3/1: 307). This untitled version was published by Ivan Turgenev in 1854 in *The Contemporary*. The decision to exclude the poem from *Dusk* was apparently made by Baratynsky, not the censor.

in Moët's stars… nor yours, Aÿ! — Both names refer to champagne, of which the Moët company was (and still is) one of the leading producers, while the French town of Aÿ, in the Marne Valley, is similarly famous for its production of the wine.

"EVERYTHING HAS ITS PACE, HAS ITS OWN LAWS"

Not published until *CCP 1914*, from a copy made by Nastasya Baratynskaya.

Aimed at Moscow's literary salons—presumably, especially those of Avdotya Yelagina and the Sverbeyevs—the epigram reflects the sentiment Baratynsky expresses to his wife in a letter from St. Petersburg after visiting the salon at the Karamzins': "The general tone of society truly satisfies the ideal one forms in youth, from books, about the height of elegance—complete naturalness and courtesy transformed into moral feeling. People in Moscow don't have the slightest idea of this." (Letter 127.)

WITH THE BOOK *DUSK*

First published, 1842, in *The Contemporary*.

The poem is addressed to *Sofya Nikolayevna Karamzina* (1802–1856), the daughter of the writer Nikolay Karamzin. With her stepmother, Yekaterina Karamzina, she hosted one of St. Petersburg's most important literary salons. Baratynsky became friends with her during his two-week visit to the city in February 1840, as he describes to his wife: "Sofya Karamzina and I are in full friendship. … She possesses genuine vivacity and unfeigned playfulness, gracefully moderated by a certain respect for decorum." (Letter 127.)

The poem was probably included with the copy of *Dusk* Baratynsky sent to Sofya Karamzina in May 1842 through Pyotr Pletnyov (see Letter 144); the poem itself appeared in *The Contemporary*, Pletnyov's journal, a few months later. On June 26, Karamzina wrote to Baratynsky: "I cannot resist the desire… to express to you my *lively* gratitude for the poetic gift I received from you; it was such a sweet surprise, as was your remembering me and the charming verses you addressed to me! Certainly, they are much too flattering; I confess I am profoundly unworthy of them, and yet I have been reading and rereading them with extreme pleasure, not from self-regard but from the heart; and to think that two years of absence have not erased from your memory this acquaintance, so short, so happy for me, which I believed to be engraved only in *my* grateful memory!" (*CCP 1914*, 1: 305, in French.)

[ON THE PLANTING OF A WOOD]

First published, 1846, in the anthology *Vchera i segodnya* [*Yesterday and Today*] under the title "Opyat' vesna" ["Again It's Spring"], almost certainly supplied by the editor, V. A. Sollogub. The poem was accompanied by Sollogub's note: "These verses were written by Ye. A. Baratynsky when he was planting a pine grove on his estate. Although it is clear that the poem was not entirely finished, in it is expressed that gemlike poetry that characterized all our poet's works, and readers will surely not complain of its placement in my Anthology" (*CCWL*, 3/1: 122). In this version, based on copies of the poem made by Nastasya Baratynskaya, the first two lines of the last stanza (lines 29–30) read: *Pust' veruyu prostyas' ya s liroyu moyey, / Chto nekogda yeyo zamenyat eti:* ["Let me believe parting with my lyre / that it will one day be replaced by these:"]—where the first line has six metrical feet instead of the usual five. In *Works 1869*, these lines were corrected as: *I pust'! Prostyasya s liroyu moyey, / Ya veruyu: yeyo zamenyat eti,* ["So be it! Parting with my lyre, / I believe: it will be replaced by these,"]. This version made two other lexical changes: in line 20, in stanza 5, the adjective describing the "glory" of the poet's opponent was changed from *zlobnoy* ["malicious"] to *groznoy* ["terrible" or "menacing"], and in line 26, the term for the surface the poet hopes will prove fertile was changed from *kryazh* [here, "solid or unplowed ground"] to *khryashch* ["gravel"]. It was in this edition that the poem was first published with the title "Na posev lesa" ["On the Planting of a Wood"], which comes from one of Nastasya Baratynskaya's copies. Although like several other titles in *Works 1869* there is no evidence that this originates with the poet, it has become well established; for this reason it is used in the present book as well, but placed within brackets.

In *CCP 1914* (where the poem's title is set in parentheses), M. L. Gofman printed a version that restored *kryazh* in line 26, as well as lines 29–30 from the poem's first publication, but where the opponent's glory in line 20 was described as *padshey* ["fallen"]. Later editions (*CCP 1936*, *CCP 1957*, *Poems 1982*, and *CCP 1989*) accepted Gofman's reading of line 20 ("fallen glory"), but otherwise followed the version in *Works 1869* (i.e. "gravel" in line 26; "And so be it!…." for lines 29–30). The editors of *CCWL*, however, use as their basic text a copy of the poem in which line 20 has *zlobnoy slavoy* ["malicious glory"]; line 26, *kryazh* ["unplowed ground"]; and lines 29–30 read: *I pust', prostyasya s liroyu moyey, / Ya veruyu: yeyo zamenyat eti,* ["And let me, parting with my lyre, / believe: it will be replaced by these,"]—the same words as in *Works 1869*, but with punctuation that somewhat changes the meaning (see *CCWL*, 3/1: 115–124 for a full discussion of the existing copies and drafts of the poem). I have used the *CCWL* text as the basis for my translation not only because of the editors' strong textological research but also because it seems very much in keeping with Baratynsky's style: for example, while a sudden exclamation such as "So be it!" [*I pust'!*] is typical of the poet, there is as a rule only one such "pivot" in a poem of this length (compare the exclamation "Madman!" [*Bezumets!*] in "What good are fantasies of freedom to the prisoner?" or "But what then?" [*No chto?*] in "A faithful record of impressions," among others) and here that pivot occurs in the penultimate stanza: "No answer!" [*Otveta net!*].

The poem was likely begun in 1842, perhaps in the spring (as the opening stanzas suggest), around the time Baratynsky tells the Putyatas of his intention to plant trees in Muranovo in the fall (Letter 145). In the summer he writes to his mother: "This fall, I will have a pleasure new for me, that of planting trees. We have a fine elderly gardener who loves his work, and I am relying on his good advice." (Letter 147.) And in August, he tells Pyotr Pletnyov: "Circumstances now keep me in a little village where I am building things, planting trees, sowing, not without satisfaction, not without love for these peaceful occupations and the beautiful nature that surrounds me." (Letter 149.)

but when he dug beneath me a hidden pit… — An allusion to Psalm 7: 15: "He has made a pit and dug it deep, and he himself shall fall into the hole that he has made." We do not know what specific incident, if any, Baratynsky is referring to in this stanza.

The younger generations my soul embraced — While some commentators have speculated that Baratynsky means Vissarion Belinsky (1811–1848) and the group around Nikolay Stankevich (1813–1840)—that is, the younger generation of the late 1830s—it seems more likely that he is thinking of Ivan Kireyevsky and his circle (see notes to "To a Coterie"), who emerged on the scene in the late 1820s and with whom Baratynsky was closely associated in the early 1830s.

dusk-enshrouded — The word rendered as "dusk-enshrouded" is *sumrachnyye*, more commonly translated as "gloomy" or "somber." Its primary meaning, however, is "characterized by dusk; twilit," deriving from *sumrak* ("dusk," "the fall of darkness"), a lexical twin of *sumerki*, the title of Baratynsky's last book of poetry—a potent connection that is worth underscoring in the translation.

"WHEN DEATH, O POET, STOPS YOUR VOICE"

First published, without a title, 1843, in *The Contemporary*.

In one of Nastasya Baratynskaya's copies, the poem is titled "Pamyat' poetu" ["In Memory of a Poet"], and throughout the nineteenth century it was generally believed that the poem was written in memory of the poet Mikhail Lermontov (1814–1841). In fact, when Ivan Turgenev republished the poem in 1854 (again in *The Contemporary*), he titled it "Na smert' Lermontova" ["On the Death of Lermontov"]. Ye. N. Kupreyanova and I. Medvedeva, however, dispute the reference in *CCP 1936* (2: 277–279), pointing out that the poem was not published until two years after Lermontov's death, and that no critic of Lermontov fit Baratynsky's "Zoilus-come-lately." What is more, Baratynsky himself, while never disputing Lermontov's abilities, did not especially like the man himself, as he says in a letter to Nastasya in 1840: "I was introduced to Lermontov, who read a splendid new poem; he is without doubt a man of great talent, but morally he didn't appeal to me. There's something uncongenial, something Muscovite about him." (Letter 121.) Kupreyanova and Medvedeva argue that the last stanza almost certainly refers to Vissarion Belinsky, who had written a very negative review of *Dusk*, in which he lambasted Baratynsky while exalting the memory of Pushkin—a poet Belinsky had criticized while alive:

> Was it so long ago that Mr. Baratynsky, together with Mr. Yazykov, composed a brilliant triumvirate, the head of which was Pushkin? But since then, for what a long time has Pushkin's colossal shadow stood alone. … Was it so long ago that every new poem by Mr. Baratynsky, when it appeared in an almanac, excited the attention of the public and interpretations and debates among reviewers? But now, quietly, modestly, a book has appeared with the recent poems of this same poet—and it is no longer talked about and debated. … Life as the prey of death, reason as the enemy of feeling, truth as the destroyer of happiness—this is the source from which flows the elegiac tone of Mr. Baratynsky's poetry and it is here that we find its greatest shortcoming. A house built on sand cannot last long; a poetry that expresses the false state of a transitory generation must itself die with that generation, for it presents in its content no strong interest for succeeding generations. … This unsustained struggle with thought has done great harm to Mr. Baratynsky's talent; it has prevented him from writing even a single creation of the kind that are recognized as the capital works of literature and that, if not for eternity, then at least for a long time survive their creators. (Published in *Notes to the Fatherland*, 1842; quoted in *Chronicle*, 392.)

While Kupreyanova and Medvedeva make a strong case for Belinsky as "Zoilus-come-lately," it is more difficult to see Pushkin as the poet whose voice was stopped "in the flower of his years." When Pushkin died, he was a married man of thirty-six with four children—middle-aged, as the nineteenth century reckoned things; also, unlike the poet's imagined fate in the poem, his death was universally mourned. Still, the poem's opening lines do recall Baratynsky's thoughts about Pushkin's last works, which he read at Zhukovsky's house in 1840. As he wrote his wife: "I spent some three hours at his place, sorting through the unpublished new poems of Pushkin. They are of an astonishing beauty, entirely new in both spirit and form. All his last pieces are distinguished by—what, do you think?—power and depth! He was just now coming into his maturity." (Letter 123.) In the end, Baratynsky is most likely not thinking of any specific poet here, or rather, the poem derives from reflections on the deaths of both Pushkin and Lermontov and, perhaps especially, on the reaction that might greet his own death when it came.

the now-silent Aonian — The muse that had inspired the poet: "Aonia" was a classical name for the region in Greece where the muses' home, Mount Helicon, was located.

Zoilus-come-lately — Zoilus (400–320 BCE) was a literary critic whose name became a byword for unjust or malicious criticism. As noted above, Baratynsky may be alluding to Belinsky.

"I LOVE YOU, GODDESSES OF SONG"

First published, 1844, in *The Contemporary*.

PRAYER

First published, 1844, in *The Contemporary*.

Nastasya Baratynskaya recorded this poem from memory a few months after her husband's death. She included it in a letter to Baratynsky's brother Sergey, dated November 11, 1844, with the comment: "I am transcribing for you a prayer by Eugène which was never written down and which I remembered one day when I was going to mass" (*CCWL*, 3/1: 146).

"WHEN THE POET, A CHILD OF DOUBT AND PASSION"

First published, 1844, in *The Contemporary*.

Addressed to Nastasya Baratynskaya. Writing to Baratynsky's mother in September 1844, Nastasya tells her, "This little poem was made for me in Paris" (quoted in *CCWL*, 3/1: 132). In *Works 1869*, it is published with the title "N. L. Baratynskoy" ["To N. L. Baratynskaya"].

THE PYROSCAPHE

First published, 1844, in *The Contemporary*, with the note "Mediterranean Sea, 1844."

In the spring of 1844, in a letter to Nikolay and Sofya Putyata, Baratynsky describes writing verses on the boat from Marseilles to Naples: "Our three-day sea voyage will stay with me as one of my most pleasant memories. I managed to escape sea sickness. In the leisure of good health, I didn't leave the deck but watched the waves day and night. ... On the ship, at night, I wrote a few verses which I will send to you, once I've corrected them a little, with the request that you pass them on to Pletnyov for his journal." (Letter 164.)

Pyroscaphe — A term used in the first half of the nineteenth century for a steam-ship, especially in France and Russia, from the Greek roots *pyro-* ("fire") and *-scaph* ("boat").

our sail opens up to the wind — Early steamships were often equipped with sails for added propulsion.

Ever since childhood, my heart's trepidation / has drawn me towards the sea-god's free kingdom — Baratynsky's desire for sea adventures is dramatically expressed in a let-ter he wrote to his mother as a fourteen-year-old boy (Letter 4); see also the notes to "The Storm."

Thetis — A sea goddess and the mother of Achilles. L. G. Frizman suggests that Baratynsky may be confusing Thetis (in Russian, *Fetida*) with the Titaness Tethys (in Russian, *Tefida*), the sister and wife of Oceanus and a personification of the sea (*Poems 1982*, 668).

Leghorn — The traditional English name for the Italian city Livorno; in Russian, Baratynsky uses the archaic name *Livurna*.

TO MY TUTOR, THE ITALIAN

First published, 1844, in *The Contemporary*, with the note "Naples, 1844." In May or June 1844, Baratynsky sent this poem and "The Pyroscaphe" to the Putyatas with the request to forward them to Pletnyov for *The Contemporary* (Letter 166).

Written in Naples in the weeks before Baratynsky's death, the poem is addressed to Giacinto Borghese (or "Bories," as his name is styled in French), who during the Napoleonic wars fled from Italy to Russia, where Baratynsky's father hired him as a tutor for his children. In the letters the young Baratynsky writes from St. Petersburg, he often sends regards to "Monsieur Bories" (as in Letter 2). In one of these letters (not included in the present selection), he appends a note that indicates the affec-tion he felt for his tutor: "My dear Monsieur Bories, I wholeheartedly thank you for your letter; it gave me great pleasure. But I beg you, stop using such horrid titles as 'your very humble servant'; there is nothing I hate more than this insipid politeness. I prefer the title 'friend'; this was the title we used when we parted. Farewell, my old friend, stay well. — Eugène." (The original, dated February 23, 1813, is printed in *Kjetsaa*, 572.)

a general most worthy — The poet's father, the retired Lieutenant General Abram Baratynsky, who hired Borghese in 1805, when Yevgeny was five years old (*Chronicle*, 51).

Moscow received us... and leaving there, alas, a precious grave behind us... — The Baratynskys moved to Moscow in 1809. Abram Baratynsky died there in March 1810 and was buried in the cemetery of the Andronnikov Monastery of the Savior. The family returned to Mara in the spring of 1811 (*Chronicle*, 56).

Ausonia — A poetic name for Italy.

the newly made cornet — A rank equivalent to ensign. Baratynsky is playing with the facts here, perhaps to obscure or minimize his humiliating years of service as a sub-officer. Although we know that Baratynsky did visit Mara at least twice during furloughs from the army (in December 1820 and October 1822), both times after first spending a few days in St. Petersburg ("the great world"), there is no record of such a visit between April 21, 1825, when he was promoted to ensign, and January 31, 1826, when his resignation from the army was accepted. His mother first saw him as a "newly made cornet" not in Mara but in Moscow, in October 1825 (see the convenient list of Baratynsky's places of residence in *Chronicle*, 422–423).

from that land, where, amazed, you watched Suvorov's soldiers / come marching into town... that land, where, one year later, you also would see him... — Commentators generally assume that these lines describe events witnessed by Giacinto Borghese in Naples; in fact, neither Suvorov's soldiers nor, indeed, Napoleon ever set foot in that city. The described events do, however, correspond with what happened in northern Italy. In the spring of 1799—some three years after Napoleon conquered the northern part of the peninsula and established several client republics there before embarking on his Egyptian campaign—General Aleksandr Suvorov (1730–1800) entered Italy leading a coalition of Russian and Austrian troops. In a string of victories culminating in the Battle of Novi, north of Genoa, in August, Suvorov's army forced the French to withdraw from nearly the entire region. In 1800, after Russia left the anti-French coalition, Napoleon, now First Consul, returned, entering Milan on June 2. Two weeks later, following the French victory in the Battle of Marengo, the Austrians withdrew from Italy and Napoleon restored the client republics.

The details Baratynsky records in these lines—the heat that could drive the dogs from the squares, the soldiers' unshaven beards, the people welcoming Napoleon with earthen lamps, the never-forgotten silver spoons—have a patina of truth, and we easily believe that Borghese did witness such events and recounted them to his wards. But he could not have witnessed them in Naples, only in some other "classical city" (Milan?) in the northern half of the peninsula.

Another possibility, however, is that Borghese experienced similar events in Naples, but with a different chronology and different protagonists. Calls for revolution, welcoming lamps, and confiscated silver could only have happened in Naples in the early months of 1799, after King Ferdinand IV fled the city to Sicily and the French General Jean Étienne Championnet, supported by the local nobility (not the poor with their earthen lamps), established the so-called Parthenopaean Republic on January 23. By the spring, however, as Suvorov's soldiers were routing the French in the north, Ferdinand's representative, Cardinal Fabrizio Ruffo, was mobilizing the poor and other royalists into an Army of the Holy Faith, with insurrections against the republicans occurring throughout the provinces—efforts supported by a British naval force under Horatio Nelson and a combined Russian-Turkish fleet under the Russian Admiral Fyodor Ushakov. Pressured by the defeats in northern Italy and the mounting successes of Cardinal Ruffo's irregular forces, the French army withdrew from Naples in April, leaving only a garrison in the Castle of St. Elmo, overlooking the city. Ruffo's army entered in mid-June, under bombardment from cannon in the castle. Peace was soon negotiated, and King Ferdinand returned a few weeks later. The king and his supporters exacted a brutal retribution, executing scores of suspected republican supporters and imprisoning or deporting hundreds of others. Could this have been when Giacinto Borghese left the city, fleeing not the French but Ferdinand? After Napoleon's triumphant return to northern Italy, Ferdinand signed an alliance with the French, but Naples remained an independent kingdom and did not become a client state until 1806, when French troops under Marshal André Masséna forced the king to flee to Sicily once more and established Napoleon's brother, Joseph Bonaparte, on the throne. By then, however, Giacinto Borghese was safely ensconced with the Baratynskys on the Tambov steppe. (For a detailed history, see John A. Davis, *Naples and Napoleon: Southern Italy and the European Revolutions (1780–1860)* [Oxford: Oxford University Press, 2006], 71–142.)

If Borghese was in fact in Naples in 1799, then either he, in his telling of the story to his wards, or Baratynsky in his retelling, switched the order of events and replaced the names of Championnet and Ushakov with the more resonant ones of Napoleon and Suvorov.

despite the blazing hours — L. G. Frizman explains this phrase as French cannon fire from the Castle of St. Elmo (*Poems 1982*, 669), but it more likely refers to the midday heat.

then still **Buonaparte,** *soon* **Napoléon** — Although by the time of his second Italian campaign, in 1800, Napoleon was already the ruler of France, with the title of First Consul, Baratynsky stresses that he was still merely the Corsican-born Napoleone Buonaparte and not yet the near-mythic Napoléon (in fact, he had begun using the French spelling of his name in 1796, after his first victories in Italy).

wondrous **condottiere** — A term that acknowledges Napoleon's military genius even as it belittles him: the *condottieri* were hired military commanders in the city-states of Renaissance Italy.

losses beyond comparing — Baratynsky is thinking of the disastrous invasion of Russia in 1812.

the Briton's mournful captive — After his defeat at Waterloo in 1815, Napoleon surrendered himself to the British, who held him captive on Saint Helena Island in the South Atlantic.

from Alpine lightning blasts returning to disfavor... Suvorov / released his warrior spirit in a volley of epigrams — After his successes in Italy, Suvorov was ordered to move his troops to Switzerland in September 1799; there Russian forces came under attack by a much larger French army. Remarkably, however, Suvorov was able to save most of his men by leading them across the Alps in the snow. The Russian Emperor Paul

I then ordered Suvorov to return to St. Petersburg, where instead of receiving a hero's welcome, he found himself in disfavor: Paul demanded his resignation and refused to receive him. The sixty-nine-year-old general, who had fallen ill on the road back to Russia, died a few months later, on May 18 (NS) / 6 (OS), 1800. Baratynsky's description of Suvorov dying "in a volley of epigrams" may relate to a witticism Suvorov supposedly uttered on his deathbed, as recounted by Baratynsky's friend Denis Davydov: "Master of the Horse Count Ivan Pavlovich Kutaysov [a favorite of the emperor's] was sent to the dying Suvorov with a demand for an account of his actions; he answered him: 'I am preparing to give an account to God and right now do not want to even think about the sovereign.'" ("Anekdoty o raznykh litsakh, preimushchenno ob Alekseye Petroviche Yermolove," in *Voyennyye zapiski* [Moscow: Voyenizdat, 1982], 311.) Although Davydov's "Anecdotes" were not published until 1860 (and then, in London), Baratynsky had very likely heard them from Davydov himself.

Upon a desolate rock, your enemy breathed his last — Napoleon died on Saint Helena Island on May 5, 1821.

and you, too, shut your eyes — Neither the commentators on the poem nor A. M. Peskov's *Chronicle* record the date of Giacinto Borghese's death, but we can estimate it as sometime around 1825, based on the fact that the tutor was hired in 1805 and Baratynsky tells us that their relationship lasted twenty years (line 18).

the house of Cicero — The Roman orator Marcus Tullius Cicero (106–43 BCE) had several residences around the Bay of Naples. L. G. Frizman suggests that Baratynsky is referring to Cicero's villa in Formia, about sixty miles north of Naples (*Poems 1982*, 670), but Formia is not mentioned in Baratynsky's list of the places he visited near Naples (in Letter 166) and, in any case, the more striking Ciceronian monument in Formia is not the orator's "house," of which little can be seen, but his much more famous tomb. Baratynsky is more likely thinking of either the excavated house in Pompeii known as the Villa of Cicero or the ruins of Cicero's villa in Pozzuoli—both are sites we know Baratynsky visited. (On the villas in Formia, Pompeii, and Pozzuoli, see Octavian Blewitt's *Handbook for Travellers in Southern Italy*, 77, 330, and 384.)

that verdurous cave... where sleeps the mighty dust of poetry's own sovereign — The Tomb of Virgil, in Naples, was indeed verdurous: "It is now clothed with ivy, and the site is concealed by a plantation of ilex and myrtle," Octavian Blewitt informs us in his 1853 *Handbook for Travellers*, 366.

Taenarum's murk — The Underworld. Taenarum, the southernmost point on the Greek mainland, is the site of a cave that the Greeks believed led to the realm of the dead. Baratynsky is using the name metonymically: in Virgil's *Aeneid*, the Cumaean Sibyl gives Aeneas directions to the Underworld through a different cave, near Lake Avernus (not far from Naples).

Marius and Sulla — Gaius Marius (157–86 BCE) and Lucius Cornelius Sulla (138–78 BCE) were generals and statesmen in the Roman Republic who led opposing forces during the civil war of 88–87 BCE. Both had villas near Naples, in Marigliano and Pozzuoli, respectively.

a face now long ago from deity demoted — The face belongs to Dionysus (Bacchus), the god of wine and ecstasy, who was often depicted in a wreath of grape leaves. Christianity demoted him from deity to demon. In Naples, in the Real Museo Borbonico (today the National Archeological Museum), Baratynsky would have seen a series of frescoes from Pompeii depicting a woman's initiation into the Dionysian mysteries.

That melancholy bard, / the child of Britain — Lord Byron (1788–1824), who lived in various parts of Italy (Venice, Ravenna, Pisa, Genoa) from 1816 to 1823, before he left to fight in the Greek war of independence. The epithet "child of Britain" (*ditya Britannii*) may be intended to suggest Byron's alter ego, the title character of *Childe Harold's Pilgrimage* (1812–1818).

NOTES TO THE LETTERS

A FEW PRELIMINARIES

within hours after Baron Delvig died... friends burned... his private papers — The burning of Delvig's papers is recorded by his nephew, A. I. Delvig, in *Moi vospominaniya* (Moscow, 1912), quoted in *Chronicle*, 251.

a collection of some three hundred letters... "disappeared in the revolutionary turmoil" — "Monsieur Modeste Hoffmann [i.e. M. L. Gofman], to whom we owe the best edition of Baratynsky (the so-called 'Academy' edition, 2 vols., St. Petersburg, 1914) tells me, in fact, that he was able to assemble nearly three hundred letters by the poet: this precious collection, which should have constituted the third volume of his edition, disappeared in the revolutionary turmoil." (Henri Mongault, "Mérimée et Pouchkine," *Le Monde Slave* 4 [1930]: 29, n. 1; quoted in *Kjetsaa*, 702.)

I. THE CORPS DES PAGES

1. TO HIS MOTHER, ALEKSANDRA BARATYNSKAYA.

he knows my uncle — Probably, Pyotr Andreyevich Baratynsky (ca. 1769–1845). At the time of the letter, Major General Pyotr Baratynsky was still in active service at the Naval Cadet Corps in St. Petersburg.

Sveaborg — A fortress and naval base near Helsingfors (Helsinki), in the Grand Duchy of Finland; today called Suomenlinna.

2. TO HIS MOTHER.

My uncle has just left for the countryside — Rear Admiral Ilya Andreyevich Baratynsky (ca. 1774–1836), recently retired, had gone to live on his estate near Podvoyskoye-Goloshchapovo.

Nikolay Antonovich — Probably Nikolay Matsnev, one of the masters at the Corps des Pages and, it seems, an acquaintance of Aleksandra Baratynskaya.

the little émigrés — *Les Petits émigrés* (1798), a novel by Madame de Genlis (see note to Letter 132).

I kiss my uncles' hands and those of my aunt — His uncles Bogdan Andreyevich (ca. 1770–1820) and Pyotr Andreyevich Baratynsky (then visiting Mara) and his aunt Yekaterina Fyodorovna Cherepanova (1782–1855), his mother's sister, who lived at Mara.

Monsieur Bories — His tutor, Giacinto Borghese (see the notes to the poem "To My Tutor, the Italian").

3. TO HIS MOTHER.

Apollon Nikolayevich — Apollon Baratynsky, a cousin of his father's.

not being able to tell you that I won the award, as I did last year — After completing the 4th Class, Yevgeny had received an award "for success in studies and good behavior" (*Chronicle*, 64).

4. TO HIS MOTHER.

the bad grades he received — See *Chronicle*, 66–67.

Florian's Estelle — The pastoral poem *Estelle et Némorin* (1788) by Jean-Pierre Claris de Florian.

BIOGRAPHICAL NOTE

"The Kamenskaya sisters have written to me…" — Aleksandra Baratynskaya's letter is quoted in *Chronicle*, 76.

6. TO HIS MOTHER.

Il le faut avouer… — Lines from "Jean qui pleure et qui ris" ["Jean Who Cries and Who Laughs"] (1772) by Voltaire.

coffee with my aunts — Probably his father's sisters Yekaterina Andreyevna Baratynskaya (1785–1840) and Mariya Andreyevna Panchulidzeva, née Baratynskaya (ca. 1782–ca. 1845).

my aunt Marfa Aleksandrovna — It is not clear who this aunt is. Baratynsky had a number of more or less distant relatives who lived near Podvoyskoye.

We paid a visit to our ancestors… — He means they visited their graves, of course. The Baratynsky family was descended from Polish nobility. The poet's ancestor Ivan Petrovich Baratynsky (d. 1708) came to Russia from Poland and entered the service of Tsar Alexis, who gave him the estate of Podvoyskoye-Goloshchapovo in the 1660s.

Podvoyskoye, whose very name seems to proclaim battles — The Slavic root -*voy*- relates to warfare.

II. ST. PETERSBURG AND FINLAND

7. TO HIS MOTHER.

Monsieur Schlechtinsky — Andrey Shlyakhtinsky was an ensign in the Jaeger Life-Guard Regiment. Baratynsky met him when he was living with his uncle in Podvoyskoye; the Shlyakhtinsky family also lived in Smolensk Province (see *True Story*, 119–120). When the ensign left St. Petersburg to join a different regiment in 1819, Baratynsky dedicated the poem "To Sh. (In an Album)" ["Sh—mu (V al'bom)"] to him. Here we find lines reflecting their youthful experiences in the countryside: "Do you remember that sweet land / where we came to know life and joy, / where we saw our first springtime, / where we burned with our first passion?…":

> Ты помнишь милую страну,
> Где жизнь и радость мы узнали,
> Где зрели первую весну,
> Где первой страстию пылали?…

who knew my father in Gatchina — In the first half of the 1790s, Abram Baratynsky had commanded the ground battalions under the Tsarevich Paul Petrovich (later Emperor Paul I), which were based at Paul's residence in Gatchina, thirty miles south of St. Petersburg.

our goddesses from Orzhevka — The daughters of Dmitry Mikhaylovich Martynov, the owner of the Orzhevka estate, not far from Mara.

Madame Ein-Gross — Little is known about this enchanting woman. M. L. Gofman refers to her as "Ye. Gerngross" (*CCP 1914*, 1: xlix).

Sophie — His sister, Sofya Abramovna Baratynskaya (1801–1844).

8. TO SERGEY UVAROV.

All this you will do — There is no record of Uvarov petitioning the emperor on Baratynsky's behalf, but whatever efforts he made did not succeed. Nikolay Konshin writes in his memoirs of Baratynsky's mood at this time: "The denial of his promotion embittered him; to the degree that the soul of a good young man could grumble, he grumbled and was angry" (quoted in *Chronicle*, 105).

10. TO HIS MOTHER.

Rochensalm — The fort at Rochensalm (in Finnish, Ruotsinsalmi) was part of the Russian fortification system in southeastern Finland designed by General Aleksandr Suvorov after the Russo-Swedish War of 1788–1790. Today the fort lies in the city of Kotka.

12. TO VASILY ZHUKOVSKY.

Kr—vich [Kristafovich]... disliked me from the first glance. — The twelve-year-old Baratynsky described a very different first encounter with Vasily Kristafovich in his first letter to his mother from the Corps des Pages (Letter 1).

Glorioso, Rinaldo Rinaldi... — Two "robber novels" by the German writer Christian August Vulpius: *Glorioso, the Great Devil* (1800; first published in Russian in 1806) and *Rinaldo Rinaldini, the Robber Captain* (1797; published in Russian in eight parts, from 1802 to 1804).

Schiller's **Karl Moor** — Baratynsky is referring to Friedrich Schiller's enormously popular play *The Robbers* (1781; published in Russian in 1793), which launched a Europe-wide vogue for works about noble-hearted outlaws. The hero of the play is Karl Moor, a young aristocrat who joins a gang of robbers after being unjustly banished from his home.

a society of avengers — The other members included Dmitry Khanykov, Pavel and Aleksandr Krenitsyn, and, later, Lev Priklonsky (*Chronicle*, 70).

that chamberlain who... is known to you because of my misfortune and also his — Pavel Nikolayevich Priklonsky, the father of Baratynsky's fellow-avenger Lev. The chamberlain's own misfortune may refer to a judicial matter in which he was involved in 1817 (Chronicle, 130).

The Christmas holidays arrived — Baratynsky is apparently misremembering: the theft took place during the Shrovetide holidays (in mid-February 1816).

he was not yet 15 years old — The theft most likely occurred on February 19, 1816— Baratynsky's sixteenth birthday. This may be a slip of the pen: he remembers it as happening during the Christmas holidays, when he would not yet have been 16.

I moved around between different Petersburg boarding schools for about a year... Finally, I went to the countryside, to my mother. — In fact, he was only in St. Petersburg a few months after his expulsion; by the fall of 1816 he was already living on his uncle Bogdan Andreyevich's estate in Podvoyskoye. He did not see his mother until late January or early February 1817, in Kirsanov, the town near Mara where she was spending the winter. It was only in the spring that he returned to Mara, and then for only a few months (*Chronicle*, 75–76, 80–83).

But when he was yet a great way off... — Luke 15: 20.

I fell into a severe nervous fever — We know of two occasions during this period when Baratynsky was ill, the most severe illness occurring in the fall of 1816 (before his reunion with his mother). On December 28 of that year, Aleksandra Baratynskaya wrote to her brother-in-law, Bogdan Baratynsky: "I cannot express my heartfelt gratitude to you for all the kindness and care you have shown Yevgeny and I am obliged to you for both his recovery and his very life. The danger he was in so presses on my heart that I forget it has passed, thanks to God and to you, and I cannot keep from feeling the most acute sorrow and terror each time it enters my thoughts." The second illness occurred in Mara, in the spring of 1817, but does not seem to have been as serious (*Chronicle*, 80–81).

the Grand Duke Nicholas Pavlovich — The future Emperor Nicholas I.

14. TO HIS MOTHER.

my colonel — Yegor Alekseyevich Lutkovsky (ca. 1785–1832), the commander of the Neyshlotsky Regiment.

Kyumen — Fort Kyumen (in Finnish, Kyminlinna, today part of the city of Kotka), about four and a half miles north of Rochensalm, was, like that fort, constructed under Suvorov's supervision in 1791. The headquarters of the Neyshlotsky Regiment moved to Kyumen in late October or early November 1824, by which time Baratynsky had already left for Helsingfors.

Rzhev — A town in Tver Province about eighty miles east of Podvoyskoye; presumably, Baratynsky thought his mother might have heard something about the uprising from their relatives.

Ar. [Arakcheyev] — Count Aleksey Arakcheyev, the emperor's closest adviser, who was famous for his ruthlessness (see the note to "The fatherland's foe, the tsar's valet").

15. TO NIKOLAY KONSHIN.

Konshin was forced to retire — On Konshin's retirement and subsequent service in Kostroma, see *Kjetsaa*, 90.

Nortman — D. A. Nordman, a local officer of Swedish descent with strong Russian sympathies (*Kjetsaa*, 72).

From idleness I chase after Annette — Anna Lutkovskaya, his commander's niece, to whom Baratynsky rededicated a few of the poems written to Sofya Ponomaryova (see note to "In an Album" ["You are adored by far too many"]) (*Chronicle*, 124).

Klercker... Düsterloh — Officers serving in Finland: Baron Carl Gustav Klercker and, possibly, Peter von Düsterloh.

Avdotya Yakovlevna — Konshin's wife, née Vasilyeva. Before Konshin's marriage Baratynsky had written the poem "To a Bride (A. Ya. V.)" ["Neveste (A. Ya. V.)"], which Konshin later published in his literary almanac *Tsarskoye Selo* (see Letter 51).

16. TO NIKOLAY PUTYATA.

"He was thin, pale... " — Putyata's recollections were first published in *Putyata*, col. 264.

18. TO IVAN KOZLOV.

if the following letter is authentic — A. M. Peskov doubts the authenticity of the letter and does not include it in his *Chronicle*. He cites two basic reasons for his decision: first, the obvious contradiction between this letter and the one to Kozlov from late March or early April 1825 (Letter 23) with regard to Baratynsky's access to journals: "We get almost all the journals here" (Letter 18) / "thank God, we don't get a single journal here" (Letter 23); and second, the unmistakable parallels, even near quotations, between this letter and an apparently genuine letter from Kozlov to Baratynsky, which lead Peskov to suspect them both to be fabrications made by the same person (*Chronicle*, 147–148). The contradiction about the receipt of journals, however, seems easily explained: Letter 18 was written in Helsingfors, the capital of the Grand Duchy of Finland, where the enlightened Zakrevskys would very likely have received "almost all the journals"; Letter 23, on the other hand, was written in the much more isolated Fort Kyumen.

I received your **Monk** — *The Monk: A Kievan Tale* [*Chernets: Kiyevskaya povest'*] was published later that year; Baratynsky would have received the poem in manuscript form.

The four verses from **The Giaour... *are beautiful in Russian*** — The verses Baratynsky quotes echo the following passage from Byron's *Giaour* (1813):

> And rushing from my couch, I dart,
> And clasp her to my desperate heart;
> I clasp—what is it that I clasp?
> No breathing form within my grasp... (lines 1285–1288)

Not knowing English, Baratynsky would have read these lines in Amédée Pichot's rather uninspired French prose translation: "Je m'élance de ma couche, et je la presse sur mon coeur désolé. Mais qu'ai-je pressé? Je ne sens dans mes bras aucun être vivant..." ("Le Giaour, Fragments d'une nouvelle turque," *Oeuvres de Lord Byron*, 4th ed., vol. 3 [Paris: Ladvocat, Libraire, 1822] p. 42.)

our celestial Peri — Aleksandra Voyeykova, for whom both Kozlov and Baratynsky (among others) shared a fascination (see the note to the poem "To A. A. V."). In Persian mythology, the *peri* were a race of spirits that had been banished from paradise but were later considered to be beautiful and good; the image was made popular throughout Europe, and especially in Russia, by the Irish poet Thomas Moore's Oriental romance *Lalla-Rookh* (1817), in particular, the section "Paradise and the Peri," which Zhukovsky (Voyeykova's godfather) translated in 1821 as "The Peri and the Angel" ["Peri i angel"].

my current protector — Count Arseny Zakrevsky (1783–1865), the governor-general of Finland.

Mnemosyne — The literary almanac co-edited by Baratynsky's friend Wilhelm Küchelbecker and Prince Vladimir Odoyevsky in Moscow. Launched in 1824, it promoted the new philosophical and literary trends of German romanticism. It ceased publication after four issues, when Küchelbecker was arrested for his part in the Decembrist uprising.

our Frérons — Élie Catherine Fréron (1719–1776) was a conservative French critic who attacked Voltaire and other Enlightenment figures. Voltaire responded with virulent epigrams and a satire, making Fréron's name synonymous with benighted reactionary criticism.

One Grech, one Bulgarin, and one Kachenovsky — In 1825, Nikolay Grech (1787–1867) was the publisher of the St. Petersburg journal *Son of the Fatherland* and Faddey Bulgarin (1789–1859) published both the *Northern Archive* (with its supplement the *Literary Pages*) and the *Northern Bee*, also in St. Petersburg. In Moscow, meanwhile, Mikhail Kachenovsky (1775–1842) was putting out the venerable *Messenger of Europe*, which Nikolay Karamzin had founded in 1802.

Polevoy's journal — *The Moscow Telegraph*, published by Nikolay Polevoy, was launched at the start of 1825.

19. TO WILHELM KÜCHELBECKER.

the mathematician Euler — Interestingly, the address "in Europe" of the great Swiss mathematician Leonhard Euler was, for much of his life, St. Petersburg, where he worked at the Russian Academy of Sciences from 1727 to 1741 and again from 1766 until his death in 1783.

a few things for your journal — Namely, "The Storm," "Leda" (see Letter 25), and an excerpt from *Eda*, as well as two other pieces that ended up being published elsewhere.

20. TO ALEKSANDR TURGENEV.

Arseny Andreyevich's aide-de-camp, Mukhanov — Aleksandr Mukhanov, an aide-de-camp to Count Zakrevsky.

21. TO HIS MOTHER.

I left a day after him with Madame [Zakrevskaya] — On Countess Agrafena Fyodorovna Zakrevskaya, see the note to "How much you have in so few days."

22. TO NIKOLAY PUTYATA.

that it may be well with thee... — Ephesians 6: 3.

Woe from Wit — Baratynsky is requesting a manuscript copy of the comedy *Woe from Wit [Gore ot uma]* by Aleksandr Griboyedov (1795–1828)—although completed in 1823, the play was not professionally staged until 1831 and not published until 1833.

Bossuet — Jacques-Bénigne Bossuet (1627–1704), a French bishop famous for his sermons.

23. TO IVAN KOZLOV.

He is risen indeed — The traditional Easter greeting in Russia.

Your "Venetian Night" — Kozlov's lilting ballad "A Venetian Night" ["Venetsianskaya noch'"], published in Bestuzhev and Ryleyev's almanac *The Pole Star* in March 1825, enjoyed enormous success. Seven years later, the composer Mikhail Glinka set the ballad's first three stanzas to music (the "description of Venice" Baratynsky admires), and the art song has been a standard in the Russian repertoire ever since.

I can hardly wait for The Monk — In Letter 18, it is clear that Baratynsky had already read Kozlov's poem in manuscript. If that letter is authentic, then Baratynsky must here be referring to the published version of the poem.

the excerpt from Eda... *"Elysian Fields"* — Like Kozlov's poem, the excerpt from *Eda* (under the title "Winter" ["Zima"]) and the poem "Elysian Fields" ["Eliziyskiye polya"] both appeared in *The Pole Star*.

God rules the bold — The first half of a Russian proverb: "God rules the bold; the devil sways the drunk" [*Smelym Bog vladeyet, p'yanym chyort kachayet*].

Whom does she lure into her house?... — Baratynsky quotes lines 65–70 from his narrative poem *The Ball*:

> Кого в свой дом она манит?
> Не записных ли волокит,
> Не новичков ли миловидных?
> Не утомлен [ли] слух людей
> Молвой побед ее бесстыдных
> И соблазнительных связей?

Flee her: no heart is in her!... — Lines 107–112:

> Беги ее: нет сердца в ней!
> Страшися вкрадчивых речей
> Обворожительной приманки,
> Влюбленных взглядов не лови:
> В ней жар упившейся вакханки,
> Горячки жар, не жар любви!

Polevoy — See note to Letter 18.

Vyazemsky — On Vyazemsky, see the note to "To Prince Pyotr Andreyevich Vyazemsky." Although Baratynsky is quite critical of Vyazemsky here and in the epigram, he would become one of Baratynsky's closest friends.

the internecine battles between Karamzin and Shishkov — In the first decades of the nineteenth century, there were heated debates over the stylistic reforms introduced by Nikolay Mikhaylovich Karamzin (1766–1826) and strongly supported by Zhukovsky, Vyazemsky, and many others. These reforms brought a large number of French borrowings and other neologisms into the language, as well as a simplified syntax, while eliminating markedly Church Slavonic forms—all with the goal of making Russian a more elegant vehicle for the refined sensibilities of the era. The Karamzinian reforms were vigorously opposed by the academician Admiral Aleksandr Shishkov (1754–1841), who wrote a series of treatises denouncing the "Frenchification" of Russian and advocating a more robust style based on the language's Slavic roots.

In journalistic war... Orlov, who also loved fistfights — Grigory Orlov, one of Catherine the Great's lovers, was famous for his love of boxing. Pushkin, as it happens, had used a similar image in a letter to Vyazemsky three years earlier: "I take issue with you only for the one epistle to Kachenovsky: how could you descend into the *arena* with this puny fist-fighter?—you knocked him off his feet, but he covered your inglorious wreath with blood, bile, and bad vodka" (*Pushkin's Correspondence*, 1: 147–148, quoted by L. G. Frizman in *Poems 1982*, 674). The Russian of Baratynsky's epigram:

> Войной журнальною бесчестит без причины
>   Он дарования свои:
> Не так ли славный вождь и друг Екатерины
> Орлов еще любил кулачные бои?

24. TO NIKOLAY PUTYATA.

We need our passions and our dreams... — From Baratynsky's poem "The Skull" (lines 25–28).

Shakespeare's plow — It is not clear what Shakespearean image Baratynsky has in mind.

Your fairy — Agrafena Zakrevskaya.

I met with the general — Count Arseny Zakrevsky, who had promised to do what he could for Baratynsky before leaving for St. Petersburg (see Letter 21).

I am writing a new nárrative poem. — *The Ball.*

Brilliant with a thousand lights... — An excerpt from an early draft of the poem's opening stanzas. The Russian:

> Блистает тысячью огней
> Обширный зал; с высоких хоров
> Гудят смычки; толпа гостей;
> С приличной важностию взоров,
> В чепцах узорных, распашных,

Ряд пестрых барынь пожилых
Сидит. Причудницы от скуки
То поправляют свой наряд,
То на толпу, сложивши руки,
С тупым вниманием глядят.
Кружатся дамы молодые,
Пылают негой взоры их;
Огнем каменьев дорогих
Блестят уборы головные.
По их плечам полунагим
Златые локоны летают;
Одежды легкие, как дым,
Их легкий стан обозначают.
Вокруг пленительных Харит
И суетится и кипит
Толпа поклонников ревнивых;
С волненьем ловят каждый взгляд:
Шутя несчастных и счастливых
Из них волшебницы творят.
В движеньи все. Горя добиться
Вниманья лестного красы,
Кавалерист крутит усы,
Франт штатский чопорно острится.

25. TO NIKOLAY PUTYATA.

[April, after the 25th…] — Baratynsky in fact dates this letter "March 29," but A. M. Peskov argues that this must be a mistake, since both this and the previous letter to Putyata (Letter 24) could not have been written before Zakrevskaya's return to Helsingfors, which could not have happened before April 5 (*Chronicle*, 157).

in Rus… — Baratynsky uses the archaic name for Russia.

BIOGRAPHICAL NOTE

"Baratynsky is an officer…" — Quoted in *Chronicle*, 158.

"I cannot express to you Baratynsky's exhilaration…" — Quoted in *Chronicle*, 159.

27. TO NIKOLAY PUTYATA.

Putyatushka — Baratynsky playfully adds the affectionate *-ushka* suffix to his friend's name.

28. TO NIKOLAY PUTYATA.

Pargolovo — A summer resort area about twelve miles north of St. Petersburg (today it falls within the city boundaries).

29. TO HIS MOTHER.

a young Finnish girl — Karolina Levander, mentioned in Letter 28.

a pleasure outing and a parting shot — A play on words in the original French: *une partie de plaisir et un coup de Parte.* Baratynsky's phrase *un coup de Parte* conflates two expressions: *une flèche de Parthe* ("an arrow of Parthia")—corresponding to the English idiom "a parting shot" (corrupted from "a Parthian shot") and meaning a cutting remark made when leaving—and *un coup de partie,* which means something like "a decisive blow."

III. MOSCOW AND MARRIAGE

Geir Kjetsaa describes Aleksandra Baratynskaya's condition as "profound hypochondria" — Kjetsaa, 122.

Denis Davydov — Denis Vasilyevich Davydov (1784–1839), who was famous both for leading guerrilla attacks against Napoleon's forces in 1812 and for his poetry celebrating the hussar's life, was a close friend of Count Zakrevsky and one of Baratynsky's most ardent supporters. His letter is quoted in *Chronicle,* 168.

30. TO NIKOLAY PUTYATA.

my mortal body, which took ill — It was a lengthy illness, which lasted from mid-October into December and provided Baratynsky with the pretext he needed for his request to retire from military service.

Aurora — Aurora Stjernvall (1808–1902), the daughter of the governor of Vyborg Province and a member of the Swedish-Finnish aristocracy, was one of the most celebrated women of her day. Baratynsky, who met the sixteen-year-old Aurora in Helsingfors, wrote her poems in both French and Russian that played on her name: *"Oh, qu'il te sied ce nom d'Aurore, / Adolescente au teint vermeil!..."* ["Oh, how the name Aurora suits you, / adolescent girl of vermillion hue..."] and "Come forth, breathe rapture on us, / You who share the name of the dawn!..." [*Vyd', dokhni nam upoyen'yem, / Soimennitsa zari!...*] (1825). More cleverly, Baratynsky teased his friend Mukhanov in "A Question for M—v" ["Zapros M—vu"], written around the same time: "Was she the real dawn / or only the northern lights?" [*Byla l' pryamoy zaryoy ona / Il' tol'ko severnym siyan'yem?*]. Mukhanov's love for Aurora, however, was real—and reciprocated; a few years later, the two were engaged and the wedding planned, but Mukhanov died suddenly in 1834 (see *Kjetsaa*, 96–97). Aurora went on to marry the wealthy Pavel Demidov in 1836. After his death in 1840, she married again in 1846, this time to Andrey Karamzin, Nikolay Karamzin's son and the nephew of Vyazemsky, another admirer (see Letter 99).

someone will write to him from here — Probably, Denis Davydov.

Oznobishin — The poet Dmitry Petrovich Oznobishin (1804–1877) was a member of the metaphysically inclined literary circle around Semyon Raich (1792–1855). Among others, the group included Fyodor Tyutchev (later one of Russia's great poets) and the writers Vladimir Odoyevsky, Stepan Shevyryov, and Mikhail Pogodin, who were part of the separate Lovers of Wisdom Society. Before he went to Finland, Putyata had also belonged to Raich's circle.

31. TO ALEKSANDR PUSHKIN.

"There is no encouragement in our country..." — Pushkin's Correspondence, 1: 479.

they have bitten off more than they can chew — Baratynsky uses the idiomatic expression, "they are sitting in someone else's sleigh" [*oni sadyatsya v chuzhiye sani*].

Küchelbecker's "Spirits" — Shakespeare's Spirits: A Dramatic Jest in Two Acts [*Shekspirovy dukhi: Dramaticheskaya shutka v dvukh deystviyakh*] (1825), a lighthearted work in which a poet is tricked into believing he has conjured spirits from Shakespeare's plays (Oberon, Titania, Puck, Ariel, Caliban, etc.).

I am not copying out Eda for you because it will be printed in a few days. — In fact, *Eda: A Finnish Tale* (published together with Baratynsky's *Feasts* [*Piry*], written in 1820) was held up by the censor and did not appear until February 1826 (*Chronicle*, 166, 175–176). This was Baratynsky's first book publication.

do for me what you did for Ryleyev — Pushkin had made a number of notes on a copy of Ryleyev's narrative poem *Voynarovsky* (1825).

Why do you refer to Lyovushka as Lev Sergeyevich?... my affection for you and your brother. — Aleksandr Pushkin had several reasons to be angry at his brother Lev— and to express his anger through the formal name-plus-patronymic address rather than the affectionate "Lyovushka": Lev Pushkin had been circulating his brother's works around St. Petersburg without his permission, was slow about arranging the publication of his collected poems, and had misappropriated his royalties (see *Binyon*, 204–205, 231–232). Baratynsky was close to both brothers, as he was, indeed, to the entire Pushkin family.

32. TO NIKOLAY PUTYATA.

Tolstoy the American — Count Fyodor Ivanovich Tolstoy (1782–1846), one of the most colorful figures of the day, was notorious for his dishonest card playing, fondness for duels, and general troublemaking. In 1803, he embarked on the first Russian circumnavigation of the globe with Admiral Johann von Krusenstern, but, as T. J. Binyon describes: "Tolstoy made himself so obnoxious on board that Krusenstern abandoned him on one of the Aleutian Islands—together with a pet female ape, which he may later have eaten. Crossing the Bering Straits, he wandered slowly back through Siberia, arriving in St. Petersburg at the end of 1805: hence his nickname 'the American.'" (*Binyon*, 96.)

Do not touch the Parnassian pen... — The epigram was published under the title "Advice" ["Sovet"] a few months later in the *Moscow Telegraph*. It may have been directed at Princess Zinaida Volkonskaya (see note to Letter 164), who had recently written an ode on the death of Baratynsky's nemesis, Alexander I (*CCWL*, 2: 153). The Russian:

> Не трогайте Парнасского пера,
> Не трогайте, пригожие вострушки!
> Красавицам немного в нем добра,
> И им Амур другие дал игрушки.
> Любовь ли вам оставить в забытьи
> Для жалких рифм? Над рифмами смеются,
> Уносят их Летийские струи:
> На пальчиках чернила остаются.

33. TO NIKOLAY PUTYATA.

this woman still pursues my imagination — Baratynsky, perhaps unwittingly, quotes his own poem "The Kiss."

34. TO ALEKSANDR PUSHKIN.

Urania — The literary almanac *Urania*, published in early January 1826 by Mikhail Pogodin, presented mainly writers from the literary-philosophical circle around Semyon Raich (see note to letter 30), such as Oznobishin and Tyutchev, and from the Lovers of Wisdom Society, such as Dmitry Venevitinov (a very gifted poet and philosopher who died in 1827 at the age of twenty-one), Shevyryov, and Vladimir Odoyevsky. All these young men were fascinated by the *transcendentalist philosophy* of Friedrich Schelling (1775–1854). Baratynsky had contributed two poems to the almanac, as had Vyazemsky, a friend and supporter of Pogodin; Pushkin, meanwhile, at Vyazemsky's urging, had contributed five poems.

a boy of about seventeen years old — Then *twenty* years old, Stepan Petrovich

Shevyryov (1806–1864) would become one of the leaders of the Slavophile movement in the 1840s.

Galich has published a poetics in the German style — *An Essay in the Science of the Beautiful* [*Opyt nauki izyashchnago*] (1825) by Aleksandr Ivanovich Galich, a professor at St. Petersburg University, was based on the aesthetics of Friedrich Schelling.

you really let the elegists have it in your epigram — "The Nightingale and the Cuckoo" ["Solovey i kukushka"], published in *Urania*, contrasts the variegated singing of the nightingale (he "warbles, and whistles, and thunders") to the monotonous repetition of the cuckoo, ending with the plea: "Deliver us, O God, / from elegiac cuckooing!"

"The simpering whining of the poets of our times" — Possibly a line (*Vytyo zhemannoye poetov nashikh let*) from a now-lost early version of Baratynsky's epistle "To Bogdanovich" ["Bogdanovichu"], probably written in 1824.

a new narrative poem on Yermak — The Cossack Yermak Timofeyevich led the Russian conquest of Siberia in the sixteenth century. Although there is no definite record of Pushkin planning a poem about Yermak, his "Imaginary Conversation with Alexander I" ["Voobrazhayemyy razgovor s Aleksandrom I] (late 1824–early 1825) ends with the tsar sending the impertinent Pushkin to Siberia, "where he would write the narrative poem 'Yermak' or 'Kochum' in varied meter with rhyme." (Kochum was the name of the khan whose empire Yermak conquered.)

your shorter poems — Pushkin's first collection of lyric poems, *Stikhotvoreniya* [*Poems*], which had appeared in late December 1825.

What are you planning to do with **Godunov?** — Pushkin finished writing *Boris Godunov* in November 1825. After his return to Moscow in September 1826, he read the play to friends on several occasions and published excerpts from it in literary almanacs, but it was only in 1830 that he received the emperor's permission to publish the entire play. Censorship, however, prevented it from being staged until 1870.

35. TO NIKOLAY PUTYATA.

the description of Finland — An excerpt from *Eda*, under the title "Finland" ["Finlyandiya"], had appeared in the *Moscow Telegraph* in December 1825.

Butkov — An official in Helsingfors.

F. V. Bulgarin — See note to Letter 18. In 1826, Baratynsky and his friends knew Bulgarin only as an unscrupulous journalist, banal writer, and generally unpleasant man with a shady past. Three years later, however, they discovered that he had for years been an informant for the tsar's secret police, the notorious Third Department (see *Binyon*, 311–312).

In your pages you play the hypocrite... — The Russian:

В своих листах душонкой ты кривишь,
Уродуешь и мненья и сказанья;

Приятельски дурачеству кадишь,
Завистливо поносишь дарованья;
Дурной твой нрав дурной приносит плод:
Срамец! срамец — все шепчут, — вот известье!
— Эх, не тужи! Уж это мой расчет:
Подписчики мне платит за бесчестье.

37. TO ALEKSANDR MUKHANOV.

My brother Irakly — Irakly Abramovich Baratynsky (1802–1859), then a lieutenant, was also serving under Field Marshal Wittgenstein in Tulchin.

after her delivery of a burden — Agrafena Zakrevskaya's daughter Lidiya was born on July 18. Baratynsky here plays on the Russian word *beremennaya* ("pregnant"), closely related to the word *bremya* ("burden").

Ladies' Night — A provisional name [*Damski vecher*] for *The Ball*.

38. TO NIKOLAY PUTYATA.

One of my brothers — Irakly (see previous letter).

our duke — Baratynsky jokingly refers to Count Zakrevsky by the German title *Herzog* (in Russian, *gertsog*).

find out if my works are being printed or not — The book of lyric poems that Baratynsky had sent to Ryleyev and Bestuzhev in 1823 (see Letter 11) was still awaiting publication. It had been put on hold in 1824 so as not to cause problems in the effort to win Baratynsky's promotion. In 1825, Baratynsky apparently took back the manuscript from Ryleyev, and by March 1826, the publication was being handled by Anton Delvig and Pyotr Pletnyov (see *Chronicle*, 24–26, 163–164, 177–178).

39. TO NIKOLAY KONSHIN.

My previous existence, disorderly and wayward — In St. Petersburg, Baratynsky "had, apparently, gained the reputation of a rake and womanizer" (I. Medvedeva, "Ranniy Baratynskiy," in *Poems 1936*, 1: 58), and many of his friends were surprised by his sudden marriage. Just a few weeks after the wedding, Lev Pushkin, a fellow carouser in St. Petersburg, wrote to Sergey Sobolevsky in Moscow: "I've been cursing you, Moscow, Muscovites, fate, and Baratynsky. You idiots, you pimps, you had to go and get him married! What are you so happy about? Just so you could do some matchmaking, a rather praiseworthy pastime, it cost you nothing to ruin a decent man. Baratynsky, in the course of three years, was a step away from marriage thirty times, and thirty times he couldn't manage it; *en était-il plus malheureux? [and was he any unhappier as a result?]* He never, not for a minute, lived without love, and when he finished loving a woman, she became loathsome to him. I say all this as proof of Baratynsky's fickle character; his youth should not be condemned to family life." (*Chronicle*, 181.)

The Saratov governor — Aleksey Davydovich Panchulidzev, the brother-in-law of Mariya Andreyevna Panchulidzeva, née Baratynskaya.

Pyotr Andreyevich — Possibly a mutual acquaintance from Finland.

40. TO NIKOLAY POLEVOY.

do me the honor of placing it in your library between Batyushkov and V. L. Pushkin — Baratynsky jokingly alludes to his reputed debt to French neoclassicism, a trait shared by both Konstantin Batyushkov (1787–1855)—one of the finest poets of the previous generation who, like Baratynsky was acclaimed for his love poetry and compared to Parny (he had also served in the army in Finland)—and the much less talented Vasily Lvovich Pushkin (1766–1830), Aleksandr Pushkin's uncle, known primarily for his light-hearted, somewhat risqué verse.

41. TO ALEKSANDR PUSHKIN.

my Tambov seclusion — Baratynsky had spent most of the second half of 1827 in Mara.

Two more Onegin *cantos* — Chapters 4 and 5 of Pushkin's *Eugene Onegin* were published together in book form in late January 1828.

Northern Flowers — The literary almanac published by Delvig.

Vasily Lvovich is writing a romantic narrative poem — Vasily Lvovich Pushkin (see note to Letter 40) was writing *Captain Khrabrov* [*Kapitan Khrabrov*], in which he pokes fun at the new romantic vogue.

Thunderclap... Zhukovsky's ballad — "Thunderclap" [*Gromoboy*], a character in Zhukovsky's ballad "The Twelve Sleeping Maidens," sells his soul to the devil (see the relevant note to the poem "The Little Demon").

42. TO NIKOLAY PUTYATA.

Forgive me, dear friend, this is the way... — An impromptu. The Russian:

Прости, мой милой, так создать
Меня умела власть господня:
Люблю до завтра отлагать,
Что сделать надобно сегодня!

I recently entered the Land Survey Office... — Baratynsky was enrolled as an of-ficial at the Land Survey Office on January 24, 1828. The position was a mere formality, and he never actually did any work there (*Chronicle*, 202). His under-standing boss was Bogdan Andreyevich Germes, a name Baratynsky has some fun with in a letter to Nikolay Yazykov (Letter 72).

Thank you for your friendly criticism... some of my changes are good for the whole. — He is referring to *Poems 1827*; many of the poems in the book had been revised, sometimes drastically, since their earlier publication in journals or almanacs.

Alcina... Magdalina — Both names refer to Agrafena Zakrevskaya (see head-notes to Letters 22 and 27 and the note to "How much you have in so few days"). The "copy" he will send her is his just-published book of poems.

43. TO ANTON DELVIG.

destroy these two pieces entirely — The poems in question may have been "In the heart's tender tongue" ["Serdechnym nezhnym yazykom"], describing a failed attempt at seduction, and "Old Man" ["Starik"], lamenting the loss of one's abil-ity to attract young women. Baratynsky possibly feared that the poems would have suggested extramarital interests on his part (see *CCWL*, 2/1: 193–194, 202–203). In the end, Delvig did publish "Old Man" in *Northern Flowers* without the author's name, and Baratynsky later included both poems in *Poems 1835*.

Will you include my portrait... ? — For some reason, the portrait was not published.

I received a letter from Pushkin... — Pushkin had read Baratynsky's *Ball* in man-uscript. The work was published under the same cover as Pushkin's own comic narrative poem *Count Nulin* [*Graf Nulin*] as *Two Tales in Verse* [*Dve povesti v stikhakh*] just a week or so after Baratynsky wrote this letter (*Chronicle*, 214).

Sofya Mikhaylovna — Delvig's wife, née Saltykova (1805–1888). Details about her taking care of Nastasya Baratynskaya (*Nastinka*), are unknown, but it must have occurred during the Delvigs' visit to Moscow in the fall of 1828. Just months after Delvig's death in 1831, Sofya Delvig married Baratynsky's brother *Sergey* Baratynsky (1807–1866)—also mentioned here—and the couple settled in Mara, where Sergey became a well-known medical doctor.

Shiryayev delivered The Double — A. S. Shiryayev was a bookseller in Moscow; the book he delivered—*The Double, or, My Evenings in Little Russia* [*Dvoynik, ili Moi vechera v Malorossii*] (1828) by Antony Pogorelsky (the pseudonym of Aleksey Perovsky [1787–1836])—was a collection of four Hoffmannesque tales that in some ways anticipated Nikolay Gogol's *Evenings on a Farm near Dikanka* (1831).

Gnedich — The poet Nikolay Ivanovich Gnedich (1784–1833) is today best known for his translation of *The Iliad* (1829).

44. TO PYOTR VYAZEMSKY.

I am already planning a novel — Like most of Baratynsky's attempts at prose fiction, we know nothing about this.

Bulgarin's Vyzhigin... *the originality of a spy's observations* — Bulgarin's picaresque novel *Ivan Vyzhigin* (1829) was an enormous success with the public. By this time, Baratynsky and his friends very likely knew that Bulgarin was a spy for the tsar's secret police (see note to Letter 35). The influential early-eighteenth-century novel *Gil Blas*, by Alain-René Lesage, had set the standard for the genre, which was by now showing its age; Vasily Narezhny's novel *A Russian Gil Blas* [*Rossiyskij Zhil'blaz*] had appeared in 1814.

I have nothing against the idea of publishing something with you — Vyazemsky, Pushkin, and Delvig were planning to produce their own journal to challenge Bulgarin's dominance in the field. *The Literary Gazette*, edited by Delvig, published its first issue on January 1, 1830.

Polevoy... Raich... Nadinka Ozerova — Baratynsky is referring to various commissions Vyazemsky had given him. On Polevoy and Raich, see the notes to Letters 18 and 30; Nadezhda Ozerova, the daughter of a senator, was at the time nineteen years old.

Sverbeyeva — Yekaterina (Katerina) Aleksandrovna Sverbeyeva, née Shcherbatova (1808–1892), was the wife of Dmitry Sverbeyev (see Letter 57). Around this time, Baratynsky dedicated to her the poem "In the Album of One Going Abroad" ["V al'bom ot"yezhayushchey"], published in *Poems 1835* as "To K. A. Sverbeyeva" ["K. A. Sverbeyevoy"].

45. TO PYOTR VYAZEMSKY.

"The Station" — Vyazemsky's poem "The Station" ["Stantsiya"] had just appeared in the almanac *The Snowdrop* along with one of Baratynsky's poems; Baratynsky is evidently referring to an offprint.

Poltava — Pushkin's historical narrative poem *Poltava*, published in book form in March 1829.

47. TO HIS WIFE, NASTASYA BARATYNSKAYA.

Marya Andreyevna's husband — Ivan Davydovich Panchulidzev (1760–1817).

Dvyatkovsky — Probably the doctor.

my dear Sophie — Nastasya Baratynskaya's younger sister, Sofya Lvovna Engelhardt.

48. TO PYOTR VYAZEMSKY.

Pletnyov — The poet, critic, and scholar Pyotr Pletnyov, who as a young man in St. Petersburg in the early 1820s had been part of the so-called "alliance of poets" with Pushkin, Baratynsky, Delvig, and Küchelbecker. His editorial and organizational skills had proved essential in the publication of both Pushkin's and Baratynsky's books of poetry.

quit-rent — In the Russian context, the quit-rent (*obrok*) was a regular payment, in goods or money, made by a serf to a landowner.

I will be in your neighborhood — Mara was about seventy-five miles from the Vyazemskys' Meshcherskoye estate.

Tiflis — The old name for Tbilisi, the capital of Georgia, which had been annexed to Russia in 1801.

49. TO IVAN KIREYEVSKY.

my Tatar homeland — He uses "Tatar" in jest, to mean "uncivilized": Mara was some four hundred miles from Tatarstan. (The Engelhardts' Kaymary estate, however, actually was in Tatarstan.)

by the Red Gate, in the house of the former Myortvy — Kireyevsky's address, where he lived with his mother and step-father, Avdotya Petrovna and Aleksey Andreyevich Yelagin. *The house of the former Myortvy* is humorously phrased: the former owner's surname is the Russian word for "dead."

Count Paskevich of Erivan — General Ivan Paskevich had led Russia's troops to victory against Persia in the War of 1826–1828, for which he was made Count of Erivan (Yerevan).

Kirsanov — The town closest to Mara.

50. TO IVAN KIREYEVSKY.

Maksimovich — Kireyevsky's friend Mikhail Aleksandrovich Maksimovich (1804–1873), a Ukrainian botanist with a strong interest in literature and folklore, was compiling material for the literary almanac *The Day Star*, which appeared in January 1830. It included an excerpt from the narrative poem *The Concubine*, which Baratynsky had just begun working on. Maksimovich had also been part of the literary-philosophical circle around Semyon Raich (see note to Letter 30).

Sobolevsky — Baratynsky's friend Sergey Sobolevsky, a writer of comic epigrams and, later, a serious book collector, was friends with most of the writers of his day. In 1822, he was given a sinecure at the Archives of the Ministry of External Affairs in Moscow, where several members of the Lovers of Wisdom group were also employed—including Kireyevsky, Shevyryov, Odoyevsky, and Dmitry Venevitinov. It was Sobolevsky who coined the label "archival youths" for this group, used later by Pushkin in *Eugene Onegin*: "The archival youths, in a throng, / look starchily at Tanya / and talk among themselves / about her with disapproval" (Chapter 7, stanza 49).

51. TO NIKOLAY KONSHIN.

the poems I promised — "The Fairy," "In the Album of One Going Abroad" (see note to Letter 44), and the epigram "What good do your noisy debates do you?" ["Chto pol'zy vam ot shumnykh vashikh preniy?"] (relating to a recent public dispute between Nikolay Polevoy and Semyon Raich).

The year is stated under my poem "The Fairy" — See the note to the poem.

52. TO PYOTR VYAZEMSKY.

your preface to F.-Vizin — Vyazemsky's "Introduction to the Life of Fon-Vizin" ["Vvedeniye k zhizneopisaniyu Fon-Vizina"], on the eighteenth-century Russian dramatist Denis Ivanovich Fonvizin (ca. 1745–1792), was published in the second issue of the *Literary Gazette*, on January 6, 1830.

Krivtsov — The wealthy Nikolay Ivanovich Krivtsov (1791–1843), an old friend of Zhukovsky's and Vyazemsky's, lived on the Lyubichi estate, only a few miles from Mara.

I am writing a narrative poem — *The Concubine*, about a man who lives openly with his gypsy mistress in Moscow.

55. TO PYOTR VYAZEMSKY.

The information about the *cholera epidemic* comes from the article "Russian Cholera Epidemic of 1829–1831," in the *Encyclopedia of Plague and Pestilence: From Ancient Times to the Present*, edited by George Childs Kohn, 3rd ed. (New York: Facts on File, 2008), 325–327.

56. TO PYOTR VYAZEMSKY.

your steppeland horse ride — Vyazemsky's poem "A Ride in the Steppes" ["Progulka v stepi"]; the poem did not arrive in time to be published by Delvig in *Northern Flowers* and was instead published in the *Literary Gazette*.

your proposal about publishing Russia's classical authors — Following up on his biography of Fonvizin (see Letter 52), Vyazemsky had suggested that Baratynsky collaborate with him on a series of biographical articles about eighteenth-century Russian writers, such as Mikhail *Lomonosov* (1711–1765) and Vasily *Tredyakovsky* (1703–1769).

Warsaw has risen up — On November 29 (NS) / 17 (OS), 1830, a group of armed insurrectionists attacked Warsaw's Belweder Palace, the seat of the tsar's brother Grand Duke Constantine Pavlovich, the viceroy of the Congress Kingdom of Poland, which had been a semi-autonomous part of the Russian Empire since 1815. Constantine fled disguised as a woman. The rebels then seized the main arsenal and took control of the city, supported by Polish civilians. The Polish army joined the uprising and a provisional government was formed on December 5 (NS) / November 23 (OS). After weeks of unsuccessful negotiations with Russia, on January 25 (NS) / 13 (OS), the Polish parliament proclaimed the removal of Nicholas I as king of Poland, essentially declaring independence. In February, the Russian army invaded Poland, and after months of war, Warsaw finally capitulated to the Russians in the late summer of 1831. The remaining Polish forces laid down their arms a few weeks later.

57. TO DMITRY SVERBEYEV.

and the same is true of Pushkin... — Pushkin had been forced by the epidemic to remain on his estate in Boldino, in Nizhny Novgorod Province, from September through November, returning to Moscow on December 5. In Boldino, he wrote an astounding quantity of superb work: Baratynsky refers to *The Little Tragedies* [*Malen'kiye tragedii*], a group of four short plays; *The Little House in Kolomna* [*Domik v Kolomne*] (the "narrative poem"); and *Onegin's Journey* [*Puteshestviye Onegina*], originally intended as the eighth chapter of his novel in verse, as well as the ninth (later Chapter 8) and unfinished tenth chapters of *Onegin* (the latter about Onegin's involvement with the Decembrists). The "folder of prose" Baratynsky mentions contained the short story collection *The Tales of the Late Ivan Petrovich Belkin* [*Povesti pokoynogo Ivana Petrovicha Belkina*] and the parodic *History of the Village of Goryukhino* [*Istoriya sela Goryukhina*]. Pushkin also wrote some thirty lyric poems in Boldino. (On Pushkin's "miraculous autumn," see *Binyon*, 338–345.)

BIOGRAPHICAL NOTE

Anton Delvig died suddenly... — Pletnyov's letter to Pushkin was written within hours of Delvig's death; it is published in *Pushkin's Correspondence*, 2: 137.

The Ladies' Journal... "reviewed" the work... — The non-review was published in May 1831, under the title "A New Work by Baratynsky, in Verse"; it is excerpted in *Chronicle*, 256.

IV: KAZAN, KIREYEVSKY, AND *THE EUROPEAN*

59. TO IVAN KIREYEVSKY.

Is your novel progressing? — Kireyevsky had begun writing the novel *Two Lives* [*Dve zhizni*] (never finished).

Ramikh — A. M. Peskov identifies this person only as "the doctor for the Kireyevsky-Yelagin family" (*Chronicle*, 256).

Yazykov — The poet Nikolay Yazykov, a close friend of both Ivan Kireyevsky and his brother, Pyotr, with whom he was collecting material on Russian folk poetry, had been living at the Yelagin house since 1829.

60. TO IVAN KIREYEVSKY.

L'Âne mort and La Confession — Novels (published in 1827 and 1830, respectively) by Jules Janin.

Salayev — A Moscow bookseller. It is not clear who *Loginov* is.

61. TO IVAN KIREYEVSKY.

Shiryayev... Kolygin — Moscow booksellers.

62. TO IVAN KIREYEVSKY.

the style of Joan — He is referring to Zhukovsky's verse drama about Joan of Arc, *The Maid of Orleans* [*Orleanskaya deva*] (1824), a translation of Schiller's *Die Jungfrau von Orleans* (1801).

63. TO IVAN KIREYEVSKY.

I am sending you my own Sismondi and Villemain — The books in question are possibly the third edition of J. C. L. de Sismondi's *De la littérature du midi de l'Europe* [*On the Literature of the South of Europe*], published in 1829, and Abel-François Villemain's five-volume *Cours de littérature française* [*Course in French Literature*] (1828–1829). It is not clear what sort of exchange Baratynsky is arranging with Kireyevsky.

Urbain — A Moscow bookseller.

64. TO IVAN KIREYEVSKY.

I'll write you a more decent letter from the village. — That is, from the Engelhardt estate Kaymary.

65. TO NIKOLAY PUTYATA.

I thank you for delivering The Concubine *to the intended recipient* — Very likely, Count Zakrevsky or his wife.

far more bad places in Eda *than in* Sara — By *Sara* he means *The Concubine*, whose heroine bears that name.

BIOGRAPHICAL NOTE

"I recently received a letter..." — *Pushkin's Correspondence*, 1: 310. The letter from Baratynsky that Vyazemsky quotes has not survived.

66. TO PYOTR PLETNYOV.

I haven't yet started on Delvig's life — Baratynsky had planned to write a biography of Delvig but apparently never did.

68. TO IVAN KIREYEVSKY.

Rousseau's Héloise — *Julie, ou La Nouvelle Héloise* [*Julie, or, The New Héloise*] (1761).

the creator of Clarissa — Samuel Richardson, author of the epistolary novel *Clarissa, or, The History of a Young Lady* (1748).

hardly as a creator — That is, as a writer of fiction.

70. TO IVAN KIREYEVSKY.

[Second half of August (?), 1831...] — Earlier editors assumed that this letter relates to the closing of *The European* in the spring of 1832. A. M. Peskov, however, argues convincingly that it had to have been written not long after the death of Yazykov's mother, which occurred in 1831, and during Yazykov's long illness from April to July or August 1831.

71. TO IVAN KIREYEVSKY.

just as one might criticize what is created in Byron's narrative poems — That is, the fictional aspects of Byron's poems.

73. TO IVAN KIREYEVSKY.

the one I sent to Yazykov — The poem "A child, I would the forest echo."

74. TO IVAN KIREYEVSKY.

Pushkin's and Zhukovsky's verses — Kireyevsky had sent him the pamphlet *On the Taking of Warsaw: Three Poems by V. Zhukovsky and A. Pushkin* [*Na vzyatiye Varshavy: Tri stikhotvoreniya V. Zhukovskago i A. Pushkina*] (St. Petersburg, 1831). The three poems, written to commemorate Russia's victory over the Polish nationalists (see note to Letter 56), were Zhukovsky's "An Old Song in a New Key" ["Staraya pesnya na novyy lad"] and Pushkin's "To the Slanderers of Russia" ["Klevetnikam Rossii"] and "The Anniversary of Borodino" ["Borodinskaya godovshchina"].

Now I am writing a short drama — Although Baratynsky completed the play and sent it to Kireyevsky, who commented on it (see Letters 75, 78, 79, 89), no draft or copy of the work has survived and we know nothing about it.

Zagoskin's novels — Mikhail Zagoskin (1789–1852) had recently published two historical novels: *Yury Miloslavsky, or, Russians in 1612* [*Yuriy Miloslavskiy, ili Russkiye v 1612 godu*] (1829) and *Roslavlev, or, Russians in 1812* [*Roslavlev, ili Russkiye v 1812 godu*] (1831).

Rozen — The poet Baron Yegor Rozen (1800–1860) was collecting material for the literary almanac *Alcyone*.

75. TO IVAN KIREYEVSKY.

in a few days I'll say the same thing to Pushkin — Pushkin was preparing a final installment of *Northern Flowers* as a memorial to Delvig and to benefit his widow and daughter (after Delvig's death, pawn tickets worth more than half his estate had disappeared). Baratynsky, of course, did not turn him down. He sent him "My Elysium," despite having already promised the poem to Kireyevsky (see Letter 73). (On Delvig's financial situation, see V. E. Vatsuro, *"Severnyye tsvety": Istoriya al'manakha Del'viga–Pushkina* [Moscow: Kniga, 1978], 231.)

76. TO IVAN KIREYEVSKY.

Vasily Lvovich Pushkin or even his brother, Sergey Lvovich — Aleksandr Pushkin's uncle (see note to Letter 40) and father, respectively.

my copyist — Nastasya Baratynskaya.

the Guizot — Probably either *Histoire générale de la civilisation en Europe* (1828) or *Histoire de la civilisation en France* (1830, in four volumes), both by the French historian François Guizot (1787–1874).

77. TO IVAN KIREYEVSKY.

literature should be viewed as "a science like other sciences... and nothing else." — Preface to *The Concubine*, in *Poems 1982*, 463.

"Mad is the artist..." — Nadezhdin's review from the *Telescope* is excerpted in *Chronicle*, 263.

in the year of my Mashenka's birth — Baratynsky's daughter Mariya (1831–?) was born in mid-October 1831.

It's not a problem that my poem was passed around — He is referring to "A child, I would the forest echo," which Baratynsky had sent to Yazykov (Letter 72).

I sent Pushkin another one, too — Baratynsky sent Pushkin both "My Elysium" and "A child, I would the forest echo" for the memorial publication of *Northern Flowers* (see note to Letter 75); he may have forgotten that he had promised both poems to *The European* (Letter 73), or Kireyevsky or Yazykov had suggested sending them to Pushkin.

78. TO IVAN KIREYEVSKY.

I forgot to call by name... — It is not clear if these two unrhymed trochaic tetrameters (*Pozabyl vse dni nedeli / Nazyvat' po imenam*) are Baratynsky's own impromptu or if he is quoting something.

my article — "A Response to Criticism" ["Antikritika"].

a story, which you remember: "The Ring" — In December 1830 or January 1831, Baratynsky and Kireyevsky had, perhaps as a mutual challenge, each undertaken the writing of a fantastic tale in prose in the style of E. T. A. Hoffmann (they were possibly inspired by Pushkin's *Tales of Belkin*, which Pushkin read to Baratynsky in early December). Kireyevsky wrote the story "The Opal" ["Opal"] (not published until 1861) and Baratynsky wrote "The Ring" ["Persten'"], in which an eccentric recluse named Opalsky appears to be controlled by a mysterious ring (*Chronicle*, 249).

the stories by the Little Russian author — The first volume of the short story collection *Evenings on a Farm near Dikanka* [*Vechera na khutore bliz Dikanki*], by Nikolay Vasilyevich Gogol (1809–1852), published in 1831. (Before the twentieth century, Ukraine was called "Little Russia.")

Zagoskin — See note to Letter 74.

I have the plan for a new long poem thought out from every angle. — Nothing seems to have come of this.

the epistle to Yazykov and the elegy you call European — The poem "Yazykov, singer of youthful wildness" ["Yazykov, buystva molodogo"], which he sent Yazykov in early November, and the poem "In days of limitless distractions," included in Letter 73 to Kireyevsky.

a veneration at a nearby hermitage — The Seven Lakes Hermitage of the Mother of God is located about four miles from Kaymary (it was largely destroyed in 1928, but is currently being rebuilt). Nastasya Baratynskaya was most likely attending a veneration of the miracle-working Seven Lakes icon of the Mother of God of Smolensk, which was said to have protected Kazan from plague in 1654. The icon is today housed in the SS. Peter and Paul Cathedral in Kazan.

79. TO IVAN KIREYEVSKY.

Here are the things for The European — "A Response to Criticism," the fantastic tale "The Ring," and the now-lost drama.

a pood of cocoa — About thirty-six pounds.

the German orthodoxy — Schelling's transcendental philosophy (see Letter 34, and the accompanying notes).

Hunter's Row — *Okhotnyy Ryad*, a major shopping street in Moscow.

80. TO IVAN KIREYEVSKY.

of the talent-killing / arrogant thought of perfection — Lines from Zhukovsky's verse epistle "To Prince Vyazemsky and V. L. Pushkin" (1814).

I'm familiar with The Tales of Belkin — Pushkin read the stories to Baratynsky not long after arriving in Moscow from Boldino (see note to Letter 57). On December 9, 1830, Pushkin told Pletnyov: "I have written five tales in prose that are making Baratynsky neigh and kick" (*Pushkin's Correspondence*, 133).

81. TO IVAN KIREYEVSKY.

Zhukovsky's new ballads — In the summer of 1831, two separate editions of Zhukovsky's ballads were published, both titled *Ballads and Tales* [*Ballady i povesti*]. The first, in two volumes, included works going back to the early 1810s, while the second, in one volume, included only work written since 1828. Baratynsky is requesting the latter.

Thank you for the cocoa — Kireyevsky must have written that he had bought (or would buy) the cocoa. As of late January, Baratynsky had not yet received it.

82. TO IVAN KIREYEVSKY.

the Guizot... — See note to Letter 76.

The terrible Artsybashev — The Kazan-based historian Nikolay Sergeyevich Artsybashev (1773–1841) had caused a scandal a few years earlier with a series of articles in the *Moscow Messenger* severely criticizing Nikolay Karamzin's *History of the Russian State* [*Istoriya gosudarstva Rossiyskago*] (1816–1826).

83. TO NIKOLAY YAZYKOV.

"To I. V. Kireyevsky..." — Yazykov's epistle to Kireyevsky is not just about the poet turning to more serious themes, but specifically about focusing on more genuinely Russian topics. Yazykov encourages his friend to "live and work in an Orthodox way / to the glory of your motherland," telling him that through his in-depth study of the Russian past "you will give us non-foreign information / and true ideas about it: / that a pure-Russian Russia / may appear to us more clearly!" From this point on, Yazykov's poetry would be increasingly marked by Slavophile views, culminating in such poems as "To Those Who Are Not Ours" ["K nenashim"] (1844).

Crowning with ivy and grapes... — The poem is an early version of the epistle "To Yazykov," first published in *Poems 1835* under numeral XXV. The Russian of this early version:

> Плющом и гроздием венчая
> Чело высокое свое,
> Бывало, муза молодая
> С тобой разгульное житье
> И удалую радость пела,
> И к ней безумна и слепа,
> То забываясь, пламенела
> Любовью грубою толпа;
> То на свободные напевы
> Сердяся в ханжестве тупом,

> Она ругалась чудной девы
> Ей непонятным божеством.
> Во взорах пламень вдохновенья,
> Огонь восторга на щеках
> Был жар хмельной в ее глазах
> Или багрянец вожделенья.
> Она высоко рождена,
> Ей много славы подобает:
> Лишь для любовника она
> Наряд Менады надевает.
> Яви ж, яви ее скорей,
> Певец, в достойном блеске миру:
> Наперснице души твоей
> Дай диадиму и порфиру;
> Державный сан ее открой:
> Да изумит своей красой!
> Да величавый взор смущает
> Ее злословного судью,
> Да со стыдом он в ней познает
> Свою Царицу и мою!

Your student elegies — The poems Yazykov wrote in the mid-1820s, when he was a student at the University of Dorpat (Tartu).

84. TO IVAN KIREYEVSKY.

if my first epistle to Yazykov hasn't been printed yet… Print the second one instead — He is asking Kireyevsky to replace his poem "Yazykov, singer of youthful wildness" (see note to Letter 78) with the one celebrating the yet-unrevealed majesty of Yazykov's muse (in Letter 83).

young Pertsov — The satirist Erast Petrovich Pertsov (1804–1837).

85. TO AVDOTYA YELAGINA.

Aleksey Andreyevich — Her husband, Aleksey Yelagin.

the magic of your seeing each other again… — Zhukovsky had been in Moscow since the fall of 1831.

in a few days you will receive enough material for an entire issue — Avdotya Yelagina was helping her son with the production of *The European*.

86. TO IVAN KIREYEVSKY.

Karamzin's **Messenger of Europe** — Karamzin launched the journal in 1802 and served as editor until 1804. It later took a much more conservative line under Mikhail Kachenovsky (see note to letter 18).

here's an epigram for you — It is not clear who the target is. In *CCP 1914*, M. L. Gofman suggested that it was possibly "provoked by N. A. Polevoy's attacks against *The Concubine* in the *Telescope*" (1: 285; a slip of the pen, surely—Polevoy's review appeared in the *Moscow Telegraph*). Later commentators have echoed Gofman, usually with greater confidence. A. M. Peskov, however, disputes the idea, arguing that Baratynsky would never consider Polevoy "one of my own" (*rodnoy*); he believes the intended target is more likely to have been "one of his actual relatives," but does not suggest who (*Chronicle*, 287; see also *CCWL*, 2/1: 273). The epigram was printed in the never-published third issue of *The European*, of which only a few copies survive.

> Кто непременный мой ругатель?
> Необходимый мой предатель?
> Завистник непременный мой?
> Тут думать нечего — родной.
> Нам чаще друга враг полезен,
> Подлунный мир устроен так.
> О как же дорог, как любезен
> Самой природой данный враг!

87. TO IVAN KIREYEVSKY.

"Up to now, our journals have been dry and worthless..." — Pushkin's letter to Kireyevsky, written February 4, 1832 (misdated by Pushkin as January 4), is found in *Pushkin's Correspondence*, 2: 409.

88. TO IVAN KIREYEVSKY.

You have understood me perfectly... — Kireyevsky had offered one of the most insightful contemporary assessments of Baratynsky's poetry as a whole: "All the truth of life is presented to us in Baratynsky's pictures in a poetic and well-proportioned perspective; in it the very discordances are not disorder but a musical dissonance that resolves in harmony. ... He reveals the possibility of poetry within reality itself, for in his profound view of life he has understood necessity and order where others see discordance and prose. ... Thus, often without transporting the imagination beyond thrice-nine lands but leaving it in the midst of ordinary life, the poet is able to warm it with such heartfelt poetry, such ideal sadness, that without tearing ourselves away from the smooth, waxed parquet, we are transported into a musical and pensively spacious atmosphere."

("Survey of Russian Literature for 1831" ["Obozreniye russkoy literatury za 1831"], quoted in *Chronicle*, 285–286.)

I'm not the least bit angry that you berate the genre I chose — Kireyevsky had written in the same article: "However, despite all the worthy qualities of *The Concubine*, it is impossible not to admit that in this genre of narrative poems... there is something conventional and unnecessary, something small, which does not allow the artist to develop his poetic idea to the full. In its very scope, the narrative poem contradicts the possibility of the free outpouring of the soul, and for the external structure, for the harmony of the transitions, for the proportionality of the parts, the poet must often sacrifice other, more essential qualities. Thus, the very love of beautiful structure and proportionality can harm the poetry when the poet works in a too constricted circle." (*Chronicle*, 286.)

89. TO IVAN KIREYEVSKY.

You analyze my attempt at drama... — We do not have Kireyevsky's analysis of Baratynsky's play, but interestingly, in his "Survey of Russian Literature for 1831" (see the notes to the previous letter), he wrote: "Baratynsky, more than any of our poets, could create for us a poetic comedy, consisting not of cold characters, not of sad witticisms and puns, but of a faithful and at the same time poetic presentation of real life as it is reflected in the clear mirror of a poetic soul, as it presents itself to a subtle and penetrating power of observation, before the judgment of a taste that is discriminating, tender, and happily developed." (*Chronicle*, 286.)

***the 8th chapter of* Onegin** — Published as a separate book in January 1832 with the cover note: "The final chapter of *Eugene Onegin*."

we will be living on our own — That is, not in his father-in-law's house.

Gorskina — Sofya Nikolayevna Gorstkina (as properly spelled) was about to be married to Prince Pyotr Aleksandrovich Shcherbatov, the brother of Baratynsky's friend Yekaterina Sverbeyeva (see note to Letter 44).

***a document from the minister of education... to ensure that students read neither the* Telegraph *nor the* Telescope** — On February 9, 1832, the head of the secret police, Count Alexander von Benckendorff had written to Prince Carl von Lieven, the minister of education, warning him that dangerous ideas were being published in Polevoy's and Nadezhdin's journals—see *Vatsuro and Gillelson*, 94.

BIOGRAPHICAL NOTE

Nicholas I issued an order — The emperor's order is quoted in *Chronicle*, 289.

"I have finally received the official prohibition..." — Kireyevsky's letter to Zhukovsky, from February 23–24, 1832, is quoted in *Pushkin's Correspondence*, 2: 412, n. 1.

Zhukovsky's intervention — Zhukovsky, Kireyevsky's great-uncle, wrote directly to the emperor: "Kireyevsky is the closest person to me: I know him completely; I answer for his life and precepts; and the prohibition of his journal falls in a certain way on me as well, for I took a rather lively interest in its publication." Zhukovsky, who was the tutor to the tsarevich, also met personally with Nicholas, assuring him that he could vouch for Kireyevsky. The tsar replied, "And who will vouch for you!" Then, according to contemporary reports, Zhukovsky said "that if he, too, was so easily not trusted, he must remove himself, [and] for two weeks he suspended his work with the heir to the throne." (Quoted in *Vatsuro and Gillelson*, 95–96.) In the view of Yury Mann, "Zhukovsky's intercession was the only thing that saved [Kireyevsky] from arrest and exile" ("Esteticheskaya evolyutsiya I. Kireyevskogo," in Ivan Kireyevsky, *Kritika i estetika* [Moscow: Isskustvo, 1979], 12).

91. TO IVAN KIREYEVSKY.

Evenings at Dikanka — Nikolay Gogol's first collection of short stories (see note to Letter 78).

Perovsky — Aleksey Perovsky, who wrote fantastic tales under the pseudonym Antony Pogorelsky (see note to Letter 43).

Yanovsky's youth — The author's full surname was Gogol-Yanovsky; he was twenty-one at the time.

Skaryatin's wedding — The artist Fyodor Yakovlevich Skaryatin, a member of Kireyevsky's circle, married Yekaterina Petrovna Ozerova on May 22, 1832. We can only speculate about why Baratynsky was interested in their wedding, but it may be worth noting that the wife and husband both died of consumption not long afterward, in 1833 and 1835, respectively, neither of them having reached the age of thirty.

92. TO IVAN KIREYEVSKY.

I am very grateful to Yanovsky for his gift... — Gogol, it seems, had sent Baratynsky the second volume of *Evenings on a Farm near Dikanka*, published in March 1832. It contained four stories, including "A Terrible Vengeance" ["Strashnaya mest'"]. Baratynsky had already received the first volume from Kireyevsky (see Letters 78 and 91).

Khomyakov's tragedy — *Dmitry the Impostor* [*Dmitriy Samozvanets*] by the poet and philosopher Aleksey Stepanovich Khomyakov (1804–1860). Khomyakov's play, published in 1833, deals with the same historical period as Pushkin's *Boris Godunov*.

My brother in Petersburg — Irakly Baratynsky, who in July 1831 had been made an aide-de-camp to the emperor.

convey my thanks to dear Karolina for translating my Transmigration of Souls — The German-Russian poet Karolina Karlova Jänisch (1807–1893), who married the writer Nikolay Pavlov in 1837, was a good friend and great admirer of Baratynsky. She translated a number of his works into German, including his "fairy tale" *The Transmigration of Souls* [*Pereseleniye dush*], which had been published in *Northern Flowers for 1829.* Her translations of Baratynsky and other Russian poets (notably, Pushkin and Yazykov) were published in Dresden and Leipzig in 1833 under the title *Das Nordlicht: Proben der neuern russischen Literatur* [*The Northern Light: Samples of Recent Russian Literature*].

Sonichka is angry... — In the early 1830s, Baratynsky's sister-in-law Sofya Engelhardt was apparently in love with Kireyevsky, a match that seems to have been encouraged by both families (though not, perhaps, by Kireyevsky himself). On *Gorskina*, see the note to Letter 89.

the receipt for you from the Trustees' Council — It is not clear what financial matter Baratynsky refers to here. The Trustees' Council (*Opekunskiy sovet*) was the body that, among other things, handled equity loans.

93. TO IVAN KIREYEVSKY.

one of the ladies here... has written me an epistle — He is referring to the writer Aleksandra Andreyevna Fuchs, née Apekhtina (1805–1853), who hosted a literary salon in Kazan. In "To A. A. F." ["A. A. F—oy"], probably written soon after this letter, Baratynsky did in fact reply to her epistle: "With brilliant verses / you greeted me flatteringly. / I know their value... / Will I forget you? Will I forget your sounds? / They have found a response in a grateful soul":

> Блестящими стихами
> Вы обольстительно приветили меня.
> Я знаю цену им...
> ....
> Забуду ли я вас? забуду ль ваши звуки?
> В душе признательной отозвались они.

When Pushkin met Aleksandra Fuchs in Kazan the following year, she read him Baratynsky's poem. In a letter to his wife he described her as "a *blue stockings*" (he uses the English phrase): "a forty-year-old unbearable woman with waxed teeth and filthy nails." He then adds: "Baratynsky has written verses to her and with astonishing shamelessness praised to the skies her beauty and genius" (Letter to Natalya Pushkina, September 12, 1833, quoted in *Chronicle*, 315). Fuchs's epistle to Baratynsky has not survived.

94. TO IVAN KIREYEVSKY.

Khomyakov's tragedy — See note to Letter 92.

Byron's Sardanapalus — Byron's play *Sardanapalus* (1821) tells of the downfall of the last king of Assyria.

better suited to Yermak than Dmitry — Khomyakov had earlier written the play *Yermak* (published in excerpts beginning in 1828, with the full play appearing in 1832), about the Cossack conqueror of Siberia (see note to Letter 34).

one on Goethe's death — See note to "On the Death of Goethe."

Khvostov-like sentiment — A reference to the neoclassical poet Dmitry Ivanovich Khvostov (1757–1835), much ridiculed for his self-importance.

our relatives — Nastasya's father and sister, Lev and Sofya Engelhardt, with whom the Baratynskys had gone to Kazan.

95. TO IVAN KIREYEVSKY.

Wieland, I think, once said... — In his *Letters of a Russian Traveler* [*Pis'ma russkogo puteshestvennika*] (1791–1792), Nikolay Karamzin records a conversation he had with the German poet C. M. Wieland (1733–1813), who told him: "If fate determined me to live on a desert island, then I would write all the same and with the same effort develop my works, with the thought that the muses would be listening to my songs" (letter dated July 21, 1789, in Nikolay Karamzin, *Izbrannyye sochineniya v dvekh tomakh* [Moscow and Leningrad: Khudozhestvennaya literatura, 1964], 1: 178).

Tsar Saltan — Pushkin's *Tale about Tsar Saltan, His Son, the Renowned and Mighty Hero Prince Gvidon Saltanovich, and the Fair Swan-Princess* [*Skazka o Tsare Saltane, o syne ego slavnom i moguchem bogatyre knyaze Gvidone Saltanoviche i o prekrasnoy tsarevne lebedi*] first appeared in the third volume of Pushkin's *Poems*, published in March 1832.

Yeruslan Lazarevich and the Firebird — Figures from Russian folk tales.

96. TO SOFYA ENGELHARDT.

My mother's letter — Presumably, forwarded to Sofya by Nastasya Baratynskaya. It has not survived.

Radcliffian, Melmothian — A reference to the gothic novels of Anne Radcliffe (1764–1823) and Charles Maturin (1782–1824), the author of *Melmoth the Wanderer* (1820).

Kiss little Sonichka for me — It is not clear who this is. It may be a slip of the pen (or transcriber's error), and Baratynsky meant to write *Sashinka* or *Sanichka*, referring to his oldest child, Aleksandra (then five years old), who possibly returned to Moscow with her grandfather and aunt. The Baratynskys' daughter Sofya (who would have been called *Sonichka*) was not born until late 1833 or early 1834.

97. TO IVAN KIREYEVSKY.

Hugo and Barbier — Victor Hugo (1802–1885) and Henri Auguste Barbier (1805–1882) had both recently published landmark works inspired by the July Revolution in France: Hugo's play *Hernani* (1830) and novel *Notre-Dame de Paris* (*The Hunchback of Notre-Dame*) (1831), and Barbier's collection of poems, *Iambes et poèmes* (1831).

V. MOSCOW SOCIETY AND THE MINUTIAE OF LIFE

98. TO IVAN KIREYEVSKY.

Here's Lapidaire *for you* — Probably the book *Daniel le Lapidaire, ou Les Contes de l'atelier* (Brussels, 1832), by Raymond Brucker and Michel Masson, who wrote under the pseudonym "Michel Raymond."

give my regards to Odoyevsky — Prince Vladimir Fyodorovich Odoyevsky (1803–1869) was a former Lover of Wisdom (and "archival youth") with whom Küchelbecker had published the almanac *Mnemosyne* in the 1820s (see notes to Letters 18, 34, and 50). He is best known today for his whimsical short stories written in the 1830s and 1840s.

99. TO PYOTR VYAZEMSKY.

D. Davydov... the pretty Zolotaryova girl — At the time of Baratynsky's letter, the poet Denis Davydov was passionately involved with the much younger Yevgeniya Dmitriyevna Zolotaryova, the daughter of a Penza landowner.

the "little bare head" whose praises you sang — Pelageya Vsevolozhskaya, whose praises Vyazemsky sang in the poem "The Little Bare Head" ["Prostovolosaya golovka"] (1829).

Aurora Stjernvall — See note to Letter 30.

100. TO PYOTR VYAZEMSKY.

M. Orlov — Mikhail Fyodorovich Orlov (1788–1842), a former major general who had been arrested for his involvement in the Decembrist uprising and exiled to his estate in Kaluga Province. He was allowed to return to Moscow in 1831. In the 1810s, he had been a member of the progressive Arzamas literary group, with Zhukovsky, Vyazemsky, and Pushkin, among others.

D. Davydov sent me the opening of your epistle to him... — Vyazemsky's poem "To an Old Hussar" ["K staromu gusaru"] (1832).

All the boys will be on hand... — Baratynsky is quoting from Vyazemsky's poem to Davydov.

I sold Smirdin the complete collection of my poems. — In December 1832, Baratynsky had, with Pushkin's assistance, come to an agreement with the St. Petersburg bookseller and publisher Aleksandr Fyodorovich Smirdin (1795–1857) to publish a three-volume edition of his collected works, and by March 1833, the St. Petersburg censor had already approved an edition in two volumes (lyric verse and narrative poems, respectively). For some reason, however, there were complications with Smirdin, and in April or May the publication rights were transferred to the Moscow bookseller A. S. Shiryayev (*Chronicle*, 303, 305–306, 309.)

101. TO PYOTR VYAZEMSKY.

publishing an almanac by Easter — Nothing came of the plan.

Chadayev — The philosopher Pyotr Yakovlevich Chaadayev (1794–1858) always wrote in French; hence, he would be appearing "in translation." In his *Lettres philosophiques*, written between 1828 and 1830, Chaadayev argued that the social advances in the West were the result of the intellectual and spiritual dynamism of the Roman Catholic Church, whereas Russia's backwardness was due to the static nature of Eastern Orthodoxy. In October 1836, Chaadayev's first "Philosophical Letter" was published, in Russian, in Nikolay Nadezhdin's *Telescope*. Chaadayev's friends were generally outraged by his pro-Catholic views, and several, including Baratynsky, planned to write a response. But two weeks later, at the orders of Nicholas I, Chaadayev was officially declared insane. He was placed under house arrest for a year, his papers were confiscated, *The Telescope* was banned, and Nadezhdin was arrested and sent to the far north of Russia.

I am very grateful to him... — See note to Letter 100.

102. TO SOFYA ENGELHARDT.

The measure is full — Baratynsky quotes the first half of a well-known line from Voltaire: "The measure is full and your hour has come" [*La mésure est comblée et vôtre heure est venue*] (from the play *L'Orphelin de la Chine* [*The Orphan of China*], 1755), essentially meaning, "Enough is enough."

103. TO IVAN KIREYEVSKY.

estate management issues — Among other things, in the summer of 1833, the Mara estate was legally divided between Aleksandra Baratynskaya and her seven children. Around the same time, Baratynsky had to deal with business concerning the Engelhardt properties, which involved a short trip to Kazan, where, by chance, he met Pushkin and introduced him to the Fuchses (*Chronicle*, 314; *Binyon*, 414–415; see also note to Letter 93).

You were recently seen at Berger's — That is, the studio of the portrait painter Philippe Berger.

105. TO IVAN KIREYEVSKY.

the program for his journal — Aleksandr Smirdin was planning to launch the monthly *Library for Reading*, which promised to present a selection of works by well-known writers on a variety of subjects (it was "a journal of literature, science, art, industry, news, and fashion," as it stated on its title page). Most importantly, Smirdin had agreed to pay his writers a fixed rate—up to 1,000 rubles a page for the best-known authors. Baratynsky published only one poem in the *Library for Reading*: the elegy "Left to Ruin," which he wrote during his present visit to Mara.

Ladvocat's **Cent et un** — The twelve-volume *Paris, ou Le Livre des cent-et-un*, an anthology of miscellaneous writing by a variety of authors, which the Parisian bookseller Camille Ladvocat had begun publishing in 1831.

Balzac's theory of walking — The essay "Théorie de la démarche" ["Theory of the Gait"], by Honoré de Balzac (1799–1850), was published in the French journal *L'Europe littéraire* in 1833.

sentilism — It is not clear exactly what Baratynsky means here; he possibly coined this word (in Russian, *sentilizm*) from the French verb *sentir*, "to smell, to taste, to feel."

106. TO IVAN KIREYEVSKY.

what Famusov says of dining... — The quote is from Act 2, scene 1, of Griboyedov's *Woe from Wit* (see note to Letter 22). Many witticisms from the play quickly entered the language as proverbs.

a haven from worldly visits... — Possibly an impromptu:

> Приют от светских посещений
> Надежной дверью запертой.
> Но с благодарною душой
> Открытый дружеству и девам вдохновений.

107. TO IVAN KIREYEVSKY.

(balance) — Written in Roman letters (i.e. in French).

Eda *and* **Feasts** — Both poems appeared in the second volume of *Poems 1835*.

a preface in verse... a musical epigraph — Neither made it into the edition. The preface is, presumably, "A faithful record of impressions"; nothing is known of the musical epigraph.

the extra poem — Almost certainly, "Left to Ruin," the only poem printed in *Poems 1835* that was not included on the list approved by the St. Petersburg censor in March 1833 (see note to Letter 100).

108. TO SOFYA ENGELHARDT.

the epistle to Vyazemsky and an epigram — See notes to "To Prince Pyotr Andreyevich Vyazemsky"; we do not know what epigram Baratynsky is referring to.

the 4th chapter of **The Concubine** — *The Concubine* was published in the second volume of *Poems 1835* under a new name: *The Gypsy* [*Tsyganka*], which already appears on the censor's list of March 1833 (*Chronicle*, 307). It is interesting that Baratynsky still refers to the poem by its old "scandalous" name (see the biographical note between Letters 57 and 58, and also Letter 78). The excised passage Baratynsky is worried about does, in fact, appear in *Poems 1835*.

109. TO HIS MOTHER.

Sashinka... Lyovushka — His two eldest children, Aleksandra (then eight years old) and Lev (then six).

the village we own in the Pereslavl District — Glebovskoye, about eighty miles northeast of Moscow.

150 arpents — About 126 acres.

110. TO HIS WIFE.

Strinyovsky — Nikolay Fyodorovich Strinyovsky, a Moscow friend originally from Tambov Province (see B. N. Chicherin, "Vospominaniya," in *Rossiyskiy arkhiv: Istoriya Otechestva v svidetel'stvakh i dokumentakh XVIII–XX vv.*, vol. 9, ed. A. D. Zaytsev et al. [Moscow: Studiya TRITE: Ros. Arkhiv, 1999], 116).

111. TO PYOTR VYAZEMSKY.

I was visiting his father — Sergey Lvovich Pushkin (1770–1848).

I lost my father-in-law — Lev Nikolayevich Engelhardt, born in 1776, died on November 4, 1836.

something for your literary anthology — Vyazemsky was putting together an almanac and had asked Baratynsky to contribute to it.

113. TO HIS MOTHER.

Heyne, Menzel — Baratynsky is probably thinking of the poet Heinrich Heine (1797–1856), who lived in Munich in the late 1820s when he first achieved fame (he moved to Paris in 1831), and the poet and historian Wolfgang Menzel (1798–1873), who, however, lived in Stuttgart.

Livonia and Courland — That is, southern Estonia and Latvia.

115. TO NIKOLAY PUTYATA.

Sonichka — Sofya Putyata, née Engelhardt.

Ivan has found a manager to fill his position. — Ivan, formerly the manager of the Skuratovo estate, was now managing the Muranovo estate.

I embrace you, Sonichka, and Nastya — Nastya, named after Baratynsky's wife, was the Putyatas' daughter.

116. TO PYOTR PLETNYOV.

The poem published in **Notes of the Fatherland** — "Clamorous day is welcome to the crowd," which appeared in mid-February. The St. Petersburg journal *Notes of the Fatherland*, which had folded in 1830, had recently been revived by the new publisher and editor Andrey Aleksandrovich Krayevsky (1810–1889), who had, in fact, been Pletnyov's assistant on *The Contemporary* in 1837.

I am sending you a few small poems — "Blessed the man who holy things discloses," "Gusting winds and violent weather," and "I am not yet ancient as a Patriarch" were published together in *The Contemporary* in early July under the title "Anthological Poems."

117. TO HIS MOTHER.

Natalie — Baratynsky's unmarried sister Natalya, then thirty years old, who lived with the Baratynskys in Moscow from about 1838 to 1841.

an excellent work by Sestenzevitch on the antiquities of Taurida — The book *Histoire de la Tauride* (1800), by the Roman Catholic Archbishop Stanisław Bohusz Siestrzeńcewicz of Mogilev (1731–1826). His name appears on the book as Stanislas Sestrencewitz de Bohusz. *Taurida* is the classical name for the Crimea.

118. TO HIS MOTHER.

the pains you took in negotiating on my behalf... — We do no know what matter Baratynsky refers to here, or who *the excellent Lapat* may be.

You are a jeweler, Monsieur Josse — A line from Molière's *L'Amour médecin* [*Doctor Love*] (1665). In the play, Josse suggests to Sganarelle that his sick daughter might revive if he gave her jewelry, to which Sganarelle replies: "You are a jeweler, Monsieur Josse, and your advice feels like that of a man who is anxious to dispose of his merchandise" (Act 1, scene 1).

The Inspector General... Dead Souls — Gogol's comedy *The Inspector General* [*Revizor*] was first published in 1836 and staged in both St. Petersburg and Moscow that same year. Gogol had begun writing the novel *Dead Souls* [*Myortvyye dushi*] in 1835, composing much of it in Rome from 1837 to 1839. He returned to Russia in the fall of 1839. The first volume of the novel was published in 1842.

VI. THE PULL OF ST. PETERSBURG

119. TO HIS MOTHER.

my aunt Sofya Ivanovna's convoy — Sofya Ivanovna Baratynskaya, née Baryshnikova (1797–1862), was the widow of Ilya Andreyevich Baratynsky (see note to Letter 2). She lived on an estate near Mara.

the dress for the little one — Most likely for the five-month-old baby, Zinaida (see Letter 117).

Natalie — Baratynsky's sister.

my brother, my sisters-in-law — Irakly, his wife, and Sofya Putyata.

a third edition of my rhymes, adding the sin of one more volume — Third, that is, after *Poems 1827* and the two-volume *Poems 1835*. The new edition would presumably consist only of works written since 1835.

120. TO HIS WIFE.

Annette ran to embrace me — Baratynsky's sister-in-law, the Armenian princess Anna Davydovna Abamelek-Baratynskaya (1814–1889), would, in fact, eventually enjoy her own degree of literary fame, not only as a woman whose beauty had been praised by Pushkin, Kozlov, Raich, and others, but also as a translator of Russian poetry into French and English (notably, works by Pushkin, Lermontov, and Tyutchev); she also translated poems by Goethe, Heine, and Byron into Russian.

Lazareva-Biron and her husband, and Prince Abamelek... his sister Catherine — Relatives of Irakly's wife.

Natalie's letter — We know nothing about the relations between Baratynsky's sister Natalya and Prince Abamelek, or the tensions between Irakly, Annette, and Natalya.

Nastinka is utterly sweet — The Putyatas' daughter, Nastasya.

Natasha's part of Atamysh — Presumably, the share belonging to Nastasya Baratynskaya's deceased sister Natalya Engelhardt (see note to "There is a lovely country, a corner on the earth") in the Engelhardts' Atamysh estate near Kazan.

121. TO HIS WIFE.

Liza Chirkova — A relation of Denis Davydov; it is not clear which *Korsakov* Baratynsky means.

we agreed to meet at the Odoyevskys' — Vladimir Odoyevsky (see note to Letter 98) had moved to St. Petersburg in 1826. He hosted a salon at his home in the 1830s and 1840s that attracted both writers and composers such as Mikhail Glinka and Aleksandr Dargomyzhsky.

Myatlev — Ivan Petrovich Myatlev (1796–1844). Baratynsky quotes the first two lines of his "Fantastic Statement" ["Fantasticheskaya vyskazka"], written in trochaic dimeters.

Zhukovsky began asking me about **his relations** — That is, the Kireyevskys and Yelagins.

Lermontov — The poet Mikhail Yuryevich Lermontov (1814–1841) had won fame with his poem on Pushkin's death, "The Death of the Poet" ["Smert' poeta"] (1837); the same poem had led to his exile in the Caucasus.

"Travels of Mme Kurdyukova in Foreign Lands" — The full title of the poem, published in 1840, might be translated "The Sensations and Remarks of Madame Kurdyukova Abroad dan l'aytranzhay" ["Sensatsii i zamechaniya gospozhi Kurdyukovoy za granitseyu, dan l'etranzhe"], that is, with the last two words in transliterated French.

my brother Lev — Lev Abramovich Baratynsky (1805–1858).

122. TO HIS WIFE.

I was at the Karamzins' — That is, the literary salon hosted by Nikolay Karamzin's widow Yekaterina Andreyevna Karamzina, née Kolyvanova (1780–1851), Vyazemsky's half-sister, and her step-daughter, Sofya Nikolayevna Karamzina—see note to the poem "With the Book *Dusk*."

123. TO HIS WIFE.

As Putyata later recalled... — In an excerpt from his notebook: "Iz zapisnoy knizhkoy N. V. Putyata," *Russkiy arkhiv* 37, no. 6 (1899): 352. Putyata, however, misremembered the date of Baratynsky's trip to St. Petersburg, giving it as "in the winter, at the end of 1837 or in 1838."

The princess — Princess Olga Stepanovna Odoyevskaya, née Lanskaya (1797–1872).

Bludov — Count Dmitry Nikolayevich Bludov (1785–1864), a founding member of the Arzamas literary group in the 1810s, had since become a central government figure. He had headed both the Ministry of Internal Affairs and the Ministry of Justice and, at the time of this letter, had just been appointed the director of the Second Department of the Chancellery, which was responsible for codifying the laws of the empire.

Sologub's tale "The Tarantass" — Count Vladimir Aleksandrovich Sollogub (1813–1882) was the author of light novels, literary sketches, and vaudeville comedies. His satirical tale *The Tarantass: Traveling Impressions* [*Tarantas: Putevyye vpechatleniya*] (1845) enjoyed considerable popular success and was published in English translation in London only five years after its Russian publication. (A *tarantass* is a covered four-wheeled carriage normally drawn by a team of three horses.)

Feofan — Archbishop Feofan Prokopovich (1681–1736), who delivered the eulogy at the funeral of Peter the Great.

They were presenting La Lectrice *with Mme Allan* — Jean-François Bayard's vaudeville comedy *La Lectrice, ou Une folie de jeune homme* [*The Reader, or, A Young Man's Folly*] (1835); Mme Allan was the famous French actress Louise Rosalie Allan-Despréaux (1810–1856).

I spent the late evening with our relatives. — That is, with the Putyatas.

124. TO HIS WIFE.

a note for Mikhey concerning Chicherin... Tell Sofya Mikhaylovna the matter is settled. — Nikolay Chicherin, the father of the political philosopher Boris Chicherin, lived on an estate near Mara. Mikhey, whom Baratynsky describes in Letter 137 as "a reliable man... my former tutor" (i.e. tutor to his children), was clearly a trusted member of the household. The details of the matter in question, and its relation to Baratynsky's sister-in-law Sofya Mikhaylovna Baratynskaya (see note to Letter 43), are not known.

Khristofor [Lazarev]'s wife — Khristofor Lazarev (1789–1871) and his wife Yekaterina Emmanuilovna, née Manuk-Bey (1806–1880), were both of Armenian descent. Their daughter Yelizaveta was married to Annette Baratynskaya's brother Semyon.

I dined at Sobolevsky's… — His good friend, Sergey Sobolevsky (see note to Letter 50).

125. TO HIS WIFE.

Pushkin's widow — Natalya Nikolayevna Pushkina, née Goncharova (1812–1863).

Vielgorsky, Sologub, and finally Vyazmitinova — Mikhail Yuryevich Vielgorsky (or Wielhorski) (1788–1856), a composer of Polish descent, and Aleksandra Nikolayevna Vyazmitinova, née Engelhardt (1767–1848), Nastasya's paternal aunt. On Sollogub, see note to Letter 123.

Neither he nor she has breathed a syllable about Natasha — That is, about Baratynsky's sister Natalya (see Letter 120).

went to the Assembly — The St. Petersburg Assembly of the Nobility, a social club for the highest nobility.

I saw the heir, the Grand Duke Michael, and the Duke of Leuchtenberg — Respectively, Tsarevich Alexander Nikolayevich (the future Alexander II); the tsar's brother, Michael Pavlovich; and Maximilian de Beauharnais, 3rd Duke of Leuchtenberg (the step-grandson of Napoleon), who the year before had married the tsar's daughter, the Grand Duchess Maria Nikolayevna.

Pavlov — The writer Nikolay Filippovich Pavlov (1803–1864), best known for his novellas, collected as *Three Tales* [*Tri povesti*] (1835) and *New Tales* [*Novyye povesti*] (1838), was closely associated with Kireyevsky and his circle ("the Moscow brethren"). An inveterate gambler, he had married Baratynsky's friend, the poet Karolina Jänisch (see note to Letter 92), in 1837, primarily, it seems, because she had recently come into a large inheritance.

126. TO HIS WIFE.

then dined at Dumé's — A restaurant (the name is possibly spelled "Dumais").

his nephew Karamzin — One of the sons of Vyazemsky's half-sister, Yekaterina Karamzina.

Taglioni's benefit — Baratynsky is referring to the famous ballerina Maria Taglioni (1804–1884). In such a benefit, she would have both starred in the performance and received all its proceeds.

my Uncle Pyotr Andreyevich — Baratynsky's sole surviving paternal uncle, who had looked after him on holidays when he was at the Corps des Pages (see notes to Letters 1 and 4), had become a lieutenant general and senator in 1821; a year after his nephew's visit, he was made an actual privy councilor, Russia's second-highest service rank.

127. TO HIS WIFE.

I saw Taglioni — See note to previous letter.

Timiryazova — Sofya Fyodorovna Timiryazova was a relation of the Krivtsovs, the Baratynskys' neighbors in Tambov Province (see note to Letter 52).

Countess Laval — Countess Aleksandra Grigoryevna Laval, née Kozitskaya (1772–1850).

Annette Blokhina — An acquaintance from Moscow society; in Letter 145 (where her name is spelled *Blakhina*), she is said to be looking for husbands for her daughters.

Annette and Sonichka — His sisters-in-law, Anna Baratynskaya and Sofya Putyata.

128. TO HIS WIFE.

Bryulov's Last Day of Pompeii — The most celebrated Russian painting of its day, the large multifigural work *The Last Day of Pompeii* was painted in Rome in the early 1830s by Karl Pavlovich Bryullov (1799–1852). Its owner, Anatoly Demidov, made a present of the painting to Nicholas I, who had it displayed at the Academy of Arts in St. Petersburg, where Baratynsky viewed it.

Krylov — Ivan Krylov (1769–1844), the author of much-beloved fables in verse.

Nikolay or Ksenofont Polevoy — Like his older brother Nikolay, Ksenofont Polevoy (1801–1867) was a journalist, literary critic, and publisher.

Le Gamin de Paris — Yet another vaudeville comedy by Bayard, first produced in 1836 (see note to Letter 123).

like an evening at the Sverbeyevs — On Yekaterina and Dmitry Sverbeyev and their salon, see notes to Letters 44 and 57.

a certain eccentric named Shishmaryov — Very likely, Afanasy Fyodorovih Shishmaryov (1790–1876), a wealthy horsebreeder known for his love of the theater.

chekmen coat — A long-sleeve ankle-length coat worn by the Turkic peoples of Central Asia and the Caucasus.

I embrace Natasha. — His sister Natalya.

129. TO HIS WIFE.

Professor Davydov... Villemain — Prof. Ivan Ivanovich Davydov (1794–1863), the chairman of the department of Russian literature at Moscow University, had published his *Lectures on Literature* [*Chteniya o slovesnosti*] a few years earlier; on Villemain's "course on literature," see note to Letter 63.

130. TO HIS MOTHER.

Perovsky — Adjutant General Vasily Perovsky invaded the Central Asian Khanate of Khiva in November 1839, but the sub-zero temperatures, low supplies, and illness of both men and camels forced him to retreat in early February; it was only in May that the troops arrived back at the Russian garrison of Orenburg, having lost over a thousand soldiers.

my dear aunt — His mother's sister, Yekaterina Cherepanova (see note to Letter 2).

my sister — Sofya Baratynskaya, who lived at Mara (see note to Letter 7); she had been his "angel" in St. Petersburg two decades earlier (Letter 9).

I was very happy... — Nastasya's postscript (in French) is printed in *Materials*, 56–57.

131. TO HIS WIFE.

Pavlov — Nikolay Pavlov (see note to Letter 125).

Orlov — Mikhail Orlov (see note to Letter 100).

132. TO HIS WIFE.

Koloshina — Countess Aleksandra Koloshina, a Moscow acquaintance.

All the commèring *I did with Vyazemsky* — See especially Letter 125.

Mme Genlis — The author Countess Stéphanie-Félicité de Genlis (1746–1830) was best known for her writings on education and children's books (at least one of which Baratynsky had read as a child—see note to Letter 2).

people told me I was very wicked — Baratynsky's unintended barb may have seemed especially harsh in light of what Chaadayev had suffered (see note to Letter 101).

134. TO HIS MOTHER.

one of our Kazan villages — The Baratynskys and Putyatas jointly owned several villages in Kazan Province, inherited from the Engelhardts.

orache — A spinach-like edible plant, also known as saltbush. Baratynsky, perhaps not knowing or not remembering the French name for the plant, uses (and strangely, capitalizes) the Russian name: *Lebeda*.

the spring crops — Again, Baratynsky uses the Russian word: *yarovyye*.

135. TO SERGEY SOBOLEVSKY.

Putyata's letter to Poltoratsky is quoted in *Chronicle*, 370.

136. TO SERGEY SOBOLEVSKY.

Dmitry Putyata — Nikolay Putyata's younger brother Dmitry Vasilyevich Putyata (1806–1869) was a highly distinguished army officer then serving as aide-de-camp to Grand Duke Michael Pavlovich; he would eventually rise to the rank of general.

137. TO NIKOLAY PUTYATA.

to get the children — The two middle children, Masha and Mitya, were in boarding schools in St. Petersburg (see the headnotes to Letters 131 and 133).

VII. MURANOVO, *DUSK*, AND PLANTING TREES

138. TO NIKOLAY PUTYATA.

our Becker — Heinrich Hermann Becker, at the time still the children's tutor. Many years later, Baratynsky's son Lev recalled: "No expense was spared on the children's education. … For German and instruction in elementary subjects [we had] the Germanized Latvian Becker, who was distinguished by his great innate mathematical abilities; for example, though he never studied algebra, he could solve algebraic problems through arithmetic." (Recounted to Ye. A. Bobrov, "Pamyati L. Ye. Boratynskomu," *Dela i lyudi* [Yuryev, 1907], quoted in *Chronicle*, 348–349.)

140. TO HIS MOTHER.

Aleksandr Antonovich — Aleksandr Antonovich Rachinsky (1799–1866) was the husband of Baratynsky's youngest sister, Varvara Abramovna (1810–1891);

his family came from Smolensk Province and were related to the Baratynskys. In the 1810s, as a guardsman in St. Petersburg, Aleksandr Rachinsky participated in the pre-Decembrist secret society known as the Sacred Artel; Delvig and Küchelbecker were also members, and it was probably Rachinsky who introduced Baratynsky to them in 1818 or early 1819 (*Chronicle*, 420).

Becker — See note to Letter 138.

141. TO NIKOLAY PUTYATA.

Twenty* desyatinas *of forest — About fifty-four acres.

142. TO NIKOLAY AND SOFYA PUTYATA.

Decree on Obligated Peasants — The information about the decree comes from David Moon, *The Abolition of Serfdom in Russia, 1762–1907* (Harlow, Essex, U.K.: Pearson Education, 2001), 42, 143–145.

"[Baratynsky's words] testify to the sympathy..." — Putyata's commentary was published in *Putyata*, col. 282.

Trinity — The Trinity Lavra of St. Sergius, in Sergiyev Posad, one of Russia's most important monasteries, was located about fifteen miles from Artyomovo.

143. TO HIS SISTER, NATALYA BARATYNSKAYA.

one of Sophie's letters — That is, from his sister Sofya in Mara.

Lise — Their cousin, Yelizaveta Ivanovna Nedobrovo, née Panchulidzeva, had decided to separate from her husband (*Chronicle*, 384).

the one who has not feared this attempt... — Nicholas I.

144. TO PYOTR PLETNYOV.

Vasilyevsky Island — A district in St. Petersburg.

145. TO NIKOLAY AND SOFYA PUTYATA.

Trustees' Council — See note to Letter 92.

Your letters… did us much good. — Sofya Putyata had spent a few days with the Baratynskys in Artyomovo in May, when she brought her daughters to them before she and her husband went abroad. She was apparently alarmed by the tensions she witnessed there, probably related to the Baratynskys' "suppositions" about an "organized coterie" (see below), and expressed her concerns in letters to her sister and brother-in-law. Nastasya assured her that everything was all right: "Do not torment yourself… over our moods; they must have given you the wrong impression… our characters are those of extreme people, too quick to accept the good side of a thing in a way that is so merry and so exaggerated that they can magnify the bad side; that is why we have made so many mistakes, always letting ourselves be carried away by our own imagination and throwing ourselves on the neck of people who should have been avoided, all for a few pleasant impressions that we embroidered at leisure; if you could hear us talk about the same things under different inspirations, you would think us quite mad in another sense as well." (From a letter, in French, dated May 23, 1842, quoted in *Kjetsaa*, 197–198.)

an organized coterie — The circle around Kireyevsky and the journal *The Muscovite*. See note to the poem "To a Coterie."

its new victims — Baratynsky was probably thinking of the literary critic Vissarion Belinsky, who had recently written the article "The Pedant: A Literary Type" ["Pedant: Literaturnyy tip"] (1842), directed against Stepan Shevyryov. Writing to her sister around the same time as this letter, Nastasya Baratynskaya explained her husband's allusions: "This society does in fact exist and on a basis that is to the highest degree vile. … The whole designated society is foaming at the mouth in fury at Belinsky… it has resolved that he must be destroyed and to harm him by all possible means." (Quoted in Russian in *CCP 1936*, 2: 279; the French original has not been published.)

Staraya Russa — At the time, a town with mineral springs and a fashionable health resort, about 180 miles south of St. Petersburg. (Annette Blakhina, or Blokhina, was compared unfavorably to Sofya Karamzina in Letter 127.)

our new home — The new house in Muranovo.

146. TO PYOTR VYAZEMSKY.

the dedication — See note to the poem "To Prince Pyotr Andreyevich Vyazemsky."

147. TO HIS MOTHER.

we have five foreigners living with us — The children's tutors.

148. TO HIS MOTHER.

25 arpents — About 67.5 acres.

Lyubichi — He is thinking of the English-style manor house of Nikolay Krivtsov (see note to Letter 52) on the Lyubichi estate, some fifteen miles west of Mara.

Vyazhlya — The Baratynsky family estate from which his father had carved out Mara—here he may simply be referring to Mara.

149. TO PYOTR PLETNYOV.

Grot — The Russian philologist Yakov Karlovich Grot (1812–1893) was a close friend of Pyotr Pletnyov. In 1841, a year before this letter, he had been appointed a professor of Russian literature and history at the Imperial Alexander University in Helsingfors (today, the University of Helsinki).

151. TO HIS MOTHER.

Natalie and Sophie — His sisters Natalya and Sofya, who both lived in Mara.

distractions, which… have been felt by the Kirsanov mail — That is, the delay in answering his mother's letter (the post office for Mara was in the town of Kirsanov).

Consuelo *and* **Zanoni** — Two novels published in 1842: *Consuelo*, by George Sand, in which religious devotion plays a central role, and *Zanoni*, by Edward Bulwer-Lytton (the French translation was published the same year as the English original), which deals with the occult philosophy of Rosicrucianism.

Annette came to see us — Irakly's wife, Anna Baratynskaya. In 1842, Irakly had been appointed the governor of Yaroslavl Province.

the Poltoratskys — The former Yaroslavl governor, Konstantin Markovich Poltoratsky, and his wife, Sofya Borisovna.

152. TO HIS MOTHER.

Mme Field — Adelaïde Field, née Percheron, had been married to the well-known Irish pianist and composer John Field (1782–1837), who lived most of his life in Russia. Baratynsky's comment about "conjugal love" is surely facetious: Adelaïde Field had left her husband in the early 1820s to pursue a solo career.

153. TO HIS MOTHER.

Tula Province... Vladimir Province — The Engelhardt estates Skuratovo and Glebovskoye were in the Tula and Vladimir provinces, respectively.

Varinka and Natalie — His sisters Varvara Rachinskaya (see note to Letter 140) and Natalya.

I heard Liszt perform — The famous Hungarian composer and pianist Franz Liszt (1811–1886) gave seven performances in Moscow between April 27 and May 16, 1843 (*Chronicle*, 397).

Thalberg — Sigismund Thalberg (1812–1871) was one of Liszt's chief rivals.

VIII. GERMANY, PARIS, AND NAPLES

155. TO HIS MOTHER.

Baron Meindorff — He means Baron Pyotr Kazimirovich Meyendorff (1796–1863), the Russian ambassador to Berlin.

Count Bludov — See note to Letter 123.

the famous gallery — The Royal Dresden Gallery, today the Old Masters Picture Gallery (Gemäldegalerie Alte Meister). The paintings Baratynsky mentions are Raphael's *Sistine Madonna* (1512) and Titian's *The Tribute Money* (ca. 1516).

Tarente Valley — He is possibly referring to the valley of the River Elbe in the area known as Saxon Switzerland, about thirty miles southeast of Dresden, a well-known sightseeing destination with striking sandstone formations.

157. TO NIKOLAY AND SOFYA PUTYATA.

My friends, my sisters, I'm in Paris! — Baratynsky quotes the opening line from Ivan Dmitriyev's poem "N. N.'s Travels to Paris and London" ["Puteshestviye N. N. v Parizh i London"] (1803).

Sobolevsky — See note to Letter 50.

Faubourg St-Germain — The Left Bank neighborhood in Paris that was home to the old aristocracy.

Lamartine — The poet and politician Alphonse de Lamartine (1790–1869), who in 1842 was still a royalist; by 1848 he was supporting the Second Republic.

Mme Aguesseau... Nodier... Thierry — Baratynsky is referring to the Marquise d'Aguesseau, the granddaughter of the eighteenth-century French Chancellor Henri-François d'Aguesseau; Charles Nodier (1780–1844), the author of gothic and fantastic tales, notably *Trilby* (1822); and the historian Augustin Thierry (1795–1856), or possibly, his less-famous brother Amédée (1797–1873), also a historian.

the Circourts — Count Adolphe de Circourt (1801–1879) and his Russian wife, Anastasie, née Khlyustina (1808–1863), who hosted a famous literary salon in Paris. The much-admired Countess de Circourt was friends with Pyotr Chaadayev and Aleksandr Turgenev, among other Russian writers, and had written articles about Russian literature in the French press. It was at the Circourts' request that Baratynsky translated twenty of his poems into French prose, although he refused to have them published (*CCP 1914*, 1: lxxxvi).

I see A. I. Turgenev almost every day — Aleksandr Turgenev (see note to Letter 17) had been traveling back and forth between Russia and Western Europe since the mid-1820s, living in Germany, Italy, London, and Paris.

Balabin — Viktor Petrovich Balabin (1811–1864), then a junior secretary at the Russian embassy in Paris.

158. TO HIS MOTHER.

everyone knocks on its doors, which are rarely carriage gates — That is, they are open only to a select few.

Mme Scarron — Françoise d'Aubigné, Marquise de Maintenon (1635–1719)—known from her first marriage as Madame Scarron—was the mistress and later secret wife of King Louis XIV of France, undoubtedly the *good company* Baratynsky mentions.

the Marquise d'A. — The Marquise d'Aguesseau (see note to Letter 157).

the Countess de F. — Countess Christine de Fontanes, the daughter of the poet Louis de Fontanes (1757–1821).

Marshal Soult — Marshal General Jean-de-Dieu Soult (1769–1851) had won fame as a general in Napoleon's Grande Armée, notably in the battles of Austerlitz and Jena.

Mme Svetchine — Sophie Swetchine (1782–1857), as her name was usually rendered in French, was born Sofya Petrovna Soymonova in Moscow. In 1799, she married General Nikolay Sergeyevich Svechin. In 1815, she converted to Roman Catholicism, strongly influenced by the philosopher Joseph de Maistre, then living in St. Petersburg. She and her husband moved soon afterwards to Paris, where she began hosting her famous salon.

Alfred de Vigny — The romantic poet and playwright (1797–1863).

Mérimée — The novelist and playwright Prosper Mérimée (1803–1870) is today best known for his novella *Carmen* (1845), the basis of Bizet's opera. He was also the author of *La Guzla* (1827), which purported to be a collection of folk ballads from

Dalmatia, Bosnia, and Croatia that were in fact written by Mérimée himself. Pushkin translated eleven of these ballads into Russian verse and included them in his "Songs of the Western Slavs" ["Pesni zapadnykh slavyan"] (1835). Mérimée, who taught himself Russian, returned the favor and in the 1850s translated works by Pushkin and Gogol into French.

the two Thierrys, Michel Chevalier, Lamartine — Michel Chevalier (1806–1879) was a liberal political economist; on the others, see the notes to Letter 157.

Charles Nodier—whom I have seen in his last days — Nodier died on January 27, 1844, about a month after Baratynsky wrote this letter.

Et vous composerez dans ce chaos fatal... — Lines from Voltaire's "Poème sur le désastre de Lisbonne" ["Poem on the Lisbon Disaster"] (1755), which Baratynsky slightly misquotes (the original of the second line is: *Des malheurs de chaque être le bonheur général* ["the general happiness from each being's misfortunes"]).

Gostiny Dvor... *the "City" in Moscow* — The first is the name of a large covered shopping complex in St. Petersburg; the second refers to Moscow's main commercial district (more properly, "China-City" [*Kitay-Gorod*]).

159. TO NIKOLAY AND SOFYA PUTYATA.

Mme Fantone — A misspelling: Countess Christine de Fontanes (see note to Letter 158).

Princess Golitsyna... Zolotnitskaya — Princess Yelizaveta Antonovna Golitsyna (1800–1866), of Polish descent, was born Elżbieta Złotnicka in Kiev, which is where Denis Davydov fell in love with her in 1817. Although she initially accepted his proposal of marriage, she later rejected him in favor of the much wealthier Prince Pyotr Alekseyevich Golitsyn, whom she married in 1820; they moved to Paris in 1837. Davydov's poem "To a Faithless Girl" ["Nevernoy"] (1817) is one of a number of poems he addressed to her. *Zolotnitskaya* (as Baratynsky Russianizes her maiden name) should not be confused with Davydov's Penza love, "the pretty Zolotaryova girl" mentioned in Letter 99—a mistake A. M. Peskov makes in his *Chronicle* (404).

the Russian custom — According to this custom, whenever you meet a priest, you should spit over your left shoulder to ward off evil, since priests are associated with death.

Saint-Beuve — The literary critic Charles Augustin Saint-Beuve (1804–1869).

Mme Ancelot — The novelist, playwright, and painter Virginie Ancelot, née Chardon (1792–1875), was the hostess of a well-known literary salon.

G. Sand — The novelist George Sand, whose real name was Amantine-Lucile-Aurore Dudevant, née Dupin (1804–1876); Baratynsky had recommended her novel *Consuelo* to his mother earlier in the year (Letter 151).

I have also met... a number of our countrymen. — The émigrés Baratynsky met in Paris—and whom he would have been wary of naming in a letter sent to Russia—included Aleksandr Turgenev's brother, the Decembrist Nikolay Ivanovich Turgenev (1789–1871), the revolutionary Nikolay Platonovich Ogaryov (1813–1877), the poet Nikolay Mikhaylovich Satin (1814–1873), and the journalists Nikolay Ivanovich Sazonov (1815–1862) and Ivan Gavrilovich Golovin (1816–1890)—see *Chronicle*, 401–402. Baratynsky's son Lev later remembered his father hosting a dinner for the émigrés: "The conversations at dinner were devoted to one general topic—the abolition of serfdom. Among those present were Sazonov and Ivan Golovin, who pronounced a remarkably compelling and eloquent speech on the topic of the emancipation of the peasants." (Recounted in Bobrov, "Pamyati L. Ye. Boratynskomu" [see note to Letter 138], quoted in *Chronicle*, 401.)

The conservative party — The ruling Orléanist party, which had brought Louis-Philippe, the "citizen-king," to the throne after the July Revolution of 1830.

160. TO NIKOLAY AND SOFYA PUTYATA.

we are twelve days younger than other nations — The Julian calendar used in the Russian Empire was twelve days behind the Gregorian calendar used in most of the rest of Europe.

161. TO NIKOLAY AND SOFYA PUTYATA.

your shared great loss — Nikolay Putyata's father, Vasily Ivanovich Putyata, died on December 4, 1843, at the age of sixty-three. He had worked at the War Ministry in 1812, during Napoleon's march on Moscow, and set up hospitals for the wounded; later, as director of the Vilnius commissary, he provided uniforms to the reserve forces and returning Russian troops. He was later appointed the War Commissar General, responsible for all provisions to the army. (See the editorial note by Pyotr Bartenev in *Putyata*, cols. 290–291.)

In one of Vyazemsky's letters to Turgenev... — Vyazemsky wrote to Aleksandr Turgenev on December 25, 1843: "My warm regards to Baratynsky. May he enjoy the full measure of Paris and, especially, may Paris enjoy the full measure of him. I do not know a more intelligent and amiable man." (*Chronicle*, 405.)

Institut des Jésuites *by Father Ravignan* — *De l'existence et de l'institut des Jésuites* (1841) by Father Gustave-François-Xavier de la Croix de Ravignan.

Guizot — The historian François Guizot (whose book Baratynsky had desired and then unexpectedly received from Kireyevsky in Kazan—see notes to Letters 76 and 82) was currently the French foreign minister and one of the dominant figures in the Orléanist party.

162. TO NIKOLAY AND SOFYA PUTYATA.

Balabin — See note to Letter 157.

164. TO NIKOLAY AND SOFYA PUTYATA.

"Now we are going directly to Naples..." — Nastasya Baratynskaya's letter to her sister-in-law, written in late March (OS) / early April (NS), is quoted in Russian translation in *Chronicle*, 408 (the original French has not been published).

Nikolinka — Baratynsky's eight-year-old son Nikolay.

I wrote a few verses — The poem "The Pyroscaphe," which Baratynsky intends for *The Contemporary.*

We saw what was possible to see in Herculaneum — Like its more famous neighbor Pompeii, the Roman town of Herculaneum, about four miles from Naples, was buried in volcanic deposits after the eruption of Mount Vesuvius in 79 BCE. The first major excavations of the site began in 1738. The excavations were difficult and expensive, and carried out "with so few hands, so little system, and in so desultory a manner that it is more surprising that so much was brought to light than that so much was left for future explorers to overcome," as Octavian Blewitt explained in his 1853 *Handbook for Travellers* (314).

Puzzoli — The Italian town of Pozzuoli (as more properly spelled) is the site of the ancient Roman settlement Puteoli. A market building was excavated here in the mid-eighteenth century, with later excavations carried out in the first decades of the nineteenth century. When a statue of the Greco-Egyptian god Serapis was discovered, the site was mistakenly assumed to be a temple of Serapis. It was identified as a marketplace only in the early twentieth century.

Philemon and Baucis — According to a story in Ovid's *Metamorphoses* (Book 8), the elderly couple Philemon and Baucis were the only ones in their town to offer hospitality to the gods Jupiter and Mercury, who were disguised as mortals. Jupiter destroyed the town but spared the couple, who, when told to name their heart's desire, asked that, when they had lived out their years, they might die at the same time. Jupiter granted their request and upon their death transformed them into interlocking oak and linden trees.

Princess Volkonskaya — The writer, singer, and composer Princess Zinaida Aleksandrovna Volkonskaya, née Beloselskaya (1789–1862) had been living in Rome since 1829. In the 1820s, she had hosted an important literary-musical salon in Moscow that was frequented by the literary lights of the day, including Baratynsky. She moved to Rome in 1829 after converting to Roman Catholicism. To commemorate her departure, Baratynsky wrote "To Princess Z. A. Volkonskaya" ["K. Z. A. Volkonskoy"], which begins: "From the tsardom of whist and winter, / where, under their double administration, / the same chill contracts / both the atmosphere and minds, / where life is a kind of heavy sleep, / she hurries to the beautiful south / under Ausonian skies, / animated, sensual, / where in pavilions, in palace porticoes / Tasso's octaves are heard...":

> Из царства виста и зимы,
> Где, под управой их двоякой,
> И атмосферу и умы
> Сжимает холод одинакой,
> Где жизнь какой-то тяжкий сон,
> Она спешит на юг прекрасный,
> Под Авзонийский небосклон
> Одушевленный, сладострастный,
> Где в кущах, в портиках палат
> Октавы Тассовы звучат...

Khlyustin... was held back in Königsberg by sudden illness. — Semyon Semyonovich Khlyustin (1810–1844) was the brother of Countess Anastasie de Circourt (see note to Letter 157); he was very likely traveling to Paris to visit his sister when he took ill. When Baratynsky wrote to Putyata from Naples, he did not yet know that Khlyustin had already died in Königsberg in March.

165. TO NIKOLAY AND SOFYA PUTYATA.

a letter... even more reassuring with regard to Nastya — The Putyatas' eldest daughter had, apparently, been seriously ill.

166. TO NIKOLAY AND SOFYA PUTYATA.

Dmitry — Nikolay Putyata's brother (see note to Letter 136).

Becker — Becker was by this time the manager of Baratynsky's timber business (see note to Letter 138 and Letter 140).

I am sending you two poems. — "The Pyroscaphe" and "To My Tutor, the Italian"; both were published in Pletnyov's journal, *The Contemporary*, just eleven days after the poet's death.

Puzzoli, Baiae, Castellammare... — All well-known sightseeing destinations near Naples with interesting ancient ruins and great natural beauty. On Puzzoli (Pozzuoli) and Herculaneum, see the notes to Letter 164.

ENDNOTE

"As we found this repugnant..." — Nastasya Baratynskaya's letter to the Putyatas, written in French, is quoted in *Kjetsaa*, 257.

"completely destroyed by grief" — The description comes from a letter, dated July 19, 1844, by the young artist Vasily Ivanovich Shternberg (1818–1845), who was then studying in Italy (quoted in *Kjetsaa*, 258, n. 1).

Aleksandr Ivanov — The artist Aleksandr Alekseyevich Ivanov (1806–1858) is today best known for his epic painting *Christ's Appearance before the People* (1857), which he worked on for twenty years. It was Ivanov who cast Baratynsky's death mask, now preserved at the Muranovo Estate Museum. On the arrangements in Naples and Ivanov's assistance to Baratynsky's family, see *Kjetsaa*, 258–259.

"On Friday (August 31) I was at the funeral..." — Pletnyov's letter to Grot is quoted in *Kjetsaa*, 259–260.

LIST OF ADDRESSEES

Baratynskaya, Aleksandra Fyodorovna, née Cherepanova (1777–1853) — Letters 1–7, 9, 10, 14, 21, 29, 109, 113, 114, 117–119, 130, 134, 139, 140, 147, 148, 150–153, 155, 158, 163

Baratynskaya, Nastasya Lvovna, née Engelhardt (1804–1860) — Letters 36, 47, 110, 120–129, 131, 132

Baratynskaya, Natalya Abramovna (1809–1855) — Letter 143

Bestuzhev, Aleksandr Aleksandrovich (1797–1837) — Letter 11

Delvig, Anton Antonovich (1798–1831) — Letter 43

Kireyevsky, Ivan Vasilyevich (1806–1856) — Letters 49, 50, 59–64, 68–71, 73–82, 84, 86–95, 97, 98, 103–107

Konshin, Nikolay Mikhaylovich (1793–1859) — Letters 15, 39, 51

Kozlov, Ivan Ivanovich (1779–1840) — Letters 18, 23

Küchelbecker, Wilhelm Karlovich (1797–1846) — Letter 19

Mukhanov, Aleksandr Alekseyevich (1800–1834) — Letter 37

Pletnyov, Pyotr Aleksandrovich (1792–1866) — Letters 58, 66, 116, 133, 144, 149

Polevoy, Nikolay Alekseyevich (1796–1846) — Letter 40

Pushkin, Aleksandr Sergeyevich (1799–1837) — Letters 31, 34, 41

Putyata, Nikolay Vasilyevich (1802–1877) — Letters 16, 22, 24, 25, 27, 28, 30, 32, 33, 35, 38, 42, 53, 65, 115, 137, 138, 141, 142, 145, 156, 157, 159–162, 164–166

Putyata, Sofya Lvovna, née Engelhardt (1814–1877) — Letters 96, 102, 108, 142, 145, 156, 157, 159–162, 164–166

Ryleyev, Kondraty Fyodorovich (1795–1826) — Letter 11

Sobolevsky, Sergey Aleksandrovich (1803–1870) — Letters 135, 136

Sverbeyev, Dmitry Nikolayevich (1799–1874) — Letter 57

Turgenev, Aleksandr Ivanovich (1784–1845) — Letters 17, 20, 26

ALPHABETICAL LIST OF TITLES AND FIRST LINES

ABOUT THE TRANSLATOR

RAWLEY GRAU studied Russian at the Friends School of Baltimore, the Johns Hopkins University, and the University of Toronto. His translations from that language include essays by the art theorists Boris Groys and Viktor Misiano. He has also translated many works from Slovene, including essays by Aleš Debeljak, fiction by Vlado Žabot and Boris Pintar, plays by Ivan Cankar and Slavko Grum, and poetry by Janez Ramoveš, Andrej Rozman Roza, and others. He lives in Ljubljana, Slovenia, and teaches English and translation at the University of Primorska in Koper.

THE EASTERN EUROPEAN POETS SERIES
FROM UGLY DUCKLING PRESSE

"In one of my last travels … to the far eastern part of
the country, I got a volume of a poet of Pushkin's circle,
though in ways much better than Pushkin—his name
is Baratynsky. Reading him forced me to abandon the
whole silly traveling thing and to get more seriously
into writing. So this is what I started to do."

Joseph Brodsky
The Paris Review

"Yevgeny Baratynsky was the most daring and dark of
the nineteenth-century poets, the only one of Pushkin's
contemporaries who can justly be compared to him.
These translations do justice to the power of the originals
and will be a revelation to readers coming to Baratynsky
for the first time."

Michael Wachtel
author of *The Cambridge Introduction to Russian Poetry*

Eastern European Poets Series #32
Ugly Duckling Presse

$25 | Poetry / Letters
ISBN 978-1-937027-13-1